JCMS Annual Review
of the European Union
in 2012

Edited by
Nathaniel Copsey
and
Tim Haughton

General Editors: Michelle Cini and Amy Verdun

WILEY
Blackwell

This edition first published 2013
© 2013 John Wiley & Sons Ltd except for editorial material and organization

Registered Office
John Wiley & Sons Ltd, The Atrium, Southern Gate, Chichester, West Sussex, PO19 8SQ, UK

Editorial Offices
350 Main Street, Malden, MA 02148--5020, USA
9600 Garsington Road, Oxford, OX4 2DQ, UK
The Atrium, Southern Gate, Chichester, West Sussex, PO19 8SQ, UK

For details of our global editorial offices, for customer services, and for information about how to apply for permission to reuse the copyright material in this book please see our website at www.wiley.com/wiley-blackwell.

The right of Nathaniel Copsey and Tim Haughton to be identified as the authors of the editorial material in this work has been asserted in accordance with the UK Copyright, Designs and Patents Act 1988.

All rights reserved. No part of this publication may be reproduced, stored in a retrieval system, or transmitted, in any form or by any means, electronic, mechanical, photocopying, recording or otherwise, except as permitted by the UK Copyright, Designs and Patents Act 1988, without the prior permission of the publisher.

Wiley also publishes its books in a variety of electronic formats. Some content that appears in print may not be available in electronic books.

Designations used by companies to distinguish their products are often claimed as trademarks. All brand names and product names used in this book are trade names, service marks, trademarks or registered trademarks of their respective owners. The publisher is not associated with any product or vendor mentioned in this book.

Limit of Liability/Disclaimer of Warranty: While the publisher and author(s) have used their best efforts in preparing this book, they make no representations or warranties with respect to the accuracy or completeness of the contents of this book and specifically disclaim any implied warranties of merchantability or fitness for a particular purpose. It is sold on the understanding that the publisher is not engaged in rendering professional services and neither the publisher nor the author shall be liable for damages arising herefrom. If professional advice or other expert assistance is required, the services of a competent professional should be sought.

Library of Congress Cataloging-in-Publication Data

ISBN 978-111851290-6
ISSN 0021-9886 (print) 1468-5965 (online)

A catalogue record for this book is available from the British Library.

Set in 11/12.5 pt Times by Toppan Best-set Premedia Limited
Printed in Singapore

1   2013

CONTENTS

JCMS 2013 Volume 51 Annual Review pp. 1–5   DOI: 10.1111/jcms.12053

Editorial: Edging Away from the Abyss – The EU in 2012

NATHANIEL COPSEY[1] and TIM HAUGHTON[2]
[1] Aston University. [2] University of Birmingham

In a year dominated by the ongoing crisis of the eurozone and the existential threat to the entire European integration project that it posed, there were two glimmers of hope. One reminded us of the achievements of the past and the other brought confidence in the future. On 10 December 2012 the European Union was awarded the Nobel Prize for Peace in recognition of its contribution to the 'advancement of peace and reconciliation, democracy and human rights in Europe'.[1] Although the announcement of the award provoked the predictable chorus of criticisms from opponents, it accorded senior EU officials and politicians some respite from the unremittingly bad news associated with the eurozone's woes. Yet for the future of European integration and achieving the goals of delivering its citizens peace and prosperity, this was not the key announcement. In July, European Central Bank (ECB) President Mario Draghi promised 'to do whatever it takes' to save the euro. His pledge brought immediate calm to the markets as the spreads between peripheral and core eurozone bonds narrowed sharply. Draghi's comments appeared to indicate that after four years of indecision, the EU's institutions, and to a lesser extent, its Member States, were finally edging away from the abyss.

The economic, political and social wounds inflicted by the eurozone crisis, however, were not to be so easily salved. The cost of restoring competitiveness and balancing national accounts through austerity and deflation was borne in human misery. By the year's end, nearly 12 per cent of the eurozone workforce was unemployed, with the rate of economic inactivity rising to a catastrophic 24 per cent among younger people. In two of the worst affected countries – Spain and Greece – youth unemployment topped an almost unheard of 50 per cent and overall unemployment was heading for almost 30 per cent of the working-age population. As a result of the draconian cuts in public spending and a precipitate drop in consumption, national budgets in most, but not all, eurozone countries (such as France) swung towards primary surpluses and current account deficits narrowed sharply. Over the course of 2012, Europe's economic, political and social crisis appeared to be bottoming out at a very low level. The prescribed medicine that we described as 'kill or cure' in the review of 2010 finally seemed to be working (Copsey and Haughton, 2011), although concerns remained about where the growth necessary to pull the EU out of its economic malaise was going to come from.

Over the course of 2012, Europe edged away from the brink of economic and political collapse. The eurozone crisis was not over, and more ignominious bail-outs were to follow, but the euro had proven its capacity for resistance – or rather its leaders had proven their will to do the right thing, paraphrasing Churchill, having exhausted all the other possibilities. What the full political and social fallout will be, however, remains to be seen.

---

[1] «http://www.nobelprize.org/nobel_prizes/peace/laureates/2012/».

© 2013 The Author(s) JCMS: Journal of Common Market Studies © 2013 John Wiley & Sons Ltd, 9600 Garsington Road, Oxford OX4 2DQ, UK and 350 Main Street, Malden, MA 02148, USA

Forecasters would be wise to keep a weather eye on Tocqueville's dictum that the 'most dangerous moment for a bad government is when it begins to reform'. By the same token, those whose sole preoccupation is how to survive from day to day are unlikely to riot. After a tentative recovery comes, perhaps in 2014 or 2015, there may still be a heavy political price to pay – an indication of which was offered by the two Greek elections in 2012 in which the radical left and the extreme right performed well.

Debates continued to rage about the cause of the crisis with politicians, pundits and protesters offering a range of different narratives. For many Eurosceptics the explanation lay in the design flaws of the single currency, what the British Foreign Secretary William Hague described as a 'burning building with no exits'.[2] While not installing a new set of fire exits and escapes, the entry into force of the European Stability Mechanism (ESM) treaty and the Fiscal Compact, combined with plans for a fully fledged banking union and an embryonic fiscal federation, at least offered the promise that future fires would be less likely to break out and would be more easily extinguished. Other narratives of the crisis continued to focus on the contemporary blame game. While criticism of bankers appeared to recede from political discourse, the real target of blame became either the undisciplined and lazy southern Europeans or the cruel and harsh Germans. Both these popular narratives highlighted that at the heart of the EU's difficulties was a crisis of trust and a crisis of solidarity (Jones, 2012; Haughton, 2012). Whatever medicines could help deal with the acute problems facing it, the EU would also need to be complemented by measures designed to help tackle these deeper chronic challenges.

The year brought an array of elections. In two strategically important countries, the United States and Russia, elections offered continuity in the form of Barack Obama's re-election and Putin's return to the presidency after his four-year sojourn as the country's prime minister. Given the salience of the Franco–German axis to European integration, many eyes turned towards France in the spring and summer of 2012 for the presidential and parliamentary elections. The incumbent centre-right Nicolas Sarkozy lost the presidential election, but by a narrower margin than was forecast. His defeat owed much to the people of France's verdict on 'Sarko's' reputation for undignified and vulgar showmanship. A second 'non' was given to the idea or notion of austerity, which the French, to the horror of their neighbours across the Rhine, collectively dismissed, seemingly out of hand. Socialist President François Hollande led his party to a solid victory in the parliamentary elections, giving the socialists control of the executive, the legislature and 21 out of 22 regions in metropolitan France. Socialists were also in charge in most large cities, including Paris. By the end of 2012, Hollande had demonstrated clearly that he was not minded to capitalize on his good fortune – showing little sign of radicalism beyond a plan to hike taxes on the very rich, which was later thrown out by the judiciary as 'confiscatory'.[3] Hollande drew the wrong lessons from the presidential election campaign. The strong showing for Marine Le Pen, Jean-Luc Mélenchon and others demonstrated that the French had not yet lost their love of radicalism, even if they were sensible enough to back a mainstream candidate in the crucial second-round play-off.

The French government's allergic reaction to the notion of real reform, born of the opposition of the core socialist vote among those employed in the large public sector

---

[2] *The Spectator*, 28 September 2011. Hague first made the remarks in 1998 when he was leader of the Conservative Party.
[3] See Lequesne in this issue.

© 2013 The Author(s) JCMS: Journal of Common Market Studies © 2013 John Wiley & Sons Ltd

(including nationalized industries), was met with scant sympathy in Berlin. Angela Merkel made no secret of her preference for Sarkozy, even going so far as to offer to campaign for his re-election – an offer that was wisely, yet politely, turned down. In the second half of 2012, the Franco–German alliance frayed, and Germany's role as Europe's 'reluctant hegemon' was confirmed (Paterson, 2011).

Yet there are grounds for optimism in Europe's crisis. For more than a decade, Europe's technocrats have pointed to the deeper malaise in the European economy. Growth has been slow and, in many places, unemployment high for a long time. The EU has also been falling further behind the United States in per capita income. Yet for many in Europe, life has simply been too good to contemplate reform. Protected labour market insiders and cosy closed-shop professionals fear – probably accurately – that they have much to lose from opening up their markets to competition from new entrants. In the meantime, a gap has opened between the protected labour market insider and the unprotected, usually young outsider, stuck on very low pay and short-term contracts with no safety or security. The crisis with its sky-high levels of unemployment has made things even worse – now there is simply no work to be had. Europe's crisis may help to overcome the sense that things cannot go on as they did before. Periods of crisis offer opportunities for change, but an essential ingredient for such change to occur is political will.

***

This is our fifth issue of the *JCMS Annual Review* as editors and we have continued our policy of commissioning special contributions from both academics and practitioners from outside the academic world. We are delighted that almost all of our regular contributors have continued for another year and we are very pleased to welcome Amelia Hadfield and Daniel Fiott to the team. Sadly, however, Dave Allen passed away in the autumn. Alongside Michael Smith he had written the contribution on 'Relations with the Rest of the World' for the past two decades. In honour of his work for this publication, but also for European Studies more broadly, we asked his long-time collaborator in conjunction with three other leading scholars in the field – Simon Bulmer, Christopher Hill and Drew Scott – to write a special tribute article highlighting Dave's contribution to the study and understanding of the European Union and the process of integration. We will certainly miss his emails updating us on the progress of his contributions, frequently accompanied by a long treatise on the fortunes of Nottingham Forest.

The EU is not the only regional grouping where individual states have realized the benefits of pooling sovereignty. As Russian Foreign Minister Sergey Lavrov argues in his contribution to this issue, the success of European integration over the past 50 years has been a source of instructive inspiration as Russia leads a process of Eurasian integration. He stresses the inextricable links between the EU and Russia, reminding readers that 'European history cannot be imagined without Russia, just as the history of Russia cannot be imagined apart from Europe'. He argues that the future of 'our common continent' will depend on harnessing the 'huge potential for partnership between Russia and the EU' and outlines in his contribution areas where such partnership can yield benefits and a number of measures which can foster and improve relations.

It is difficult sometimes for politicians and citizens in the EU to think about broader strategic questions when we are stuck in an economic malaise. In 2012, debates about the

© 2013 The Author(s) JCMS: Journal of Common Market Studies © 2013 John Wiley & Sons Ltd

merits of austerity measures and policies needed to extricate Europe from its difficulties and place it in on a path towards sustained and sustainable growth remained heated not just in academic seminars and summits, but on the streets of Athens, Lisbon and Madrid. In their contribution, Paul de Grauwe and Yuemei Ji argue that the budgetary austerity imposed on Member States such as Greece, Portugal and Spain 'has been too intense and has been influenced too much by panic in financial markets'. They do not deny that a degree of austerity is needed to return these countries to sustainable government finances. Rather, 'the *timing* and the *intensity* of the austerity programmes have been dictated too much by the market sentiments of fear and panic instead of being the outcome of rational decision-making processes'. Moreover, they recommend that while the debtor nations have no other option than to continue on the path of austerity, the creditor nations, especially Germany, 'should offset the deflationary consequences of these austerity programmes by policies allowing for some fiscal stimulus'.

In her contribution to the *JCMS Annual Review* former prime minister of Slovakia, Iveta Radičová, who sat around the European Council table in 2010–12, focuses on the unemployment which blights the social and economic landscape of Europe. She draws stark contrasts between the EU experience and the United States in areas of productivity, investment and innovation, highlighting two areas where innovation can be nurtured and helped: reducing the costs of patenting, and ensuring we have a well-educated and equipped workforce. However, she cautions against the arguments for simply pumping money into education, reminding us that 'success of policies should be judged against objective criteria, desirable aims, not the proportion of GDP that is spent'.

French presidents have played a central role in the process of European integration over the past six decades. The 1960s were the decade of de Gaulle, who oversaw the launch of the common agricultural policy. Pompidou unblocked the enlargement process in the 1970s. In the 1980s and early 1990s, François Mitterrand made Europe one of the main focuses of his presidency. Given the French presidential election and the changing of the guard in the Elysée, we commissioned Christian Lequesne of Sciences Po in Paris to assess the state of France's relations with the EU and what the Hollande presidency will mean for Europe. Lequesne argues that at the core of European integration for the first three decades was the 'unbalanced balance' between France and Germany, whereby the economic power of the latter was complemented by the attributes of the former in the international system. The end of the cold war and the enlargement of the Union diluted the importance of the relationship between France and Germany, although the eurozone crisis helped to bring back the salience of the duo in the form of what was dubbed 'Merkozy'. Despite hope that Hollande's victory might bolster the anti-austerity agenda and a new image of Europe, the first few months of the new president's term were underwhelming. Lequesne maintains that in contrast to the last French Socialist president who did much to shape the Europe of his day, Hollande was not in such a strong position as Mitterrand, weakened both by his less-than-dominant position inside the *Parti Socialiste*, and the fact that the EU was 'less delegitimized' in public opinion in 1983 than 30 years later.

The theme of legitimacy is an undercurrent running through Gerda Falkner's *JCMS Annual Review* lecture assessing compliance in the EU. The aim of the lecture is to invite a leading scholar of the EU to reflect deeply on European integration, to challenge the received wisdom and to offer some fresh thinking on policy prescriptions. Following in the footsteps of Vivien Schmidt (2009), Kalypso Nicolaïdis (2010), Loukas Tsoukalis

© 2013 The Author(s) JCMS: Journal of Common Market Studies © 2013 John Wiley & Sons Ltd

(2011) and Erik Jones (2012), who examined central themes of European integration such as solidarity, sustainability and democracy, Falkner looks at the question of whether the EU is becoming what she terms a 'non-compliance community'. In doing so, she argues that the notion of 'non-compliance' now needs to to go beyond simple transposition, implementation and enforcement of directives and look at deeply worrying trends, such as threats to the rule of law, to fundamental values and to the principle of sticking to decisions agreed between Member States in Council meetings. Non-compliance, she maintains, strikes at the very heart of the integration project as it erodes trust and encourages non-compliance by others. For Falkner, decisive action is needed to ensure the EU will continue to be perceived as a trustworthy actor by the outside world and its citizens.

We would like to thank all the contributors to this issue of the *JCMS Annual Review* for their efforts and efficiency in producing such excellent copy within the usual tight time constraints. We would also like to thank the editors of the *JCMS*, Michelle Cini and Amy Verdun, for their continuing support over the past year and hope our relationship will continue to be as productive in the future.

References

Copsey, N. and Haughton, T. (2011) 'Editorial: 2010, Kill or Cure for the Euro?' *JCMS*, Vol. 49, No. S1, pp. 1–6.

Haughton, T. (2012) *An SUV on a Road to Nowhere? Solidarity, Unanimity and Vulnerability in the European Union* (Washington, DC: Center for Transatlantic Relations). Available at: «http://transatlantic.sais-jhu.edu/publications/articles/Tim%20Haughton%20An%20SUV%20on%20a%20Road%20to%20Nowhere%20Solidarity.pdf».

Jones, E. (2012) 'The JCMS Annual Review Lecture: European Crisis, European Solidarity'. *JCMS*, Vol. 50, No. S2, pp. 53–67.

Nicolaïdis, K. (2010) 'The JCMS Annual Review Lecture – Sustainable Integration: Towards EU 2.0?' *JCMS*, Vol. 48, No. S1, pp. 21–54.

Paterson, W. (2011) 'The Reluctant Hegemon? Germany Moves Centre Stage in the European Union'. *JCMS*, Vol. 49, No. S1, pp. 57–75.

Schmidt, V. (2009) 'Re-envisioning the European Union: Identity, Democracy, Economy'. *JCMS*, Vol. 47, No. S1, pp. 17–42.

Tsoukalis, L. (2011) 'The JCMS Annual Review Lecture: The Shattering of Illusions – And What Next?' *JCMS*, Vol. 49, No. S1, pp. 19–44.

© 2013 The Author(s) JCMS: Journal of Common Market Studies © 2013 John Wiley & Sons Ltd

JCMS 2013 Volume 51 Annual Review pp. 6–12　　　　　　　　　　　　　　　　DOI: 10.1111/jcms.12047

State of the Union
Russia–EU: Prospects for Partnership in the Changing World

SERGEY LAVROV
Minister of Foreign Affairs, Russian Federation

It gives me great pleasure to address the readers of such an influential publication as the *JCMS Annual Review* and share my views regarding relations between the two biggest players in Europe – the Russian Federation and the European Union. The importance of this subject should not be underestimated because the future of our common continent in the 21st century will primarily depend on the EU and Russia – and their interaction.

European history cannot be imagined without Russia, just as the history of Russia cannot be imagined apart from Europe. For centuries, Russia has been involved in shaping European reality in its political, economic and cultural dimensions. Yet the debate of how close Russia and its west European partners can be and to what degree Russia is a European country has also been going on for centuries. This debate was somewhat put aside during the cold war, when the European continent was essentially divided into spheres of influence by the two superpowers. But in recent years, when Europeans have agreed to leave behind the era of the bloodiest and most devastating wars in the history of mankind and when the walls of irreconcilable ideological confrontation have been torn down, we have an unprecedented opportunity to fulfil the dream of a united Europe.

There is definitely a huge potential for partnership between Russia and the EU. After all, our countries have about 650 million people living on the territory of more than 21 million square kilometres. There are many things that bring us together: the complementarity and interdependence of our economies, the objective indivisibility of European security, extensive human contacts and common cultural roots. The fact that European culture in the broad sense spans the area to the Pacific coast is definitely Russia's historic achievement.

We have accomplished a lot in the past two decades. Russia and the EU have agreed to establish four 'common spaces' and prepared road maps to implement them. Trade between Russia and the EU exceeds US$400 billion, which is commensurate with the EU's trade with the United States or China. Total EU investment in the Russian economy exceeds US$260 billion, and Russian investment into the EU countries amounts to US$75 billion. Last August, Russia joined the World Trade Organization (WTO), and now that we have the same trading rules our interaction should intensify and expand.

In 2010, we launched the Partnership for Modernization initiative, where we jointly implement innovative, research and technological projects. In the future, we may see production and technology alliances in areas like the energy industry, aircraft manufacturing, shipbuilding, the automotive industry, medicine and the pharmaceutical industry. This will certainly make these industries and our economies in general more competitive and help them adapt to new challenges in the globalizing world.

© 2013 The Author(s) JCMS: Journal of Common Market Studies © 2013 John Wiley & Sons Ltd, 9600 Garsington Road, Oxford OX4 2DQ, UK and 350 Main Street, Malden, MA 02148, USA

We have a number of sectorial dialogues where we work to harmonize our technical regulations and remove barriers for trade. We focus on creating better conditions for mutual investment and interaction between small and medium-sized businesses. We are pleased that most of the EU countries have shown interest in this concrete synergetic work and signed bilateral agreements with Russia on partnership for modernization.

Energy resources are Russia's top exports. We top the list of the EU's major energy suppliers. Russia provides the EU with a third of its oil and natural gas and almost a quarter of its coal and petrochemicals. The EU simply does not have another partner that can guarantee secure deliveries in such amounts. Even at the time of the cold war, our country strictly fulfilled all its obligations. Today, we are much better positioned to guarantee a reliable gas supply to European consumers in the decades to come. Last year, the Nord Stream pipeline that connects the gas grids of Germany and other EU countries with Russia's integrated gas transport network became fully operational. Construction of the South Stream is under way as well.

There are numerous indications that we need each other – and not just on earth, but in space as well. On 14 March 2013, the Russian Federal Space Agency (Roscosmos) and the European Space Agency (ESA) signed a co-operation agreement in Paris to work in partnership on the ExoMars programme for the robotic exploration of Mars, Jupiter and the Moon in 2016–18.

However, the fundamental questions regarding the extent and the prospects of the Russia–EU relationship remain. The new version of Russia's Foreign Policy Concept, approved by President Vladimir Putin on 12 February, sets the strategic goal of creating a common economic and human space from the Atlantic to the Pacific. In this context, I would like to quote something European Commission President José Manuel Barroso said at the conference on Russia–EU partnership that took place in Moscow in March:

> I think it is important, even when we take concrete decisions be it in daily life, in politics or business, to have a long-term vision. The long term vision is a common economic and human space from Lisbon to Vladivostok with free travel of people, free exchange of goods and services, very close overall cooperation. (Barroso, 2013)

So, can we say that in developing their bilateral partnership Russia and the EU share the same, clearly visualized goal? Obviously, it would be premature to say that today. The strategic goals of Russia–EU relations have not yet become reality affecting daily affairs. To borrow an expression used by José Manuel Barroso, the situation will only change if Russia–EU interaction goes from a 'partnership of necessity' to a 'partnership of choice'. And this means that our relationship needs strategic trust as a strong foundation.

We can only achieve a fundamentally new, higher level of partnership if we regard each other as equal partners, respect each other and take into account each other's interests. I have to say that we see some inertia in the way the EU treats its relations with Russia. This is due to the Union's general tradition of developing ties with neighbouring countries only if they approach EU standards and follow EU policies. In fact, it seems that recently our European partners have even somewhat abandoned our common understanding regarding the consistent development of Russia–EU co-operation. For instance, Russia is seriously concerned about the EU's steps to implement the Third Energy Package, which it portrays as a measure to improve antitrust regulations. Of course, we do not question the EU's right

© 2013 The Author(s) JCMS: Journal of Common Market Studies © 2013 John Wiley & Sons Ltd

to regulate its markets, but we expect it to abide by its international legal obligations. In the situation with the Third Energy Package, which is retroactive and affects the investments that Russian companies had made in EU countries before this document was adopted, our partners violated Article 34 of the current Russia–EU partnership and co-operation agreement as well as bilateral investment promotion and protection agreements between Russia and EU Member States.

The Third Energy Package has already created problems for practical co-operation. Certain EU countries are now less appealing to Russian businesses, and systemic risks are higher. In some cases, we see *de facto* expropriation of Russian companies' assets. We never expected to face this kind of situation in the EU. Such preposterous decisions may erode trust and damage the foundations of our partnership. Therefore, we hope the EU responds positively to Russia's proposals for amending the situation, which we presented to the European Commission at the Russia–EU summit in Brussels on 20–21 December 2012. We suggest signing a special agreement that would minimize the negative effect the Third Energy Package will have on our energy co-operation. Also, we hope that the joint road map for Russia–EU energy co-operation until 2050 signed on 22 March 2013 in Moscow will further stimulate energy co-operation.

We are also concerned because of the antitrust investigation the European Commission launched last year against Gazprom – a company that makes a significant contribution to energy security on the European continent. One of the accusations is that Gazprom allegedly 'imposed unfair prices on its customers by linking the price of gas to oil prices'. But this formula (which, incidentally, was first introduced by the Dutch) has never been questioned before and is used by other companies supplying natural gas to Europe as well. If sanctions are introduced against Gazprom, it will be difficult for the company to work on the markets where it faces open discrimination.

In this situation, we observe with interest current discussions in the EU about the distribution of powers between Brussels and Member States. As far as we understand, the Lisbon Treaty has catalogued different categories of powers within the EU, but has not provided explicit answers for all the questions. Some in the EU think that it should never get involved in matters which can be better taken care of at a local or national level, and the EU will obviously have to clarify these matters in the medium term.

In addition to the negative effect this problem has on energy co-operation where Brussels seeks to impose the principles of the Third Energy Package on all Member States, it also affects the issue of visa facilitation between Russia and EU Member States.

EU rules in no way negate the principle of subsidiarity and proportionality in relation to other countries. In fact, the Treaty on European Union says that in areas which do not fall within its exclusive competence the EU shall act only if Member States cannot achieve their objectives at a national level. Perhaps our partners should follow this wise principle more often? Most of the areas where we co-operate, including transport, energy, trans-European networks and issues of freedom, security and justice, are not within the EU's exclusive competence. We know from experience that attempts to restrain EU Member States in their relations with Russia often only hamper our strategic partnership, whereas agreements that we initially make with individual countries may then be successfully implemented at the EU level.

Our co-operation has long outgrown the limits of the 1994 partnership and co-operation agreement. Yet, while working on a new framework agreement, we face

© 2013 The Author(s) JCMS: Journal of Common Market Studies © 2013 John Wiley & Sons Ltd

attempts by Brussels to take advantage of the talks in order to get further economic benefits in addition to the terms on which Russia joined the WTO. There should be no illusions: Russia will never accept a lopsided agreement. In general, we regard it as a framework, strategic agreement that would outline key areas for developing our co-operation, set goals for the future and define ways to achieve them.

We are disappointed with insufficient progress towards visa-free travel for short-term visits between Russia and the EU. The visa regime has long been an anachronism in our relations. From the technical point of view, Russia and EU Member States have been ready to waive visas for each other. This issue is symbolic; it exemplifies all the differences between Russia and the EU. It is ironic that our western partners, who were so adamant about freedom of movement when negotiating the Helsinki Final Act, are now reluctant to create conditions for free human communication on the European continent.

Of course, when considering future relations between Russia and the EU, we should consider the rapidly changing global context. It often seems that these considerations are not always taken into account sufficiently – and this while the world is undergoing transformation. The global balance of power is shifting, and a new, polycentric system of international relations is emerging, where Europe will no longer play a central role. International affairs are becoming more complex and less predictable as destabilizing tendencies aggravate. Concepts and views that used to seem unquestionable are undergoing radical change. Developed nations no longer drive global growth; the factor of civilizational identity is becoming more prominent; the plurality of development models is becoming evident. Changes are taking place at all levels and in all areas. As many experts observe, for example, the crisis made the dichotomy between Europe's north and south more evident, whereas the traditional division into west and east is less prominent now. Under these circumstances, clinging to obsolete concepts from the past era would inevitably result in big mistakes. With the current fluid situation, one should not take the traditional system of international alliances for granted. It is obvious that history will make us reconsider our views on a lot of things.

The global economic situation, affected by financial difficulties in some leading economies, requires responsible and consolidated action. Nobody can avoid the effect of global economic processes, and no country or a group of countries – no matter how big or powerful they are – can handle today's challenges on their own. The International Monetary Fund (IMF) predicts global gross domestic product (GDP) growth at 3.3 per cent in 2013 and 4.0 per cent in 2014. At the same time, the eurozone is expected to shrink by 0.3 per cent this year and grow by 1.1 per cent in 2014. Russia's growth last year of 3.4 per cent was above all of the other G8 countries. I only mention these figures to encourage our European colleagues to take into account the situation on the ground.

We genuinely hope our European partners emerge from the period of stagnation as soon as possible. We believe they will find appropriate solutions. This is why we still keep about 40 per cent of our foreign exchange reserves in euros. And this is not just well-wishing – Russia regularly participates in working out collective decisions in the IMF in order to support distressed European economies. We take part in multilateral efforts to overcome the consequences of the global financial and economic crisis. As the current chair in the G20, Russia has proposed an agenda that seeks to achieve sustainable, well-balanced growth in the global economy and create new jobs. We put emphasis on

© 2013 The Author(s) JCMS: Journal of Common Market Studies © 2013 John Wiley & Sons Ltd

stimulating investment and making regulation more transparent and efficient. We think the primary objective for the G20 is to strengthen global governance institutions, create new effective instruments for removing existing disparities and for stimulating growth in all the parts of the world, and to ensure close co-ordination of economic policies.

At the same time, it is clear that there is no magic solution for Europe or for any other part of the world. The situation requires serious and long-term effort which may employ unconventional approaches, such as adjusting one's model of economic development and generally rebuilding trust in the economic regulation system.

Also, Russia–EU relations should certainly take into account the new reality that emerges as Commonwealth of Independent States (CIS) nations progress towards closer Eurasian integration. Russia, Kazakhstan and Belarus have established the Customs Union (CU) and the Common Economic Space (CES) with a market of 165 million consumers. It is based on universal integration principles consistent with the WTO standards and is harmonized in terms of macroeconomic policies, competition rules, technical regulations, transport, natural monopolies' tariffs, and agricultural and industrial subsidies. Last year, the Eurasian Economic Commission – a permanent organ for these two formats – was established. It oversees matters of customs tariffs and technical regulations, trade regimes with third countries, competition, macroeconomic and energy policies, and some other issues. Gradually, it will assume responsibility for other matters as well.

It took 40 years for the European Coal and Steel Community to evolve into the full-fledged European Union. The CU and the CES are developing much faster, in part because we take into account the EU's experience as the most successful integration project so far. We will do our best to further develop and improve Eurasian integration mechanisms and produce the regulatory framework for the CU and the CES. Our integration is already yielding specific, practical results, as illustrated by GDP growth and trade statistics. In 2012, trade between the CU member states grew by 8.7 per cent; in 2011, it grew by 33.9 per cent. The establishment of the CU and the CES helped improve the investment climate in the three countries, created more favourable conditions for doing business including small and medium-sized businesses, and created new jobs. The number of people in the CU and CES countries registered as unemployed by the end of 2012 was 16.8 per cent lower than in 2011, with the unemployment rate at 5.2 per cent. I think many of our European partners can only wish they had these kind of figures.

There is no intention on our part, nor could there be, to restore the Russian Empire or the Soviet Union in any shape or form. That would be naïve and impossible. Yet close integration based on different values, with a new political and economic foundation, is certainly what our times call for. It reflects objective trends of this globalization era, including the increasing role of regional alliances. This is not our invention. We just follow current trends based on pragmatism and common sense. It is only natural to take advantage of economic, infrastructural, logistic and transport connections we inherited from the time when our countries were all parts of the same state.

The new union will be open for interested countries to join. We expect it to become a hub effectively connecting Europe and the Asia-Pacific. Of course, the parameters of Eurasian integration are for participating nations to determine, just as it is up to the EU Member States to decide how the EU should develop. But I strongly believe that further Eurasian integration, in formats that are complementary and compatible with the processes under way in the EU, meets our common interests.

© 2013 The Author(s) JCMS: Journal of Common Market Studies © 2013 John Wiley & Sons Ltd

With the CU and the CES as the foundation, we expect to establish the Eurasian Economic Union (EEU) by 1 January 2015. The purpose of the Union is to make maximum use of mutually beneficial economic ties among the CIS nations. This project is our priority. We expect the EEU to become a unification model that will shape the future not only of our three countries, but also that of other post-Soviet nations.

As far as we can see, the EU understands that Eurasian integration is an objective reality and would like to work out mechanisms for interacting through EU institutions, primarily the European Commission, going from the level of experts, where this interaction actually works, to a higher level. We can only welcome this approach. In this context, it would be appropriate to quote former French minister and MEP Rachida Dati:

> Don't wave the red rag of a new cold war, a bloc against a bloc. We must work for a union of unions, an alliance of the European Union and the Eurasian Union. Naturally, this cannot happen overnight. But we must have the courage to set such a long-term goal in developing relations with Russia and its Eurasian partners. (Dati, 2013)

Generally speaking, there can be no doubt that defining additional opportunities for economic growth based on a new, high-technology foundation with maximum co-operation between Russia and the EU could become one of the most promising areas where we can work together in the years to come. At the same time, we clearly cannot take Russia–EU ties to a fundamentally new level in one leap. We can only develop our bilateral partnership gradually, step by step. Here are a few areas which we think we could start with. First, we can develop energy co-operation, leading in the future to a single European energy complex. Russia is ready to advance in this direction on the basis of transparency, without politicizing energy co-operation. We hope that common sense and wisdom, which have always been typical of the statesmen who initiated European integration, will eventually prevail. Second, a new Russia–EU framework agreement, which would outline key areas of our future interaction and ways of achieving common objectives, should be signed at an early date. Third, the signing of an agreement to waive visas for short-term trips would be a serious confirmation of the strategic nature of the Russia–EU partnership and make a real contribution to removing the dividing lines that still remain on the European continent. Fourth, we should develop co-operation in foreign policy and security. To ensure common and indivisible security in the Euro-Atlantic region, all the parties that play a major role in these matters in Europe and neighbouring regions should actively participate in this work. If there is political will, we may find a formula that would allow us to increase our co-operation in foreign policy and security without jeopardizing the EU's autonomy as regards decision-making in the common security and defence policy (CSDP) or Russia's sovereignty as a country that is not seeking membership of the EU. The need for this is obvious. One may simply take a look at what is happening south of Europe, in the Middle East and North Africa. We think that differences in our approaches to settling this region's problems, including the crisis in Syria, are exaggerated, while opportunities for joint action for the purpose of improving stability and finding political solutions to conflicts remain underestimated.

We stand for co-operation as equal partners in crisis management. We are convinced that the Seville modalities for Russia's participation in EU crisis management operations/ missions as the only possible form of our interaction should be replaced with co-operation based on equality, which befits strategic partnership between Russia and the EU. If the

© 2013 The Author(s) JCMS: Journal of Common Market Studies © 2013 John Wiley & Sons Ltd

EU signs an agreement based on equality, that would be a sign of mutual respect, as is appropriate for strategic partners. At the same time, the EU would have no obligation to participate in crisis management operations conducted by Russia, and Russia, similarly, would have no obligation to participate in operations conducted by the EU. The parties will decide whether they want to co-operate under the agreement on a case-by-case basis, considering the circumstances in each particular case.

As a confidence-building measure, we think it would be important for Russia and the EU to boost their military co-operation. The military-to-military working group established on the EU's initiative in 2010 became an organic part of the Russia–EU dialogue, assuming responsibility for a number of matters: exchanging assessments on the current situation and possible developments in crisis-hit regions, using Russia and EU's peace-keeping potentials, fighting piracy.

Russia will continue pursuing a dual-track approach, simultaneously developing partnership with the EU and its Member States. However, to make this progress stable and uninterrupted, we need common understanding of our joint mission, which is to secure an appropriate role for Europe in the world and to increase its contribution to international stability and global development.

I believe that today we need to be creative rather than cling to predetermined views. The idea of synergy and combining our potentials rather than trying to distance ourselves from each other on the common European continent is what we need in this era of globalization, as the world becomes increasingly interdependent. Incidentally, such an approach would deliver the countries which the EU describes as 'common neighbourhood' from having to choose between the eastern and western directions of developing co-operation.

I think that a careful study of the prospects and outlooks for establishing a common Russia–EU space is a subject that deserves close attention from Russian and EU experts. Analysis that would substantiate the viability of Russia's and the EU's joint efforts in economic and other fields could make an important contribution to the process of forming a strategic bilateral alliance.

Together, we can achieve a lot – politically, economically and in addressing key international problems. There are many things on the Russia–EU agenda. What results and how soon we will be able to achieve them will depend on the degree of our openness for interaction, for working together in order to produce compromise solutions that take into account both parties' interests.

References

Barroso, J.M. (2013) 'Speech by President Barroso at the Russia–European Union Potential for Partnership Conference: "Moving into a Partnership of Choice"'. European Commission. Available at: «http://europa.eu/rapid/press-release_SPEECH-13-249_en.htm».

Dati, R. (2013) 'Europe is Missing Its Chance: The EU will Commit a Grave Mistake if it Ignores the Eurasian Union' ('Европа упускает свой шанс: ЕС совершит большую ошибку, проигнорировав Евразийский союз'). Rossiyskaya Gazeta. Available in Russian at: «www.rg.ru/2013/04/17/dati.html».

© 2013 The Author(s) JCMS: Journal of Common Market Studies © 2013 John Wiley & Sons Ltd

JCMS 2013 Volume 51 Annual Review pp. 13–30

DOI: 10.1111/jcms.12051

The JCMS Annual Review Lecture
Is the European Union Losing Its Credibility?*

GERDA FALKNER
Institute for European Integration Research, University of Vienna

I. Non-compliance with EU Policies: Why Worry?

In recent years, non-compliance (the failure to respect the rules) with European Union policies has received ever more attention in both public debates and scholarly writings. But why should we worry about it? No policy has ever been implemented exactly to the letter of what seems to be intended from a reading of the policy as it appears 'on the books'. In the absence of data comparing the national and the supranational levels, there is no way to verify in a quantitative sense if the EU's compliance deficiencies are actually worse than the average at the national level. What is more, not even the most law-abiding society functions without any breaches of rules, so why should the EU – especially as it is a 'compound' polity (Schmidt, 2004) at a greater distance from the daily lives of its people and their affairs?

Several arguments speak against this benign perspective. First, the EU's landmark function is 'integration through law' and the rule of law is the very foundation stone on which the community has been built. If the law visibly degenerates into a 'dead letter', then the project loses its basic function. Therefore, even if the EU's non-compliance rate were as good or bad as the national average, this still implies that the phenomenon is more critical for the Union's survival.

Second, the EU's legitimacy is less solidly anchored than is the case in most other political systems, both at the level of a constitution that might serve as a point of identification and with regard to deeply founded feelings of belonging within 'its society'. De-legitimization of its basic function (integration through law) will therefore endanger its continued existence more profoundly than would be the case with a typical 'nation-state'.

Third, the EU is currently in a state of turmoil. Many hold that it is even at a decisive moment in its history. Tensions are mounting as the financial market crisis affects some countries over-proportionally, while others are reluctant to share the burden in times of economic downturn. The EU's leaders cannot find a consensus with regard to interpreting

*A much longer version of this lecture will be published as a working paper. See «http://eif.univie.ac.at/falkner/publications.php» for further information. The *Annual Review* editors, Nathaniel Copsey and Tim Haughton, have provided stimulating and in-depth comments. My research was in part carried out during a visiting professorship in Paris at Sciences Po and the Interdisciplinary Research Centre for the Evaluation of Public Policies (LIEPP). I am grateful for feedback and support to, *inter alia*, Christopher Bickerton, Renaud Dehousse, Jean Leca, Christian Lequesne, Imola Streho, Desmond King and Olivier Rozenberg. Helpful feedback was also given by Michael Nentwich and Darina Malová, and during presentations of parts of this article – for example, in Panel 548 on 'Judicial Policy-Making as a Mode of EU Governance', Sixth General Conference of the European Consortium for Political Research, University of Iceland, Reykjavik, and at the conference 'Europeanization: Do We Still Miss the Big Picture?', Université Libre de Bruxelles, May 2012 (I owe the expression 'non-compliance community' to Stella Ladi during the discussions there). Thanks for research support to Stephanie Liechtenstein and Veronika Pollak, and for language revisions to Whitney Isaacs. The usual disclaimer applies.

© 2013 The Author(s) JCMS: Journal of Common Market Studies © 2013 John Wiley & Sons Ltd, 9600 Garsington Road, Oxford OX4 2DQ, UK and 350 Main Street, Malden, MA 02148, USA

the sources of the crisis – not to mention effective solutions. What makes things worse is that internal homogeneity was always low in the EU, but it has recently shrunk even more and continues to do so for various reasons. Enlargement has imported ever more disparate economic, social, legal and political systems into the Union. In a situation of increasingly centrifugal forces and great instability, a growing perception that the EU might become a non-compliance community could indeed be disastrous.

However, non-compliance with EU rules has recently happened at an increasing number of levels; with increasing frequency and greater visibility to a broad audience; and in fields of very direct relevance for basically all citizens and politicians. All of this has contributed to a degree of politicization of the EU's compliance problem that was unknown in earlier phases of the integration process, notwithstanding the fact that not all of the non-compliance phenomena are indeed novel. Although there is no theory available to predict when and how non-compliance develops from a minor weakness into a systematic danger to any political system, the indicators just mentioned suggest that the EU's 'compliance deficit' should be taken rather seriously and that efforts are needed to prevent the situation from possibly reaching a 'tipping point' and ruining the EU's credibility.

Politicization has already happened not only in the Member States, where some fear that their own commitment to the rule of law is not fully matched elsewhere (an argument that is unfortunately exploited heavily by populist parties or practices that have been gaining ground virtually everywhere in the EU); it has even reached the very peak of the EU's polity. One indicator that the problem is perceived to have become quite serious is that it was a major subject in EU Commission President Manuel Barroso's 2012 State of the Union Address to the European Parliament (Barroso, 2012). The EU executive leader discussed two elements of the EU's non-compliance problem: non-compliance with summit decisions; and non-compliance with the EU's basic democratic values. Not mentioned were further layers of non-compliance with EU policies that are nonetheless virulent, and include: multiple deviations from agreed rules regarding economic and monetary union (EMU); failure to implement and adequately enforce EU law in the Member States; lack of respect for European Court of Justice (ECJ) judgments; and non-compliance with deals struck in the past as incorporated in the present EU integration mode (in other words, the United Kingdom's stated desire to withdraw from earlier compromise solutions). This article will cover them one by one, in brief.[1] All these phenomena deserve attention as they form part of the EU's overall compliance problem, even if the actors whose behaviour is not in line with relevant rules differ between these categories. In fact, it makes the situation even more worrying that not only Member State governments and other national institutions break EU rules, but that this also seems to be the case at times with EU institutions.

Overall, I argue that rather than perfect compliance, 'credibility' is indeed crucial: the EU needs to restore the confidence that its commitments are both real and binding.

---

[1] For a fuller version, see Falkner (forthcoming). Further potential compliance problems not discussed here include: do the Commission and the European Central Bank always stick to the *acquis communautaire* when they negotiate with bail-out countries as part of the Troika? Is the EU indeed enforcing the rules specified in external agreements, for example, for social and competition policies in the partner states, considering that the EU has hardly ever suspended bilateral trade agreements due to third party violations of non-trade-related contents? On this latter question, see Falkner and Müller (2013). Consider, furthermore, that during the March 2013 European Council the EU's leaders initially did not demand that their much vaunted guarantee on bank savings up to €100,000 per saver should be respected in Cyprus.

Credibility implies that the EU's policies need to be effective, even if each and every detail of all policies ever adopted may not always be implemented exactly as originally formulated. On the basis of a renewed trust in the EU's achievement of its goals and hence its overall reliability, a modicum of continuing slack in policy implementation will certainly not endanger the success of European integration as a whole. In a nutshell, the argument is that in order to be sustainable in a broad sense (Nicolaïdis, 2010), the European integration process needs a sufficiently high degree of trust that its commitments will be upheld. Clearly one prerequisite of solidarity as discussed in last year's *JCMS Annual Review* Lecture (Jones, 2012) is that the Union can only build on the basis of trust and credibility. In fact, all the recent *JCMS Annual Review* lecture-givers seem unanimous in their call for decisive action to uphold the EU's credibility and to steer it out of what can be seen as a current crisis of trust. This contribution joins their calls.

Non-compliance with Summit Decisions

Among the problems mentioned by Commission President Barroso is that heads of state and government publicly question the solutions adopted at summits, even directly afterwards.

> On too many occasions, we have seen a vicious spiral. First, very important decisions for our future are taken at European summits. But then, the next day, we see some of those very same people who took those decisions undermining them. Saying that either they go too far, or that they don't go far enough. And then we get a problem of credibility. A problem of confidence. (Barroso, 2012)

Indeed, this kind of 'non-compliance' gave the media ample room for putting disunity on display in recent times. At the eurozone summit on the fringes of the European Council meeting of 29 June 2012, the heads of state or government, according to various press sources[2] and the official European Council website, decided, *inter alia*, 'that EFSF/ESM [European Financial Stability Facility/European Stability Mechanism] funds can be used flexibly to buy bonds for Member States'.[3] However, no more than two days later, the deal was already challenged and the markets' 'post-summit euphoria was dealt a blow. [. . .] A report outlining the Finnish government's position delivered to the parliament on Monday said: Due to [the] intervention of Finland and, among others, the Netherlands, the possibility of ESM operations in the secondary markets was blocked'.[4] The Finnish government declared on its website that:

> At the euro area summit in Brussels on 28–29 June, Prime Minister Jyrki Katainen stated, in the context of the discussion on the euro area summit statement, that Finland will not approve operations in the secondary markets because experience has shown them to be ineffective and because the EFSF and ESM resources are limited. Finland's position was reported in public on the Friday.[5]

[2] See even the German weekly *Der Spiegel*: «http://www.spiegel.de/politik/ausland/angela-merkel-erleidet-bei-eu-gipfel-niederlage-a-841653.html».
[3] European Council website: «http://www.european-council.europa.eu/home-page/highlights/summit-impact-on-the-eurozone».
[4] «http://euobserver.com/economic/116848» and «(http://euobserver.com/institutional/116818».
[5] Government Communications Department, Press Release 223/2012: «http://www.finland.eu/Public/default.aspx?contentid=252828&nodeid=35742&culture=en-US».

© 2013 The Author(s) JCMS: Journal of Common Market Studies © 2013 John Wiley & Sons Ltd

It is hard to find reliable information on such sensitive and behind-the-scenes processes. Various readings seem possible – all of which relate to non-compliance in one way or another. Either these governments were actually outvoted in the European Council, which would have been non-compliance with the treaty regarding the summit decision-making rules. Or alternatively, the European Council decided unanimously on something that was later not accepted by the Finnish and, less noticeably, the Dutch governments. That would have been non-compliance with summit agreements. One reason could be negative press and parliamentary criticism at home. One possible course of events is that nobody disagreed (or continued to disagree) the moment the decision was taken at the European Council, but the next day, the Finnish government realized that this would be hard to sell at home. President of the European Council Herman Van Rompuy stated in any case 'that all decisions had been taken unanimously and no other type of decision was possible'.[6] German Chancellor Angela Merkel stressed as well that during a summit one always needs to find unanimous agreement, and that this had happened.[7] Additionally, it comes to mind that both of the two camps could have informed the media of their perceived and/or desired outcome, based on discussions that had only brought a less than perfectly clear consensus and that the different versions told to the public allowed for all of them to appear as the winner. The course of events may have been less than fully unintended since it was possibly the only way to let both camps appear to have won the battle. A final scenario is that it was a simple but serious misunderstanding that resulted from the enormous pressures placed on all people involved in EU summitry. Politicians and officials work around the clock, including the negotiators and the press officers who feed the websites and the media, and the possibility for human error is thus much increased.

It is not important here to discuss which of the versions[8] is most plausible. It suffices to show that on yet another level a problem of non-compliance has become a matter of debate. Crucially, the problem is by no means singular. The example shows how non-transparent the proceedings of the important and widely publicized EU summits actually are. In the future, a problem of credibility may result from such incidents not only with regard to the much-feared markets, but also the EU's media and citizens.

II. EMU

> This, Honourable Members, reveals the essence of Europe's political crisis of confidence. If Europe's political actors do not abide by the rules and the decisions they have set themselves, how can they possibly convince others that they are determined to solve this crisis together? (Barroso, 2012)

It is undisputed that multiple deviations from agreed rules regarding the EMU occurred over time. This section very briefly summarizes just some of the most salient issues.[9]

---

[6] *Agence Europe*, 4 July 2012.
[7] *Tageszeitung TAZ*, 5 July 2012.
[8] The EU institutions could apply a quick, hands-on strategy and disseminate widely future summit communiqués – ideally in all official languages at the same time – but this only touches the most superficial level of the problems involved and could actually bring about detrimental secondary effects since the leaders would be well aware of this.
[9] For supporting documentation, see the working paper version (Falkner, forthcoming).

© 2013 The Author(s) JCMS: Journal of Common Market Studies © 2013 John Wiley & Sons Ltd

Convergence Criteria and Statistical Reporting

Eurostat, the Commission's department for collecting and publishing official data, witnessed repeated debates about the quality of its data even before the 1990s. EMU, however, clearly made remaining doubts or weaknesses even more problematic. Regarding the Maastricht Treaty's convergence criteria for joining the euro (which set targets regarding price stability, government finances, exchange rates and long-term interest rates), many if not all Member States made their statistics look better.[10] Greece obviously did so to a particularly severe extent and, with the benefit of hindsight, it seems hardly possible that the other governments could not have noticed. Reportedly, one of the largest investment banking and securities firms, Goldman Sachs, was instrumental in the Greek government's legal circumvention of the Maastricht rules and masking the true extent of the Greek deficit. In 1998, the deficit may have been lowered by 0.14 per cent via a hidden credit from Goldman Sachs and later again via a derivatives deal[11] which other EU countries have possibly used as well.[12] It needs mentioning that the relevant EU documents remain closed to the public since the EU General Court in Luxembourg announced that the European Central Bank (ECB) is allowed to refuse access on the grounds of potential negative consequences on the financial markets.[13]

In 2004, at the very latest, the EU partners must have been highly alarmed since creative accounting practices understating the budgetary deficit problem were discovered in an external audit. Nonetheless, the Commission's 2005 proposals to extend Eurostat's powers were blocked by a number of Member State governments, including Germany, who did not want to subject their statistical offices to EU scrutiny. When the Ecofin Council was confronted with 'renewed problems in the Greek fiscal statistics' in November 2009, it invited the Commission to prepare a report and suggest remedies (European Commission, 2010, p. 3). The Commission admitted that 'recent developments, in particular, the inaccuracy of the Greek government deficit and debt statistics, have [. . .] demonstrated that the system for fiscal statistics did not sufficiently mitigate the risk of substandard quality data being notified to Eurostat', and expressed the need to grant Eurostat extended powers in the field of fiscal statistics. These powers were granted by the Council in August 2010 (European Commission, 2010, p. 2).

In any case, much time and credibility had been lost before rather evident shortcomings were addressed. In the eyes of the citizens, it may also have harmed the EU's reputation that its statistics office itself was part of a major scandal around forged tenders and paybacks in the early 1990s.[14] And, what was even more shocking, because of its poor record in investigating corruption cases such as the 'multimillion scandal surrounding Eurostat',[15] Commission President Romano Prodi subsequently also needed to reform the EU's own anti-fraud unit. This suggests that while criticism may seem justified with

---

[10] Generally, the trustworthiness of public debt statistics has been called into question by the International Monetary Fund and there still seems to be ample room for improvement (e.g. *Der Standard*, 6 November 2012).
[11] See, for example, the BBC News report: «http://www.bbc.co.uk/news/world-europe-17108367».
[12] *Der Spiegel*, 8 February 2010.
[13] «http://europa.eu/rapid/press-release_CJE-12-156_en.htm».
[14] In 2003, all directors were replaced. See, for example: «http://www.stern.de/wirtschaft/news/maerkte/affaere-bereichert -euch-510460.html».
[15] *The Telegraph*, 16 November 2003 («http://www.telegraph.co.uk/news/worldnews/europe/1446869/Prodi-turns-on-EUs -failing-fraud-squad.html»).

© 2013 The Author(s) JCMS: Journal of Common Market Studies © 2013 John Wiley & Sons Ltd

regard to reporting, compliance and corruption at the Member State level, the very same is unfortunately the case at the EU level.

Budget Deficit Ceilings, Fiscal Pact, Bail-Out Clause

Once EMU was in force, compliance with the criteria specified in the Maastricht Treaty did not significantly improve. For example, the annual budget deficit ceilings were by no means always respected – not even by the prosperous countries, and partly without the severe economic downturns that might have made that justifiable. The Commission tried, largely in vain, to make the governments enforce the rules of their so-called 'Stability and Growth Pact' (originally from 1997) against themselves, even in ECJ proceedings (C-27/04). It seems evident that if these criteria had always been respected, in both spirit and letter, the financial and budgetary crisis might have hit less badly than it did.[16]

The financial crisis finally made the heads of state and government design new means to convince the markets that their budgetary reforms would hold in the future. Most importantly, the intergovernmental Treaty on Stability, Coordination and Governance (TSCG, or 'Fiscal Compact') was signed by 25 EU Member States (all but the United Kingdom and the Czech Republic) in March 2012. The novel feature is that it requires its signatory states to enshrine key provisions of the EU's Stability and Growth Pact as well as an automatic correction mechanism in permanent national law. Its efficiency cannot be judged as yet. What is of relevance here, however, is that the Fiscal Compact seemed problematic in legal terms to renowned experts. Paul Craig (2012), to give one example, questioned if and to what extent a treaty outside the confines of the Lisbon Treaty can confer new powers on EU institutions, and whether existing powers of EU institutions can actually be used in such a context. Although the ECJ (C 370/12) and national constitutional courts have thus far upheld, at least in essence, what the EU's polity had agreed upon, it seems that further ad hoc agreements and day-to-day practice of EMU rules might want to aim for caution. In terms of public acceptance, the EU would certainly not want to appear as a political system that regularly casts doubt upon the respect of its own constitutional and other rules.

One more case in point which underlines the relevance of that argument is the controversy about the 'no bail-out clause' of the EU treaties. Article 123 Treaty on the Functioning of the European Union (TFEU) (ex Article 101 Treaty establishing the European Community, TEC) states that:

> Any [. . .] type of credit facility with the European Central Bank or with the central banks of the Member States [. . .] in favour of [. . .] governments [. . .] shall be prohibited, as shall the purchase directly from them by the European Central Bank or national central banks of debt instruments.

Most recently, however, the ECB with its covered bond purchase programmes chose a pathway that is seen by some as nonconformity with the 'no bail-out provision' of the Treaty. In essence, the debate is – not least because the German Constitutional Court had stressed that aspect on 12 September 2012 – being shifted away from a ban of one instrument (bailing out countries) towards a framing where the legality of its use depends

---

[16] Corrections of weaknesses may bring further problems in the near future, for example, inclusion of parts of public sector deficits transferred into the accounts of extra-budgetary bodies, corporations and similar bodies.

on the intentions of those who use it. If they employ the instrument in order to reach a goal that is according to the treaties (particularly, the primary objective of the European System of Central Banks, price stability; Article 127 TFEU), what may amount to a bail-out could indeed be legal.[17]

This is not the place to go into any detail of this truly complex and political matter. In general, desperate times may call for desperate measures. From the perspective of compliance, however, it needs mentioning that harm is already being done if the world sees EU actors such as the ECB, the Commission, Member State governments, European Parliament members, the Bundesbank and so on choosing opposing interpretations. In short, the question here is not which version is the 'right' one. What matters for the sake of this argument is that the public legitimacy of the EU may be in danger if such debates and law-suits become a regular feature of EU politics. The risk becomes all the greater if this is not the sole contentious issue but if, as discussed in the section to follow, the most basic values and principles of the EU are also openly put at risk.

III. Basic EU Principles: Can They be Enforced?

Article 6(1) of the Treaty on European Union (TEU) provided that 'the Union is founded on the principles of liberty, democracy, respect for human rights and fundamental freedoms, and the rule of law, principles which are common to the Member States'. Under the Lisbon Treaty, in Article 2, the new formulation lists instead:

> the values of respect for human dignity, freedom, democracy, equality, the rule of law and respect for human rights, including the rights of persons belonging to minorities. These values are common to the Member States in a society in which pluralism, non-discrimination, tolerance, justice, solidarity and equality between women and men prevail.

Article 7 TEU stipulates that a risk of a breach of values may trigger the prevention mechanism and a 'serious and persistent breach' of values, the penalty mechanism. In case of 'a clear risk of a serious breach' of values mentioned, the Council may, according to Article 7 TEU, address appropriate recommendations to that state. After inviting the government of the Member State in question to submit its observations, the Council – meeting in the composition of the heads of state or government – may determine the existence of a 'serious and persistent breach' by a Member State of values mentioned in Article 2. Based on that determination, the Council, acting by a qualified majority, may decide to suspend certain rights deriving from the TEU, including the voting rights of the representative of that Member State government in the Council. The procedural rule for determining a breach of the EU's basic values is unanimity, without taking the vote of the Member State in question into account. This seems the key reason why this procedure has not been used so far, given the severe controversies about the state of democracy in Hungary and Romania.

In Hungary, Victor Orban's national-conservative Fidesz Party came to power[18] with a two-thirds majority of representatives after the elections of 25 April 2010. In 2011, a new

---

[17] For a legal analysis of developments in economic governance, see Amtenbrink's contribution to this issue.
[18] Technically in a coalition with the Christian Democratic People's Party, often described as a satellite party – for example, by Batory (2010).

© 2013 The Author(s) JCMS: Journal of Common Market Studies © 2013 John Wiley & Sons Ltd

constitution was adopted in haste, partly in the middle of the night, that attracted considerable criticism both nationally and internationally. The same applied to various sweeping legal provisions whose revision would also need a two-thirds vote in the future – not an easy task under less clear electoral outcomes. Critics hold that democratic checks and balances, and the EU's democratic values were undermined.[19] Several Hungarian rules of relevance in the field of the rule of law, basic rights and the separation of powers were questioned by the EU Commission for collision with EU secondary law, for example, concerning data protection, non-discrimination on grounds of age in employment, the independence of the central bank and – involving the potentially greatest danger to the basics of Hungarian democracy – the freedom of press. EU Commission Vice-President Neelie Kroes repeatedly expressed concerns, requested changes and even launched infringement proceedings. The Hungarian parliament passed amendments, but insufficiently so. The Council of Europe, the Organization for Security and Cooperation in Europe (OSCE) and non-governmental organizations such as Amnesty International were not satisfied and some even criticized the lack of action by the European Commission. It should be noted that Hungary happened to hold the EU Presidency during the first half of 2011 (Ágh, 2012).

The Commission finally set up a high-level group on media freedom and pluralism that suggested that Hungary 'put itself in a position of potential danger to media freedom and the Government would be wise to consider how to get out of it'.[20] Commissioner Kroes alluded to Article 7 proceedings but referred matters to the Council of Europe,[21] which on 11 May 2012 issued 66 recommendations with regard to the Hungarian media law.[22] Kroes continued to pressurize via the media, but did not initiate proceedings at the EU level. Just as this article was being finalized, most of the controversial provisions adapted earlier have been newly passed in the Hungarian parliament, restoring 'many of the most contentious elements of the new basic law'.[23] The Commission has announced new proceedings with the ECJ and even Article 7 is once again being debated on a daily basis.

In Romania, political instability is, *inter alia*, connected to the economic and financial crisis (see Phinnemore and Papadimitriou, 2013; Gallagher, 2008) and to a conflict between President Traian Basescu (centre-right) and Prime Minister Victor Ponta (social democrat). It may have fuelled the conflict that Ponta's own mentor and former prime minister Adrian Nastase was sentenced to two years in jail on corruption charges, and that the pre-membership adaptations to EU standards regarding law and justice were at best superficial (Gugiu, 2012). The power struggle involved various issues closely related to democratic principles: a procedure to suspend the president, emergency decrees, the removal of the Constitutional Court's powers to review parliamentary decisions, the replacement of high-level office holders such as the ombudsman who can challenge institutions' actions in the Constitutional Court, and the Constitutional Court's authority. Defying a Constitutional Court ruling upholding Basescu's claim that this was the president's job, Ponta travelled to Brussels in June 2012. Thanks to EU intervention (and due

---

[19] See, for example, Dawson and Muir (2012), and the Venice Commission, the Council of Europe's advisory body on constitutional matters: «http://www.venice.coe.int/webforms/documents/?country=17&year=all».
[20] Speech 12/80 to the European Parliament Civil Liberties, Justice and Home Affairs Committee, Brussels, 9 February. Available at: «http://europa.eu/rapid/press-release_SPEECH-12-80_en.htm?locale=en».
[21] Speech 12/80.
[22] «http://hub.coe.int/c/document_library/get_file?uuid=fbc88585-eb71-4545-bc5d-b727e35f59ae&groupId=10227».
[23] *Financial Times*, 4 March 2013 and 5 March 2013.

to a less than 50 per cent turnout in the referendum), the president stayed in power. The Commission's pressure on Romania also led to the revocation of two controversial decrees (on powers of the Constitutional Court and on referendum rules). However, the conflict is only under truce and this struggle cast serious doubt on 'the solidity of Romania's democracy and respect for the rule of law in the country'.[24]

The EU frequently hinted that fundamental principles are at stake, but Article 7 proceedings were not started. Just as in the Hungarian case, alternative means were chosen to increase pressure on Romania. In this case, the country's wish to join the border-free Schengen zone provides some leverage. Originally, both Romania and Bulgaria were expected to enter in spring 2011, but the enlargement was repeatedly blocked.[25] This further example of an indirect fight for improving democratic standards in a Member State by the EU is quite controversial and bears a great risk of antagonizing EU Member States since, in principle, Romania fulfils the formal criteria for Schengen.[26] Various actors, however, argue that the Schengen area 'is not just about technical border control, as evaluated by the Commission, but also about proper functioning of the justice system and the guarantees it provides'.[27] In the aftermath of the latest critical Commission report, Prime Minister Victor Ponta voiced that Romania would implement all the recommendations made by the Commission. This may be seen as a victory for the EU Commission, but it needs mentioning that the dire financial situation of the country gave crucial backing to the political pressures via the International Monetary Fund.[28]

All in all, can foundational principles of the EU such as liberty, democracy, respect for human rights and fundamental freedoms, and the rule of law, be efficiently protected? The good news is that thanks to the EU, there are at least some checks and balances outside individual countries. The bad news is that the EU treaties do not (yet) offer an effective framework to fight threats to democratic principles in the Member States. Determining a breach under Article 7 TEU needs unanimity minus the government concerned in the European Council, plus a two-thirds majority of MEPs. This seems to be the main explanation why it has not yet been used. However, continued non-usage could turn into a very obvious sign of weakness on the part of the EU, and pressurizing by other means may not have the desired effects. What is more, to continue with mainly 'indirect' means in the fight against non-compliance with the EU's basic principles could in the long run invite criticism that the EU acts in a less than transparent, reliable and rule-based manner.[29]

Additionally, as long as no formal proceedings under Article 7 TEU are executed, voting rights in the Council cannot be withdrawn. All leaders of EU states, regardless of their credentials, will continue to participate in the central decisions. Indeed, this is a painful issue: who qualifies in a more than formal sense to be a member of the team in the EU's major decision-making body? Should it be open even to those who tamper with crucial issues of democracy and human rights? Or should the EU – if an important case comes up – contemplate the withdrawal of membership rights not only for reasons of

---

[24] *Financial Times*, 26 November 2012.
[25] *Agence Europe*, 8 March 2013.
[26] *Agence Europe*, 31 January 2013 and 5 February 2013.
[27] Commission Vice-President Viviane Reding, quoted in *Agence Europe*, 4 September 2012.
[28] *Financial Times*, 17 July 2012.
[29] It may even expose the EU 'to charges of hypocrisy and a lack of transparency' (Dawson and Muir, 2012, p. 473).

© 2013 The Author(s) JCMS: Journal of Common Market Studies © 2013 John Wiley & Sons Ltd

procedure, but also for the very sake of protecting itself from the effects this may have both on the outcome of decision-making and the impression that the EU gives to its own people and the world at large?

It is understandable, however, that the Union does indeed act with extreme caution. In addition to the great sensitivity of the matter, it is also obvious that in recent times, there are more than one or two top-level politicians whose democratic credentials have been questioned in one or another dimension, or have even been tried in court proceedings.[30] The EU needs to be very careful in order to prevent a meltdown of democratic systems in Europe, particularly at times of profound economic crisis. In that light, the Article 7 proceedings may indeed appear as a dangerous choice and Commission President Barroso may be right to ask for an alternative 'between the "soft power" of political persuasion and the "nuclear option" of Article 7 of the Treaty' (Barroso, 2012).

IV. Non-compliance with EU Law in the Member States and Enforcement Shortcomings

This section covers what is usually discussed under the heading of non-compliance with EU law. In terms of the ongoing crisis, all of the phenomena highlighted above may seem much more important. Nevertheless, any in-depth analysis of the EU's non-compliance problem cannot ignore these issues.[31] Overall, there is no reason as yet to believe that EU law is actually obeyed in a regular manner, particularly when the application and enforcement (not only the first step of transposition of directives) is concerned. Regarding these later phases of the compliance process, our knowledge is still exceedingly scarce but there are structural weaknesses that make the expectation of swift application seem an illusion. Effective law enforcement needs a number of basic pillars to work adequately: public administrations, labour inspectorates, court systems, media and civil society institutions that could act as whistleblowers and intermediate potential problems. In several new Member States (Falkner, 2010), but also realistically in at least some of the older ones (Falkner et al., 2005), these essential infrastructures have been found wanting as they did not work with a high enough degree of effectiveness as to deserve trust in their capacity to indeed secure that EU rules be applied.

At least regarding the first step of compliance with most EU standards, the transposition of directives into national law, there is good news. Just a couple of years ago, only 11 per cent of 90 cases studied saw both timely and correct transposition (Falkner et al., 2005). Significant improvements seem to have happened lately due to increased investment by the EU Commission. Three initiatives, although falling short of solving the compliance problems overall, have helped in specific cases: the internal market scoreboard, EU pilot and SOLVIT (see Martinsen and Hobolth, forthcoming). Both the number of formal infringement proceedings launched and the seizures of the ECJ have recently been decreasing. The number of open infringement cases even fell from 2,900 in the year 2009 to 1,775 by the end of 2011 (European Commission, 2011, part 2.2). In other words, the portion of non-compliance that is discovered and followed up by the European Commission is tackled more efficiently, both by itself and by the Member States.

---

[30] For details, see Falkner (forthcoming).
[31] They are discussed in greater length in the working paper version of this article; see Falkner (forthcoming).

© 2013 The Author(s) JCMS: Journal of Common Market Studies © 2013 John Wiley & Sons Ltd

However, even the Commission's reports are not unequivocally positive: 'The correct application of EU law continues to present challenges for the Member States [. . .] with late transposition becoming increasingly problematic' (European Commission, 2011, part 4 conclusions). The Commission is thus in agreement with the almost unanimous voice of researchers stating that further improvements are needed as 'the scale of the compliance gap appears worrying' (Toshkov *et al.*, 2010, p. 5). A review of the explanations of compliance offered in numerous qualitative studies revealed that factors related to administrative capacity and co-ordination seem to have the greatest explanatory leverage (Toshkov *et al.*, 2010).

It is true that non-compliance issues 'below' the level of transposition into national law only attract attention occasionally – but if they do so, the harm for the EU's reputation in the eyes of the citizens is enormous. A case in point is the 2013 'horse meat scandal' where a variety of national and EU laws have evidently been disrespected and adequate checks were lacking.[32]

V. Non-compliance with ECJ Judgments and Even Penalization Proceedings

During the pre-1992 era, non-compliance with verdicts of the EU's court soared. Every year about four so-called 'second judgments' were handed down because a Member State had not complied with earlier ECJ judgments on the same case. No effective EU weapon against such forms of Member State non-compliance existed. The Maastricht Treaty set up procedures to penalize disobedient Member States[33] with a lump sum or penalty payment.

Did this change the EU's state-of-law performance? Little is known about the use[34] and effect of these proceedings.[35] It is safe to say that the Commission has been extremely cautious in exercising these powers. In total, there were only 16 such ECJ rulings by the end of 2012. However, between 2006 and 2010, an average of 108 cases of Member State non-compliance were being condemned each year in first judgment, compared to less than one second judgment annually. This seems to suggest that the Commission regards second proceedings and penalization as an exceptional means to demonstrate power in selected cases, and not as the standard means to be applied whenever Member States do not comply with ECJ judgments.

The Commission is indeed quite successful in court when it actually chooses to use this instrument since the ECJ has essentially followed the Commission's views. Does this make the penalization proceedings a powerful weapon? The author rather doubts this since there are manifold signs that one cannot always consider the problem solved, at least in a profound sense, when the Commission treats a second judgment to be finally implemented correctly (see also Kilbey, 2010). Among the cases studied in depth, it seems that about 50 per cent have some, at least related, problems persisting. Another argument to that effect is that the fines seem quite sincere only at first sight. Looking at the relevant frame of comparison – the national budgets – makes the amounts seem small indeed. Consider even the case of Greece, the country with most penalization judgments (six by

---

[32] *Agence Europe*, 26 February 2013.
[33] Now contained in Article 260 TFEU (the Lisbon Treaty).
[34] But see Kilbey (2010).
[35] At the time of writing, an in-depth political science project was still under way at the Institute for European Integration Research (EIF), University of Vienna, funded by the Jubilee Fund of the Austrian National Bank (project 13261). Nikolas Rajkovich and Florian Steininger co-operated in the study.

© 2013 The Author(s) JCMS: Journal of Common Market Studies © 2013 John Wiley & Sons Ltd

January 2013): the amount of fines until mid-2011 (c.€34,500,000) approximates just 0.54 per cent of the annual social expenses of the Greek state.[36] This suggests that even a less wealthy state can in fact afford to keep paying the EU's fines. Maybe this is what makes the Commission so very prudent in its use of the seemingly most powerful weapon; since no direct intervention in domestic affairs is possible for the EU, penalization could easily boil down to a 'paper tiger' with quite narrow limits.

VI. Unravelling Historical Compromises that Built the Very Basis of Major EU Projects

Ever since its origins in the mid-1950s, the EU found a compromise solution between market-making as the core ambition, and a limited degree of re-regulation in fields such as competition policy and social policy. The pact with liberalization going hand-in-hand with some degree of harmonization (the 'market-plus' model) has been extended in various EU treaty reforms to cover further fields such as, importantly, environmental policy (since the Single European Act in 1986).

The United Kingdom signed up to the initial deal when it joined the EEC in 1973 and it explicitly agreed to all further treaty reforms, as well. Prime Minister Cameron and his Conservative Party, however, now want to undo all this in order to get a 'market-only' model. Should the renegotiation be unsuccessful, the possibility of leaving the Union via a referendum has been threatened.[37] This begs discussion as a novel type of non-compliance problem in the wider, but potentially even narrow, sense. The United Kingdom is withdrawing from the existing *acquis* and threatening to no longer apply parts of it. While Cameron stresses that continued 'access to the Single Market is vital for British businesses and British jobs'[38] he wants to get rid of existing policies surrounding this. On 'Cameron's possible shopping list' are the social and employment directives, environmental policy and regional and fishing policies.[39] From the perspective of credible commitments, in any case, the firmest rejection of any insinuation to reopen done deals seems in place. To give in to Cameron's wish to cherry-pick and unravel the EU's existing policies would be like opening Pandora's box since leaders of other states could not resist the pressure to undo compromises they or any powerful lobby in their country might at any point consider to be less than advantageous.

VII. Where to Go? Towards 'Compliance for Credibility'

> We cannot belong to the same Union and behave as if we don't. (Barroso, Speech/12/596, p. 2)

Each of the sections above has hinted at potential or already real compliance problems, at least in a wider sense. My conclusion is that, as unfortunate as any single non-compliance aspect may be (or not), it is the overall impression of the EU as a credible and authoritative body that matters most. Under the condition that any of the non-compliance phenomena discussed appears as a singular weakness, no fundamental danger will result. In a state of

---

[36] Reportedly at €6,400,000,000 (*Die Presse*, 3 August 2011).
[37] *Financial Times*, 23 January 2013.
[38] «http://www.number10.gov.uk/news/david-cameron-eu-speech/».
[39] *Financial Times*, 23 January 2013.

© 2013 The Author(s) JCMS: Journal of Common Market Studies © 2013 John Wiley & Sons Ltd

rather 'generalized non-compliance',[40] by contrast, the EU would no longer be perceived as a trustworthy actor either by its people or by the outside world. And once the EU is indeed seen as a 'non-compliance community' decay seems a foregone conclusion: why should anyone take it seriously?

In that light, policy recommendations and the renewed promotion of good ideas already voiced by various EU actors seem an urgent matter. Humans including politicians follow both the 'logic of appropriateness' and the 'logic of consequentiality' for different reasons and at different times,[41] and democratic governance involves balancing between diverse motivations and modes of action. Hence, both rule-oriented prescriptions based on sanctions and value-oriented measures connected to relevant beliefs can be usefully employed by the EU when striving for improvements to the status quo. One should start with promoting the basic, fundamental values involved and improving the provision of related data and comparative statistics.

First, the rule of law can, unfortunately, not be taken as a 'given', even in today's Europe. Therefore, a relevant campaign should be put in place throughout the EU. People can be convinced, but much more effort is needed to make them aware that law abidance is of crucial value in stable democracies and hence worth fighting for (see also Dawson and Muir, 2012, p. 476). Good compliance examples should be spread in television spots and newspapers. For example, politicians from Nordic countries (whose culture of law abidance is comparatively good)[42] could publicly explain that they dutifully implement even directives with costly effects for their country because they trust that, in turn, the EU partners will do the same with directives they may find difficult. Business people should argue that they depend on a level playing field in the EU's internal market not only in the books, but in practice. Campaigning for the rule of law could even have an additional, indirect benefit as well: the EU would, in the longer run, be less associated with infringements and fraud of agricultural subsidies and more with its role as a watchdog for democracy and basic rights throughout the EU – a role it has started to play during recent years.

Second, additional (and finally appropriate) resources for the Commission are indispensable with regard to improved EU-level control of the application of EU law. If not the daily process of application, then at least the framework conditions for its functioning need to be controlled much more tightly from the EU level. The open method of co-ordination (OMC)[43] could be used with regard to court systems, labour inspectorates and administrative capacity. With regular reporting duties resulting in relevant cross-country data sets that can be used for naming and shaming as well as harvesting examples of good practice, all national infrastructures should be supported that are needed to uphold the practice of the rule of law. Spreading best practice models could help activists among the citizens and the media throughout the EU promote democracy since, typically, even the leading countries can improve on some specific facets.

Third, an 'OMC democracy' could be set up overlooking all basic building blocks that are indispensable for a properly working democracy, such as political parties (adequate

---

[40] Thanks to Christopher Bickerton for suggesting the expression.
[41] See the work by March and Olsen (for example, March and Olsen, 1989).
[42] See, for example, Falkner *et al.* (2005, pp. 317ff.) and Sverdrup (2004).
[43] The open method of co-ordination is a multiform process of reporting, benchmarking, establishing best practice and so on. It involves a communicative process among a large variety of national and supranational actors (Kröger, 2009; Hartlapp, 2012).

© 2013 The Author(s) JCMS: Journal of Common Market Studies © 2013 John Wiley & Sons Ltd

and transparent funding, intraparty democracy procedures, etc.), civil society organizations (working conditions, transparency of funding, etc.) and freedom of the media. The OMC goes beyond data comparison, which is however in itself a task to be specified.

Fourth, these OMCs should be supported by bodies or units with the task to develop useful indicators and collect, compare and publicize relevant data. This could mean strengthening the human rights agency and/or establishing observatories (in the Commission or in academia)[44] or scoreboard task forces within the Commission. At least for the judicial systems, the case of Hungary has triggered relevant developments: EU Commissioner for Justice Viviane Reding announced a procedure to assess its members' democratic standards and a 'scoreboard on judicial systems'.[45]

Fifth, great care is needed to respect best practice during the process of law-making, too. It is not viable to set standards that are simply unrealistic targets for some of the Member States (or to fail to exempt new Member States); at times, more differentiation may be needed – as demanded by Vivien Schmidt in her 2009 article in the *JCMS Annual Review* (Schmidt, 2009; see also Piris, 2012). For example, it seems with the benefit of hindsight quite evident that some of the EU environmental policy directives contained unfeasible goals considering the state of affairs in states like Greece.[46] If such circumstances continue to be neglected, non-compliance may develop into a 'weapon of the weak' for those who are outvoted in the Council but incapable of complying even if they wanted to.[47] Admittedly, striking a balance between the ambition and the feasibility of targets will surely not be an easy task, and the same is true when considering if a government's commitment can actually be trusted to be real if it does not protest against a particularly demanding new joint regulatory standard.

Sixth, law-making at the higher level, and implementation at the lower one, seems a plausible distribution of labour, in principle. However, that cannot function properly if the indispensable equipment for effective enforcement is missing on the lower level. Recent problems discussed in this contribution indicate a danger that EU law might be degrading towards a 'dead letter' in some places for structural reasons. Even if the problems of having EU law applied, particularly in the new Member States, is now said to 'toughen the pre-membership process', and even if the EU strives in the future only to let in 'those which are fully prepared to assume their responsibility join the EU',[48] it seems that an important instrument may be given up if new Member States (such as Croatia by mid-2013) would, in the future, not have to undergo a process like the co-operation and verification mechanism applied to Bulgaria and Romania. Giving up these monitoring systems seems unduly optimistic with regard to the short-term reform capacities preceding accession and

---

[44] See the European Observatory on Counterfeiting and Piracy set up in the Commission («http://ec.europa.eu/internal _market/iprenforcement/observatory/index_en.htm»). At the European University Institute in Florence, the European Union Democracy Observatory (EUDO) has four observatories responsible for data-gathering, reporting and fostering dialogue; in the fields of citizenship, public opinion and the media, political parties and representation, and institutions. So far, its 'Observatory on Institutional Change and Reform' is devoted to the analysis of institutional reforms of the EU, not in the Member States, but this could possibly be further developed given the necessary means.
[45] *Agence Europe*, 14 September 2012.
[46] Since the 1970s, Member States need to ensure that waste is disposed of without harm to health or the environment. Notwithstanding relevant ECJ judgments against Greece, including with penalization, 'some 78 illegal landfills continue to operate in violation of EU waste legislation and 318 are still in the process of being rehabilitated' by March 2013 («http://europa.eu/rapid/press-release_IP-13-143_en.htm»). The Commission has therefore taken Greece to the Court again.
[47] Thanks to Renaud Dehousse for this argument.
[48] EU Commissioner for Enlargement Stefan Füle, cited in *Agence Europe*, 10 October 2012.

© 2013 The Author(s) JCMS: Journal of Common Market Studies © 2013 John Wiley & Sons Ltd

with regard to the political dynamics that make stopping envisaged enlargement difficult, even if there may be visible shortcomings in some areas.

If the first group of measures above did not even demand any significant legal reforms, a second group would go much further and establish either new rules or even innovative institutions at the European level. This may seem outrageous in the light of the long-standing ideas of democracy and the rule of law being located first and foremost in 'sovereign nation-states'. However, that may no longer be sufficient. Democracy is under pressure when national politics are ever more prone to instability, parliamentary majorities are ruthlessly exploited for anti-democratic means, populism abounds, the media no longer perform their classic control function and the economy is in trouble. In such circumstances, it seems not only prudent but sensible to contemplate additional and innovative checks and balances in order to make sure that the basic democratic pillars are fully supported. This task should involve representatives from all levels of EU governance – local, national, European – and from multiple segments of society. Crucially, it could combine actors with different, reinforcing kinds of legitimacy (politics, academics, civil society, legal and technical experts). The EU's great potential for collaboration and discourse could hence be turned into a resource, as a means of both enabling and restraining national politicians. The idea is not to supersede national systems, but rather to use European means to stabilize and, where appropriate, improve democracy in the Member States. With major challenges ahead, a two-level system of checks and balances seems indispensable.

This brings to mind a number of promising possibilities including provision of expert advice and discourse when it comes to the basic architecture of democracy. Constitutional reforms and changes concerning pillars of democratic life such as electoral and media laws should, before being voted on at the relevant national level, be checked (possibly at a later point even approved) at the EU level. For example, an 'EU Council for Democracy and Rule of Law'[49] could vet all major reform projects according to basic common principles. Its composition needs in-depth consideration but representatives from the EU institutions are possible candidates as well as representatives of the national constitutional courts and the ECJ[50] and independent experts such as political scientists and lawyers from an academic background. Possibly, this institution could become an independent agency (the dynamics of party politics need to be kept at bay) at the European Parliament since the latter is directly legitimized by the EU's citizens.

Who is best suited to perform highly sensible functions in terms of safeguarding basic democratic principles at the European level[51] and complementing the at times sterile debates in individual states? As far as the collection of data is concerned, the legitimacy of well-trained personnel in expert institutions such as the EU Commission, the Council of Europe,[52] the EU's Human Rights Agency and so on may be appropriate. When it comes to making judgments and innovative proposals, a board of truly independent wise

---

[49] Or 'EU Council for Fundamental EU Values' or 'EU Council for Democratic Principles and Fundamental Rights'.

[50] There is an interesting debate among specialized lawyers over the possibility of having fundamental rights checked by national- and EU-level courts under a 'reversed solange' doctrine. For the details, see Von Bogdandy *et al.*, 2012.

[51] This raises complex issues of legitimacy as well as politicization (De Wilde and Zürn, 2012) that cannot be discussed in depth here. See, for example, the *JCMS* 50th Anniversary Special Issue on the evolution of the EU's polity (Mattli and Stone Sweet, 2012).

[52] EU co-operation with the Council of Europe would warrant in-depth consideration that is, however, beyond this article's scope.

© 2013 The Author(s) JCMS: Journal of Common Market Studies © 2013 John Wiley & Sons Ltd

(wo)men – possibly political scientists and constitutional lawyers – might be better placed. When decisions concerning the withholding of funds or even suspending voting rights come into play, the highest level of political legitimacy is clearly indispensable. For good reasons, the TEU provides for the determination of a serious and persistent breach by a Member State of values mentioned in Article 2 to be agreed in the Council (in such cases, composed of the heads of state or government) upon assent by the European Parliament. At times, the courts might also be appropriate umpires, including the ECJ and the national (constitutional) courts.

With regard to Article 7 TEU, the excessively high quota – all governments minus one, and EP assent – for determining the breach of basic EU values could be replaced by, for example, simple majorities in both the Council and the EP in cases where an advisory opinion of the ECJ (and potentially, of the new 'EU Council for Democracy and Rule of Law' mentioned above) supports the motion.

Commission Vice-President Viviane Reding proposed that the talks about establishing a 'European minister of finance' should be complemented by an 'EU minister of justice' charged with enforcing the rule of law in the EU.[53] Although possibly perceived by some countries as overly interventionist, this could certainly be an effective pathway to make EU standards that are still dead letters into living rights.

Establishing EU-wide rules for independent supervisory agencies in the Member States is also a relevant idea. With regard to the freedom of press relevant proposals have been made by a high-level working group set up by EU Commission Vice-President Neelie Kroes. They refer to the harmonization of media laws across the EU and regulation of the media by independent agencies based on EU-wide principles with powers to investigate complaints and impose fines and orders.[54] Similarly, the European Parliament's Civil Liberties Committee recently recommended that the European Commission and the European Fundamental Rights Agency carry out an annual audit of media laws, monitoring, for example, the concentration in the media industry and the extent to which the new laws allow governments to interfere with the media across the EU. The Committee recommended non-legislative action as well as expanding the audio-visual services directive to ensure full application of the European Charter of Fundamental Rights, particularly full independence and adequate resources for national media watchdogs.[55]

These suggestions are bold. However, decisive action is needed so the EU will continue to be perceived as a trustworthy actor by the outside world and its citizens, and not a 'non-compliance community'. This is a major goal to be achieved without delay. What indeed matters are credible commitments. If non-compliance spreads – and a tipping-point even in terms of basic legitimacy of the political system might be close – any policies formally adopted by the EU will not find the trust of economic operators, global partners or the European people themselves. But trust is crucial. Even (or maybe particularly) markets judge credibility, not *de facto* compliance. If the essential, high level of trust in the EU's overall ability to deliver and meet its goals can be restored, there will be little cause to worry about minor problems of continuing slack in policy implementation.

---

[53] Interview with *Frankfurter Allgemeine Zeitung*, 18 July 2012 (translated by the author).
[54] *Financial Times*, 21 January 2013.
[55] *Agence Europe*, 23 February 2013.

© 2013 The Author(s) JCMS: Journal of Common Market Studies © 2013 John Wiley & Sons Ltd

References

Ágh, A. (2012) 'The Hungarian Rhapsodies: The Conflict of Adventurism and Professionalism in the European Union Presidency'. *JCMS*, Vol. 50, No. S2, pp. 68–75.

Barroso, J.M.D. (2012) 'State of the Union Address'. Speech 12/596, 12 September. Available at: «http://europa.eu/rapid/press-release_SPEECH-12-596_en.pdf».

Batory, A. (2010) 'Electronic Briefing 51: Europe and the Hungarian Parliamentary Elections of April 2010'. Available at: «https://www.sussex.ac.uk/webteam/gateway/file.php?name=epern -election-briefing-no-51.pdf&site=266».

Craig, P. (2012) 'The Stability, Coordination and Governance Treaty: Principle, Politics and Pragmatism'. Legal Research Paper Series No. 47, University of Oxford.

Dawson, M. and Muir, E. (2012) 'Enforcing Fundamental Values: EU Law and Governance in Hungary and Romania'. *Maastricht Journal of European and Comparative Law*, Vol. 19, No. 4, pp. 469–76.

De Wilde, P. and Zürn, M. (2012) 'Can the Politicization of European Integration be Reversed?' *JCMS*, Vol. 50, No. S1, pp. 137–53.

European Commission (2010) 'Report on Greek government deficit and debt statistics'. *COM*(2010) 1 final, 8 January.

European Commission (2011) '29th annual report on monitoring the application of EU law'. *COM*(2012) 714, 11 November.

Falkner, G. (2010) 'Institutional Performance and Compliance with EU Law: Czech Republic, Hungary, Slovakia and Slovenia'. *Journal of Public Policy*, Vol. 30, pp. 101–16.

Falkner, G. (forthcoming) 'Is the EU a Noncompliance Community? Towards "Compliance for Credibility"'. Working Paper. For further information, see: «http://eif.univie.ac.at/falkner/ publications.php».

Falkner, G. and Müller, P. (2013) 'Comparative Analysis: The EU as a Policy Exporter?' In *EU Policies in a Global Perspective: Shaping or Taking International Regimes?* (London: Routledge).

Falkner, G., Treib, O., Hartlapp, M. and Leiber, S. (2005) *Complying with Europe: EU Harmonisation and Soft Law in the Member States* (Cambridge: Cambridge University Press).

Gallagher, T. (2008) *Modern Romania: The End of Communism, the Failure of Democratic Reform and the Theft of a Nation* (New York: New York University Press).

Gugiu, M.R. (2012) 'EU Enlargement and Anticorruption: Lessons Learned from Romania'. *Journal of European Integration*, Vol. 34, No. 5, pp. 429–46.

Hartlapp, M. (2012) 'Deconstructing EU Old Age Policy: Assessing the Potential of Soft OMCs and Hard EU Law'. *European Integration Online Papers*, Vol. 16, No. 3. Available at: «http:// eiop.or.at/eiop/texte/2012-003a.htm».

Jones, E. (2012) 'The JCMS Annual Review Lecture: European Crisis, European Solidarity'. *JCMS*, Vol. 50, No. S2, pp. 53–67.

Kilbey, I. (2010) 'The Interpretation of Article 260 TFEU (ex 228 EC)'. *European Law Review*, Vol. 35, No. 3, pp. 370–86.

Kröger, S.E. (2009) 'What We Have Learnt: Advances, Pitfalls and Remaining Questions in OMC Research'. *European Integration Online Papers*, Vol. 13, No. S1. Available at: «http:// eiop.or.at/eiop/index.php/eiop/issue/view/21».

March, J.G. and Olsen, J.P. (1989) *Rediscovering Institutions* (New York: Free Press).

Martinsen, D.S. and Hoboth, M. (forthcoming) 'Transgovernmental Networks in the European Union: Improving Compliance Effectively'. *Journal of European Public Policy*.

Mattli, W. and Stone Sweet, A. (eds) (2012) 'Special Issue: Regional Integration and the Evolution of the European Polity'. *JCMS*, Vol. 50.

Nicolaïdis, K. (2010) 'The JCMS Annual Review Lecture – Sustainable Integration: Towards EU 2.0?' *JCMS*, Vol. 48, No. S1, pp. 21–54.

Phinnemore, D. and Papadimitriou, D. (2013) 'Romania: Uneven Europeanization'. In Bulmer, S. and Lequesne, C. (eds) *The Member States of the European Union* (Oxford: Oxford University Press).

Piris, J.-C. (2012) *Future of Europe: Towards a Two-Speed EU* (Cambridge: Cambridge University Press).

Schmidt, V.A. (2004) 'The European Union: Democratic Legitimacy in a Regional State?'. *JCMS*, Vol. 42, No. 5, pp. 975–97.

Schmidt, V.A. (2009) 'Re-envisioning the European Union: Identity, Democracy, Economy'. *JCMS*, Vol. 47, No. S1, pp. 17–42.

Sverdrup, U. (2004) 'Compliance and Conflict Management in the European Union: Nordic Exceptionalism'. *Scandinavian Political Studies*, Vol. 27, No. 1, pp. 23–43.

Toshkov, D., Knoll, M. and Wewerka, L. (2010) 'Connecting the Dots: Case Studies and EU Implementation Research'. Working Paper 10/2010 (Vienna: Institute for European Integration Research). Available at: «http://eif.univie.ac.at/downloads/workingpapers/wp2010-10.pdf».

Von Bogdandy, A., Kottmann, M., Antpöhler, C., Dickschen, J., Hentrei, S. and Smrkolj, M. (2012) 'Reverse Solange: Protecting the Essence of Fundamental Rights against EU Member States'. *Common Market Law Review*, Vol. 49, No. 2, pp. 489–519.

© 2013 The Author(s) JCMS: Journal of Common Market Studies © 2013 John Wiley & Sons Ltd

JCMS 2013 Volume 51 Annual Review pp. 31–41   DOI: 10.1111/jcms.12042

From Panic-Driven Austerity to Symmetric Macroeconomic Policies in the Eurozone

PAUL DE GRAUWE[1] and YUEMEI JI[2]
[1] London School of Economics and Political Science and Centre for European Policy Studies. [2] University of Leuven

Introduction

On 6 September 2012 the European Central Bank (ECB) announced its 'Outright Monetary Transactions' (OMT) programme, which promised to buy unlimited amounts of sovereign bonds during crises. It is interesting to quote Mario Draghi who justified the OMT programme as follows:

> [Y]you have large parts of the euro area in a bad equilibrium in which you may have self-fulfilling expectations that feed on themselves. [. . .] So, there is a case for intervening [. . .] to 'break' these expectations, which [. . .] do not concern only the specific countries, but the euro area as a whole. And this would justify the intervention of the central bank.[1]

After long hesitation the ECB appears to have made the fateful, but correct, decision to become a lender of last resort, not only for banks but also for sovereigns, thereby re-establishing the stabilizing force needed to protect the system from market fears and panic that have destabilized the eurozone.

The effect of this announcement was quite dramatic. It took away the fear factor that dominated the eurozone in 2012: the fear that the eurozone could collapse soon. By taking away this existential fear, the ECB made it possible for government bond spreads to decline dramatically. Thus the decision of the ECB was a game changer and put meat onto the bones of Mario Draghi's July 2012 promise to 'do whatever it takes' to save the euro.[2]

Will this new role for the ECB be sufficient to save the eurozone? The question is analyzed in this article in two steps: first, we look at the risks that have been created by austerity; and second, we ask what kind of macroeconomic policies would be most appropriate.

I. The Risks Created by Austerity

Since the outburst of the sovereign debt crisis in 2010, macroeconomic policies in the eurozone have been dictated by financial markets. This is made clear in Figure 1, which shows the average interest rate spreads[3] in 2011 on the horizontal axis and the intensity of

---

[1] *Financial Times*, 11 September 2012.
[2] For an overview of developments in the eurozone during 2012, see Hodson's contribution to this issue.
[3] These are defined as the difference between each country's ten-year government bond rate and the German ten-year government bond rate.

© 2013 The Author(s) JCMS: Journal of Common Market Studies © 2013 John Wiley & Sons Ltd, 9600 Garsington Road, Oxford OX4 2DQ, UK and 350 Main Street, Malden, MA 02148, USA

Figure 1: Austerity Measures and Spreads in 2011

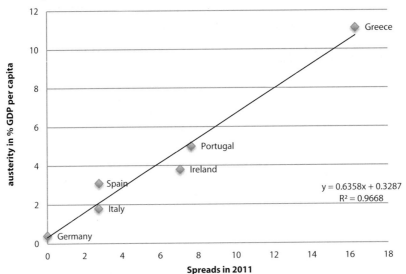

Source: *Financial Times*, available at: «http://www.ft.com/cms/s/0/feb598a8-f8e8-11e0-a5f7-00144feab49a.html# axzz2JSOwncys», and Datastream.

austerity measures introduced during 2011 as measured by the *Financial Times*[4] (as a percentage of per capita gross domestic product [GDP]). These measures are in the spirit of the 'narrative approach' to measuring exogenous changes in fiscal policies and avoid the endogeneity problem inherent in using headline budget deficit numbers (see Romer and Romer, 2007). These measures contain the decisions made in the countries under pressure to reduce spending and increase taxes. The estimated impact of all these measures on disposable income is then used as indicators of austerity. Although this painstaking work was only done for the six countries labelled in Figure 1, the statistics are illuminating for developments in the eurozone as a whole.

It is striking to find a very strong positive correlation. The higher the spreads in 2011, the more intense were the austerity measures. The intensity of the spreads can be explained almost uniquely by the size of the spreads (the R^2 is 0.97). Note the two extremes. Greece was confronted with extremely high spreads in 2011 and applied the most severe austerity measures amounting to more than 10 per cent of GDP per capita. Germany, which did not face any pressure from spreads, did not undertake any austerity measures.

A cautionary note should be made here. The sample consists of only six countries. Too strong generalizations even when the correlation is very high are out of place. With the exception of Germany, the countries in Figure 1, however, are those that were subjected to the most intense austerity programmes. It is, therefore, instructive to discover that these are also the countries whose spreads increased the most.

[4] *Financial Times*, available at: «http://www.ft.com/cms/s/0/feb598a8-f8e8-11e0-a5f7-00144feab49a.html# axzz2JSOwncys».

© 2013 The Author(s) JCMS: Journal of Common Market Studies © 2013 John Wiley & Sons Ltd

There can be little doubt: financial markets exerted different degrees of pressure on countries. By raising the spreads they forced some countries to undertake severe austerity programmes. Other countries did not experience increases in spreads and as a result did not feel much urge to apply the austerity medicine. Note that it was not just the pressure of the markets that was at work here: the movements of the markets affected the views of key political and economic actors in Europe, which created pressure for the adoption of austerity measures.

The question that arises is whether the judgement of the market (measured by the spreads) about how much austerity each country should apply was the correct one. There are essentially two theories that can be invoked to answer this question. According to the first theory, the surging spreads observed from 2010 to the middle of 2012 were the result of deteriorating fundamentals (for example, domestic government debt, external debt, competitiveness). Thus, the market was just the messenger of bad news, but not the cause of that bad news. Its judgement should then be respected. The implication of that theory is that the only way these spreads can be reduced is by improving the fundamentals, mainly through austerity programmes aimed at reducing government budget deficits and debts.

Another theory, while accepting that fundamentals matter, recognizes that collective movements of fear and panic can have dramatic effects on spreads. These movements can drive the spreads away from underlying fundamentals, very much like in stock markets when prices can be gripped by a bubble pushing them far away from underlying fundamentals.[5] The implication of that theory is that while fundamentals cannot be ignored, there is a special role for the central bank that has to provide liquidity in times of market panic (De Grauwe, 2011b).

The decision by the ECB in 2012 to commit itself to unlimited support of the government bond markets was a game changer in the eurozone. It had dramatic effects. By taking away the intense existential fears that the collapse of the eurozone was imminent, the ECB's lender of last resort commitment pacified government bond markets and led to a strong decline in the spreads of the eurozone countries. Whether this decision will be sufficient to permanently stabilize the eurozone is the subject of the next section.

The decision of the ECB provides us with an interesting experiment to test these two theories about how spreads are formed. Figure 2 provides the evidence. On the vertical axis we show the change in the spreads in the eurozone from the middle of 2012 (when the ECB announced its OMT programme) to the beginning of 2013. On the horizontal axis we present the initial spread – that is, the one prevailing in the middle of 2012. We find a surprising phenomenon. The initial spread (in 2012 Q2) explains almost all the subsequent variation in the spreads. Thus the country with the largest initial spread (Greece) experienced the largest subsequent decline; the country with the second largest initial spread (Portugal) experienced the second largest subsequent decline, and so on. In fact, the points lie almost exactly on a straight line going through the origin. The regression equation indicates that 97 per cent of the variation in the spreads is accounted for by the initial spread.[6] Thus it appears that the only variable that matters to explain the size of the decline

[5] For a classic analysis, see Calvo (1988) and Eaton and Gersovitz (1981). Similar analyses have been made for banks – for example, Diamond and Dybvig (1983).
[6] We undertook an ordinary least squares (OLS) regression test. The estimated coefficients are significant at the 99 per cent level.

© 2013 The Author(s) JCMS: Journal of Common Market Studies © 2013 John Wiley & Sons Ltd

Figure 2: Change in Spread and Initial Spread from 2012 Q2 to 2013 Q1 (in %)

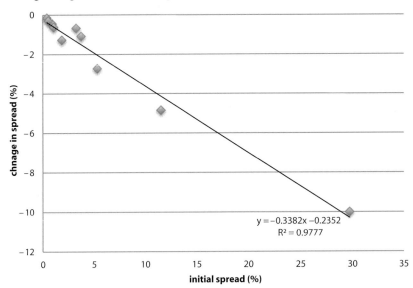

$y = -0.3382x - 0.2352$
$R^2 = 0.9777$

Source: Datastream (Oxford Economics).

in the spreads since the ECB announced its determination to be the lender of last resort (OMT) is the initial level of the spread. Countries whose spread had climbed the most prior to the ECB announcement experienced the strongest decline in their spreads, which is a remarkable feature.

In De Grauwe and Ji (2012) we provided evidence that prior to the regime shift made possible by the ECB a large part of the surges in the spreads were the results of market sentiments of fear and panic that had driven the spreads away from their underlying fundamentals. The evidence provided by Figure 2 tends to confirm this. By taking away the fear factor, the ECB allowed the spreads to decline. We find that the decline in the spreads was the strongest in the countries where the fear factor (as measured by the initial spreads) had been the strongest.

What about the role of fundamentals in explaining the decline in the spreads observed since the middle of 2012? In Figure 3 we provide some evidence. We selected the change in the government debt/GDP as the fundamental variable. It appears from many studies (Aizenman and Hutchinson, 2012; Attinasi *et al.*, 2009; Beirne and Fratzscher, 2012; De Grauwe and Ji, 2012) that the debt/GDP ratio is the most important fundamental variable influencing spreads. We observe two interesting phenomena in Figure 3. First, while the spreads declined, the debt/GDP ratio continued to increase in all countries after the ECB announcement. Second, the change in the debt/GDP ratio is a poor predictor of the declines in the spreads (as can be seen from the regression equation). Thus the decline in the spreads observed since the ECB announcement appear to be completely unrelated to the changes of the debt-to-GDP ratios. If anything, the fundamentalist school of thinking would have predicted that as the debt-to-GDP ratios increased in all countries, spreads should have increased rather than declined.

© 2013 The Author(s) JCMS: Journal of Common Market Studies © 2013 John Wiley & Sons Ltd

Figure 3: Change in Debt/GDP and Spread since 2012 Q2

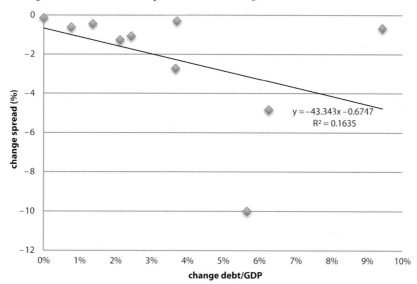

$y = -43.343x - 0.6747$
$R^2 = 0.1635$

Source: Datastream (Oxford Economics).

From the previous discussion one can conclude that a large component of the movements of the spreads since 2010 was driven by market sentiments. These market sentiments of fear and panic first drove the spreads away from their fundamentals. Later as the market sentiments improved thanks to the announcement of the ECB, these spreads declined spectacularly – once again out of line with fundamentals.

We can now give the following interpretation of how the spreads exerted their influence on policy-makers and led them to apply severe austerity measures. As the spreads increased due to market panic, these increases also gripped policy-makers. Panic in the financial markets led to panic in the world of policy-makers in Europe. As a result of this panic, rapid and intense austerity measures were imposed on countries experiencing these increases in spreads. The imposition of dramatic austerity measures was also forced by the fact that countries with high spreads were pushed into a liquidity crisis by the same market forces that produced the high spreads (De Grauwe, 2011a). This forced these countries to beg 'cap in hand' for funding from the creditor countries.

We are not arguing that the debtor countries do not need to return to sustainable public finances or that they can avoid budgetary austerity. Rather, we argue that the budgetary austerity imposed on these countries has been too intense and has been influenced too much by panic in financial markets.

How well did this panic-induced austerity work? We provide some answers in Figures 4 and 5. Figure 4 shows the relation between the austerity measures introduced in 2011 and the growth of GDP over 2011–12. We find a strong negative correlation. Countries that imposed the strongest austerity measures also experienced the strongest declines in their GDP. This result is in line with the International Monetary Fund's recent analysis (IMF, 2012).

One may argue that this is the price that has to be paid for restoring budgetary orthodoxy. But is this so? Figure 5 may lead us to doubt this. It shows the austerity

© 2013 The Author(s) JCMS: Journal of Common Market Studies © 2013 John Wiley & Sons Ltd

Figure 4: Austerity (2011) and GDP Growth (2011–12)

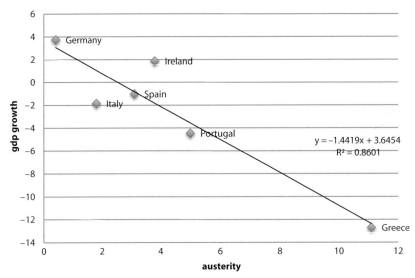

Source: *Financial Times*, available at: «http://www.ft.com/cms/s/0/feb598a8-f8e8-11e0-a5f7-00144feab49a.html#axzz2JSOwncys», and Datastream.

Figure 5: Austerity (2011) and Increases in Government Debt/GDP (2010 Q4–2012 Q3)

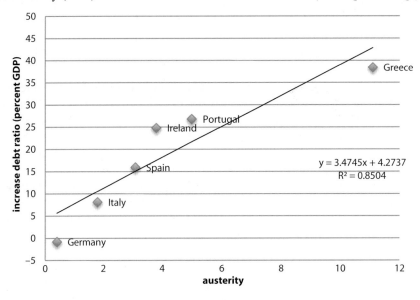

Source: *Financial Times*, available at: «http://www.ft.com/cms/s/0/feb598a8-f8e8-11e0-a5f7-00144feab49a.html#axzz2JSOwncys», and Datastream.
Note: The Greek government/debt ratio excludes the debt restructuring at the end of 2011 that amounted to about 30 per cent of GDP.

© 2013 The Author(s) JCMS: Journal of Common Market Studies © 2013 John Wiley & Sons Ltd

measures and the subsequent change in the debt-to-GDP ratios.[7] It is striking to find a strong positive correlation. The more intense the austerity, the larger the subsequent increase in debt-to-GDP ratios. This is not really surprising, as we have learned from the previous figure that those countries that applied the strongest austerity also saw their GDP (the denominator in the debt ratio) decline most forcefully. Thus, it can be concluded that the sharp austerity measures that were imposed by market and policy-makers' panic not only produced deep recessions in the countries that were exposed to the medicine, but also that up to now this medicine did not work. In fact it led to even higher debt-to-GDP ratios and undermined the capacity of these countries to continue to service the debt. Thus the liquidity crisis that started all this risks degenerating into a solvency crisis.

II. What Kind of Macroeconomic Policies?

The previous results show the power of financial markets in affecting macroeconomic outcomes. They also show how financial markets have split the eurozone in two, forcing some (the southern European countries, the 'periphery') into bad equilibria and others (mainly northern European countries, the 'core') into good equilibria. The southern European countries (including Ireland) are also the countries that have accumulated current account deficits, while the northern European countries have built up current account surpluses.

The first best policy would have been for the debtor countries to reduce spending and for the creditor countries to increase spending. The southern European countries have no other option than to continue reducing spending relative to output (or to increase output relative to spending) so as to eliminate their current account deficits and to reduce their external debt. At the same time, however, the northern creditor countries that spend too little relative to their output should do the reverse. As a result, the inevitable deflationary forces arising from budgetary austerity in the south can be offset by demand stimulus in the northern European countries.

Instead, under the leadership of the German government and the European Commission, tight austerity was imposed on the debtor countries, while the creditor countries continued to follow policies aimed at balancing the budget. This has led to an asymmetric adjustment process in which most of the adjustment has been done by the debtor nations. These countries have been forced to reduce wages and prices relative to the creditor countries (an 'internal devaluation') without compensating wage and price increases in the creditor countries ('internal revaluations'). Thus the burden of the adjustments to the imbalances in the eurozone between the surplus and the deficit countries is borne almost exclusively by the deficit countries in the periphery. This creates a deflationary bias that explains why the eurozone has been pulled into a double-dip recession as can be seen from Figure 6.

Yet macroeconomic policies in the eurozone could be organized differently. A more symmetric macroeconomic policy could be implemented. This symmetric approach should start from the different fiscal positions of the member countries of the eurozone. In Figures 7 and 8 we show this difference. We present the government debt ratios of two

[7] In Greece there was a debt restructuring at the end of 2011 which reduced the government's debt by about 30 per cent of GDP. We do not take this into account in the Greek numbers as we want to measure the total effect of austerity on the government debt ratios.

© 2013 The Author(s) JCMS: Journal of Common Market Studies © 2013 John Wiley & Sons Ltd

Figure 6: Growth of GDP in Eurozone

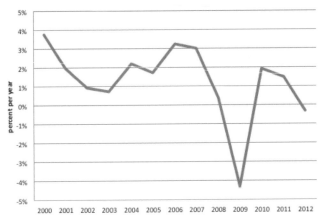

Source: European Commission, AMECO.

Figure 7: Gross Government Debt Ratios in Creditor Countries of the Eurozone (% of GDP)

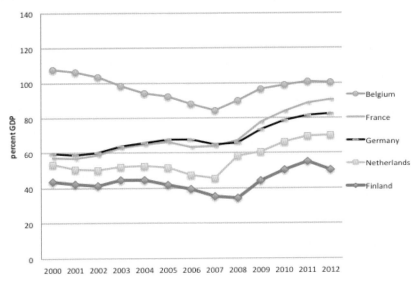

Source: European Commission, AMECO.

groups of countries in the eurozone: the debtor and the creditor countries. One observes from Figures 7 and 8 that while the debtor countries have not been able to stabilize their government debt ratios (in fact these are still on an explosive path), the situation of the creditor countries is dramatically different. They have managed to stabilize these ratios. This opens a window of opportunity to introduce a rule that can contribute to more symmetry in the macroeconomic policies in the eurozone.

Here is the proposed rule. The creditor countries that have stabilized their debt ratios should stop trying to balance their budgets now that the eurozone is entering a new recession. Instead they should stabilize their government debt ratios at the levels they have

© 2013 The Author(s) JCMS: Journal of Common Market Studies © 2013 John Wiley & Sons Ltd

Figure 8: Gross Government Debt Ratios in Debtor Countries of the Eurozone (% of GDP)

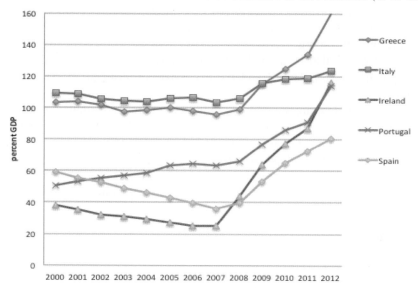

Source: European Commission, AMECO.

achieved in 2012. The implication of such a rule is that these countries can run small budget deficits and yet keep their government debt levels constant. Germany, in particular, which in 2013 is close to achieving a balanced budget, could afford to have a budget deficit of close to 3 per cent of GDP while keeping its debt-to-GDP ratio constant. This would provide a significant stimulus for the eurozone as a whole. It would also make it easier to deal with the current account imbalances between the north and the south of the eurozone noted earlier. By stimulating spending the northern countries would wind down the surpluses they have accumulated against the south. This is a necessary condition for the south to be able to reduce its current account deficits *vis-à-vis* the north.

Whether the symmetric rule proposed here will be implemented very much depends on the European Commission and on domestic politics in Germany. The European Commission should take the lead and should invoke exceptional circumstances – that is, the start of a recession that hits the whole eurozone and threatens to undermine its stability – and urge the creditor countries to stop temporarily trying to balance their budgets. As an alternative rule, the European Commission should convince the creditor countries that it is in their – and the eurozone's – interests that they stabilize their government debt ratios instead.

Conclusions

Two conclusions can be drawn from the previous analysis. First, since the start of the debt crisis financial markets have provided misleading signals. Led by fear and panic they pushed the spreads between different kinds of government debt in the eurozone to artificially high levels and forced countries lacking the cash into intense austerity pro-ducing great suffering in these countries. They also gave these same misleading signals to the European authorities – in particular the European Commission which went on a crusade trying to enforce more austerity. Thus financial markets acquired great power in that they spread panic into the world of the European authorities which translated the market panic into enforcing excessive austerity. While the ECB finally acted in September 2012, it could also be argued that had it acted earlier much of the panic in the markets might not have occurred and the excessive austerity programmes could have been avoided.

Second, panic and fear are not good guidelines on which to formulate sound economic policies. These sentiments have forced countries into quick and intense austerity that not only led to deep recessions, but also to much suffering by millions of people. Up to now, moreover, austerity has not helped to restore the sustainability of public finances. On the contrary, the same austerity measures led to significant increases of the debt-to-GDP ratios of the countries forced to engage in austerity, thereby weakening their capacity to service their debts (Blyth, 2013).

In order to avoid misunderstanding: we are not saying that southern European countries will not have to go through austerity in order to return to sustainable government finances. They will have to do so. What we are claiming is rather that the *timing* and the *intensity* of the austerity programmes have been dictated too much by the market sentiments of fear and panic instead of being the outcome of rational decision-making processes.

All this creates new risks for the eurozone. While the ECB's decision in 2012 to be a lender of last resort in the government bond markets eliminated the existential fears about the future of the eurozone, the new risks for the future of the eurozone have now shifted into the social and political sphere. As it becomes obvious that the austerity programmes have been dictated by financial markets and have produced unnecessary suffering for the millions of people who have been thrown into unemployment and poverty, resistance against these programmes is likely to increase. This resistance may lead millions of people to wish to be liberated from what they perceive to be shackles imposed by the euro, undermining not only the single currency, but also the European integration project.

These social and political risks arising from excessive austerity could be reduced by symmetric macroeconomic policies. While the debtor nations in the eurozone have no other option than to continue onto the path of austerity (albeit at a slower pace than the one imposed by panicky financial markets), the creditor nations should offset the deflationary consequences of these austerity programmes by policies allowing for some fiscal stimulus. We have argued that the creditor countries that have stabilized their debt-to-GDP ratios have the financial capacity to do so.

The responsibility of Germany is key here. This is the leading eurozone country that has accumulated the largest current account surpluses during more than a decade. These surpluses also made it possible for the periphery countries to accumulate large current account deficits. Thus, the responsibility of the unsustainable imbalances in the eurozone is shared between debtor and creditor countries. For every reckless debtor there must have been a reckless creditor. The acceptance in the north of Europe that the responsibility of the euro crisis is a shared one would make it possible for the northern eurozone countries – in particular Germany – to take their share in the burden of rebalancing the eurozone instead of putting all the burden onto the shoulders of the debtor nations.

© 2013 The Author(s) JCMS: Journal of Common Market Studies © 2013 John Wiley & Sons Ltd

References

Aizenman, J. and Hutchinson, M. (2012) 'What is the Risk of European Sovereign Debt Defaults? Fiscal Space, CDS spreads and Market Pricing of Risk'. Paper presented at the 'The European Sovereign Debt Crisis: Background and Perspectives' conference, organized by Danmarks Nationalbank/JIMF, 13–14 April.

Attinasi, M., Checherita, C. and Nickel, C. (2009) 'What Explains the Surge in Euro Area Sovereign Spreads during the Financial Crisis of 2007–09?' ECB Working Paper 1131, December. Frankfurt: European Central Bank.

Beirne, J. and Fratzscher, M. (2012) 'Pricing and Mispricing of Sovereign Debt in the Euro Area during the Crisis'. Paper presented at the 'The European Sovereign Debt Crisis: Background and Perspectives' conference, organized by Danmarks Nationalbank/JIMF, 13–14 April.

Blyth, M. (2013) *Austerity: The History of a Dangerous Idea* (Oxford: Oxford University Press).

Calvo, G. (1988) 'Servicing the Public Debt: The Role of Expectations'. *American Economic Review*, Vol. 78, No. 4, pp. 647–61.

De Grauwe, P. (2011a) 'The Governance of a Fragile Eurozone'. CEPS Working Document, Economic Policy, May. Available at: «http://www.ceps.eu/book/governance-fragile-eurozone».

De Grauwe, P. (2011b) 'The European Central Bank: Lender of Last Resort in the Government Bond Markets?' CESifo Working Paper 3569, September (Munich: Centre for Economic Studies and Ifo Institute for Economic Research).

De Grauwe, P. and Ji, Y. (2012) 'Mispricing of Sovereign Risk and Macroeconomic Stability in the Eurozone'. *JCMS*, Vol. 50, No. 86, pp. 866–80.

Diamond, D.W. and Dybvig, P.H. (1983) 'Bank Runs, Deposit Insurance and Liquidity'. *Journal of Political Economy*, Vol. 91, No. 3, pp. 401–19.

Eaton, J. and Gersovitz, M. (1981) 'Debt with Potential Repudiation: Theoretical and Empirical Analysis'. *Review of Economic Studies*, Vol. 48, pp. 289–309.

International Monetary Fund (IMF) (2012) *World Economic Outlook* (Washington, DC: IMF).

Romer, D. and Romer, C. (2007) 'The Macroeconomic Effects of Tax Changes: Estimates Based on a New Measure of Fiscal Shocks'. Discussion paper, March (Berkeley, CA: University of California).

© 2013 The Author(s) JCMS: Journal of Common Market Studies © 2013 John Wiley & Sons Ltd

JCMS 2013 Volume 51 Annual Review pp. 42–54　　　　　　　　　　　DOI: 10.1111/jcms.12040

A New Socialist President in the Elysée: Continuity and Change in French EU Politics*

CHRISTIAN LEQUESNE
CERI – Sciences Po, Paris

Introduction

In May 2012, France elected a new president of the Republic and a new parliament. The socialist candidate François Hollande won the presidential election with a majority of 51 per cent against the right-wing incumbent Nicolas Sarkozy. For the first time in the history of the Fifth Republic, the *Parti Socialiste* won both the presidency of the Republic and the majority of the seats at both the National Assembly and the Senate. The Party also controls the executives of all the French regions, except one (Alsace) and some major cities (Paris, Lyon, Nantes, Strasbourg).

François Hollande's main task is to reform a French economy that has to contend with a large public deficit, a low rate of growth and a high rate of unemployment. These domestic economic challenges give rise to domestic debates closely connected to other debates on the relationship with Germany, the future of the EU and especially of the eurozone. Coming from a political party strongly divided on EU issues, what is the new French president's policy with regard to Europe?

This article begins by recapitulating the fundamentals of France's EU politics that create a path dependency for any newly elected president. It analyzes the connections between the economic challenges the new president has to cope with and the EU debates. Finally, it analyzes the role President Hollande and the socialist government are prepared to play within the EU foreign and security framework.

I. The Path Dependency of France's EU Politics

In a book published ten years ago, Craig Parsons emphasized the strong role that the ideas of the political and administrative elites have played in the development of France's EU politics. For Parsons, ideas have clearly shaped French interests throughout the process of the construction of Europe (Parsons, 2003). Following his thesis, we can observe that French elites – outside the far right and the far left – have shared common beliefs about what France should and should not be within the European Community/European Union. If these beliefs do not necessarily correspond to the reality of the EU in 2013, they have been, and still are, strongly embedded in the minds of the French policy-making elite, forming a kind of *doxa*.

* I would like to thank Wilfred Suddath, intern at CERI, for his research assistance, and civil servants from the French Ministry of Foreign Affairs whom I interviewed. My gratitude goes also to Nat Copsey and Tim Haughton for their constructive comments on the early draft.

© 2013 The Author(s) JCMS: Journal of Common Market Studies © 2013 John Wiley & Sons Ltd, 9600 Garsington Road, Oxford OX4 2DQ, UK and 350 Main Street, Malden, MA 02148, USA

   The first belief has to do with France which must defend, as a founding Member State of the EU, the model of a 'core Europe' built around Franco–German co-leadership. It explains why any French government has appeared cautious towards every new enlargement of the EU that could challenge the Franco–German core. The second belief has to do with an EU that should be a *Europe puissance* going beyond the model of a civil power. Nobody has never clearly defined what a '*Europe puissance*' is, but the notion refers to the necessity of an institutional system combining both supranationality and intergovernmentalism, and the necessity of an EU security and defence policy. The third belief is that France has to fight against any political temptation coming from the other Member States to limit the role of the EU to the single market. The EU should be considered as a 'political' project that includes regulatory policies and welfare policies based on the highest common denominator – that is to say the social model (currently in crisis) of the 'old' continental countries of western Europe.[1]

   The year 1989 represented a historic and dramatic change in the course of French EU politics. Before 1989, the French administrative and political elites strongly believed in a model of 'quiet functionalism' (Lequesne, 2008) based on a step-by-step delegation of concrete policies (mainly economic) to the EC/EU that would foster in the end (nobody said exactly when) a closer political union. This belief legitimized the political support to the European Monetary System in 1979, the Single European Act in 1986, the economic and monetary union (EMU) in 1993 (although initiated in 1988 before the end of the cold war). In the cold war period, French political and administrative elites assumed that Paris had to work closely with Bonn because no step was possible within the EC/EU without a preliminary Franco–German agreement. The relationship between France and Germany, guaranteed by the Elysée Treaty of 1963, was seen in Paris as effective mainly because it rested upon an 'unbalanced balance': the economic power of the divided Germany had to be complemented by the attributes of France in the international system, such as its independent nuclear bomb or its permanent seat on the United Nations Security Council. For the French elite, the German partner had also to be contained: Georges Pompidou agreed in 1969 to the United Kingdom's membership because he wanted to counterbalance the economic rise of Germany as well as Chancellor Brandt's new *Ostpolitik* (Krotz and Schild, 2013). Finally, the French elite had before 1989 no real concern about the borders of the EC/EU as they were confined by the cold war to the 'little' western Europe.

   After 1989, all these references embedded by the French elite about what a legitimate EC/EU should be were destabilized. The end of the cold war was really for them a critical juncture (Auer, 2012). Doubts emerged immediately after German reunification became a reality. The end of the complementary asymmetry between Paris and Berlin (and not Bonn anymore) was perceived as a potential threat to France's role in the EU. The perspective of rapid enlargement towards the new democracies of central and eastern Europe, supported by Berlin, was seen as a contradiction to the model of a *Europe puissance* only fitting with the 'little Europe'. In parallel to the end of the cold war, the diffusion of the neo-liberal paradigm in Europe, from the mid-1980s onwards, added to fears among the French elite that the EU could become no more than a single market. The new countries of central and eastern Europe were rapidly suspected of being Trojan horses for both neo-liberalism and Atlanticism (Lequesne, 2008).

---

[1] See also A. Leparmentier, 'Petit catalogue des opinions chic', *Le Monde*, 4 April 2013.

© 2013 The Author(s) JCMS: Journal of Common Market Studies © 2013 John Wiley & Sons Ltd

Although there was broad consensus on European issues prior to 1989, there were significant differences of opinion which were manifested in party competition. During the first direct elections to the European Parliament (EP) in 1979, a controversy arose over supranationality issues on the right of the political spectrum between the liberals of the *Union pour la Démocratie Française* (UDF), led by Simone Weil, and the Gaullists of the *Rassemblement pour la République* (RPR), led by Jacques Chirac. The latter accused the former of being supporters of federalism and, therefore, to be the representatives of the 'party of the foreigners' selling off France's national sovereignty. In 1983, the *Parti Socialiste* was also split on the issue of whether to stay within the exchange rate mechanism of the European monetary system (EMS) (MacCarthy, 1987). But as in several Member States, there was no noticeable debate in French public opinion on the future of the EC/EU before 1989. The only real exception was in 1954 over the European Defence Community which was rejected by the French parliament because of the strong suspicion of both the Communists and the Gaullists about a remilitarization of Germany (Aron and Lerner, 1956). In general, Ronald Inglehard's thesis on the 'permissive consensus' of public opinion towards European issues was valid in the French pre-1989 context (Inglehard, 1970). However, the mobilization of French public opinion changed with the Treaty of Maastricht in 1993 and has never declined since then (Brouard *et al.*, 2007). The treaty, which is to a certain extent a counterpart to German reunification, made Euroscepticism more explicit, both on the right and on the left of the political spectrum, and even more so on the far right and far left.

Euroscepticism has changed in nature in France over the past 20 years (Rozenberg, 2012). During the referendum on the Maastricht Treaty in September 1992 (won by socialist President Mitterrand with a small majority of 51 per cent), the main argument of the Eurosceptics inside the left and the right was the defence of national sovereignty. During the referendum campaign on the European Constitutional Treaty (lost in May 2005 by Gaullist President Chirac with 'no' garnering 54 per cent of the votes), the main argument was the protection of the national welfare state against the liberalization provided by the single market. A majority of the left-wing electorate (especially the voters of the *Parti Socialiste*) said 'no' in 2005 when they had said 'yes' in 1992. The *Parti Socialiste*, split on the 2005 referendum, has never overcome the consequences of the cleavage: it remains a very divided party on the European issue. If we consider that, in the last ten years, the moderate left parties have been the most pro-European supporters, the French difference comes from the patchwork nature of the *Parti Socialiste*, combining social democrats and neo-Marxists representing a statist and protectionist tradition of socialism (Bergounioux and Grunberg, 2007).

II. A New Socialist President Facing an Economic Crisis

François Hollande, candidate of the *Parti Socialiste*, was elected president of the Republic against the incumbent Nicolas Sarkozy in May 2012 with 51.64 per cent of the votes. Inside his party, Hollande is a centrist who supports the social market economy. Contrary to some other leaders of the *Parti Socialiste*, such as Laurent Fabius who was appointed minister of foreign affairs in 2012, Hollande was never openly opposed to the ratification of EU institutional reforms, either by the National Assembly or through a referendum. He

© 2013 The Author(s) JCMS: Journal of Common Market Studies © 2013 John Wiley & Sons Ltd

supported the ratification of both the Treaty of Maastricht and the European Constitutional Treaty.

François Hollande was elected president in 2012 without being profiled long in advance for the post. He won the primary election inside the *Parti Socialiste* because the main potential candidate – Dominique Strauss-Kahn, Director-General of the International Monetary Fund (IMF) – became ineligible after having been arrested for an alleged sexual offence in New York in 2011. As an MP and mayor of Tulle in Central France, Hollande has a long experience of politics inside the *Parti Socialiste*. He was the head of the party from 1997 to 2008, a particularly long period which explains some trends in his political style. Inside the *Parti Socialiste*, which is divided on several issues (not only the EU), Hollande acted mainly as a compromise builder who learned how to balance the different sensitivities and orientations.

During the presidential campaign, the EU was not an important issue as such. In France, a presidential campaign is always more concentrated on domestic objectives, but the split in the *Parti Socialiste* in 2005 also did not encourage EU proactivism. Hollande's manifesto, called 'Sixty Commitments for France' (Hollande, 2012), stressed a number of issues on the EU: a renegotiation of the Europe Budgetary Discipline Treaty (EBDT, the so-called 'Fiscal Compact'), an EU budget for the period 2013–20 focusing more on innovative policies, and a reform of EU trade policy taking more into consideration the social and environmental constraints.

The EU appeared in the campaign through the debate on the state of the French economy that dominated the public sphere as is now the case in almost all other elections in the other Member States. Ending his five-year mandate with a public deficit of 5.2 per cent and growth of 1.7 per cent, Nicolas Sarkozy, candidate of the centre-right party *Union pour un Mouvement Populaire* (UMP), focused his discourse on the need to re-launch the growth and the competitiveness of the French economy by reducing the public deficit. He strongly endorsed the German orthodox view that more cuts should be made to the French public budget. Sarkozy, despite letting the public deficit accumulate during his presidential mandate (2007–12), supported together with German Chancellor Angela Merkel the negotiation of the EBDT. Signed on 2 March 2012 by 25 EU Member States (the United Kingdom and Czech Republic remaining outside), the EBDT established compulsory balanced budgets for national governments (the 'budgetary golden rule'), controlled by new EU rules. For the first time in the history of the Franco–German relationship since 1949, a German chancellor – Angela Merkel – declared explicitly her support for the re-election of a French president – Nicolas Sarkozy. This official support during the campaign provided a boulevard for the left and the press to lampoon the outgoing president with the nickname '*Merkozy*'. Arnaud Montebourg, the more left-wing candidate for the primary inside the *Parti Socialiste*, rekindled anti-German slogans, saying that Merkel represented a Bismarkian style of politician.[2] Without giving way to such anti-German rhetoric, Hollande denounced forcefully the subordination of Sarkozy's economic policy proposals to Merkel and stressed that the EBDT should be re-negotiated to enhance the new priority of growth.

Once elected in May 2012, Hollande launched however very pragmatic policies. First, he appointed as prime minister the mayor of Nantes, Jean-Marc Ayrault, and as minister for economics and finances, Pierre Moscovici. They both represent the centrist, pro-EU

---

[2] A. Montebourg, 'Question d'info', *LCP – Assemblée Nationale*, 2011. Available at: <<http://www.dailymotion.com>>.

© 2013 The Author(s) JCMS: Journal of Common Market Studies © 2013 John Wiley & Sons Ltd

orientation inside the *Parti Socialiste*. On the EBDT, Hollande and Moscovici agreed with their EU partners not to have a re-negotiation of the EBDT (which in any case was not acceptable for Merkel, and therefore probably not a runner anyway) but rather an additional 'compact for growth and jobs' announced at the European Council in Brussels on 29 June 2012. This addition was enough for the socialist government to convince its majority to ratify the EBDT in parliament. After a short debate in the National Assembly, the EBDT was ratified by a majority of 477 out of 538 deputies on 9 October 2012. The vote was approved with a left–right consensus: 285 MPs from the *Parti Socialiste* and 187 from the UMP. Only 20 socialist MPs, but all the green MPs and all the *Front de Gauche* (far left) MPs voted against.

On economic policy in general, Ayrault made a priority the reduction of the public deficit by decreasing public spending and increasing drastically the taxes both for individuals and companies – a move which was much criticized on the centre-right. The Ayrault government's objective is to reach the 3 per cent public deficit target set up by the Treaty of Maastricht at the end of 2013. Beyond the rhetoric on growth, the economic policy of the socialists and the greens (represented by ministers within the coalition) does not differ a lot from the German economic orthodoxy on the necessity of budgetary restraint: it focuses on cuts to public spending and, for instance, on not replacing civil servants as they retire (a policy inherited from the Sarkozy era). It shows clearly that the social democratic line is dominant in the government, with the risk for Hollande of losing the support of part of his electorate. Contrary to François Mitterrand in 1983, Hollande does not have such a strong leadership inside the *Parti Socialiste* to impose his policy of rigour. Furthermore, the European Commission does not believe that the French public deficit can reach the 3 per cent target by the end of 2013. It published a forecast of a deficit of 3.7 per cent in March 2013.

Hollande increased substantially taxes for individuals and firms (by 5.3 per cent between 2012 and 2013). In December 2012, the Constitutional Court annulled the project to tax incomes exceeding €1 million a year at a level of 75 per cent. The judges considered that such a tax would be confiscatory and punitive. In general, the increase in taxes exercises pressure on the part of the middle classes who have sometimes voted for the *Parti Socialiste*. It explains the reason why, by spring 2013, Hollande was the president of the Fifth Republic with the lowest level of public support including among the citizens who voted for him a year previously. On 1 April 2013, only 31 per cent of French citizens approved of his policies; and 54 per cent of the left-wing voters declared themselves to be unsatisfied.[3] This disillusionment in public opinion benefits parties at both extremes (the far right *Front National* and the far left party *Front de Gauche*) that are both populist and Eurosceptic parties. It also prevents Hollande from adding structural reforms to the budgetary measures in order to increase the overall competitiveness of the French economy in the absence of the possibility of devaluation.

Competitiveness has remained a topic much discussed by experts and politicians. In November 2012, the former chairman of the Franco–German company EADS, Louis Gallois, produced a report on how to improve French competitiveness. Among his proposals, Gallois asked for a necessary increase in industrial research, aid for small and

---

[3] IFOP-*Paris Match* Survey, 28–29 March 2013, available at: «http://www.parismatch.com».

© 2013 The Author(s) JCMS: Journal of Common Market Studies © 2013 John Wiley & Sons Ltd

medium-sized enterprises (SMEs) and improved social dialogue. Germany is presented throughout the report as a source of inspiration (Gallois, 2012).

Hollande has limited room for manoeuvre, however, though not for institutional reasons (the *Parti Socialiste* controls the government and the parliament), but rather because his reformist line – implying rigour and perhaps recession – is very much criticized inside his own party. Hollande's problem is his lack of leadership over the dominant *Parti Socialiste*. Furthermore, the political conditions for a social dialogue on future structural reforms (rents, flexibility of the work market) between the government and the unions are more difficult in France than in Germany. Even if French membership of trade unions is the lowest among the Organisation for Economic Co-operation and Development (OECD) countries in 2012 (7 per cent), the workers' unions – with the exception of the *Confédération Française Démocratique du Travail* (CFDT) are not strong supporters of new structural reforms of the French economy.

The debates in France about economic policies have a direct link to the commitment in the eurozone. On the reform of the eurozone, Hollande's policies did not mark a drastic turning point in 2012 compared to Sarkozy's options. He supported a mutualization of sovereign debts through the creation of eurobonds as well as more direct intervention by the European Central Bank in the management of the debt (Hollande, 2012). *Vis-à-vis* Chancellor Merkel, Hollande had no other option than to compromise. Despite the refusal of Paris to replace Jean-Claude Junker with the German minister for finances, Wolfgang Schäuble, in the presidency of the Eurogroup, the logic of compromise between the *Elysée* and the *Kanzleramt*, and between the German and the French treasuries, was observed. Prime Minister Ayrault, who speaks fluent German as a former teacher of the language, also supported the deals between Paris and Berlin.

The main source of difference between Merkel and Hollande has to do with the institutional design of the eurozone. President Hollande is not in favour of a new reform of the treaties that would delegate more power to the European institutions to co-ordinate fiscal and tax policies, while Berlin seems to wish it in accordance with the theory of 'crowning politics' ('*Krönung Politik*') considering that the EMU should be crowned by a kind of institutional federalism (Guérot, 2012). French Minister of Foreign Affairs Laurent Fabius participated only in the final few meetings of the informal Westerwelle[4] Committee, which suggested in September 2012 a new institutional reform of the EU to codify the policy changes in the eurozone (Westerwelle, 2012). The French government considered that policy substance – what it calls '*intégration solidaire*' – should have priority over institutional reform (Schild, 2013).

This position could be explained in two ways. The first has to do with the differing conception of 'legitimacy' in France and in Germany: the German scenario for an institutional reform of the eurozone focuses on an increase in democratic legitimacy and, therefore, emphasizes the empowerment of the EP (Guérot, 2012). For the French, the executive has the legitimacy and therefore the role of the European Council should be enhanced (Klau, 2012). The second explanation for the French reluctance to undertake an institutional reform of the EU treaties was the ratification process. Any change in the EU Treaty requires from the government a political (not constitutional) obligation to organize

---

[4] The Future of Europe Group was comprised of the foreign ministers of Austria, Belgium, Denmark, France, Italy, Germany, Luxembourg, the Netherlands, Poland, Portugal and Spain. It was chaired by German Foreign Minister Guido Westerwelle, and the group produced an informal final report on the future of the EU on 17 September 2012.

© 2013 The Author(s) JCMS: Journal of Common Market Studies © 2013 John Wiley & Sons Ltd

a referendum. Hollande had no wish to take this risk and find himself in the same lame duck position as President Chirac after the negative referendum of 2005. In the political system of the Fifth Republic, any president who loses a referendum is considerably delegitimized (Cohendet, 2012).

The difficulty in promoting an alternative (but also credible) neo-Keynesian model over the German economic model creates a problem of leadership for France in Europe. In Paris, more and more politicians and analysts had to admit that Germany had become by 2013 the *de facto* leader of the EU as its economic reforms had delivered results and, therefore, won legitimacy. The fears about Germany's economic policy (Beck, 2012), which imposed recession on the EU, were present among the leftist tendency of the *Parti Socialiste* at the moment when the two countries celebrated the 50th anniversary of the Franco–German Elysée Treaty. In his speech in Ludwigsburg, in September 2012, Hollande declared that the most urgent task for both countries is 'to create the conditions for growth' (Hollande, 2012). The reference to growth was a message to Germany. On the other side, the recovery of the German economy since 2010 was a problem for the Franco–German tandem.

Hollande's EU politics were very much concentrated on finding solutions to the economic problems at home. It explains why he did not speak about grand designs and projections for the future of the EU. France's leadership within the EU-27 seems to depend on Hollande's ability to succeed in his reform of the French economy. Although his discourse on the reform of the eurozone seems to stick less to Germany than Sarkozy, the margin of manoeuvre for Paris *vis-à-vis* Berlin remains limited in concrete policy terms.

III. Foreign Policy: A French Ambition for Europe?

If the French governments – of whatever political colour – have historically supported the Community Method for the development of EU economic policies, they have, in parallel, always defended the intergovernmental method for the development of a foreign and security policy. President Pompidou was particularly proactive when the 'Six' decided to set up in 1970 a co-ordination of their national foreign policies outside the existing treaties, called 'European political co-operation'. It was also the French government that insisted in 1993 on having a pillar structure in the Treaty of Maastricht, with a second pillar defining the rules of an intergovernmental common foreign and security policy (Keukeleire and MacNaughtan, 2008). However, the intergovernmentalism that the French have been prepared to accept in the field of EU foreign and security policy has always been tempered by the acceptance of new institutions at the EU level. In this regard, the French approach goes beyond a classic neo-realist conception of how a national foreign policy shall be conducted and matches well with the model that Daniel C. Thomas calls 'normative institutionalism' (Thomas, 2011).

When Sarkozy decided in 2009 that France should reintegrate into the command structure of Nato, which President De Gaulle had left in 1966, the *Parti Socialiste* expressed its strong disagreement. As an MP belonging to the opposition, Hollande wanted to pass a vote of no confidence in France's reintegration.[5] The main reasons to be against were twofold. First, Sarkozy's decision intervened at a time when Nato was changing its identity

[5] Speech at the French National Assembly, 8 April 2008.

© 2013 The Author(s) JCMS: Journal of Common Market Studies © 2013 John Wiley & Sons Ltd

to become a global organization. Hollande considered that the American project to redeploy Nato in conflicts outside Europe was not acceptable. Second, the normalization of the *de facto* work of the French armies within Nato would decrease the autonomy of French diplomacy *vis-à-vis* its western allies, and the United States in particular. However, during the presidential campaign of 2012, Hollande did not put at the forefront of his agenda the withdrawal of France from the Nato command structure. He simply made clear that he would commission a report to assess the benefits of the full reintegration of the French troops inside the transatlantic organization if he won the election.

Hubert Védrine, Mitterrand's former diplomatic adviser and Jospin's former foreign affairs minister, who expressed strong views against reintegration in 2009,[6] was in charge of writing the report. Interestingly, he concluded very pragmatically in favour of France remaining in the Nato command structure with a number of conditions: deploying all the means to be influential, which means not hesitating about opposing the United States; resisting the idea that Nato should become a political organization; insisting on the transatlantic vocation of Nato operations; and, finally, not giving up on proper capacities to analyze threats within the French army. In addition to that, Védrine's report emphasized that France should remain the EU Member State that pushes most for a 'real common strategy' within the EU. He questioned the opportunities for France to stimulate with the United Kingdom a more ambitious security and defence policy, and suggested alternative scenarios within a 'Weimar+ Triangle', composed of France, Germany, Poland, Italy and Spain (Védrine, 2012).

This last set of remarks about how to get a 'real' EU defence policy underlines a series of problems for the French government, which are both domestic and European. The domestic problem is the regular decline in the defence budget over the past ten years. If France has still, together with the United Kingdom, the largest national budget for defence, it is a decreasing one. In 2013, it still corresponds to 2.3 per cent of gross domestic product (GDP) (in comparison with 2.6 per cent in the United Kingdom and 1.3 per cent in Germany).[7] The European problem is the relationship with the United Kingdom. French politicians and military experts have increasing doubts about what political input they can expect from the United Kingdom to develop the EU security and defence policy. In December 2010, Sarkozy signed with British Prime Minister David Cameron, a Franco–British treaty to reinforce bilateral co-operation in the area of defence. The main objective of this agreement was co-operation in the manufacture of weapons. However, the British government did not accept any reference in the treaty to a more ambitious EU defence and security policy. For the French, the strictly bilateral approach of the Cameron government keeps the United Kingdom away from the expectations of the Saint-Malo Agreement signed by Tony Blair in 1998 (Charillon, 2013).

The issue is complicated, as the British Army remains the only one among the EU-27 to have the necessary resources for launching military operations outside Europe. The discrepancy in the United Kingdom between military resources and political cautiousness about a future EU security and defence policy puts the French government in a delicate position. On the one hand, Hollande continues as if the main *raison d'être* of a Franco–British relationship remains defence. On the other hand, the French ministries of foreign

---

[6] H. Védrine, 'Pourquoi il faut s'opposer à une France atlantiste', *Le Monde*, 5 March 2009.
[7] *Le Monde*, 28 March 2013.

© 2013 The Author(s) JCMS: Journal of Common Market Studies © 2013 John Wiley & Sons Ltd

affairs and defence, which were producing a new *White Book on Defence and National Security* during 2013, began to consider political alternatives to the Franco–British relationship based on the 'Weimar +' scenario.[8] This alternative would, however, imply that the German Bundestag decides to increase the defence budget and German society gets over its historical inhibition about military operations abroad. In practice, it is with the British Army that outside operations were co-organized, as was the case for Libya in March 2011, after the German government abstained on Resolution 1973 at the UN Security Council.

Another option is for French troops to intervene alone with the political backing of the other EU members, as was the case in Mali in January 2013. With regard to Africa, Hollande said explicitly during the presidential campaign that he wanted to depart from the policy of *Françafrique* which has been characterized as supporting undemocratic governments in sub-Saharan Africa just because their leaders are favourable to French interests. After his election, he repeated this commitment in his Dakar speech of October 2012. In practice, the situation has been more nuanced. While Hollande decided in March 2013 not to intervene in the Central African Republic to protect the dictator François Bozizé against the advance of the Seleka rebels who took power in Bangui, his decision was quite different in Mali two months previously. Although the Malian regime had been created in a military coup in 2012, Hollande decided to protect Bamako's regime from Islamist groups who had imposed sharia law in the north of the country. The socialist government would of course have preferred that France led a European intervention in Mali to avoid any accusation of neocolonialism. If the decision-making of the EU security and defence policy would not yet allow a quick decision on such an intervention, it is also doubtful that any of the other Member States would have accepted to be fully part of such a mission.

In 2008, former President Sarkozy proposed to launch a Union for the Mediterranean (UfM) (Dehousse and Menon, 2009). The original project, set up directly by the Elysée Palace against the Quai d'Orsay,[9] was conceived exclusively for the countries bordering the Mediterranean Sea. However, Angela Merkel's strong opposition to this restrictive approach led to an amendment of the original plans. The UfM was opened to all the 27 Member States and was finally included in the EU neighbourhood policy to replace the Euro-Mediterranean Dialogue set up in 1995 by the Barcelona Process (Lequesne, 2008). The UfM consists of funding a series of concrete projects between the two banks of the Mediterranean, from solar energy to sea depollution. Signed in 2008 with the authoritarian governments of the southern bank of the Mediterranean, the UfM was seriously delegitimized by the Arab Spring.

Hollande wrote in his electoral manifesto: 'I will develop France's relationship with the countries of the Southern Bank of the Mediterranean on the basis of an economic, democratic and cultural project' (Hollande, 2012), but he did not re-launch the UfM which was too much identified with his predecessor. More generally, French diplomacy does not know exactly how to deal with the Arab Spring's results, balanced between a long

---

[8] Commissioned in July 2012 by President Hollande to a committee of experts, chaired by Jean-Marie Guéhenno, former Deputy Secretary-General of the UN, the *White Book on Defence and National Security* is a report that takes an inventory of 'the national strategies and the necessary capacities' the French government should adopt within the next 15–20 years to answer the main security challenges.
[9] The French Ministry of Foreign and European Affairs.

© 2013 The Author(s) JCMS: Journal of Common Market Studies © 2013 John Wiley & Sons Ltd

tradition of intervention in the Maghreb and the wish to respect the sovereignty of the newly elected governments. In the end, the UfM continues formally, but does not spend its funds.

Hollande has been in favour of an EU policy that develops strategic partnerships with the main emerging countries. Following on from the previous right-wing government, he supported, in general, a reform of the international system that would give more leverage to the emerging countries (Telo and Ponjaert, 2013). However, such a policy should not decrease France's own influence. In his election manifesto, he stated: 'I will plead for a reform of the United Nations, in particular for an enlargement of the Security Council where France should keep its seat and its veto power' (Hollande, 2012). There is no commitment in favour of sharing an EU seat in the UN Security Council.

If there is no particular enthusiasm among French diplomats for the job done by Catherine Ashton as the High Representative for Foreign Affairs and Security Policy, they accept the principle of exchanging and co-ordinating their positions inside the new European External Action Service (EEAS) and the 140 EU delegations (Lequesne, 2013). The presence of a senior French diplomat (Pierre Vimont) in the post of executive secretary of the EEAS is seen as a guarantee to control the process of resources mutualization in the field of foreign policy.

On the EU–Russia relationship in particular France has fewer economic interests at stake than Germany or Italy. France is indeed much less dependent on the gas supplies from Russia and the level of French investments in Russia is far behind that of Germany. For this reason, France is not pushing very hard to get a renewal of the political and co-operation agreement signed in 1994 between the EU and Russia. The main concern of the French government with Russia is the handling of global diplomacy. Under the Sarkozy presidency, the posture consisting of an avoidance of any criticism of Russian domestic politics, because the Russians were such useful allies in fighting Muslim fundamentalism and nuclear proliferation in rogue states, was challenged inside the Quai d'Orsay by a pro-western group of diplomats who emphasized the differences in values.[10] Hollande's presidency has seen the return of the pragmatists on Russia, disconnecting the diplomacy from values and human rights issues. This policy, however, was not successful in its attempt to influence Russian support for Bachar el Assad's regime in Syria. The French government was the first among the 27 to recognize officially, in November 2012, the Syrian National Coalition (SNC) as the only legitimate representative of the Syrian people and of the future government of a democratic Syria. Paris shared with London the view that weapons should be delivered to the SNC, but had to cope with the strong opposition of the Obama administration that feared a generalization of violence in the Middle East.[11]

Finally, the enlargement of the EU was not a priority during the Sarkozy presidency and is not one for the Hollande presidency either. On Turkey, the Erdogan government expected after the 2012 election that the new socialist president would facilitate a re-opening of the enlargement negotiations partially frozen in 2006. There is no statement from Hollande, before or after his election, mentioning any strong opposition to Turkish membership of the EU. In general, the opposition is less strong in France on the left

---

[10] This group, which was also a strong supporter of having France back in the Nato Command Structure, deserves to be the subject of further research.
[11] *Le Point*, 14 November 2012.

© 2013 The Author(s) JCMS: Journal of Common Market Studies © 2013 John Wiley & Sons Ltd

side than at the right side of the political spectrum, even if the cleavage has never been so clear. To take two examples inside the Ayrault administration, Minister for Economy and Finance Moscovici has several times declared himself in favour of Turkish membership while Minister of Foreign Affairs Fabius said before he took office that he was against. Nevertheless, there is no incentive for any French government to fight for a quick enlargement to include Turkey as two-thirds of French public opinion remains opposed to the idea. In 2013, there was, however, a symbolic gesture from the socialist government in favour of the reopening of a new chapter in negotiations (Chapter 22 on regional policy). The decision was not publicized in France and any further steps remain very much constrained by Merkel's opposition to any option going beyond a 'privileged partnership'.

Although France had not objected to Croatia's membership since 2006 as long as Zagreb co-operated with the International Tribunal for ex-Yugoslavia, there is no particular enthusiasm for a rapid enlargement to Western Balkan countries. Hollande did not contest the Thessaloniki Declaration of the EU to move towards an enlargement with the Western Balkan countries, but considered the Copenhagen criteria should be strictly applied and that a resolution of the Kosovo problem is a prerequisite to any serious decision. The normalization agreement between Belgrade and Pristina, initialled on 19 April 2013 under Catherine Ashton's assistance, is considered by the French government to be a very preliminary step in a longer process. As is the case in many EU Member States, the French government does not want to repeat with Kosovo the Cyprus experience of letting a divided country enter the EU. In the bilateral negotiations between the two parts, the French government – which recognized Kosovo in 2008 – tried nevertheless not to isolate Serbia. The nationalist President Nikolić and neo-socialist Prime Minister Dačić considered that France is their strongest ally *vis-à-vis* the German chancellor who seems close to Pristina's interests.[12]

Any further enlargement of the EU, after Croatia, will depend to a great extent on French public opinion. France is the only EU Member State that, in 2005, made compulsory in its constitution that a referendum be held in order to ratify any further enlargement. This provision was voted for by the UMP's MPs in order to balance President Chirac's acceptance of negotiations with Turkey, but will be used for any candidate country. According to Article 88-5 of the French Constitution, the only means of bypassing a referendum is to get the agreement of three-fifths of each chamber in favour of a parliamentary procedure (Rozenberg, 2012). Whatever the majority, it will not be easy to get such agreement because of the political sensitivity of the French public towards enlargement but also direct democracy. Ever since the Treaty of Maastricht, it is difficult for any president of the Republic to escape a referendum on an EU issue as public opinion and political parties will immediately raise the spectre of the democratic deficit.

Conclusions

Looking at French politics since 2012 is a good case study to point out how EU Member States cannot separate domestic politics issues from EU political issues (Bulmer and Lequesne, 2012). For any government of an EU Member State, the focus can of course be put more on one side or the other of the same intertwined process. In the first two years

[12] Interviews in Belgrade, 20 March 2013.

© 2013 The Author(s) JCMS: Journal of Common Market Studies © 2013 John Wiley & Sons Ltd

of his presidency, Nicolas Sarkozy tried to enhance his legitimacy at the domestic level by being proactive in the resolution of EU crises. The French EU Presidency of 2008 was entirely dedicated to crisis management with its 26 EU partners (Rozenberg, 2012). French public opinion perceived that France was still an influential actor in the EU and that the president was the guardian of Gaullist 'heroism'. Hollande's position since his election was very different as his electorate expects him to find solutions that will improve the French economy without touching the welfare state too much. The new French president is in the opposite situation to François Mitterrand in 1981, who started with an economic policy inspired by 'old socialism' methods but was able to move in 1983 towards an economic policy compatible with the commitments of France in the European Community. He used the single market project as a means to convince the *Parti Socialiste* that France can no longer follow a Keynesian policy alone (Mazzucelli, 1997). Hollande initiated in 2012 an economic policy that should be compatible with the reform of the eurozone, but had to cope more and more with the pressures of his electorate to draw back to a neo-Keynesian policy ignoring rigour and structural reforms. There are two big differences between the margin for manoeuvre of both presidents: first, their leadership inside the *Parti Socialiste*, and second, the state of the EU was less delegitimized in public opinion in 1983 than it is in 2013.

Hollande is coping with a contradiction that illustrates what Europeanization means for any political leader in the EU. One the one hand, he would like to lead domestic policies which remain compatible with Germany because he knows that economic interdependence at the EU level is a constraint from which it is difficult to escape. On the other hand, he has to take into account the pressures coming from his domestic scene to follow an economic policy infringing German budgetary orthodoxy. There are two kinds of domestic pressures with which he has to cope. First, the sovereignists (both at the far left and at the far right) argue that states in the end can only count on their own choices and that sharing policies within the EU is nonsense. Second, the left-wing neo-Keynesians (especially inside the *Parti Socialiste*) argue that he should impose within the EU an alternative economic policy going against the negative effects of budgetary rigour for societies. Both groups do not accept that the recovery of the German economy since 2010 has imposed its *de facto* leadership in the EU (Paterson, 2010).

Hollande is a leader trapped by a dilemma on which he has not decided what to do yet: remain close to Germany, in continuity of Nicolas Sarkozy's policy, and impose economic reforms to a reluctant public, or depart from the German way to abandon structural reforms and satisfy the majority of his electorate. The fact that he seems to have no real space between these two options illustrates the fact that the balance of power between France and Germany is very different from what it was in the past and that the borders between EU and domestic politics are extremely porous.

References

Aron, R. and Lerner, D. (1956) *La querelle de la CED: Essais d'analyse sociologique* (Paris: Armand Colin/FNSP).

Auer, S. (2012) *Whose Liberty is It Anyway? Europe at the Crossroads* (London: Seagull Books).

Beck, U. (2012) *Das Deutsche Europa* (Berlin: Suhrkamp).

Bergounioux, A. and Grunberg, G. (2007) *Les socialistes français et le pouvoir: l'ambition et le remords* (Paris: Hachette).

Brouard, S., Grossmann, E., and Sauger, N. (2007) *Les Français contre l'Europe : les sens du référendum du 29 mai 2005* (Paris: Presses de Sciences Po).

Bulmer, S. and Lequesne C. (eds) (2012) *The Member States of the European Union* (Oxford: Oxford University Press).

Charillon, F. (2013) 'Jacques Chirac, l'OTAN et la défense européenne: Un pragmatism à l'épreuve du brouillard stratégique'. In Lequesne, C. and Vaïsse, M. (eds) *La politique étrangère de Jacques Chirac* (Paris: Riveneuve Editions), pp. 107–19.

Cohendet, M.-A. (2012) *Le président de la République* (Paris: Dalloz).

Dehousse, R. and Menon A. (2009) 'The French Presidency'. *JCMS*, Vol. 47, No. S1, pp. 99–111.

Gallois, L. (2012) *Pacte pour la compétitivité de l'industrie française* (Paris: Commissariat Général à l'Investissement).

Guérot, U. (2012) 'Noces d'or franco-allemandes: le couple est-il fini?' *Politique Etrangère*, Vol. 77, No. 4, pp. 755–68.

Hollande, F. (2012) *Les soixante engagements pour la France*. Available at: «http://www.parti-socialiste.fr».

Inglehard R. (1970) 'Regional Integration and Public Opinion: Theory and Research'. *International Organization*, Vol. 24, No. 4, pp. 764–95.

Keukeleire, S. and MacNaughtan, J. (2008) *The Foreign Policy of the European Union* (Basingstoke: Palgrave Macmillan).

Klau, T. (2012) 'Three French Conundrums: The Voters, The President and the Country'. ECFR Reinvention of the European Project. Available at: «http://www.ecfr.eu».

Krotz, U. and Schild, J. (2013) *Shaping Europe: France, Germany and Embedded Bilateralism from the Elysée Treaty to Twenty-First Century Politics* (Oxford: Oxford University Press).

Lequesne, C. (2008) *La France dans la nouvelle Europe: Assumer le changement d'échelle* (Paris: Presses de Sciences Po).

Lequesne, C. (2013) 'The European External Action Service: Can a New Institution Improve the Coherence of the EU Foreign Policy?' In Telo, M. and Ponjaert, F. (eds), pp. 79–86.

MacCarthy, P. (ed.) (1987) *The French Socialists in Power, 1981–1986* (New York: Greenwood Press).

Mazzucelli, C. (1997) *France and Germany at Maastricht: Politics and Negotiations to Create the European Union* (New York: Garland).

Parsons, C. (2003) *A Certain Idea of Europe* (Ithaca, NY: Cornell University Press).

Paterson, W. (2010) 'The Reluctant Hegemon? Germany Moves Centre Stage in the European Union'. *JCMS*, Vol. 49, No. S1, pp. 57–75.

Rozenberg, O. (2012) 'France: Genuine Europeanization or Monnet for Nothing?' In Bulmer, S. and Lequesne, C. (eds).

Schild, J. (2013) 'Politischer Führungsanspruch auf schwindender Machtbasis: Frankreichs Europapolitik unter François Hollande'. *Integration*, Vol. 36, No. 1, pp. 3–16.

Telo, M. and Ponjaert, F. (eds) (2013) *The EU's Foreign Policy: What Kind of Power and Diplomatic Action?* (Farnham: Ashgate).

Thomas, D.C. (ed.) (2011) *Making EU Foreign Policy: National Preferences, European Norms and Common Policies* (Basingstoke: Palgrave Macmillan).

Védrine, H. (2012) *Rapport pour le président de la République française sur les conséquences du retour de la France dans le commandement integer de l'OTAN, sur l'avenir de la relation transatlantique et les perspectives de l'Europe de la défense*. Unpublished.

Westerwelle, G. (2012) *Final Report on the Future of the Eurogroup*, 17 September. Available at: «http://www.auswaertiges-amt.de».

© 2013 The Author(s) JCMS: Journal of Common Market Studies © 2013 John Wiley & Sons Ltd

JCMS 2013 Volume 51 Annual Review pp. 55–62

DOI: 10.1111/jcms.12048

Shock to the System: Division, Unemployment and the Common Sense of European Institutions*

IVETA RADIČOVÁ
FSEV Comenius University

Introduction

The European Union's motto is 'United in Diversity'. The divisions between countries in today's EU revolve around three main axes: economic and social institutions (north versus south), political and civic institutions (east versus west) and governmental and financial institutions (small versus large government). This contribution investigates the hypothesis that the major factor behind attitudes towards international and supranational integration comprises differences between countries about what the role of institutions should be. The heterogeneity of national institutions plays a crucial role both in the European integration process and the ability of Member States to respond to the challenges they face. Moreover, differences between countries correlate with their environments and institutions, together with the interaction between these environments and institutions. The effects of so-called 'global shocks' over the past 40 years and the impact of the EU's common regulations have had varied consequences across the Member States in terms of economic and political performance.

I. The Economic and Social Environment

From the end of World War II until the end of the 1960s, European unemployment was very low. In the 1970s, however, it started to rise, increasing further in the 1980s, and again at points in the 1990s and in the 2010s – albeit with a high degree of variation across the EU. Labour Force Survey data show that unemployment follows a cyclical pattern: from the lows of 4 per cent in the early 1970s up to 12 per cent in 1980, before falling back to 7 per cent in the late 1990s, only to rise again to 10 per cent in the early 1990s, before dropping to below 5 per cent in 2004, only to increase again to over 11 per cent by September 2012.[1] The assumption often drawn from these trends that as a country experiences economic growth the number of jobs grows and unemployment falls[2] and, conversely, that as the economy slows and goes into recession unemployment tends to rise, however, has not stood up to empirical scrutiny.

---

* Iveta Radičová was prime minister of the Slovak Republic from 2010 to 2012. This article stems from a lecture given at the University of Birmingham in February 2013.

[1] For full details, see: «http://www.ilo.org/dyn/lfsurvey/lfsurvey.home and http://laborsta.ilo.org/».
[2] Although any mismatches between the skill requirements of the new jobs and the skills of those available for work may slow this process.

© 2013 The Author(s) JCMS: Journal of Common Market Studies © 2013 John Wiley & Sons Ltd, 9600 Garsington Road, Oxford OX4 2DQ, UK and 350 Main Street, Malden, MA 02148, USA

While heterogeneity across the EU has always been present, it is more marked today, to the point where talking about 'European unemployment' is misleading. Unemployment is low in many countries. September 2012's Eurostat showed unemployment stood at 4.4. per cent in Austria, 5.2 per cent in Luxembourg and 5.4 per cent in Germany and the Netherlands. Such figures stand in stark contrast to other countries where the rates are much higher such as in Spain (25.8 per cent) and Greece (25.1 per cent) (Eurostat, 2012). Compared with the previous year, the September 2012 figures showed that the unemployment rate increased in 20 Member States and fell in seven. The largest falls were observed in Lithuania, Estonia and Latvia, whereas the highest increases were in Greece, Cyprus and Portugal.[3]

High unemployment rates may be the result of high flows in and out of unemployment and/or a high average duration of unemployment (that is, citizens unemployed for a long period of time). The evolution of the unemployment rate and unemployment duration across the EU shows that the increase in the unemployment rate has come with a large increase in the duration of unemployment. In all countries, high unemployment is associated with higher unemployment for some groups, in particular the young and the unskilled. In general, depressed labour markets have demonstrated not only higher unemployment, but also lower participation and employment rates.

To understand the trajectory of unemployment it is instructive to remind ourselves of the shocks the European economy has faced. In the space of a decade, Europe suffered two major oil price increases. The first was triggered by the Arab oil embargo of 1973–74, the second by the Iranian revolution in 1979 and the Iran–Iraq War of 1980. Another consequence of these shocks was the considerable slowdown of total factor productivity (TFP) growth. The annual rate of growth of warranted wages decreased dramatically. This last shock was created by changes in real interest rates. Such changes affect capital accumulation, and so, at a given wage (and thus a given ratio of employment to capital), shift the demand for labour. Such shifts reflect either a technological bias away from labour or a decrease in the wage relative to the marginal product of labour. In either case, the implication is an adverse shift in labour demand and thus a potential source of unemployment.

While in the 1970s the discussion of the rise of unemployment focused primarily on shocks, the persistence of high unemployment for another two decades has led to a shift in focus from shocks to labour market institutions, particularly labour market rigidities. These institutions either increase the equilibrium unemployment rate (such as unemployment insurance systems), change the nature of unemployment but have an ambiguous effect on the equilibrium unemployment rate (for example, employment protection), or have an impact mostly on wages not on unemployment (for example, components of the so-called 'tax wedge'). There is enough heterogeneity in labour market institutions within Europe potentially to explain differences in today's unemployment rates. Neither the view that labour market institutions have been stable through time nor the view that labour market rigidities are a recent development, however, is correct.

Adverse shocks can explain the general increase in unemployment. Differences in institutions can explain differences in outcomes across countries. These differences

---

[3] For an overview of economic developments in the EU Member States, see Hodson's and Connolly's contributions to this issue.

© 2013 The Author(s) JCMS: Journal of Common Market Studies © 2013 John Wiley & Sons Ltd

have become stark and exposed due to the debt and financial crises of recent times. Two points are illustrative here: the shocks of the 1970s and 1980s led to high unemployment, triggering changes in institutions, but these were only partial and poorly carried out in some European countries; and high duration of unemployment leads to a loss of skills and morale and thus renders many of the long-term unemployed in effect unemployable.

We can identify four general trends in unemployment across Europe. First, the initial increase in unemployment in Europe was primarily due to adverse and largely common shocks. Second, different institutions led to different initial outcomes. Collective bargaining and/or inflation could be used to reduce real wage growth and determine the size of the increase in unemployment. Third, the increase in unemployment in most countries led to changes in institutions as most governments tried to limit increases in unemployment through employment protection and to reduce the pain of unemployment through more generous unemployment insurance. Fourth, most governments in Europe have partly reversed the initial change in institutions due to financial pressures and intellectual arguments, but this reversal has been partial and sometimes perverse. The different paths chosen may well explain the differences in unemployment rates across European countries today.

Several explanations are relevant here to explain these trends. The role of shocks and the interaction with collective bargaining emphasized by initial theories, the role of capital accumulation and insider effects emphasized by the theories focusing on persistence, and the role of specific institutions clarified by flow-bargaining models, all explain important aspects of the evolution of European unemployment. We would predict that the more favourable the macroeconomic environment and an improvement in institutions should lead to a substantial decline in unemployment.

Several trends in the job market are worthy of attention. In 1995, for instance, services accounted for about two-thirds of the total EU economy, rising to three-quarters in 2010. Indeed, in recent times job creation was driven by the service sector, while the primary and secondary sectors have lost about ten million jobs since the mid-1990s. The growth in services and the decline in primary and secondary employment are also reflected in the demand for qualifications. Whereas in 2000 just 22 per cent of jobs required higher education qualifications, 29 per cent required just basic qualifications. A decade later, the position had been reversed. That is not to say that all manufacturing industries lost jobs; the car industry, for instance, has bucked the trend. Moreover, although there has been a relative decline in manufacturing industry it is important to recall that for every job in manufacturing it is estimated that a further complementary job is needed in a related business service. In total, some 74 million jobs across the EU depend on manufacturing. The high-technology sector, in contrast, represented just 5.5 per cent of total employment and about 8 per cent of the EU's gross domestic product (GDP). Perhaps the most sobering statistic was the impact of the crisis on growth. The crisis cut growth potential by a quarter, mainly as a result of job losses and limited working hours. Ageing will reduce our workforce and this will further reduce our capacity to grow.

Although all advanced countries are welfare states to some degree, the extent of the redistribution varies substantially. Some stark and enlightening comparisons can be drawn by looking at both the EU and the United States. By just about any measure, taxes in the latter are lower and there is less support for the unemployed than in the former. The difference in institutions may explain the striking contrast between the American and European experiences. In those countries where there is no upward trend in unemployment, we should expect to see a marked rise in wage inequality. I would suggest that growing American inequality and growing European unemployment are different sides of the same coin.

It is indeed instructive to contrast the EU experience with the United States. Central to the differences are productivity, investment and innovation. In terms of productivity, over three-quarters of the gap between EU income and the United States is explained by the slower growth of productivity in the EU. Regarding investment, the EU lags behind the United States in hardware, software and communications equipment. If the EU matched the levels of the United States, about 5 per cent could be added to the GDP level by 2020. Innovation is key to a successful economy, but such innovation needs to be nurtured and helped. Whereas it currently takes, on average, 15 days to start a business in Europe (with considerable variation between Member States), across the Atlantic it takes just six. Speed appeals to young innovators. It is perhaps no surprise that more than half of the leading innovators in the United States are 'young' (born after 1975). Whereas in the United States young leading innovative companies account for 35 per cent of the total, in the EU it is just 7 per cent. In the EU firms have much less access to venture capital and many administrative barriers to overcome. Innovation is not helped by the fact that the costs of patenting in the EU averages close to €35,000, whereas in the United States it is just $1,850.

Great innovative ideas and the experience needed to turn ideas into practice will come from a workforce well educated and equipped with the right skills. About 80 million people in the EU, however, have only low or basic skills. Only about one person in three aged 25–34 has completed a university degree, compared to well above 50 per cent in Japan and more than 40 per cent in the United States. Particularly worrying is the lack of information technology (IT) professionals. On current trends, the EU may lack 700,000 IT professionals by 2015. It is not just in the field of IT, but education more broadly, where the trends are worrying. Every year, for instance, 6 million young Europeans drop out of school with at best a lower secondary education. The easy solution here is to suggest more money, but there is little correlation between spending on primary and secondary education per pupil and the results of the Organisation for Economic Co-operation and Development (OECD) programme for international student assessment (PISA). Many countries with high spending levels only show around average PISA reading scores.

High productivity growth need not imply favourable employment performance, or vice versa. There is a strong tendency on the part of policy-makers to presume that economic problems must be one-dimensional – that growth and job creation are both aspects of some underlying quality, typically labelled with words such as 'competitiveness'. The available evidence suggests, however, that the unemployment problem has a life of its own and is not simply part of a generalized deterioration in economic performance. Significant differences in the overall economic and social environments created the gap – and resultant tensions – between two clusters of European countries: north and south.

II. Political and Civic Environment

The consequences of the current crisis have been drastic. We have *lost* about €2,000 billion between 2007–10 due to the crisis, which corresponds to the entire GDP of France or 11 per cent of Europe's cumulative debt. GDP has slowed substantially and no fewer

© 2013 The Author(s) JCMS: Journal of Common Market Studies © 2013 John Wiley & Sons Ltd

than 25.7 million people are now unemployed in the EU (representing 11.6 per cent of the working-age population in September 2012). Youth unemployment is particularly high, running at over 20 per cent, and twice the average level. Debts have increased for households, non-financial corporations and states. In the eurozone, sovereigns and banks face significant refinancing requirements for 2012, estimated at 23 per cent of GDP. Moreover, gross debt-to-GDP ratios will rise further to around 91 per cent in the eurozone by 2017, although the EU is not alone. The debt-to-GDP figure is forecast to reach 130 per cent in the G7 and 256 per cent in Japan by then.

So, what we can do? There are several possible answers. One view is that investment in human capital – both in basic education and in retraining for older workers – can reverse the tendency toward greater inequality. A second view suggests improvements in the welfare system, especially decreasing expenditures, which would reduce social contributions and hence lower the cost of labour. A third view – what was dubbed the 'Swedish model' in the past – advocates an 'active manpower policy' with subsidized employment for those who otherwise would be unemployed seen as the way to cut through the otherwise agonizing trade-off between mass unemployment and mass poverty. Economic stagnation and high unemployment in several countries will have an impact on remittances with potential repercussions on countries highly dependent on external demand and financial flows. The eurozone's real problems, however, concern fiscal policy and bank/financial market regulation.

The current crisis has been created by two factors: the sharp rise in European unemployment rates, and the emergence of large budget deficits in countries with extensive welfare states and lower productivity. The 2009 crisis, therefore, is the product of the interaction among several underlying forces: mispriced risk, macroeconomic policy misbehaviour over many years, weak prudential policies and frameworks and missing structural reforms.

Policy concern with European unemployment tends to come in waves, reflecting the rise and fall of the unemployment statistics. 'Eurosclerosis' was the major issue in the mid-1970s, but was nearly forgotten in the wave of 'Europhoria' during the rapid growth of 1987–90. Now the consensus is that this growth was no more than a business cycle recovery, with little bearing on underlying structural problems. Markets became increasingly integrated, with enormous cross-border bank lending but supervision and regulation remained at a national level. The European Central Bank (ECB) was explicitly not allowed to be a lender of last resort, yet markets operated under the assumption that the authorities (governments and central banks) would be ready with a safety net if things went wrong. The perception that economies or banking systems were too big or too complex to fail underlay the idea that their liabilities had implicit guarantees. The consequences of these circumstances is that market forces did not function properly, sovereign and credit risks were underestimated and mispriced, resulting in large cross-country divergences in fiscal and external current account balances. Therefore, the eurozone has had to develop new mechanisms of support for heavily indebted members while implementing severe fiscal restraint. Concerns were present about bailing out investors and burdening public debts, and by the markets that other sovereigns could consider debt restructuring as a partial alternative to strong fiscal restraint and support from eurozone peers. The process was followed by the European Banking Authority's (EBA) stress tests. The eurozone had neither a clear road map nor visibly available resources to recapitalize banks found to be in need of more capital.

© 2013 The Author(s) JCMS: Journal of Common Market Studies © 2013 John Wiley & Sons Ltd

The EU and eurozone agreed on several solutions and policy measures during a succession of meetings. The heads of state and government met no fewer than 27 times at summits and informal meetings during a four-year period from 2009 to fix the problems. The solutions proposed included the creation of the European Stability Mechanism (ESM) and the European Financial Stability Facility (EFSF) and their combination, three-year, long-term refinancing operations (LTROs) by the ECB; bank recapitalization plans by the EBA; implementation of the ESM treaty in mid-2012; improvement of fiscal governance and policy co-ordination; national measures to strengthen fiscal balances; and the introduction of structural reforms.

Despite policy steps to contain the debt and banking crises there remain continued high risks to financial stability. Empirical studies present evidence that the labour rate share is typically counter-cyclical – rising during recessions and falling during recoveries (Blanchard, 2006; Krugman, 1994; Leaker, 2009; Freeman and Nickell, 1988). In most economies during the current crisis, labour compensation has actually increased, except in Greece, Ireland, Spain and the United States. During the recovery, although all components of GDP increased, profits rebounded quite strongly in most economies, leading to a decline in the labour share. Labour compensation increased in all countries, with the exception of Portugal and Spain. We are facing an overall downward trend in the labour share because of the 'college premium' (the premium on wages of those with a Bachelor's degree), the 'superstar effect' (the disproportionate compensation of the top 1 per cent of the income distribution and the 'hollowing out' of the middle class as a result of skill-biased technological change) or the offshoring of medium-skill jobs, and low wages and unemployment.

Leaving aside the hopeful effects of education and training, there are two main alternatives: Europe can become more like the United States, or it can try to become more like Sweden used to be – that is, the welfare state can be scaled back, increasing the incentives for firms to offer and for workers to accept low-wage employment, or governments can try to subsidize employment at acceptable wage levels. The political problems with either alternative are obvious. Attempts to scale back the protections that have discouraged employment in Europe will lead – indeed, already have led – to massive protests. On the other hand, if employment is to be subsidized, the money must be found somewhere – a difficult task when the budgets of many high-unemployment nations seem already to be dangerously out of control.

There is no painless solution, but the challenges call for more policy action in fiscal, monetary and structural fields. In terms of the first, medium-term fiscal consolidation plans need to be implemented, whereas in the second not only does a very accommodative monetary policy stance need to be implemented, but ample liquidity needs to be provided to help repair household and financial sector balance sheets. Moreover, structural reforms are needed in many fields including health care systems, labour and product markets, the housing and financial sectors, and education. Above all, time is not on our side. The crisis needs to be resolved without delay.

Rich countries with smaller governments tend to grow more quickly than big governments. There is evidence to suggest that low marginal tax rates are associated with higher economic growth. The level of the top rates of individual income and corporate income tax combined with marginal tax rates is another axis dividing countries into two clusters – with small and big governments. Bourne and Oechsle's (2012) statistical analysis is supportive of the assertion made by supply-side economists that the growth performance

© 2013 The Author(s) JCMS: Journal of Common Market Studies © 2013 John Wiley & Sons Ltd

of countries with smaller governments will be better than those with bigger governments. Furthermore, small governments do not appear to deliver worse social outcomes. Significantly higher growth meant more resources to devote to public service provision, even if it dedicates less as a proportion of GDP.

There are several policy implications of these statistical findings. First, politicians should recognize the potential for tax rate cuts to stimulate economic growth. Second, these tax cuts have to be financed – that is, paid for by cutting government expenditure. Cutting the size of the state also helps to generate economic growth by improving the efficiency of the economy and encouraging entrepreneurial behaviour. When considering public services there is a tendency to focus on inputs rather than outcomes. The success of policies should be judged against objective, desirable aims – not the proportion of GDP that is spent.

III. Diversity, Identity and the Communist Past

There is one more important difference among EU countries: those countries with a communist past that had to go through a subsequent process of transition versus those (mostly old Member States) that have not experienced communism. Even though in people's minds the 1989–91 revolutions in Europe, which brought the fall of communism, have become one of the most positive events in modern history, we still cannot say that the majority in those states that overthrew communism has enthusiastically embraced the new way of life, which was formed during a complicated social and economic transformation. The democratization of totalitarian regimes itself was not linear, simple or without serious perils. The problems with the consolidation of democracy and establishment of democratic institutions tied to the tendencies towards authoritarianism and the undermining of democratic institutions accompanied the transition towards a new regime.

Behind people's insistence on the strong role of the state in the former communist states lies their critical reaction to social inequalities, which grew significantly under the new economic conditions and recent crises. The public was not ready for the deepening social differentiation. The communist era instilled in their minds an ideal of equality, which refused differences in the compensation of workers based on their varying productivity or added value for society. After 1989 'eastern' societies started to disappear, and under the influence of the new social differentiation the important part of the population has come to believe that the new economic differences among people are less just than under socialism. In addition to the terrible consequences of debt and the financial crisis, people are dissatisfied with the level of corruption, the weak rule of law, the lack of transparency and the weakness of the judicial system. In general there are low levels of confidence in government and democratic institutions and doubts about the legitimacy of the EU decision-making process.

Negative expectations in these countries anticipated the deepening of social inequalities and the concentration of wealth in the hands of individuals at the expense of the majority of the population, rising unemployment, the worsening of interpersonal relations, the selling off of national assets to foreign capital, but also the departure of the most talented persons to work abroad. Nonetheless, it is not all doom and gloom. The positive expectations have focused mostly on the potential of reforms to increase the opportunities for gifted and able individuals, bringing adequate goods and services and increasing the possibilities for the improvement of the environment.

© 2013 The Author(s) JCMS: Journal of Common Market Studies © 2013 John Wiley & Sons Ltd

In the short term, the majority of the population will probably evaluate the direction of their respective countries and the achievements of their political representatives above all through the prism of their own wallets. For the fulfilment of the modernization challenges, however, it will be crucial to what extent the decisions of their political representatives focus on long-term investments into education and the environment, as well as the support for a real equality of opportunities, respect for human rights and non-discrimination.

Conclusions

Democratization is the protection of diversity. The story of contemporary Europe is unique in the complementary and parallel strengthening of national identities together with the respect for the spirit and values of Europe. Several profound changes took place in one historical moment: the transition of totalitarian regimes, the emergence of new independent states, and the enlargement and strengthening of a supranational union. The evaluation of a regime is significantly connected not only to expectations, but also to the reflection of one's own gains and losses, which the change of the regime has brought. From this perspective, two opposing streams will always emerge: the first open to trans-formation, characterized by the will for significant socio-economic change (supporters of the post-1989 regimes); the second closed to transformation and rejecting it. This diversity is the natural result of diverse political values and economic orientations, differing social and cultural capital, political affiliations concentrated around basic political subcultures and the socio-demographic differentiation of society.

Unemployment blights contemporary Europe. It has negative consequences for both individuals and societies. The former do not fulfil their talents and the latter are deprived of the contributions to economic wealth and prosperity. A close examination of the causes of unemployment across the continent and further afield points to huge variations. We should learn lessons from these contrasting experiences and formulate our policies accordingly. Europe's motto may be 'United in Diversity', but for the sake of all citizens of the EU we should formulate fiscal, monetary and social policies in order to ensure low levels of unemployment across the EU.

References

Blanchard, O. (2006) 'European Unemployment: The Evolution of Facts and Ideas'. *Economic Policy*, Vol. 21, No. 45, pp. 5–59.

Bourne, R. and Oechsle, T. (2012) *Small is Best: Lessons from Advanced Economies* (London: Centre for Policy Studies). Available at: «http://www.cps.org.uk/files/reports/original/120522105633-smallisbest.pdf».

Eurostat (2012) 'Euro Area Unemployment at 11.6%, EU 27 at 10.6%'. Available at: «http://epp.eurostat.ec.europa.eu/cache/ITY_PUBLIC/3-31102012-BP/EN/3-31102012-BP-EN.PDF».

Freeman, R. and Nickell, S. (1988) 'Labour Market Institutions and Economic Performance'. *Economic Policy*, Vol. 3, No. 6, pp. 63–80.

Krugman, P. (1994) 'Past and Prospective Causes of High Unemployment'. *Economic Review*, Vol. 79, No. 4, pp. 49–98.

Leaker, D. (2009) 'Unemployment Trends since the 1970s'. *Economic and Labour Market Review*, Vol. 3, No. 2, pp. 37–41.

JCMS 2013 Volume 51 Annual Review pp. 63–69   DOI: 10.1111/jcms.12043

David Allen: A Tribute

SIMON BULMER,[1] CHRISTOPHER HILL,[2] DREW SCOTT[3] and MICHAEL SMITH[4]
[1] University of Sheffield. [2] University of Cambridge. [3] University of Edinburgh. [4] Loughborough University

Dave Allen, who died in October 2012, was a long-time contributor to the *JCMS Annual Review*. For 20 years, he wrote – together with Mike Smith – the article in the *Annual Review* on 'Relations with the Rest of the World'. Thanks to the expansion of the European Union (EU) during the 1990s and 2000s, and the changing focus of its external actions, this article varied in its scope and coverage, but Dave's energy and interest in the subject matter always gave it a special flavour. In many ways, the *Annual Review* was the ideal outlet for Dave's eclectic and practical approach to the problems of EU policy-making, and to the substance of EU policies. In approaching these subjects, Dave took a position best described as that of a passionate European, but not necessarily that of a Europhile – he could see the contradictions and the eccentricities of EU policies as well as their growing impact on the world.

A key to this approach was Dave's recognition that the internal and external development of EU policies and institutions had not done away with the national state. He was always keen to point out that the EU, whatever else it might be, was and is not a state; not only this, but the Union came embedded in a world of states, some at least of which have been strengthened rather than weakened by the process of European integration, others of which have claimed the 'right of resistance' to the deepening of the integration process, at least in formal terms, and still others of which have very different sets of priorities in their pursuit of 'great power' status.

This tribute pursues and develops these themes – the coexistence of the EU and the national state, and the interactions between them internally and externally – in four areas which were central to Dave's academic interests and which relate closely to themes that have emerged from successive years of the *Annual Review*. The first is the relationship between the United Kingdom and the EU, which was an enduring focus of Dave's attention. The second is the exploration of EU policies and their impact in Member States, and particularly regional and structural policies. The third is the making of the common foreign and security policy, and the final area is the EU's relationship with the global arena.

I. Britain and the EU

Since he was appointed to a lectureship at Loughborough University in 1972 in the very early years of European Studies and ahead of the United Kingdom's accession in 1973, it is scarcely surprising that the relationship of Britain and the European Community became one of Dave's research interests. Coming from an international relations background, his early work placed Britain's relationship with the EC in a foreign policy context (Allen, 1988). Indeed, his publications covered wider relations with western

© 2013 The Author(s) JCMS: Journal of Common Market Studies © 2013 John Wiley & Sons Ltd, 9600 Garsington Road, Oxford OX4 2DQ, UK and 350 Main Street, Malden, MA 02148, USA

Europe, the role of the Foreign and Commonwealth Office/foreign secretary and extending to British policy on nuclear weapons (Allen, 2010a). His later work also followed the academic trend towards Europeanization, looking at the adaptation of British politics, its political system and policy, especially foreign policy, to EU membership (Allen, 2005, 2013).

When addressing Britain's relationship with western Europe, one of Dave's key arguments was that the decline from global status repeatedly led to policy-makers being concerned that EC solutions were too narrow or parochial. Prime Minister Callaghan's rejection of joining in the European Monetary System in 1978–79 was cited as a case in point. In the period prior to the end of the cold war, Dave was keen to emphasize that there was much more to British diplomacy in western Europe than its troubled relationship with the EC. This position in fact reflected the organization of the FCO at the time, where EC business was set apart from bilateral relations and other European international organizations. His emphasis on Britain's role in European defence through the North Atlantic Treaty Organization (Nato) – an organization with which it was completely at ease – was a corrective to those who only focused on the 'awkward' relationship with the EC. Linking up with his work on foreign policy co-operation (see below), Dave charted the FCO's growing diplomatic engagement with EC partners and its efforts to resist any Franco-German challenge to Nato supremacy on security and defence.

Already in the mid-1980s Dave was developing the argument for which his work on Britain and the EU is best known. Initially, the argument focused on the way that successive British governments treated the EC as a foreign policy issue, and consequently did not feel the need to build a domestic consensus behind membership or spell out to the public the implications for sovereignty and autonomy. This failure contrasted with his observation of the way that the morale of the FCO was revived by foreign policy co-operation with its partners.

The end of the cold war and the gathering of pace in integration brought important changes to the context of British diplomacy. From close inside knowledge Dave charted the incremental realignments within the FCO into an 'EU Command'. He noted the concern in some quarters of the FCO that the scale of resources allocated to EU missions was neglecting some other parts of the world – a bias that Foreign Secretary Hague has come to address since 2010. His earlier interpretation of Britain's insecure domestic consensus for European integration came to be expressed in the language of Europeanization. He argued specifically that the adaptation of Whitehall to working with the EU was not mirrored by similar adjustment in the wider political context (Allen, 2005). In short, and writing during the final years of the Blair governments, he saw the United Kingdom as a 'Europeanised government in a non-Europeanised polity'. In his final publication on Britain and the EU he captured the consequences of the Labour governments' failure to build domestic support for the EU as 'towards isolation and a parting of the ways?' (Allen, 2013).

Dave's work has therefore highlighted key problems over the 40 years of EU membership: that Britain is a key player in (western) European politics; that its engagement with the EC/EU was never properly explained in a way to build a domestic consensus; and that the adaptation of governmental machinery was inadequate for a settled EU relationship. Now a possibly redefined relationship or parting of the ways lies ahead. Alas,

© 2013 The Author(s) JCMS: Journal of Common Market Studies © 2013 John Wiley & Sons Ltd

it will be left to Dave's former colleagues in the academic community to chart the political denouement after the next general election.

II. Regional and Structural Policies

The first connection that many undergraduate students are likely to have had with Dave Allen was through his contribution to what has long been the textbook of choice for all serious students of the EU – *Policy-Making in the European Union*. In later editions Dave authored the chapter on the regional and structural policies of the EU (having written on competition policy in earlier editions), reflecting not only his interest in this particular policy domain but additionally his much wider engagement with the EU policy process (Allen, 2010b). For it was the EU policy process that really engaged Dave's interest – in particular perhaps the role that compromise and 'deal-making' played in the dynamics of EU-level policy-making. It was no coincidence that for many years Dave took great pleasure delivering a range of training courses for British civil servants helping prepare them for the style of negotiation they would encounter as they engaged the EU segment of the United Kingdom's diplomatic activities.

One of the most interesting aspects of the structural funds for Dave was the multi-level governance (MLG) architecture in which they were, at least formally, located. While Dave had little doubt that MLG had considerable potential both to improve the design and delivery of EU-level policies and to buttress the legitimacy of the EU as a system of governance, as a practical proposition he found it less convincing. Notwithstanding the 'region-friendly' reforms introduced by the Maastricht Treaty (in particular establishing the Committee of the Regions and the new recitals on subsidiarity) and despite attempts to transfer greater authority to regions (and indeed arguably to the Commission as well) via the design and implementation of the structural funds, he remained sceptical that genuine MLG was possible in a Union that was, first and foremost, a creation of and for *nation-states*.

Dave's scepticism was not based on a particularly pessimistic view of the future development of EU regional development policies. Instead, his argument was that the funding of this policy was part of the wider multi-annual budget agreement reached between the EU Member States and, accordingly, the implementation stage (which for some represented the core of EU multi-level governance but for Dave was anchored in the prior intergovernmental budget deal) 'did not constitute a significant stage in the policy process' (Allen, 1996a, p. 222). This did not preclude an influential role for the Commission in ensuring that in its disbursement the structural funds would favour the principles of 'concentration' and 'programming' – both of which had been witnessed. But it was to insist that Member States retained the decisive role in determining the design and implementation of the structural funds.

Dave's work on EU regionalism permitted him regular incursions into another subject of very real interest to him – namely the ambitions of some governments in EU sub-state jurisdictions for full 'independence in Europe' (an issue that was *always* discussed on the many visits he made to his much-loved Scotland!). Leaving the politics to one side, it is fair to say that Dave saw no real contradiction between the self-determination ambitions of politicians in, say, Scotland, Catalonia or Flanders, and the wider cohesion of the EU as a whole. Indeed he was a critic of the view that regarded 'subsidiarity' as a principle only to be applied in mediating the division of powers between the EU and national levels of government. Why could this not equally be applied in determining the infranational division of competences?

Dave's untimely death has robbed the academic profession of a gifted intellect and highly engaging (and entertaining) communicator. Those of us interested in the development and governance of EU policies, especially at the level of the Brussels 'beltway', will feel this loss particularly acutely. There are countless aspects of Dave Allen's academic work that warrant, and have received, the acclaim of his peers. His many contributions to our understanding of the complex world(s) of EU policy-making were immense, but perhaps more important for his many graduate students was that his intellectual judgement in interpreting these developments was quite simply second to none.

III. EPC and the CFSP

Dave Allen was present at the creation of what has become known – still rather optimistically – as 'European foreign policy'. European political co-operation (EPC) was born in 1969–70, just before he was appointed at Loughborough. Although some established figures such as Geoffrey Goodwin and Roger Morgan quickly saw the potential of the foreign ministers' meetings provided for in the Luxembourg Report, Dave was in the vanguard of his own generation in being fascinated by the way the EEC was moving tentatively towards an external political profile and experimenting with new diplomatic mechanisms.

He quickly became an authority on both these dimensions, producing two widely read volumes, first with Reinhardt Rummel and Wolfgang Wessels on EPC as a platform for a future European foreign policy (one of the first serious discussions of that idea) and then on Europe's role in relation to what was then called the 'Arab–Israeli conflict', with Alfred Pijpers (Allen *et al.*, 1982; Allen and Pijpers, 1984). Both illustrated Dave's preference for collaborative work, and his eager involvement with the small network of people in continental Europe which had begun to spring up. At the time, some of the latter were suspicious of foreign policy co-operation, as a British attempt to revive intergovernmentalist threats to integration, despite the hostility of the British Atlanticists to any kind of joint European venture. Dave characteristically had little time for either anxiety, being quick to see both the added value which co-operation would bring to any national foreign policy, and the way in which foreign policy had the potential to revive a faltering European project.

When EPC was replaced by the CFSP (common foreign and security policy) in 1993 Dave was in a position to educate those many new enthusiasts for a European foreign policy who were unaware that it had not suddenly emerged as a product of the post-cold war world. At the same time, he did not fall into the error of the 'nothing new under the sun' analysts overly influenced by history. He saw that incremental change in procedures could lead to qualitative change in policy, and even in identity. This is why he developed the idea of 'Brusselization' in European foreign policy, whereby the increasing tendency to allow CFSP committees and staffs to coexist with the EU's institutions proper, in Brussels, created new possibilities for 'consistency' across the range of Europe's economic and political diplomacy, and removed some of the more theological barriers to the harmonization of national policies (Allen, 1998). On the other hand, as he also spotted at

© 2013 The Author(s) JCMS: Journal of Common Market Studies © 2013 John Wiley & Sons Ltd

a very early stage, there was an evident tendency to fall back on procedural change as a substitute for substantive foreign policy achievements (Wallace and Allen, 1977).

As has already been noted, Dave's good political judgement meant that he never suspended belief in the resilience of the state and its determination to retain the freedom of international manoeuvre which the bigger units, especially, associated with their sovereign independence. Indeed, he was one of the few analysts to be able to integrate successfully a realist view about the entrenched power of states with an historical under-standing of the changed conditions under which Member States had to operate – by virtue of the opportunities which the EU offered them, as well as their relative decline in global terms. This subtle dualism was behind his inspired extension of Alan Milward's paradigm to foreign policy. Dave's essay 'The European Rescue of National Foreign Policy?' concluded that EPC/CFSP had created 'for large and small states alike [. . .] the means for preserving (and in some cases advancing) a degree of autonomy in the contemporary international system' (Allen, 1996b, pp. 303–4). For Eurosceptics and integrationists alike this paradox was not easy to digest, but it rang true. For Dave profoundly understood the subject to which he devoted his career, combining academic and political wisdom with the result that his views carried real conviction for all those who read him or heard him speak. They will continue to do so.

IV. The EU and the Global Arena

Dave was persistently – and often contentiously – involved in the study of the EU's role in the global arena. In a way, this was a natural concomitant of his concern with the question 'who speaks for Europe?' and the process of 'Brusselization' described in the previous section (Allen, 1998). Three questions lay at the core of what interested and occasionally infuriated Dave. First, what kind of international actor was the EU? Second, what kind of influence could the EU wield in the global arena? And finally, was the EU capable of taking a strategic approach to the conduct of its relations with key partners and institutions in the global arena?

As noted at the beginning of this tribute, the starting point for much of Dave's analysis of the EU's international role was that it was not, is not and will not be a state in any conventional sense of the word. Indeed, because it is an entity in which the key political actors are (still) national states and their governments, this was bound to be a basic constraint on the scope and depth of the EU's international activity. Another basic constraint was that while the EU was what others might call 'post-sovereign', the global arena continued to be dominated by entities that were predominantly sovereign. In such a world, the pursuit of some kind of post-sovereign utopia was just that – utopian – and was bound to end in exposure of the EU's inherent limitations. For Dave, the key test of this line of thinking was the EU's relationships with major external actors. The United States, the EU's most significant 'other', remains defiantly sovereignist, and acts both unilaterally and in other fashions in pursuit of its national interests. Equally, the EU's relations with Russia or with India were conditioned fundamentally by the hybrid nature of the EU as an actor, and by the resolutely sovereignist orientations of these two major partners (Allen, 1997, 2012). Faced with this kind of challenge, it was no surprise to Dave that EU positions were often subject to fragmentation, decay and defection in ways that limited their impact.

© 2013 The Author(s) JCMS: Journal of Common Market Studies © 2013 John Wiley & Sons Ltd

This brings us to the second major area of Dave's interest in the EU's world role. What kind of influence could or should the EU be in the global arena? There were really two key areas in which EU influence might be sought. The first was in the effects membership of the Union might have on Member State foreign policies, and the second was the impact of the Union on the broader structure of world politics. With regard to the first, we have already noted the uneven but nonetheless significant influence of 'Brusselization' – a form of Europeanization at the level of foreign policy, but often a thin veneer for the national priorities of Member States. As just noted, the pervasive possibility of defection from Union positions and the ploughing of national furrows is a key element in this set of tensions.

At the global level, a central focus of Dave's attention was the modifying effect that the Union might have on global structures and patterns of interaction. The notion of the EU's 'presence' which he developed with Mike Smith during the 1990s was an attempt to find a way of expressing the fact that the EU was not without impact, while not having the structural characteristics of the national state (Allen and Smith, 1990, 1998). This process of structuring, not only of patterns of interaction but also of patterns of expectations and of priorities, provided a way of allowing for the EU's undoubted influence while not making the unsustainable claim that it was – or was on the way to being – a state. It also provided a way of accounting for the EU's intangible as well as its tangible impacts, and thus for pointing out variations in the EU's 'actorness' across issue areas and institutional contexts.

Dave's concern with the nature of the EU as an actor and with its influence fed naturally into one of his most recent areas of academic work: the investigation of the EU's diplomatic strategies. As part of a network dealing with the diplomatic system of the EU, Dave was especially involved in the development of ideas about 'strategic diplomacy' – the notion that the post-Lisbon Treaty EU should be able to develop a more consciously strategic use of its diplomatic machinery and thus pursue strategic relationships with key international partners and rivals. Dave became increasingly sceptical about the potential for such a strategic diplomacy as he explored both the diplomatic process within the EU and the pursuit of 'strategic partnerships' with key emerging powers, and especially with India (Allen, 2012). Dave's conclusion was that, on the one hand, the EU was incapable of acting in a truly strategic way, either because of institutional constraints or because of the basic tension between the Union and its Member States, and that, on the other hand, India in particular was an unlikely candidate for strategic partnership because of its defensiveness and its concentration on consolidating its regional status as a South Asian 'great power'. The result was stalemate in any efforts to secure diplomatic advantage for the EU – a situation in which the possibility of defection by Member States with interests in the region only became more likely.

Conclusions

This has not been a purely 'academic' essay or a review of a body of work. Rather, it is an appreciation not only of the issues and problems that inspired Dave Allen to think, talk and write about European integration, but also of the contribution that he made over 40 years to critical thinking and debate about the key processes of co-operation within and around the 'European' institutions. All four of us have been touched and stimulated not only by Dave's scholarship, but also by his friendship. The same applies to many new and long-established students in the field, and he will be sorely missed by all of us and all of them.

References

Allen, D. (1988) 'Britain and Western Europe'. In Smith, M., Smith, S. and White, B. (eds) *British Foreign Policy: Tradition, Change and Transformation* (London: Unwin Hyman).

Allen, D. (1996a) 'Cohesion and Structural Adjustment'. In Wallace, H. and Wallace, W. (eds) *Policy-Making in the European Union* (3rd edition) (Oxford: Oxford University Press).

Allen, D. (1996b) 'Conclusions: The European Rescue of National Foreign Policy?' In Hill, C. (ed.) *The Actors in Europe's Foreign Policy* (London: Routledge).

Allen, D. (1997) 'EPC/CFSP, the Soviet Union and the Former Soviet Republics: Do the Twelve have a Coherent Policy?' In Regelsberger, E., Schoutheete, P. de and Wessels, W. (eds) *Foreign Policy of the European Union: From EPC to CFSP and Beyond* (Boulder, CO: Lynne Rienner).

Allen, D. (1998) 'Who Speaks for Europe? The Search for a Coherent and Effective External Policy'. In Peterson, J. and Sjursen, H. (eds) *A Common Foreign Policy for Europe? Competing Visions of the CFSP* (London: Routledge).

Allen, D. (2005) 'The United Kingdom: A Europeanised Government in a Non-Europeanised Polity'. In Bulmer, S. and Lequesne, C. (eds) *The Member States of the European Union* (Oxford: Oxford University Press).

Allen, D. (2010a) 'The United Kingdom's Nuclear Deterrent and the 2010 Strategic and Defence Review'. *Political Quarterly*, Vol. 81, No. 3, pp. 385–96.

Allen, D. (2010b) 'The Structural Funds and Cohesion Policy: Extending the Bargain to Meet New Challenges'. In Wallace, H., Pollack, M. and Young, A. (eds) *Policy-Making in the European Union* (6th edition) (Oxford: Oxford University Press).

Allen, D. (2012) 'The EU and India: A Strategic Partnership but Differing Strategies'. Paper presented at the UACES Annual Conference, Passau, September.

Allen, D. (2013) 'The United Kingdom: Towards Isolation and a Parting of the Ways?'. In Bulmer, S. and Lequesne, C. (eds) *The Member States and the European Union* (2nd edition) (Oxford: Oxford University Press).

Allen, D. and Pijpers, A. (eds) (1984) *European Foreign Policy-Making and the Arab–Israeli Conflict* (London: Butterworth Scientific).

Allen, D., Rummel, R. and Wessels, W. (eds) (1982) *European Political Cooperation: Towards a Foreign Policy for Western Europe* (London: Butterworth Scientific).

Allen, D. and Smith, M. (1990) 'Western Europe's Presence in the Contemporary International Arena'. *Review of International Studies*, Vol. 16, No. 3, pp. 19–38.

Allen, D. and Smith, M. (1998) 'The European Union's Security Presence: Barrier, Facilitator or Manager?' In Rhodes, C. (ed.) *The European Union in the World Community* (Boulder, CO: Lynne Rienner).

Wallace, W. and Allen, D. (1977) 'Political Cooperation: Procedure as a Substitute for Policy'. In Wallace, H., Wallace, W. and Webb, C. (eds) *Policy-Making in the European Community* (Chichester: John Wiley & Sons).

© 2013 The Author(s) JCMS: Journal of Common Market Studies © 2013 John Wiley & Sons Ltd

JCMS 2013 Volume 51 Annual Review pp. 70–79   DOI: 10.1111/jcms.12056

The 2012 Danish Presidency of the Council of the European Union: Bridging Exclusion*

IAN MANNERS
University of Copenhagen

Introduction

> You're an out, a small out, and you're new. We don't want to hear from you. (Nicolas Sarkozy, in Barker and Parker, 2011)[1]

Holding the rotating Presidency of the Council of Ministers of the European Union (EU) is a challenging task for any Member State, but in the context of the global financial and eurozone crisis, the perceived decline of EU influence in the world and the growing resentment of EU citizens to austerity measures, the 2012 Danish Presidency was always going to be particularly difficult. As the remark from French President Nicolas Sarkozy to newly elected Danish Prime Minister Helle Thorning-Schmidt during the European Council meeting around 2 a.m. on Friday 9 December 2011 suggests, the Danish Presidency began early and in considerable difficulty (Gardner, 2012).

The Danish task was made even more demanding by the historical context of its relationship to the Treaty on European Union (TEU). However, the changes to the role of the rotating Presidency introduced by the trios from 2007 and the Lisbon Treaty from 2009 held the potential to help overcome these difficulties. It would be simple to suggest that the newly elected centre-left government (after ten years out of office) or the relative size of Danish governmental bureaucratic and diplomatic capacity were defining features of the Presidency. But they were not.

Evaluating Presidencies is never an easy task for both subjective and comparative reasons (see Manners, 2003; Quaglia and Moxon-Browne, 2006; Fernández, 2008; Adler-Nissen, 2012a). Evaluations are subjective in the sense that ambition, expectation and impression are all important in our reading of Presidencies. A balance has to be struck between internal evaluations of a 'pragmatic Presidency' and external evaluations of an 'invisible Presidency'. Comparative evaluations are exceptionally difficult, especially comparing historically with Presidencies prior to the trio and Lisbon. In this respect, the Danish Presidency could only conceivably be compared with the Spanish, Belgian, Hungarian and Polish Presidencies that preceded it.

* I am very grateful to the *JCMS Annual Review* editors, Nathaniel Copsey and Tim Haughton, and in particular Rebecca Adler-Nissen, Mette Buskjær Christensen, Mads Dagnis Jensen, Dorte Sindbjerg Martinsen, Jens Ladefoged Mortensen, Peter Nedergaard, Julie Hassing Nielsen and Marlene Wind for their help and comments.

[1] The authenticity of this quote is uncertain, with most sources referring to the *Financial Times*, but its validity is questioned. See also Charlemagne (2012); Gardner (2012); Kantner (2012).

© 2013 The Author(s) JCMS: Journal of Common Market Studies © 2013 John Wiley & Sons Ltd, 9600 Garsington Road, Oxford OX4 2DQ, UK and 350 Main Street, Malden, MA 02148, USA

This assessment will examine three sides of the Danish Presidency: its historical context, the Danish priorities and the most difficult challenges.[2] It will conclude that the Presidency was largely a function of the political and economic context in which Denmark found itself during January to June 2012. This conclusion is broadly in line with the work of Fernández (2008) and Adler-Nissen (2012a) who argue that the Presidency must be judged in terms of the defence of community interests rather than 'national interests'. In this context, the Presidency appeared to perform relatively well in some areas such as administrative co-ordination, keeping some policies moving and the interactive role of the Minister for European Affairs. The Presidency appeared unable to do too much in areas that were outside of its reach, such as the eurozone, the budget or external action. The Presidency appeared to encounter difficulty in areas that were a 'bridge too far', such as green growth, Schengen reform and co-ordination within the trio. Could Denmark have performed better if it were a 'full member' of the EU? This is of course difficult to judge, but at least it would have stood a chance as a eurozone member, which was not the case during 2012.

I. Context: Danish Self-Exclusions and the Lisbon Treaty

More than any of the other 26 Member States, the context of Denmark's historical relationship to the EU is critical in understanding its Presidency. Denmark had a 40-year relationship with the European institutions; it was entering its seventh Presidency demonstrating it had plenty of positive experience in the job. More importantly, some of its crucial diplomatic players, including Secretary of State Claus Grube and Permanent Representative Jeppe Tranholm-Mikkelsen, had extensive knowledge and experience of the EU. Denmark's previous experience of holding the Presidency in 2002 had been widely represented as a success – particularly for reaching agreement on EU enlargement (Friis, 2003). The changes since 2002 could not have been more striking – the Danish exclusions from the TEU, as well as the changes of EU enlargement, the trio and Lisbon Treaty, and the economic crisis had transformed Denmark's relationship to the EU (DIIS, 2008; Manners, 2011).

Danish Self-Exclusions

In 1993 the Danish government was forced to negotiate a series of opt-outs from the TEU in the areas of economic and monetary union (EMU), justice and home affairs (JHA) and in the security and defence policy (SDP). Up until 1999 these opt-outs did not really matter in institutional terms because the third stage of EMU had not occurred, while co-operation in JHA and SDP remained largely intergovernmental (Manners, 2000). From 1999 all this changed for Danish membership as it moved from 'opt-outs' to 'self-exclusion'. It is important to remember that the opt-outs were the result of a referendum and not party politics or government initiative. Every Danish government since 1993 has wished to remove some or all of these opt-outs in some way. Hence the term 'self-exclusion' is far more appropriate to describe the extent to which, after 1999 they exclude

---

[2] For good empirical overviews of the Presidency, see Adler-Nissen *et al.* (2012); Jensen and Nedergaard (2012); Christensen and Nielsen (2013); and the special issue of *Økonomi & Politik*, Vol. 85, No. 3, 2012, on 'Det danske EU-formandsskab foråret 2012'.

© 2013 The Author(s) JCMS: Journal of Common Market Studies © 2013 John Wiley & Sons Ltd

Denmark from the benefits of being a fuller, policy-making Member State (DIIS, 2008; Kantner, 2012). In this respect Adler-Nissen (2012b, p. 131) has described Denmark as a 'quasi-member'.

Denmark has maintained a fixed exchange rate policy against Germany's currency since 1982, pegged first to the deutschmark (1982–99) and then to the euro (1999–date). From 1979 to 1999 Denmark was a full member of the exchange rate mechanism (ERM) with a target currency fluctuation band of plus or minus 2.25 per cent. In 1999 Denmark joined the ERM II system with a nominal fluctuation band of plus or minus 2.25 per cent – in practice the actual currency fluctuation band is less than 1 per cent against the euro.

There are four wider consequences of Denmark's exclusion from the third stage of EMU. First, many assume that the Danish kroner is free-floating, but it is actually pegged in a fixed exchange rate policy against the euro – the 'krone-uro' (Bentow, 2000). Second, the fixed exchange rate policy brings both economic benefits in terms of stability and the possibility of floating, but economic costs in terms of finance, investment and trade (Flam, 2009; Aabo and Pantzalis, 2011). Third, a political consequence is that Denmark is excluded from participation in the Eurogroup of finance ministers and full membership of the European Central Bank (ECB) (Dyson and Marcussen, 2010). The final consequence was that while Denmark joined the Treaty on Stability, Co-ordination and Governance during its Presidency, leadership on issues related to economic governance came from the four presidents of the European Council, Commission, Eurogroup and the ECB.

Denmark participates to the fullest extent possible in the areas of JHA, although this was complicated as external border controls, asylum, immigration and the prevention and combating of crime were transferred to supranational policy-making in an area of freedom, security and justice (AFSJ) (Manners, 2000).[3] Prior to the Lisbon Treaty, Denmark participated intergovernmentally in many areas of AFSJ, but was excluded from supranational policy-making except for Schengen and areas of parallel agreement (for example, the Dublin Regulation), where it aligns its national legislation on civil law and asylum with that of the EU. In other areas of AFSJ Denmark has unilaterally introduced similar rules under Danish law (Adler-Nissen and Gammeltoft-Hansen, 2010, p. 145). The Lisbon Treaty brought police and judicial co-operation in criminal matters (PJCC) into EU supranational policy-making with 'opt-in' rules for the United Kingdom and Ireland. Denmark may change its exclusion to a more inclusive 'opt-in' position through a referendum.

The wider consequences of Denmark's exclusion from the supranational aspects of AFSJ include, first, the way the country participates in Schengen and parallel agreement areas as a taker, not maker, of policy. Second, in other areas of border control, asylum, immigration and civil law, Denmark engages in the national shadowing of EU policies, but cannot lead on policies in these areas. Third, in police and criminal law Denmark could be systematically excluded as the Stockholm Programme slowly moves the AFSJ from intergovernmental to supranational legislation. However, the indications from the European Asylum Support Office and other agreements suggest that Denmark sought full status but wound up with a hybrid observer/associate status similar to European free trade agreement (EFTA) states (Comte, 2010; Monar, 2012). The final consequence is that while Denmark chaired the JHA council during its Presidency, it did not participate on the same basis as the other Member States.

[3] For developments in the realm of JHA in 2012, see Monar's contribution to this issue.

© 2013 The Author(s) JCMS: Journal of Common Market Studies © 2013 John Wiley & Sons Ltd

As a leading international advocate of the 'comprehensive approach' to international conflict, Denmark seeks to combine the civilian and military aspects of peacekeeping and conflict management. Denmark cannot do this in EU SDP as it is excluded from military co-operation within the EU's common foreign and security policy (CFSP). In general, the Nordic influence on the development of civilian crisis management and civilian SDP has been relatively large (Björkdahl, 2008; Jakobsen, 2009). This exclusion has become more expansive with the growth of CFSP and CSDP activities over the past decade. It has also led to the withdrawal of Danish forces as Nato-led peacekeeping operations in Macedonia and Bosnia-Herzegovina became EU-led. Danish exclusion from the Nordic battle-group and the European Defence Agency reflect two minor aspects of a much wider problem as the diplomatic, civilian and military aspects of SDP became integrated into the European External Action Service (EEAS) after the Lisbon Treaty.[4]

The wider consequences of Denmark's exclusion from SDP are fourfold. First, its ability to shape the post-Lisbon construction of the EEAS has been largely restricted to the activities of Poul Skytte Christoffersen and Michael Matthiessen, both of whom were international, rather than national, diplomats during 2010–11. In contrast, fellow Nordic countries Sweden and Finland have senior staff in the EEAS as Director of the EU intelligence analysis centre (EU INTCEN) and Chair of the political and security committee, although neither country is a member of Nato. Second, EU SDP operations have increasingly involved the overlapping and interlaced deployment of military and civilian missions in regions such as the former Yugoslavia, Congo, Chad/Sudan and Somalia. Third, EU SDP operations in the Somali regions such as EUNAVFOR – Operation Atalanta, EUTM Somalia and EUCAP NESTOR have been specifically aimed at improving maritime security critical for Danish shipping. Fourth, the combination of Danish exclusion from CSDP operations and the construction of the EEAS have enforced Denmark's Nato preference, for example, in Nato air missions over Libya in 2011.

The Trio of Poland–Denmark–Cyprus

The Danish Presidency was the middle member of the fourth trio since 2007, consisting of Poland–Denmark–Cyprus (PDC). Following the Spain–Belgium–Hungary trio, the Danish trio was the first post-Lisbon Treaty group to have two new Presidencies in it. Furthermore, none of the members could be considered central players in Europe-wide attempts to deal with the crisis of the eurozone. The PDC trio created some difficulties for Denmark as Poland was eager and ambitious in its first Presidency, acting more like a larger state despite relative lack of experience (Pomorska and Vanhoonacker, 2012). In contrast, Cyprus had relatively little capacity and ambition, and was almost entirely consumed by banking crises and relations with Turkey.[5] Despite these difficulties, initial administrative co-ordination with Poland was good, in spite of disagreements over green growth. However, the trio resulted in little agreement on the 18-month programme of the Council, which meant the work had to be done in the Council Secretariat, potentially weakening the trio agenda management role of the Presidency. The trio Presidencies were intended to facilitate co-ordination and allow older members to help newer members, but the eurozone crises completely overshadowed the PDC trio, with Denmark not well placed

---

[4] For an overview of developments in EU foreign relations in 2012, see Hadfield and Fiott's contribution to this issue.
[5] For an account of the Cypriot Presidency, see Christou's contribution to this issue.

© 2013 The Author(s) JCMS: Journal of Common Market Studies © 2013 John Wiley & Sons Ltd

to help, particularly Cyprus, in this respect. According to Jensen and Nedergaard (2012), the trio had a 'moderate to low scope of goals as well as a moderate to low depth of coordination', compared with previous trios. It also could be argued that the process of drawing up the trio programme had a socializing effect on the participants (Adler-Nissen, 2012a).

The Lisbon Treaty Changes for Denmark

The Lisbon Treaty changes regarding, in particular, the President of the European Council, the High Representative of the Union for Foreign Affairs and Security Policy, the EEAS, the legal basis of the Eurogroup, the consolidation of all areas of AFSJ in the supranational treaty base and the enhanced status of the European Parliament (EP), made the Danish Presidency radically different to all of those that preceded it (Beach, 2012). While these changes appear more immediate than those of the Danish exclusions, it is the combination that proved challenging for Denmark. The extent to which the President of the European Council ran the European Councils, the review of eurozone governance (with the other three Presidents), as well as seeking to steer the multi-annual financial framework (MFF) largely relegated the Danish Presidency to a supporting role in the larger issues of the time. The three roles of the High Representative of the Union for Foreign Affairs and Security Policy in acting as foreign minister representing the EU with the help of the EEAS, chairing the Foreign Affairs Council and acting as deputy Vice-President of the Commission raised a number of questions over what role Danish Foreign Minister Villy Søvndal was to play during the Danish Presidency. Similarly, EEAS diplomatic relations, delegations, operations, missions and negotiating roles brought together tasks formerly shared between the Commission, the Council Secretariat and the Presidency that left less space for a local Danish co-ordinating role in third countries. The Eurogroup was placed on a legal basis by the Lisbon Treaty, which put it at the centre of attempts to shape EU economic governance, especially through the role of the President of the Eurogroup (one of the four Presidents), excluding the Danish Presidency from involvement. After the Lisbon Treaty, AFSJ policy-making, together with the consolidation and separation of tasks within Commission DG Justice (rights) and DG Home Affairs (free movement), moved beyond the policy-making fragmentation and lack of democratic oversight of the intergovernmental JHA and PJCC, especially through the Stockholm Programme. In this respect, the Danish Presidency found itself chairing Council meetings discussing AFSJ policies it could not participate in on the same basis as other members. Finally, the Lisbon Treaty meant that the EP experienced an increase in co-decision responsibility over areas including agriculture, immigration and the budget. Through these new powers, the EP sought to extend its control of the Commission appointments, the High Representative and the EEAS. To respond to this development, the Danish Presidency created a minister for European affairs position and appointed Nicolai Wammen to the post.

II. Priorities: A Responsible, Dynamic, Green and Safe Europe

While the centrality of steering the MFF negotiations was known years ahead of the Danish Presidency, the other priorities began to take shape about two years in advance. While Denmark has a long history of environmental advocacy, after the events of the

© 2013 The Author(s) JCMS: Journal of Common Market Studies © 2013 John Wiley & Sons Ltd

Copenhagen UN Climate Change Conference of the Parties 15 in December 2009, and the appointment of Connie Hedegaard as European Commissioner for Climate Action in February 2010, it became clear that green growth would be important to any Danish government holding the EU Presidency. However, this primary priority of green growth was soon overshadowed by the European sovereign debt crisis, particularly that of Greece, during 2011. Hence by November 2011 the five main priorities of the Danish Presidency were: overcoming the eurozone debt crisis; setting a new green growth agenda; making progress on negotiations over the EU's next MFF; making progress on JHA issues, including Schengen and asylum; and external matters – for example, free trade agreements (Tranholm-Mikkelsen, 2011; Pop, 2011).

The Danish Presidency priories were finalized late in December 2011 and publicly presented in January 2012 (MFA, 2012a). The priorities were broadly similar to the *Europe 2020 Strategy* of smart, sustainable and inclusive growth: *A Responsible Europe* (economics); *A Dynamic Europe* (competitiveness); *A Green Europe* (green growth); and *A Safe Europe* (security). Not only had green issues dropped down the agenda, but issues which Denmark was excluded from (eurozone and AFSJ) had risen up the agenda. It is also striking that unlike most Presidencies, and especially compared with the focus on enlargement in the 2002 Danish Presidency, no real priority was given to external action. Like the Spanish, Belgian and Hungarian Presidencies that preceded it, the Danish Presidency demonstrated the effects of the Lisbon Treaty and the EEAS.

A Responsible Europe

The main focus of the EU during the Danish Presidency was dealing with economic governance and eurozone reform – areas in which Denmark played very little role in agenda management. It has been argued that for Finance Minister Margrethe Vestager, 'Denmark's position outside the eurozone meant that influence on economic and financial affairs was often only marginal and she remained a spectator as the group of 17 tried to get to grips with the crisis' (Gardner, 2012). As was clear since the Lisbon Treaty, and demonstrated by the conclusions of the March and June European Council meetings, agenda management of *A Responsible Europe* was led by Herman Van Rompuy, President of the European Council, together with Presidents of the Commission, Eurogroup and the ECB.[6] In contrast, the Danish Presidency was generally acknowledged to have played a positive agenda management role in handling the MFF during the first half of 2012.

A Dynamic Europe

The secondary focus of the EU during the Danish Presidency was the issue of addressing the *Europe 2020 Strategy* goal of 'smart growth' though revitalizing the single market and developing a knowledge-based economy. In many respects this agenda has not changed since the 2000 Lisbon Strategy, although the low growth/high unemployment economic crises of 2012 raised this issue up the political agenda. Largely because of the flawed economics of austerity – for example, in the reduction of research and investment in the draft MFF – the Danish Presidency found very little opportunity for innovation in this

[6] See Dinan's contribution to this issue.

© 2013 The Author(s) JCMS: Journal of Common Market Studies © 2013 John Wiley & Sons Ltd

long-standing weakness in EU policy. The one shining light, and unforeseen in the Danish priorities, was the surprise agreement on unified patent system reform.

A Green Europe

The priority of sustainable or green growth would have been an issue the Presidency might have wanted to push hard on. Certainly Denmark was ambitious in the environmental area, especially on energy, chemicals, pollution and the UN Rio+20 Conference. While the Presidency was successful in chemical regulation, ship pollution and Rio+20, it was blocked in energy efficiency reforms by heavyweight anti-green governments in the United Kingdom, Germany and Poland (EEB, 2012). Most unfortunately, the greatest opposition to the Danish Presidency's advocacy of long-term climate and energy road maps 2050 appears to have come from its trio partner, Poland, although an unwillingness to push more at the international level also appeared to be a problem.

A Safe Europe

The Danish exclusions from the EU were also felt in the priority area of a safe Europe, particularly in the context of counter-terrorism and the civil war in Syria. While the Danish programme made no mention of a comprehensive approach, military or defence policies, the EU's crisis management concept was implemented in three new integrated civilian missions during the Presidency: EUCAP NESTOR (Horn of Africa); EUAVSEC South Sudan; and EUCAP Sahel Niger. The Danish Ministry of Foreign Affairs found itself struggling to describe the 'Adoption of a framework for more comprehensive approach in third countries' without using the terms 'military' or 'defence' (MFA, 2012b). These combined effects of the Lisbon Treaty changes to external representation and the Danish exclusions from the EU led to the observation that a safe Europe was not really a priority for the Danish Presidency, or at best was overshadowed by the other priorities. However, as Dehousse and Menon (2009, p. 100) have argued, 'a Presidency can only really accomplish objectives devised and set by others', thus it may be that Denmark may have sowed seeds for a more comprehensive approach to EU crisis management in the future.

III. Challenges: Bridging Exclusion

This combination of rapidly changing context and externally driven priorities ensured that the 2012 Danish EU Presidency was deeply challenging. But, was the Presidency better or worse than others? As discussed, it can only genuinely be compared with the four that preceded it. On these terms it can be favourably compared with the Belgian and Hungarian Presidencies (Drieskens, 2011; Ágh, 2012), although it clearly had structural disadvantages compared to Belgium (despite its caretaker government) and advantages compared to Hungary (because of its repressive government). For all the reasons discussed, it cannot be compared to the 2002 Danish Presidency or the Spanish and Polish ones that preceded it. The Danish exclusions from the EU and the Presidency strategy of focusing on the manageable and achievable tasks in the post-Lisbon era make such a comparison inappropriate.

© 2013 The Author(s) JCMS: Journal of Common Market Studies © 2013 John Wiley & Sons Ltd

There are three conclusions that can be drawn from the Presidency relating to the relatively successful *bridge-building* activities, the largely *out of reach* areas of policy, and the very difficult areas which were a *bridge too far* for the Danish Presidency.

Bridge Building

At its outset the Danish Presidency was regularly portrayed as a 'bridge over troubled water' by both the foreign ministry and European press (Wammen, 2012). According to the foreign ministry, the ambition of the Presidency was to act as a bridge over troubled water and to demonstrate that co-operation works and is able to achieve results (Jensen, 2012). In this respect the Presidency was relatively successful in the three bridge-building activities of administrative co-ordination, the role of the Europe minister, and relations between eurozone and non-eurozone members. The Presidency largely succeeded in co-ordinating the chairing activities of the Council of Ministers and bridging the administrative gaps between the trio (Jensen and Nedergaard, 2012). Danish Minister for European Affairs Nicolai Wammen was able to provide co-ordination between ministries, Member States, institutions and councils. Finally, the Presidency was able to go some way towards bridging the large gap between eurozone and non-eurozone members in the discussion of economic governance proposals and the 'Two Pack' regulations on surveillance and monitoring the eurozone. The obvious comparison in this respect between Denmark, the United Kingdom and the Czech Republic helps illustrate the gaps.

Out of Reach

However, what was also clear to the Danish Presidency was that a number of policy areas were largely out of reach of significant Danish agenda management and brokerage/mediation. With one of these – the MFF – Denmark did its best to steer negotiations towards settlement in the future, but the two others – eurozone governance and external action – were subject to Danish exclusions and the effects of the Lisbon Treaty, leaving them largely out of reach. The eurozone was the dominant policy area during the Danish Presidency, but the leading roles were taken by the four Presidents, as well as important euro-states such as Germany. The budget was the second most important policy area during the Danish Presidency. However, the timing and inter-institutional dynamics meant that significant negotiations left it largely out of reach, although there is a feeling that the presentation of the negotiating box and discussions of Horizon 2020 were important. In the area of external action, the ongoing events of the Arab uprisings (particularly Syria), bilateral trade negotiations and continuing enlargement (Serbia) were important. In the post-Lisbon context, these areas were largely out of reach for the Danish Presidency, although many of the secondary topics were manageable.

Bridge too Far

Unfortunately, there were a number of very difficult areas which were a bridge too far for the Danish Presidency, although this perception came from outside, and not inside, the Presidency. The Danish Presidency ran into difficulties with its trio partner Poland on the

© 2013 The Author(s) JCMS: Journal of Common Market Studies © 2013 John Wiley & Sons Ltd

low carbon road map to 2050, but also with green growth more generally. Danish Justice Minister Morten Bodskov was attacked from many sides when he presented the unanimous decision of ministers for amendment to the Schengen borders code to the EP. While this was a little unfair, given the strong pressure from France, Italy, the Netherlands and other Member States, there is a sense that as a Member State with special provisions for participation in JHA, the Danish Presidency was being blamed for wider concerns about lack of EP democratic oversight. The EP suspended JHA co-operation with the Presidency until the next Presidency, although Cyprus is not a member of Schengen. The lack of co-ordination in only the second post-Lisbon trio suggests problems for future trios. While some Presidencies (such as Poland) still seek to run pre-Lisbon Presidencies, others (such as Cyprus) experienced severe structural and capacity problems. This made Denmark's problems all the more challenging, particularly as the institutional diversity (EMU, JHA, SDP) between the trio was so striking.

The 2012 Danish EU Presidency was broadly in line with what informed outside observers had expected: an experienced, smaller Member State taking the role of Council Presidency in a post-Lisbon environment, but with its hands tied behind its back. In many respects, the Danish Presidency played smart and went for the achievable; in other respects, the advocates and critics of the Presidency need to rethink what is achievable. Like all Presidencies over the past five years, the 2012 Danish EU Presidency was not what it used to be. But then, Presidencies probably never were.

References

Aabo, T. and Pantzalis, C. (2011) 'In or Out: The Effect of Euro Membership on the Exercise of Real Business Options'. *European Journal of Finance*, Vol. 14, No. 4, pp. 259–84.

Adler-Nissen, R. (2012a) 'Formandskabets prioriteter: Når EU's dagsorden bliver en national ambition'. *Økonomi & Politik*, Vol. 85, No. 3, pp. 4–14.

Adler-Nissen, R. (2012b) 'Danish Presidency Risks Being Hoist on Its Referendum Petard'. *Europe's World*, Spring, p. 131.

Adler-Nissen, R. and Gammeltoft-Hansen, T. (2010) *Straitjacket or Sovereignty Shield? The Danish Opt-Out on Justice and Home Affairs and Prospects after the Treaty of Lisbon* (Copenhagen: DIIS).

Adler-Nissen, R., Nielsen, J.H. and Sørensen, C. (2012) *The Danish EU Presidency 2012: A Midterm Report* (Stockholm: Swedish Institute for European Policy Studies).

Ágh, A. (2012) 'The Hungarian Rhapsodies: The Conflict of Adventurism and Professionalism in the European Union Presidency'. *JCMS*, Vol. 50, No. S2, pp. 68–75.

Barker, A. and Parke, G. (2011) 'False Assumptions Underpinned British Strategy'. *Financial Times*, 16 December.

Beach, D. (2012) 'Fremtidens ledersløse formandskaber'. *Økonomi & Politik*, Vol. 85, No. 3, pp. 63–74.

Bentow, D. (2000) 'Krone-uro'. *Børsen*, 18 September.

Björkdahl, A. (2008) 'Norm Advocacy: A Small State Strategy to Influence the EU'. *Journal of European Public Policy*, Vol. 15, No. 1, pp. 135–54.

Charlemagne (2012) 'To Opt In or Not to Opt In: That is the Question Denmark Still Wrestles with in the Euro Crisis'. *The Economist*, 14 January.

Christensen, M.B. and Nielsen, J.H. (2013), 'Can a Small Non-euro Member State Holding the EU Presidency Make a Difference in Times of EU Economic Crisis'. In Dabrowska-Klosinska, P. (ed.) *Polish Yearbook of European Studies*, YPES 15/2012.

© 2013 The Author(s) JCMS: Journal of Common Market Studies © 2013 John Wiley & Sons Ltd

Comte, F. (2010) 'A New Agency is Born in the European Union: The European Asylum Support Office'. *European Journal of Migration and Law*, Vol. 12, No. 4, pp. 373–405.

Danish Institute for International Studies (DIIS) (2008) *De danske forbehold over for den Europæiske Union: Udviklingen siden 2000* (Copenhagen: DIIS).

Dehousse, R. and Menon, A. (2009) 'The French Presidency'. *JCMS*, Vol. 47, No. S1, pp. 99–111.

Drieskens, E. (2011) 'Ceci n'est pas une présidence: The 2010 Belgian Presidency of the EU'. *JCMS*, Vol. 49, No. S1, pp. 91–102.

Dyson, K. and Marcussen, M. (2010) 'Transverse Integration in European Economic Governance: Between Unitary and Differentiated Integration'. *Journal of European Integration*, Vol. 32, No. 1, pp. 17–39.

European Environmental Bureau (EEB) (2012) *The EEB's Assessment of the Environmental Dimension of the Danish Presidency of the European Union* (Brussels: EEB).

Fernández, A.M. (2008) 'Change and Stability of the EU Institutional System: The Communitarization of the Council Presidency'. *Journal of European Integration*, Vol. 30, No. 5, pp. 617–34.

Flam, H. (ed.) (2009) *EMU at Ten: Should Denmark, Sweden and the UK Join?* (Stockholm: Centre for Business and Policy Studies/SNS).

Friis, L. (2003) 'The Danish Presidency: "Wonderful Copenhagen"'. *JCMS*, Vol. 41, No. S1, pp. 49–51.

Gardner, A. (2012) 'A Professional, Pragmatic Presidency'. *European Voice*, 5 July.

Jakobsen, P.V. (2009) 'Small States, Big Influence: The Overlooked Nordic Influence on the Civilian ESDP'. *JCMS*, Vol. 47, No. 1, pp. 81–102.

Jensen, C.S. (2012) 'The Danish EU Presidency 2012', presentation, 30 June.

Jensen, M.D. and Nedergaard, P. (2012) 'Erfolgreiche Koordination in turbulenten Zeiten: die dänische Ratspräsidentschaft im ersten Halbjahr 2012'. *Integration*, Vol. 35, No. 4, pp. 258–73.

Kantner, J. (2012) 'Dane Seeks a Spot at Europe's Top Table'. *New York Times*, 11 January.

Manners, I. (2000) *Substance and Symbolism: An Anatomy of Cooperation in the New Europe* (Aldershot: Ashgate).

Manners, I. (2003) 'The British Presidency of 1998: New Labour, New Tone?' In Elgström, O. (ed.) *European Union Council Presidencies: A Comparative Analysis* (London: Routledge).

Manners, I. (2011) 'Denmark and the European Union'. In Wind, M. and Martinsen, D.S. (eds) *EU som et politisk system: Udviklinger og udfordringer* (Copenhagen: Forlaget Columbus).

Ministry of Foreign Affairs (MFA) (2012a) *Europe at Work: Programme of the Danish Presidency of the Council of the European Union 2012* (Copenhagen: MFA).

Ministry of Foreign Affairs (MFA) (2012b) *Europe at Work: The Results of the Danish Presidency of the Council of the European Union 2012* (Copenhagen: MFA).

Monar, J. (2012) *The External Dimension of the EU's Area of Freedom, Security and Justice: Progress, Potential and Limitations after the Treaty of Lisbon.* SIEPS Report 2012:1 (Stockholm: Swedish Institute for European Policy Studies).

Pomorska, K. and Vanhoonacker, S. (2012) 'Poland in the Driving Seat: A Mature Presidency in Turbulent Times'. *JCMS*, Vol. 50, No. S2, pp. 76–84.

Pop, V. (2011) 'Danish EU Presidency to Focus on Euro Crisis'. *EU Observer*, 23 November.

Quaglia, L. and Moxon-Browne, E. (2006) 'What Makes a Good EU Presidency? Italy and Ireland Compared'. *JCMS*, Vol. 44, No. 2, pp. 349–68.

Tranholm-Mikkelsen, J. (2011) 'The Priorities of the Danish Presidency of the EU', European Policy Centre talk, 23 November.

Wammen, N. (2012) 'The Presidency has Worked for Growth in Europe'. *Politiken*, 1 July.

© 2013 The Author(s) JCMS: Journal of Common Market Studies © 2013 John Wiley & Sons Ltd

JCMS 2013 Volume 51 Annual Review pp. 80–88

DOI: 10.1111/jcms.12031

The Cyprus Presidency of the EU: 'Real Achievements' in a 'Filoxenos Topos'

GEORGE CHRISTOU
University of Warwick

> In a few words, our aspiration was to move [. . .] European integration a small step further, and I think that the important results of our presidency reflect that we succeeded in this. (Mavroyiannis, quoted in *Cyprus News*, 2013)

Introduction

The rotating Presidency of the European Union (EU) held for the first time by Cyprus between July and December 2012 was always going to be a challenge given its own domestic economic difficulties, the continued division of the island and the fractious process of EU enlargement towards Turkey. Even before Cyprus had begun its tenure on 1 July 2012 Turkey refused to recognize the Presidency and to co-operate with the Council during Cyprus' term of office. As if this was not enough of a challenge, Cyprus also had to grapple with the turmoil in Greece and its own exposure to the Greek debt crisis, the broader fallout from the eurozone crisis, and the peaceful and not so peaceful transitions in its immediate southern neighbourhood. Indeed, Cyprus neared its Presidency term preparing a bail-out bid as well as a programme of priorities for the EU. In addition to this, there was also the issue of resource for what is a 'small Member State' in EU terms, and questions over whether it could administer and manage an effective Presidency with a Permanent Representation that under 'normal' circumstances employed approximately 80 staff. The pre-Presidency context presented an extraordinary set of obstacles for Cyprus, and there was certainly some trepidation as to how it would perform: the outcome, however, demonstrated that Cyprus was able to adapt, learn and act as honest and impartial broker for its six-month term with a modicum of success.

Cyprus was the third Member State of a Presidency trio made up of Poland (July–December 2011) and then Denmark (January–July2012).[1] It prepared for the Presidency for over two years, and recognized it as one of the most significant and important responsibilities it had undertaken in its history. The seriousness with which it treated its role, particularly as one of the relative newcomers having joined in May 2004 was reflected first of all in the separation of the Cyprus problem – the island's division between Greek south and Turkish Cypriot north[2] – from its responsibilities and obligations as holder of the Presidency of the Council of the EU. Negotiations between the leaders of the

---

[1] On the Danish Presidency see Manners in this issue.

[2] Following intercommunal strife in 1963 and 1967 and the attempted coup against President Makarios by the Greek military junta in 1974, Turkey invaded and occupied 37 per cent of the island. Cyprus has remained divided between the Greek-Cypriot south and the Turkish-Cypriot north since then despite numerous attempts to negotiate a viable solution. See, for example, Ker-Lindsay (2009, 2011).

© 2013 The Author(s) JCMS: Journal of Common Market Studies © 2013 John Wiley & Sons Ltd, 9600 Garsington Road, Oxford OX4 2DQ, UK and 350 Main Street, Malden, MA 02148, USA

Figure 1: Presidency Priorities and Logistics

Priorities: 1. Europe, more efficient and sustainable; 2. Europe, with a better performing and growth economy; 3. Europe, more relevant to its citizens, with solidarity and social cohesion; 4. Europe in the world, closer to its neighbours

Cyprus Presidency: 230 Cypriot officials (approx.), 184 days, over 1,500 meetings

Cost: €46 million (€61.7 was actually allocated by the Cyprus House of Representatives)

In Brussels: 30 sessions of the Council of Ministers, 63 ambassador-level meetings, and 1,400 technocrat-level meetings. Over 60 visits by Cypriot ministers to the European Parliament

In Cyprus: 225 conferences and meetings (including 15 informal ministerial councils) attended by over 19,000 delegates. 140 meetings of non-governmental organizations and 350 cultural events

Twitter: @#cy2012eublogs!

Source: *Cyprus News*, January 2013.

two communities under United Nations auspices were effectively postponed during this period, and Cyprus aimed to ensure its neutrality on enlargement, precisely because of the Turkish issue and the deteriorating relations between Turkey and the EU. Having said this, the Cyprus Presidency did not seek to exclude Turkish-Cypriots, but rather sought to involve them, with many Turkish-Cypriot non-governmental organizations (NGOs) participating in meetings to draft the Presidency programme.[3]

Second, resource mechanisms were bolstered and logistical and administrative processes were put in place for the lifetime of the Presidency to ensure that it could run as smoothly as possible. Additional flights to the tune of six per week were provided by Cyprus Airways for the Presidency period, the post of (Deputy) Minister of European Affairs (Andreas Mavroyiannis) was created specifically for the Presidency and an additional 150 civil servants (approximately) were redeployed from Nicosia to Brussels. Furthermore, 'small' teams were deployed (typically three to four officials)[4] to work intensively on each issue area in order to ensure, on a practical level, that the Cyprus Presidency was able to pursue its priorities and achieve its stated objectives.

In addition, and again to avoid 'domestic' problems impacting negatively on the Presidency as it has with newer Member States in the recent past (for example, Hungary, in 2011 and the Czech Republic in 2009),[5] Cyprus took the decision to 'Brusselize' the Presidency as much as possible (see Figure 1); so while a newly refurbished conference centre provided a location for informal ministerial meetings in Nicosia, the bulk of the other meetings would be facilitated by the larger Cypriot representation drafted in for the Presidency[6] in Brussels.[7] In this sense, an interesting comparison can be made between the preparations of Cyprus and those of Slovenia in 2008, where 'domestic politics' was

[3] *Cyprus News*, January 2013. This does not imply that all Turkish-Cypriots were satisfied with the level or scope of representation; clearly they were not and demonstrated this through protests in Brussels in June 2012 before the start of the Cyprus Presidency.
[4] This varied according to issue area and is in comparison to the resource that larger Member States usually deploy whereby there might typically be 10–12 officials working on each issue.
[5] See Ágh (2012) and Beneš and Karlas (2010), respectively.
[6] While there is a perception (from the outside at least) of Cyprus being dependent on Greece within the EU, the Presidency demonstrates the extent to which the Cypriots were able to work independently towards achieving their Presidency programme and goals.
[7] *European Voice*, 21 June 2012; *Euractiv*, 25 June 2012.

© 2013 The Author(s) JCMS: Journal of Common Market Studies © 2013 John Wiley & Sons Ltd

virtually suspended for the period of the Presidency in order to insure against any potential spoilers and to demonstrate that 'smaller' and newer Member States could be trusted and relied upon to deliver an effective Presidency programme (see Kajnč, 2009; Krašovec and Lajh, 2009).

EU institutional changes after the Lisbon Treaty and their potential impact on the rotating Presidency have been well documented (see, for example, Dinan, 2011), and some have made the argument that it might become even 'more pivotal than ever for the smooth running of the EU legislative machine' given the potentially central role of the Presidency in interacting with an ever more self-confident European Parliament (EP) following the extension of the co-decision procedure to an increased number of policy areas after Lisbon (Pomorska and Vanhoonacker, 2012, p. 77).

The Cyprus Presidency aimed to play the role of honest broker in those areas in which it sought to move forward and make progress upon within the Presidency agenda (discussed below). This contribution analyzes the extent to which it has managed to achieve this aim and indeed, how it has fared in achieving its programmatic ambitions through its ability to lead and forge compromise, particularly on issues that are notoriously difficult to agree such as the multi-annual framework for the period 2014–20. It will begin by briefly providing an overview of the Cypriot Presidency's strategic programme and will assess how it performed in its self-assigned honest broker role across key areas of its agenda, despite the internal and broader challenges and obstacles that it has faced. The article will conclude with some overall thoughts on the performance of Cyprus and its implications for the rotating Presidency more broadly.

I. Keeping It Modest but 'Relevant': Issues and Performance

The rationale that underpinned the Cyprus Presidency was one of narrowing the scope of its programme in order to ensure it maximized its effectiveness – perhaps not a surprise given its size and resources. To this end, it outlined four main strategic priorities that were designed[8] primarily to work towards a more effective Europe, contribute to sustainable growth and lay the foundations for a more prosperous and socially cohesive EU polity underpinned by the principle of solidarity. In short, its overarching symbolic theme was to work *Towards a Better Europe*, and there was recognition that for the EU to overcome the crisis it had to re-engage with and reinforce its core values in particular in relation to its citizens, especially the younger generation of Europeans. The Cyprus Presidency was innovative in its approach to engagement from the outset, which included a bloggers' event in Brussels on 26 July in order to encourage dialogue and open debate and demonstrate how social media might facilitate a better understanding of EU policy processes and close the 'input' gap between citizens and EU policy-makers.[9] Ultimately, such an initiative was also an attempt to expose the Presidency to the wider European public, particularly as many Presidencies often come and go unnoticed in the broader public sphere nationally, regionally and internationally. The socio-economic context in Europe and the fact that Cyprus only had one specific national priority in the form of maritime

[8] This was designed as part of the broader 18-month Trio programme approved by the General Affairs Council on 21 June 2011.
[9] For more details, see «http://www.cy2012.eu/index.php/en/news-categories/areas/the-presidency/press-release%97 bloggers-across-europe-gathered-to-meet-the-cyprus-presidency».

© 2013 The Author(s) JCMS: Journal of Common Market Studies © 2013 John Wiley & Sons Ltd

policy among the many issues programmed for its Presidency meant that it could exercise flexibility within the policy process. It also enhanced Cyprus' ability to mediate and find compromise on the many other thornier topics for debate during its term of office. On some issues it succeeded in gaining agreement, on others this proved more difficult to achieve even though general progress was made on all fronts and concrete platforms for moving forward were put in place for its successor, Ireland.

The Multi-annual Financial Framework

There is no doubt that the Multi-annual Financial Framework (2014–20) (MFF) (Priority 1) was the main focus of the Cyprus Presidency given its overarching impact. The MFF caused Cypriot diplomats the most difficulty in playing their role as honest broker as they attempted to find a compromise that would be agreeable to Member States and the EU institutions (the European Commission and the EP). While the Cypriots were determined that the Presidency would be conducted in the spirit of '*Filoxenos topos*' (literally translated: 'hospitable place') in order to work towards a *Better Europe*, the arena within which negotiations for the MFF took place proved to be anything but. In an age of austerity, where supranational and national philosophies clashed and, indeed, where there was no consensus between Member States on whether the budget for this period should be cut, maintained or increased, it was always going to be a difficult task to agree on an outcome that accommodated the diversity of views that existed during the short lifespan of not just the Cyprus, but also Danish, Presidencies.

In general, there was a determination among 'net contributors' that the MFF should be reflective of the budgetary discipline and consolidation efforts in Member States, and that it should incorporate 'smart' spending that would deliver sustainable growth embedded within the Europe 2020 Strategy. To this end the proposal presented by the Commission in June 2011 for the MFF to raise the budget from €976 billion to €1.025 trillion was not seen in a positive light by the EP as it argued that this would be insufficient to meet the goals of the Europe 2020 strategy, while Member States such as Germany and the United Kingdom sought to cut the budget[10] to make it more reflective of cuts in various domestic contexts. The Cyprus Presidency had the impossible task of finding a compromise so that agreement on the MFF could be reached by December 2012. It had to strike a balance between cutting enough to satisfy net contributors and what they had promised to their domestic audiences and ensuring that the cuts were not so severe that the aims embedded in Europe 2020 would be jeopardized. It sought to do this through revising the 'negotiating box', which proposed a reduction in the budget of over €50 billion, but which still sought to emphasize the importance of growth and jobs to the European economy. However, while the full force of the informal and formal machinery had been put to work to construct this compromise, it received severe criticism and was rejected by the Commission and the EP for sending out the wrong signal and proposing 'the deepest cuts [. . .] precisely in those policy areas that are considered vital for stimulating competitiveness, growth and employment'.[11] More specifically, there was grave concern because the cuts were proposed in areas such as cohesion policy and the Commission's flagship

[10] The United Kingdom insisted on a €200 billion cut, while Germany insisted on a €130 billion cut (reflective of a budget that amounts to 1 per cent of Members' GDP) (*Euractiv*, 31 October 2012).
[11] *Euractiv*, 31 October 2012.

© 2013 The Author(s) JCMS: Journal of Common Market Studies © 2013 John Wiley & Sons Ltd

Connecting Europe Facility (CEF) that sought to accelerate infrastructure development in transport, energy and information and communication technology (ICT). The Cypriot proposal to cut spending to Europe's poorest regions from 2.55 to 2.36 per cent of a recipient country's economic output, not surprisingly, was also unpopular with newer Member States. Nevertheless, 'net contributors' such as Sweden (in line with British demands), called for four times the cuts proposed by the Cyprus Presidency.

The fractious debate on the MFF continued and even though an extraordinary meeting of the European Council was held at the end of November 2012 in the hope of reaching agreement, the gap was simply too wide to bridge. Indeed, what the issue of the MFF demonstrated was the increasingly important role of the permanent President in negotiations in situations where the rotating Presidency is unable to secure compromise. While there existed intensive co-operation between the Cyprus Presidency and the Permanent Presidency, Herman Van Rompuy effectively led the process of negotiation, eventually putting forth proposals (the 'negotiating box') through which agreement was reached by Member State governments at the European summit on 7–8 February.[12] Again, though, the Irish Presidency made little running here; it was Van Rompuy who steered a path to compromise and eventual agreement. As Van Rompuy (2013) recognized: 'As a compromise, it is perhaps nobody's perfect budget, but it does reconcile everybody's views'. So the negotiations for the MFF can be seen less as a success story for the Cyprus Presidency and more as a diplomatic victory for the political machinery and leadership of the permanent President.[13]

The Single Supervisory Mechanism

Agreement on the Single Supervisory Mechanism (SSM) (Priority 2) was heralded as one of the 'real' achievements of the Cyprus Presidency, particularly in the context of crisis in the Union and the attempts to move towards a more integrated economic and monetary union.[14] It was a priority area for the Presidency which effectively gave a mandate to the European Central Bank (ECB) to supervise, directly and indirectly, credit institutions from participating EU Member States, and to create the foundation for a common banking union. While there was a general consensus among European leaders (of those in and out of the eurozone) that the SSM supervised by the ECB would be desirable, the Cyprus Presidency had to navigate around concerns about such a system in relation to how this might impact on the 'independence' and reputation of the ECB, participation for non-members of the eurozone and a level playing field between those in and out of the SSM. The initial agreement tabled by the European Commission on 29 June 2012 suggested that the eurozone should denote the geographical coverage of the SSM, with the possibility of only close supervisory co-operation from those Member States outside rather than representation in the governance of the SSM. However, this was not deemed inclusive enough, and at the European Council on 18 October, consensus was reached for 'equitable treatment' of members and non-members alike in the participation of the SSM[15] and this was also reflected in the final agreement. Thus although the United Kingdom, Sweden and

[12] For details, see European Council (2013). For an initial assessment of the outcome, see Zuleeg (2013).
[13] At the time of writing the EP had not endorsed the MFF agreement negotiated by Member State governments.
[14] See Hodson's contribution in this issue.
[15] European Council Conclusions, October 2012.

© 2013 The Author(s) JCMS: Journal of Common Market Studies © 2013 John Wiley & Sons Ltd

the Czech Republic had stated from the outset that they would not participate, this does leave the door open for other non-members to become involved.

A further issue with which the Cyprus Presidency had to deal with was that of the legal framework for the SSM which was based on two Regulations: the SSM Regulation and the European Banking Authority (EBA) Regulation. On the latter the EP has the power of co-decision, whereas on the former it has only a consultative role (due to its legal base, Article 127 (6)). The United Kingdom insisted that any reform of the EBA should involve those Member States not involved in the SSM, thus potentially creating a tension and possible constraint for those making decisions on the *inside*. While this was not entirely satisfactory as an outcome for any participants in the SSM, the lack of any alternative and the British right of veto helped the Cyprus Presidency to facilitate agreement aligned with the position of the United Kingdom. Final agreement between Member State governments was reached after an extraordinary meeting of the Ecofin Council on 12 December, which had important implications not only for creating the foundation for an integrated financial union more broadly, but specifically, for allowing the European Stability Mechanism (ESM) to contribute directly to bank recapitalization that will allow a virtuous circle to evolve between banks and sovereign debts.

The EU Unitary Patent Package

Another issue for which the Cyprus Presidency has claimed success is securing an agreement on the EU unitary patent package (Priority 2) – an issue that has been controversial and under discussion at the EU level for almost 30 years. The objective of achieving a common patent agreement was underpinned by the aims of boosting innovation, fostering technological and scientific advances, enhancing competitiveness and growth in the internal market, and ultimately, creating a cheaper, simpler and more efficient system that would increase patent activity among small and medium size enterprises (SMEs) in particular. Here, it is fair to say that the Cyprus Presidency fulfilled successfully its role as an honest broker in carving out a compromise that was acceptable to the EP and that would break a historic deadlock. The problem at the heart of the deadlock was legal, with concerns from the EP about compatibility of any such package with the EU *acquis*. The critical point in the negotiations for the package came at the European Council meeting in June 2012 where Member States, despite agreement with the EP at the first reading stage, decided to delete Articles 6–8 from the Patent Regulation – this because a compromise could not be reached on the seat (geographical location) of the central division of the Unified Patent Office!

The central problem for the Cyprus Presidency then was twofold: first, to regain the trust of the EP without which final endorsement would be impossible; and second, to find a compromise text that was fully compliant with the EU *acquis* and in particular Article 118 of the Treaty. The proposed compromise came in the form of a new Article and through reinstating the deleted Articles 6–8 in another component of the patent package – namely the Unified Patent Court Agreement. The new Article 5 was proposed to be inserted into another component of the package – the Regulation of Unitary Patent Protection – and would give rights to the patent holder to prevent 'third parties from acts against which the patent provides protection' (Cyprus Presidency, 2012). The compromise, while ultimately legal in nature, also proved to be politically astute as it addressed the EP's 'red lines' in previous negotiations, which included among them compatibility with Article 118 and the insistence that the role of the European Court of Justice and the EP would be respected and retained in any final agreement. Article 5 also ensured patent holders would be protected across the EU, while reinstating Articles 6–8 guaranteed a homogeneous patent case law. In essence, then, the compromise, while by no means securing full support, did draw majority support, particularly from the relevant EP rapporteurs and from Internal Market and Services Commissioner Michel Barnier. This was no mean feat, especially with regard to the EP as it faced sustained pressure from big business and certain political groups (GREEN/EFA) in the EP that had serious concerns about the Unitary Patent Regulation.[16] The end result, however, demonstrated that the Cyprus Presidency could act effectively in its role as mediator and, in this case, demonstrate its competence through bringing about agreement that had historically been impossible to reach.

Conclusions: Challenges, Outcomes and 'Real' Achievements?

There were many other achievements during the Cyprus Presidency such as those on maritime policy (the 'Limassol Declaration'), which were especially important to Cyprus, and the contentious issue of Schengen governance (Priority 3) where agreement was reached with the EP on the Reception Conditions Directive, despite the inter-institutional crisis that manifested itself during the Danish Presidency. Seemingly more minor but equally as important, the Cyprus Presidency negotiated free trade agreements between the EU and Japan and the EU and Singapore, and some progress was made on enlargement and development issues (Priority 4);[17] with the European Commission developing the 'positive agenda' in order to ensure that some momentum was maintained with the Turkish accession process.

At the outset of the Presidency there existed some apprehension about the ability of Cyprus to run an efficient and effective Presidency, which Cypriot officials worked hard to dispel before and during the six months that they were in the driving seat. The broader issues that might have hindered the effectiveness of the Presidency and its work were put to one side, and the Cypriots ensured that its agenda was free of any contentious issues that directly reflected its own national self-interest. One might argue that being a 'small state' holding the Presidency for the first time did not bring with it any high expectations from other EU Member States, EU institutions and external observers in terms of which issues and challenges could be adequately addressed. However, the outcome demonstrated that despite having fewer resources the intensity of work through smaller teams and a deliberately narrow programme resulted, in general, in effective brokerage and mediation across a plethora of issues within its priority areas. Indeed the Cypriot Presidency received praise from the Commission President, José Manuel Barroso, for its 'dedication and hard work' in 'delivering real achievements in the last six months' and also from Herman Van Rompuy who spoke of excellent co-operation during the Presidency, particularly with regard to the MFF. Of course, the MFF also highlighted the limitations of the Cyprus Presidency, although it cannot automatically be concluded that a larger state with more

[16] See «http://www.unitary-patent.eu».
[17] «http://www.cy2012.eu».

© 2013 The Author(s) JCMS: Journal of Common Market Studies © 2013 John Wiley & Sons Ltd

capacity would have achieved greater success in gaining agreement on what was a truly discordant issue. However, this issue perhaps reflected more than any other the extent to which alternative institutional dynamics (European Council) and actors (the Permanent President) can take the lead and set the tone when the rotating Presidency exhausts its options for seeking compromise.

The Cyprus Presidency's 'functional, pragmatic and results-oriented approach'[18] cultivated a positive momentum in the areas in which it concerned itself, and even if this did not always lead to the conclusion of an 'agreement' it certainly provided a platform from which the subsequent Presidency could work constructively with the relevant EU institutions and actors. While inexperienced in the Presidency role, the Cypriots realized that a modest but relevant agenda would be more realistically achievable than one with grand ambition. Leadership was provided – perhaps not in the conventional way – but through a Brusselization of the process, with officials that quickly and effectively learned the Presidency 'ropes'. Cyprus certainly managed to promote Europe as a '*filoxenos topos*' during its Presidency, and to project an image of itself as a reliable albeit small Member State. However, it remains to be seen what the post-Presidency ramifications of its own dire domestic financial situation will be, and indeed, the extent to which the freeze with Turkey will impact on reunification talks in Cyprus and Turkey–EU relations in the future.

References

Ágh, A. (2012) 'The Hungarian Rhapsodies: The Conflict of Adventurism and Professionalism in the European Union Presidency'. *JCMS*, Vol. 50, No. S2, pp. 68–75.

Beneš, V. and Karlas, J. (2010) 'The Czech Presidency'. *JCMS*, Vol. 48, No. S1, pp. 69–80.

Cyprus News (2013) 'Cyprus EU Presidency Hailed for Its "Real Achievements"'. *Cyprus News*, No. 279, January, London edition.

Cyprus Presidency (2012) 'Press Release: "Unitary Patent Closer to the Finishing Line"'. Available at: «http://www.cy2012.eu/index.php/en/news-categories/areas/competitiveness/press-release-unitary-patent-closer-to-the-finishing-line».

Dinan, D. (2011) 'Governance and Institutions: Implementing the Lisbon Treaty in the Shadow of the Euro Crisis'. *JCMS*, Vol. 49, No. S1, pp. 103–21.

European Council (2013) 'Conclusions (Multi-annual Financial Framework)'. EUCO 37/13, 8 February, Brussels. Available at: «http://www.consilium.europa.eu/uedocs/cms_data/docs/pressdata/en/ec/135344.pdf».

Kajnč, S. (2009) 'The Slovenian Presidency: Meeting Symbolic and Substantive Challenges'. *JCMS*, Vol. 47, No. S1, pp. 89–98.

Ker-Lindsay, J. (2009) 'A History of Cyprus Peace Proposals'. In Varnava, A. and Faustmann, H. (eds) *Reunifying Cyprus: The Annan Plan and beyond* (London: I.B.Taurus).

Ker-Lindsay, J. (2011) *The Cyprus Problem: What Everyone Needs to Know* (Oxford: Oxford University Press).

Krašovec, A. and Lajh, D. (2009) 'The European Union: A Joker or Just an Ordinary Playing Card for Slovenian Political Parties?' *Journal of Communist Studies and Transition Politics*, Vol. 25, No. 4, pp. 491–512.

Pomorska, K. and Vanhoonacker, S. (2012) 'Poland in the Driving Seat: A Mature Presidency in Turbulent Times'. *JCMS*, Vol. 50, No. S2, pp. 76–84.

[18] *Cyprus News*, January 2013.

© 2013 The Author(s) JCMS: Journal of Common Market Studies © 2013 John Wiley & Sons Ltd

Van Rompuy, H. (2013) 'Op-Ed by President Herman Van Rompuy: A Budget for the Future', Brussels, 15 February. Available at: «http://www.consilium.europa.eu/uedocs/cms_Data/docs/pressdata/en/ec/135463.pdf».

Zuleeg, F. (2013) 'The EU Multiannual Financial Framework (MFF): Agreement but at a Price' (Brussels: European Policy Centre)' Available at: «http://www.epc.eu/pub_details.php?cat_id=4&pub_id=3306».

© 2013 The Author(s) JCMS: Journal of Common Market Studies © 2013 John Wiley & Sons Ltd

JCMS 2013 Volume 51 Annual Review pp. 89–102

DOI: 10.1111/jcms.12037

EU Governance and Institutions: Stresses Above and Below the Waterline

DESMOND DINAN
George Mason University

Introduction

The composition of the European Council, the institution at the tip of the EU governance iceberg, changes constantly, reflecting the rise and fall of national leaders as well as, less frequently, the arrival of a new Commission President or European Council President. Some changes in national leadership are more consequential than others for the institution's functioning and effectiveness. Changes in the leadership of the European Union's larger, more influential Member States are the most consequential of all. Accordingly, the election of François Hollande as president of France[1] in May 2012, following a campaign in which he was highly critical of German Chancellor Angela Merkel, who in turn made no secret of her preference for Hollande's opponent, Nicolas Sarkozy, was highly significant for the European Council and, potentially, for the Franco–German direction of the EU.

Hollande's victory in a contest overshadowed by serious economic concerns was one of two key personnel changes which had a major impact on EU institutional affairs in 2012. The other was the election of Martin Schulz as President of the European Parliament (EP). As soon as he took office, in January, Schulz sought to fashion a new, overtly political model for the EP Presidency, in contrast to the more reserved, ceremonial model followed by his predecessors. Thriving on confrontation, Schulz denounced the excessive role of the European Council in the eurozone crisis, which, he claimed, accentuated intergovernmentalism, undermined parliamentary scrutiny and weakened the legitimacy of EU governance. Restricted to delivering a speech to national leaders immediately before the official opening of each summit, Schulz demanded full membership in the EU's most exclusive institution. Schulz's forcefulness, acumen, nationality (German) and ambition to become the next Commission President enhanced his public profile and political presence.

Criticism of 'summitization' of 'ever more frequent meetings of the European Council' was a constant refrain in Schulz's speeches throughout 2012 (see, for instance, Schulz, 2012a). Undoubtedly, meetings of national leaders in the European Council and the Euro summit (restricted to leaders whose countries were in the eurozone), as well as in bilateral and plurilateral settings, have proliferated since the onset of the crisis. The institutional ascendancy of the European Council and the EP, thanks in part to the Lisbon Treaty, was bound to cause friction between the two institutions. Schulz's election as EP President brought latent tension to the fore.

[1] See Lequesne's contribution to this issue.

© 2013 The Author(s) JCMS: Journal of Common Market Studies © 2013 John Wiley & Sons Ltd, 9600 Garsington Road, Oxford OX4 2DQ, UK and 350 Main Street, Malden, MA 02148, USA

The European Council's insistence that legislative decisions deemed essential for resolving the eurozone crisis be taken as early and quickly as possible in the co-decision procedure irritated Schulz and other Members of the European Parliament (MEPs), and strengthened a move already under way to amend the EP's rules of procedure with regard to first-reading agreements. Separately, the EP fiercely resisted a decision taken by the Council of Ministers in June 2012 to use a legal base for review of the Schengen regime that excluded the co-decision procedure, thereby severely restricting the EP's role. MEPs went on the warpath, breaking off negotiations with the Council on a number of Schengen dossiers and threatening to withhold funds. Schulz left the European Council in no doubt about the EP's annoyance.

At the core of these issues lay a profound set of questions: where was EU governance going in the post-Lisbon period? What difference was the eurozone crisis making? At one level, the age-old dichotomy of a more intergovernmental versus a more supranational EU seemed to be in play, with Schulz, Commission President José Manuel Barroso and some national leaders fiercely defending the apparently embattled Community Method. At another level, key characteristics of good governance – representation, participation, inclusiveness, efficiency, credibility, transparency – were central to the dispute over Schengen and efforts to improve the quality of first-reading decision-making.

I. The Tip of the Iceberg

Leaders of EU Member States meet each other, in various configurations, almost all the time. The European Council, the most inclusive and prominent forum for such meetings, convened seven times in 2012, on four formal, two informal and one extraordinary occasion. Leaders of the eurozone members often met separately, either just before or after meetings of the European Council or on special occasions, such as in July, at the height of the crisis when the situation in Greece required urgent action. In addition, national leaders met in various combinations, convened either as stand-alone meetings or opportunistically on the margins of other events. For instance, a number of national leaders availed of their presence at the award ceremony for the Nobel Peace Prize, in Oslo on 10 December, to discuss EU affairs. As European Council President Herman Van Rompuy observed in his annual report, in 2012 'we again witnessed how European politics are increasingly playing into national political debates. National leaders also meet each other frequently [outside the European Council], a clear sign of a new sense of co-responsibility' (Council General Secretariat, 2013, p. 23).

Meetings of national leaders, especially in the European Council and the Euro summit, attract a lot of attention. The intensity and duration of the crisis has increased both the frequency of EU summits and the level of media interest. By their nature, summits highlight the role of key individuals in diplomacy and decision-making, and emphasize personal attributes and interpersonal dynamics. There is a risk on the one hand of glamorizing and trivializing such events; and on the other hand of attaching excessive importance to them.

Changing Franco–German Dynamics

It can be difficult, under the circumstances, to assess the genuine significance of a change of membership in the European Council. The entrance of a new French or German leader is bound to affect bilateral (Franco–German) and multilateral (intra-EU) relations, however minimally. In the case of François Hollande, who campaigned implicitly against Merkel, the effect would have to be considerable. Inevitably, speculation arose about the long-term impact of Hollande's presidency on Franco–German leadership in the EU. Temperamentally, Hollande – a self-described 'normal' president – was much more in tune with the unflappable Merkel than was the notoriously excitable Sarkozy. Yet politically, Hollande and Merkel were opposites – Hollande being on the centre-left and Merkel on the centre-right. The history of Franco–German relations in the EU shows that the leaders of both countries usually manage to overcome personal and political differences, as well as deep-rooted national disparities on fundamental economic and institutional issues. Hollande and Merkel were well aware of that tendency and of their countries' special responsibility to provide joint direction in the EU, especially in the run-up to the 50th anniversary, in January 2013, of the Elysée Treaty of Franco–German friendship.

However, the old verities of Franco–German relations may no longer apply in an EU of nearly 30 Member States enduring a deeply debilitating political and economic crisis, and with a German chancellor conspicuously promoting the national interest and seemingly bereft of European idealism. Germany's preponderant power and unyielding position on austerity and structural reform have deeply alienated other Member States – not just those struggling to stay afloat financially. Though far from isolated within the European Council, Merkel must have felt slighted by the widespread euphoria with which other leaders greeted Hollande's victory. For them, Sarkozy's defeat meant not only the departure of an unpopular member of the European Council, but also a stinging rebuke for the hegemonic duo known derisively as 'Merkozy'.

The possible repercussions of Hollande's victory, specifically for the functioning of the European Council, featured prominently in the election campaign. Sarkozy's seemingly uncritical attachment to Merkel compounded the president's unpopularity in France. Conversely, Hollande's emphasis on investment and stimulus spending, as an antidote to excessive austerity, boosted the socialist contender's electoral prospects. Merkel's support for Sarkozy inevitably prompted allegations of foreign interference in French affairs. Yet the emergence of a European angle in the French presidential election was hardly a cause of concern, even if the issue – the poor health and even the survival of the eurozone – was inherently worrisome.

The tide against 'Merkozy' was already turning by the time Hollande arrived in the European Council. On 20 February, 12 EU leaders wrote to Van Rompuy and Barroso reminding them, and the other members of the European Council, that:

> [T]he crisis we are facing is also a crisis of growth. The efforts that each of us are taking to put our national finances on a sustainable footing are essential. Without them, we will not lay the foundations for strong and lasting economic recovery. But action is also needed to modernize our economies, build greater competitiveness and correct macro-economic imbalances. We need to restore confidence, among citizens, businesses and financial markets, in Europe's ability to grow strongly and sustainably in the future and to maintain its share of global prosperity. (Cameron *et al.*, 2012).[2]

[2] The signatories were: David Cameron (United Kingdom), Mark Rutte (The Netherlands), Mario Monti (Italy), Andrus Ansip (Estonia), Valdis Dombrovskis (Latvia), Jyrki Katainen (Finland), Enda Kenny (Ireland), Petr Nečas (Czech Republic), Iveta Radičová (Slovakia), Mariano Rajoy (Spain), Fredrik Reinfeldt (Sweden) and Donald Tusk (Poland).

© 2013 The Author(s) JCMS: Journal of Common Market Studies © 2013 John Wiley & Sons Ltd

Sarkozy and Merkel were conspicuously absent from the list of signatories. Indeed, they had not been consulted on the initiative.

The heating up of the French presidential campaign further weakened Merkel's ability almost single-handedly to determine the EU's response to the crisis. Hollande's victory, moreover, put a definite social democratic stamp on the growing opposition to Merkel. According to Hannes Swoboda, leader of the Socialists and Democrats (S&D), the political group in the EP of the Party of European Socialists:

> The times are changing, a new wind is blowing. [. . .] The French elections will change the climate [. . .] because other forces that have similar intentions or ideas to François Hollande will be strengthened. [. . .] The web of cooperation at EU level will change. This includes the European Council, which might become more courageous to come forward with some ideas that until now they have been hiding.[3] (*Agence Europe*, 4 May 2012)

Danish Prime Minister Helle Thorning-Schmidt, another social democrat, was jubilant, especially as Denmark held the rotating Council Presidency in the first half of 2012.[4] She pointed out that job creation and growth – Hollande's two main objectives – were also the Danish Presidency's priorities.[5] Though now President of the EP, the social democratic Schulz did not disguise his partisan preference for Hollande and expressed delight that a counterweight was forming against Merkel. Moreover, Schulz was keenly aware of the domestic repercussions for Merkel of Hollande's victory, which coincided with defeats for Merkel's Christian Democratic Party in regional elections.

Sensitive to the significance of Hollande's victory and eager for the new French leader to meet his EU counterparts before what was being billed as a decisive European Council meeting at the end of June, Van Rompuy called for a special meeting of the European Council to take place on 23 May. By that time Hollande and Merkel had already held a bilateral summit, at which it was abundantly clear that the tone and substance of Franco–German relations had changed dramatically. As if to emphasize the point, the special meeting of the European Council did not begin with a joint Franco–German position or policy statement. A mini-summit in Rome on 22 June, between Hollande, Merkel, Italian Prime Minister Monti and Spanish Prime Minister Mariano Rajoy saw Monti, who did not belong to any national or European political party, attempting to mediate between Hollande and Merkel. Monti, who had growing doubts about Merkel's austerity policy, soon abandoned any pretence of neutrality and slipped into the Hollande camp. This was apparent at the June summit, when Merkel found herself on the defensive.

The June meeting of the European Council represented a turning point not for the eurozone crisis – that came later when European Central Bank (ECB) President Mario Draghi pledged to do whatever is needed within the institution's mandate to save the euro[6] – but for relations among key national leaders. The European Council adopted the compact for growth and jobs (Growth Pact) – a pledge to take all possible steps to tackle unemployment, address the social consequences of the crisis and improve economic competitiveness (Council General Secretariat, 2012). Nobody disputed the desirability of growth, which was precisely what austerity and budget discipline aimed to foster. Yet the

---

[3] *Agence Europe*, 4 May 2012.
[4] See Manners' contribution to this issue.
[5] *Agence Europe*, 7 May 2012.
[6] See Hodson's contribution to this issue.

© 2013 The Author(s) JCMS: Journal of Common Market Studies © 2013 John Wiley & Sons Ltd

word 'growth' became a catch-all for measures to stimulate economic activity other than seemingly arbitrary and widespread budget cuts. Merkel was not about to renegotiate the treaty on stability, co-ordination and governance (Fiscal Pact), signed by 25 national leaders on 2 March – the prime ministers of Britain and the Czech Republic being the odd ones out. Nor was she willing (at least not yet) to contemplate mutualizing the sovereign debts of eurozone members by agreeing to issue eurobonds.

Nevertheless, Merkel had acquiesced in the Growth Pact and made considerable concessions to Monti and Rajoy at the June summit on the functioning of the European Stability Mechanism (ESM), the permanent eurozone bail-out fund. Merkel's new-found flexibility once again demonstrated the interplay between domestic and European politics. In order to secure ratification in the German parliament of the ESM and the Fiscal Pact, her signature measure to deal with the crisis, Merkel needed support from the opposition Social Democratic Party. The votes on ratification were due to take place immediately after the summit. Accordingly, Merkel agreed to approve the Growth Pact – a preference of the Social Democrats. This, in turn, made Merkel vulnerable to pressure from Monti and Rajoy to ease conditions for receiving aid from the ESM, without which they threatened to block the Growth Pact. Hitherto Merkel had resolutely opposed such concessions. 'By making the growth pact a condition of their approval of the ESM in the Bundestag', a member of Merkel's party fumed, 'the SPD and the Greens exposed the German chancellor to extortion in Brussels [. . . and] betrayed German interests'.[7]

For the rest of the year, Merkel and Hollande sparred over how to resolve the crisis. Merkel repeatedly called for 'more Europe', meaning a massive transfer of sovereignty from the national to the European level. Deeper political integration, involving far-reaching institutional reforms, would complement the shift of responsibility for fiscal and economic policy-making to Brussels and Strasbourg. This could come about only through major treaty change, which would be time-consuming and contentious. Hollande was less ambitious. The notion of convening a convention and negotiating treaty change would hardly appeal to someone whose political party had been torn apart during the disastrous 2005 French referendum campaign on the Constitutional Treaty. He preferred to focus on issues affecting the stability of the eurozone and holding back economic growth that could be tackled immediately.

The distance between Hollande and Merkel made it unlikely that the European Council would agree at its December meeting on a far-reaching plan for 'completion' of economic and monetary union (EMU). Indeed, the 'road map for the achievement of genuine economic and monetary union', which the European Council adopted, was a far cry from what Van Rompuy proposed in a series of reports presented to national leaders in June, October and December, prepared with the assistance of Barroso, Eurogroup President Jean-Claude Juncker and ECB President Draghi. In particular, the European Council did not endorse the final report's call for a three-stage, time-specific plan (Van Rompuy *et al.*, 2012). Merkel successfully resisted the idea of establishing a munificent EU-level mechanism to help counter country-specific economic shocks, fearing that it would cost Germany too much and possibly reward countries that were not serious about structural reform. She also managed to limit the scope of the single supervisory mechanism to large

[7] *Spiegel Online*, 2 July 2012.

© 2013 The Author(s) JCMS: Journal of Common Market Studies © 2013 John Wiley & Sons Ltd

banks and those already receiving state support, thereby shielding most German institutions from it.[8]

Especially in view of the Van Rompuy report that preceded it, the December European Council marked a disappointing, but not entirely unexpected, end to a year of hectic summitry. Merkel's commitment to far-reaching EU reform increasingly looked more rhetorical than real. Hollande seemed bereft of ideas that might have a meaningful impact on high unemployment and sluggish economic performance throughout the EU. The two leaders were uninterested in working closely together. According to Janis Emmanouilidis, an analyst of EU summits, the December European Council 'demonstrated once again that the Franco–German tandem does not function [. . . and] that the process towards a more ambitious renewal of the EU/EMU [. . .] will not be possible without a rapprochement between Germany and France' – a rapprochement unlikely to happen before the German federal elections of September 2013 (Emmanouilidis, 2012, pp. 10, 11).

Regardless of what might happen later in 2013, the idea of an indispensable Franco–German engine of integration may simply be outmoded. Germany is the undisputed hegemon in the EU (Paterson, 2011). Yet Germany most likely prefers not to try to lead alone, even if it were possible for it or any other country to do so. With which of the other big Member States might Germany form a 'privileged partnership' (Simonian, 1985)? The United Kingdom has marginalized itself, thanks to Prime Minister Cameron's pandering to Eurosceptic elements within and to the right of his Conservative Party. Italy and Spain are unreliable interlocutors due to chronic economic and (in Italy's case) political problems. Poland under Prime Minister Donald Tusk would like to hitch itself to Germany's wagon, but the fragility of post-World War II and post-cold war reconciliation, and Poland's non-membership in the eurozone, weakens the possibility of a German–Polish engine in the EU. By contrast, the historical foundations of the Franco–German alliance are deep and strong, though the divergence in economic performance between both countries presents a greater impediment to a fully functional partnership than personality differences between the chancellor and president. Therefore, a well-oiled Franco–German engine may be harder to achieve than in the past, and would likely be less effective in a larger, more complex EU.

The European Parliament President

Though not a member of the European Council, the EP President operates at the highest level of EU politics. In keeping with a long-standing arrangement between the two largest political groups in the EP, which other political groups and even some members of the largest groups deeply resent, Martin Schulz, a Social Democrat, replaced Jerzy Buzek, a Christian Democrat, as President in January 2012, halfway through the EP's 2009–14 term. A much more forceful personality than the courtly, old-fashioned Buzek, Schulz seemed determined to turn the office of President into a powerful political platform. Resentful of his exclusion from the European Council and of that institution's prominence throughout the crisis, Schulz focused his considerable ire on the seemingly endless rounds of EU summits.

Decrying 'decisions which affect all of us being taken by heads of government behind closed doors', Schulz described the pervasiveness of summits as:

---

[8] *Spiegel Online*, 27 December 2012; see also Emmanouilidis, 2012.

© 2013 The Author(s) JCMS: Journal of Common Market Studies © 2013 John Wiley & Sons Ltd

> a reversion to a form of European politics which I thought had been consigned to the history books: it is reminiscent of the era of the Congress of Vienna in the 19th century, when Europe's leaders were ruthless in their defense of national interests and democratic scrutiny was simply unheard of. [. . .] The plethora of summits, the growing fixation with meetings of the Heads of State and Government, is severely diminishing the part played by the only directly elected Community institution, the European Parliament, in decision-making processes. [. . .] The [EP] will not stand idly by and watch this process continue [. . .] I issue a challenge to anyone who claims that more Europe can be achieved with less parliamentarianism [. . .] we must have a seat at the table at European summits. I see my role as President of the EP, as President of one of the three main EU institutions, as being one of countering this fixation with summits, this ongoing trend towards the renationalization of policy-making. (Schulz, 2012b)

For all his bluster, Schulz was generally liked by the national leaders and, having been a long-time leader of the Socialist Group in the EP, had a strong rapport with those on the centre-left. National leaders on the centre-right were more wary of him. Whatever she thought of Schulz personally, Chancellor Merkel, a Christian Democrat, saw him as a political opponent in European and, to an extent, national politics. Regardless of these personal and political likes or dislikes, however, national leaders collectively wanted to keep the EP at arm's length from the European Council.

The European Council President

Managing relations between the European Council and the EP, as well as other EU institutions, is one of Van Rompuy's most important responsibilities. Given the EP's seemingly unquenchable thirst for power and prominence, European Council–EP relations became increasingly strained following implementation of the Lisbon Treaty. As the European Council's point of contact with the EP, Van Rompuy was in frequent touch with Schulz and also spoke regularly at EP plenary sessions in 2012. A number of MEPs attacked Van Rompuy specifically for pandering – as they saw it – to the Merkel–Sarkozy duopoly and, after Sarkozy's departure, for being too deferential to Merkel. In November 2012, Van Rompuy found himself caught between the European Council and the EP in a dispute over a nomination to the governing council of the ECB. Flexing its political muscles, the EP insisted that a woman be appointed; the European Council stuck to its guns and appointed Yves Mersch, from Luxembourg (though Spain objected to Mersch's appointment for other reasons). The EP raked an unapologetic Van Rompuy over the coals.[9]

Working with the post-Lisbon rotating Council Presidency has not posed as much of a challenge for the European Council President, though Van Rompuy has had to forge a special relationship every six months with a different set of politicians and senior officials representing the Presidency country. Two small Member States (Denmark and Cyprus) were in the Council Presidency in 2012.[10] Denmark held the Presidency in the past; Cyprus was a newcomer to the role. Traditionally, small Member States have cherished being in the Council Presidency, especially when the country's leader presided over the European Council and the foreign minister presided over the Foreign Affairs Council. Experience of the European Council Presidency in the past has made it difficult for some older Member States to come to terms with the post-Lisbon arrangement. By the same token, missing out

---

[9] *Europolitics*, 16 November 2012.
[10] See Manners' and Christou's contributions to this issue.

© 2013 The Author(s) JCMS: Journal of Common Market Studies © 2013 John Wiley & Sons Ltd

on presiding over the European Council and the Foreign Affairs Council has made holding the rotating Presidency a bittersweet experience for newcomers.

In the event, Denmark adjusted well to the new regime and performed admirably during its term in office, despite being at the centre of a dispute between the Council and the EP over Schengen governance (see below). Nevertheless the social democratic prime minister often criticized Van Rompuy for his allegedly uncritical adhesion to Merkel's pro-austerity policy. Cyprus' limited diplomatic resources and animosity toward Turkey complicated the country's Presidency and, by extension, Van Rompuy's dealings with it. The fact that Denmark is not a eurozone member, and therefore could not preside over the Euro summit, highlighted the value of having a standing European Council and Euro summit President, especially during the height of the eurozone crisis in mid-2012.

As for chairing the European Council, the outcome of the French election can hardly have been unwelcome to Van Rompuy. Hollande's ascendancy, and with it the ending of the Franco–German duopoly (at least for a while), gave Van Rompuy – hitherto seen as beholden to Merkel and Sarkozy – welcome room to manoeuvre. Thereafter he was markedly more independent of Merkel. Sarkozy's departure also changed the tone of the European Council in ways that were more congenial to Van Rompuy's style. Sarkozy was notoriously heavy-handed, making it difficult for Van Rompuy to call him to order. Hollande and Merkel are more restrained. Regardless of the tension generated by the eurozone crisis, meetings of the European Council were often testy when Sarkozy was present, and during the presence as well of the mercurial Silvio Berlusconi, prime minister of Italy, who resigned in December 2011. Subsequently, meetings of the European Council became less dramatic and more business-like.

Before Sarkozy's departure, the European Council elected Van Rompuy, again by acclamation, for a second term, in March 2012 (European Council, 2012a). Van Rompuy had incumbency on his side; implicit in the Lisbon Treaty was the assumption that the office-holder would be re-elected for a second two-and-a-half-year term. Van Rompuy had ruffled a few feathers in the job, but not to the point of alienating key supporters. There was no reason for a majority of European Council members to look for another candidate. Upon beginning his second term, Van Rompuy secured another prize: the presidency of the Euro summit.

'As guardian of the unity of the 27', Van Rompuy remarked at the time of his re-election, 'I have insisted all along on involving all Member States – all 27 even when it was about the 17 of the Eurozone – and all institutions' (European Council, 2012b). That may be so, but the launch of the Euro summit emphasized the distinction within the EU between the eurozone and non-eurozone members – a distinction resembling that between first- and second-class citizens. Reflecting developments in the EU, fissures erupted within the European Council not only between the eurozone members and non-members, but also between and among the big and small Member States and between the United Kingdom and the rest. The challenge of facilitating cohesion under such circumstances made it difficult for Van Rompuy to drive forward the work of the European Council, as called for in the treaty. To say that this has been a taxing time for the European Council and for Van Rompuy would be a gross understatement.

Van Rompuy's undoubted success as European Council President, despite these challenges, owes much to his ability, experience and skill. Van Rompuy is a competent chairman; a team-builder; a safe pair of hands. Being in the Presidency full-time brings one

© 2013 The Author(s) JCMS: Journal of Common Market Studies © 2013 John Wiley & Sons Ltd

big advantage over a rotating presidency: an ability to focus exclusively and continuously on European Council business. Van Rompuy had the opportunity to travel throughout the EU in order to consult constantly, between meetings, with the other members of the European Council, including the Commission President, and with the High Representative. Those meetings gave Van Rompuy an unparalleled awareness of the perspectives and positions of each player, which was extremely advantageous when preparing the European Council's agenda and chairing the meetings themselves.

Having a small but highly effective *cabinet* and being able to draw on the resources of the Council secretariat-general, Van Rompuy has the necessary staff and administrative support to carry out his responsibilities efficiently. However, the retirement in October 2012 of Frans Van Daele as *chef de cabinet* noticeably dented the *cabinet*'s effectiveness, and to an extent Van Rompuy's effectiveness as well, at least for a short but crucial time in the ongoing euro crisis and in the negotiations for a new multiannual financial framework (MFF). Formerly a senior Belgian diplomat with extensive experience at the highest levels of EU governance, Van Daele was Van Rompuy's most trusted adviser and a powerful figure behind the scenes at European Council meetings and in the forefront of the preparatory and follow-on work (Howorth, 2011).

Though highly fraught politically because of the intensity of national interests, concluding a new MFF constitutes routine business in that the calendar of the negotiations is determined far in advance. It is not unusual for such tense negotiations to go down to the wire. In this case, Van Rompuy made it clear that his office – not that of the Cypriot Presidency – would conduct the negotiations, which usually conclude at the level of the European Council. Van Rompuy convened a special session of the European Council in November 2012 to try to reach an agreement, but the summit ended in acrimony, perhaps in part because of inadequate planning.

Van Rompuy has limited scope within the European Council for pushing his own agenda. His position is inherently weaker than that of even the weakest Member State. Though he may once have led a small but influential Member State, Van Rompuy is deliberately stateless as President of the European Council. His influence depends on the foundation within the treaty of the office of European Council President, on his own abilities, on the forcefulness of his ideas and, just as in the case of presidencies under the old system, on the susceptibility of the other heads of state and government as well as prevailing political and economic circumstances. Nevertheless, having an inherently weak platform from which to launch major initiatives and, in Van Rompuy's case, build 'more Europe', may have strengthened the President's capabilities as an honest broker – one of the traditional responsibilities of the rotating Presidency.

Circumstances including the depth of the euro crisis and political realities like the reluctance of key national leaders to empower the European Council President have limited Van Rompuy's opportunities for political leadership and policy entrepreneurship. Partly for that reason, Van Rompuy has not become the public face of the EU. Nor has he supported calls to strengthen the President's visibility and popular legitimacy by holding an EU-wide election for the office. Instead, Van Rompuy laboured quietly and consistently throughout 2012 to hold the European Council together and manage the escalating eurozone crisis. At the very least, it seems fair to conclude that without the standing Presidency and without Van Rompuy, the European Council and the EU as a whole would have fared a lot worse during an extremely testing time.

© 2013 The Author(s) JCMS: Journal of Common Market Studies © 2013 John Wiley & Sons Ltd

II. Below the Waterline

If summitry represents the tip of the EU governance iceberg, the co-decision procedure occupies much of the mass below the waterline. The emergence and refinement of the procedure over time reflects the successful assertion by the EP of its rights, as the directly elected institution strove for equality with the Council in EU legislative decision-making. Though inherently complex, co-decision has operated well in practice, thanks in large part to the proliferation of first-reading agreements. However, dissatisfaction within the EP with the unintended consequences of early agreements came to a head in 2012, resulting in a potentially significant change in the EP's rules of procedure. At the same time, the Council and the EP squared off in a dispute over co-decision with considerable political ramifications: the appropriate legal base for a review of the Schengen regime.

First-Reading Agreements

Schulz made an intriguing reference to co-decision during his inaugural speech as EP President in January 2012: 'If our Parliament is to become more visible, if greater attention is to be paid to its views, a rethink of the issue of first-reading agreements is also essential' (Schulz, 2012b). He was referring to the fact that the number of first-reading agreements on legislative proposals from the Commission now stands at about 80 per cent of all cases.[11] This seems like a good thing, given that first-reading agreements improve the efficiency of legislative decision-making, though studies have shown that such agreements do not necessarily save as much time as their proponents claim (Toshkov and Rasmussen, 2012). The proliferation of first-reading agreements, involving intense negotiations between representatives of the Commission, the EP and the Council Presidency (the so-called 'trilogues'), has nonetheless come at a political cost. Many MEPs resent what they see as the exclusive involvement of a small number of their colleagues in the decision-making process, and the lack of opportunity for the EP as a whole to have a meaningful say in important public policy issues. An academic assessment of first-reading or 'early' agreements referred to the phenomenon as 'secluded decision-making' (Reh *et al.*, 2011).

Growing dissatisfaction among MEPs over the prevalence and conduct of first-reading agreements resulted in the EP adopting a report in November 2012 to amend its rules of procedure with a view to making early agreements more transparent and participatory. Based to some extent on existing practices in certain EP committees, a completely revised 'Rule 70 on Interinstitutional Negotiations in Legislative Procedures' came into effect in early December (European Parliament, 2012a). It includes the following key provisions:

- Such negotiations shall not be entered into prior to the adoption by the committee responsible, on a case-by-case basis for every legislative procedure concerned and by a majority of its members, of a decision on the opening of negotiations. That decision shall determine the mandate and the composition of the negotiating team. Such decisions shall be notified to the President, who shall keep the Conference of Presidents informed on a regular basis.
- The negotiating team shall be led by the rapporteur and presided over by the Chair of the committee responsible or by a Vice-Chair designated by the Chair. It shall comprise at least the shadow rapporteurs from each political group.

[11] *Europolitics*, 20 November 2012.

© 2013 The Author(s) JCMS: Journal of Common Market Studies © 2013 John Wiley & Sons Ltd

- Any document intended to be discussed in a meeting with the Council and the Commission ('trilogue') shall [indicate] the respective positions of the institutions involved and possible compromise solutions and shall be circulated to the negotiating team at least 48 hours, or in cases of urgency at least 24 hours, in advance of the trilogue in question.
- After each trilogue the negotiating team shall report back to the following meeting of the committee responsible. Documents reflecting the outcome of the last trilogue shall be made available to the committee.
- If the negotiations lead to a compromise, the committee responsible shall be informed without delay. The agreed text shall be submitted to the committee responsible for consideration. If approved by a vote in committee, the agreed text shall be tabled for consideration by Parliament in the appropriate form, including compromise amendments.
- Any decision by a committee on the opening of negotiations prior to the adoption of a report in committee shall be translated into all the official languages, distributed to all Members of Parliament and submitted to the Conference of Presidents.
- At the request of a political group, the Conference of Presidents may decide to include the item, for consideration with a debate and vote, in the draft agenda of the part-session following the distribution, in which case the President shall set a deadline for the tabling of amendments.

Regardless of the new rule, the extent of the EP's involvement in the informal, pre-proposal stage of legislative decision-making is an important factor in the discussion about inclusiveness and deliberation. For instance, the Internal Market and Consumer Protection (IMCO) Committee engaged the Commission well before the Commission proposed its Single Market Act I (April 2011) and Single Market Act II (October 2012) to strengthen the internal market – a perpetual work in progress. The committee's pre-legislative work involved own-initiative reports, expert studies, hearings and consultations with other MEPs. According to an IMCO member:

> If you do your policy development and strategic work upfront that is effectively [. . .] a first reading. [The] second reading is then the detail. I do not think that we have short-circuited the process or diminished the transparency of it at all. If anything, we have given people more opportunities to engage with us on the issues that we would have done if we had simply waited for the Commission to send us a proposal.[12]

Extensive EP involvement in the pre-proposal stage depends to a great degree on the policy field in question. The nature of the eurozone crisis, which required rapid decision-making, precluded the possibility of leisurely Commission–Council–EP legislative planning. This, in turn, fuelled the frustration of many MEPs, including President Schulz, over what looked like *diktats* from the European Council to enact legislation as quickly as possible in response to the escalating crisis. Such frustration emerged especially during enactment in 2011 of the 'Six Pack' of legislative proposals to strengthen the Stability and Growth Pact, and the subsequent 'Two Pack' aimed at further strengthening surveillance mechanisms in the eurozone, agreed to in early 2013. The legislative agenda generated by the crisis put a heavy burden on the EP's Economic and Monetary Affairs Committee

[12] Quoted in *Europolitics*, 19 September 2012.

© 2013 The Author(s) JCMS: Journal of Common Market Studies © 2013 John Wiley & Sons Ltd

(ECON), which hitherto was rarely involved in co-decision. Intense pressure to reach agreement, combined with the committee's relative inexperience, accelerated moves within the EP to revise Rule 70 on early agreements. Whether the new procedures will allay MEPs' concerns, improve transparency and participation, and enhance the quality of legislative decision-making, however, remains to be seen.

Schengen Review [13]

A dispute between the Council and the EP that flared in 2012 over co-decision and the Schengen regime was less procedural than profoundly political. At issue was a pronounce-ment by the Council, under the Danish Presidency, that it would interpret the legal basis of reform of the Schengen evaluation mechanism so as to exclude co-decision, thereby in effect robbing the EP of a central role in Schengen governance. The EP promptly retaliated by suspending progress on a number of Schengen-related proposals in the legislative pipeline and by threatening to cut funding. At the same time, the EP's legal affairs committee (JURI) confirmed that co-decision was indeed the appropriate procedure for the proposed Schengen review. For the ever-combative Schulz, the Council's decision was further evidence of rampant intergovernmentalism in the EU at a time when a number of Schengen members appeared to be unilaterally reinstating border controls. According to Schulz:

> It is without precedent that in the middle of the legislative process, one co-legislative chamber excludes the other. The [Justice and Home Affairs] Council's approach [. . .] represents a slap in the face of parliamentary democracy and is unacceptable to the directly elected representatives of European citizens. (European Parliament, 2012b)

What Schulz called 'a serious inter-institutional incident' and what *Europolitics* called an 'institutional declaration of war' by the Council was a black-eye for the Danish presi-dency.[14] It fell to the Cypriot Presidency to try to repair the damage. The fact that Cyprus was not in the Schengen area and faced considerable criticism for its handling of migrants did not increase the country's relatively limited diplomatic leverage. An exasperated Schulz raised the issue before the European Council in October 2012, saying that:

> the EP regards the position adopted by the Council [. . .] on the Schengen evaluation mechanism as a direct challenge to its rights [. . . and] as unacceptable. Parliament is calling on the Council to resume negotiations, so that the two institutions, as equal partners in the legislative process, can find a satisfactory solution consistent with the Community method. (Schulz, 2012c)

The issue remained unresolved at the end of 2012, though both sides – the Council and EP – seemed eager to reduce tension, avoid bringing a case before the Court of Justice and resume collaboration on Schengen issues. Nevertheless, the eruption of the dispute dem-onstrated a willingness on the part of Member States to limit the EP's involvement in a politically sensitive policy area and, correspondingly, the determination of the EP, under Schulz's feisty leadership, to fight tenaciously for its rights.

---

[13] For an overview of developments in the field of justice and home affairs, see Monar's contribution to this issue.
[14] Europolitics, 14 June 2012; see also European Parliament, 2012c.

© 2013 The Author(s) JCMS: Journal of Common Market Studies © 2013 John Wiley & Sons Ltd

Conclusions

The year 2012, like 2011 before it, saw a 'surfeit of summits' in the EU thanks to the continuing eurozone crisis (Dinan, 2012). A change of leadership in France following François Hollande's election had a major impact on personal and political dynamics within the European Council, and on Franco–German direction of the EU. Increasingly isolated, Chancellor Angela Merkel had greater difficulty promoting a policy of austerity in response to the crisis. The prominence of the European Council during the crisis and the non-eurozone membership of Denmark and Cyprus – the two countries in the rotating Presidency in 2012 – demonstrated the utility of having a standing European Council President. Herman Van Rompuy, the first holder of the post-Lisbon position, continued to perform admirably under difficult conditions and was re-elected for a second term in March 2012.[15]

Though not a member of the European Council, the EP President operates at the summit of EU governance. Martin Schulz, who became President in January 2012, immediately put a political stamp on what was, traditionally, a ceremonial position. Even after his term in office ends in June 2014, Schulz hopes to remain at the top in the EU, possibly by becoming European Commission President. To that end, he advocated in 2012 the idea that European political parties should announce before the next EP elections, scheduled for mid-2014, their choice for European Commission President. Given that the European Council must, under the terms of the Lisbon Treaty, take the outcome of EP elections into account when selecting the Commission President, Schulz hopes, if the European Socialists either win a majority of seats or form a majority coalition, to secure the European Council nomination.

In the meantime, the EP was at the centre of other noteworthy developments in EU governance in 2012. These included a potentially important change in the EP's rules of procedure to improve transparency and participation in first-reading agreements involving the co-decision procedure, which account for the vast majority of EU legislative outcomes. The EP also took governments to task for the Council's decision to relegate the EP to a minor role in the Schengen evaluation mechanism. This seemingly arcane procedural issue was, in fact, profoundly political. As Schulz was quick to point out, the Council's decision smacked of rampant intergovernmentalism, of the kind epitomized by the centrality of the European Council in tackling the eurozone crisis. For Schulz and other defenders of the Community Method, the behaviour of national governments at the tip and in the mass of the EU governance iceberg throughout 2012 was a cause of serious concern.

References

Cameron, D. *et al.* (2012) Joint Letter to President Van Rompuy and President Barroso, 20 February. Available at: «http://www.number10.gov.uk/news/joint-letter-to-president-van-rompuy-and-president-barroso/».

Council General Secretariat (2012) Council Conclusions, Brussels, 28–29 June. Available at: «http://www.consilium.europa.eu/uedocs/cms_data/docs/pressdata/en/ec/131388.pdf».

Council General Secretariat (2013) *The European Council in 2012* (Luxembourg: Publications Office of the European Union).

[15] For an assessment of the first holder of another post-Lisbon position, the External Action Service's Catherine Ashton, see Hadfield and Fiott's contribution to this issue.

© 2013 The Author(s) JCMS: Journal of Common Market Studies © 2013 John Wiley & Sons Ltd

Dinan, D. (2012) 'Governance and Institutions: Impact of the Escalating Crisis'. *JCMS*, Vol. 50, No. S2, pp. 85–98.

Emmanouilidis, J. (2012) 'Steps but No Roadmap towards GEMU: The Results of a Disappointing Summit', post-summit analysis (Brussels: European Policy Centre).

European Council (2012a) 'President Van Rompuy Elected for a Second Term', 1 March. Available at: «http://www.european-council.europa.eu/home-page/highlights/president-van-rompuy-re-elected-for-a-second-term».

European Council (2012b), 'Acceptance Speech by President of the European Council Herman Van Rompuy', 1 March. Available at: «http://register.consilium.europa.eu/pdf/en/12/st00/st00036.en12.pdf».

European Parliament (2012a) Decision of 20 November on amendment of Rule 70 of Parliament's Rules of Procedure on interinstitutional negotiations in legislative procedures, 2011/2298(REG). Available at: «http://www.europarl.europa.eu/sides/getDoc.do?pubRef=-//EP//TEXT+TA+P7-TA-2012-0422+0+DOC+XML+V0//EN».

European Parliament (2012b) 'EP Decides to Suspend Cooperation with Council on Five JHA Dossiers until Schengen Question is Resolved', 14 June. Available at: «http://www.europarl.europa.eu/news/en/pressroom/content/20120614IPR46824/html/EP-suspends-cooperation-with-Council-on-five-justice-and-home-affairs-dossiers».

European Parliament (2012c) 'EP Conference of Presidents Rejects Approach of Justice and Home Affairs Council on Schengen', 7 June. Available at: «http://www.europarl.europa.eu/the-president/en/press/press_release_speeches/press_release/2012/2012-june/press_release-2012-june-5.html».

Howorth, J. (2011) 'The "New Faces" of Lisbon: Assessing the Performance of Catherine Ashton and Herman Van Rompuy on the Global Stage'. Paper presented at the EUSA biennial conference, Boston, MA, 3–5 March. Available at: «http://euce.org/eusa/2011/papers/10i_howorth.pdf».

Paterson, W. (2011) 'The Reluctant Hegemon? Germany Moves Centre Stage in the European Union'. *JCMS*, Vol. 49, No. 1, pp. 57–75.

Reh, C., Héritier, A., Bressanelli, E. and Koop, C. (2011) 'The Informal Politics of Legislation: Explaining Secluded Decision Making in the European Union'. *Comparative Political Studies*, 15 December. Available at: «http://cps.sagepub.com/content/early/2011/12/05/0010414011426415.full.pdf+html».

Schulz, M. (2012a) 'A Return to Long-Term Thinking'. Speech, Berlin, 6 November. Available at: «http://www.europarl.europa.eu/the-president/en/press/press_release_speeches/speeches/sp-2012/sp-2012-november/speeches-2012-november-1.html».

Schulz, M. (2012b) 'Inaugural Speech as President of the European Parliament', 17 January. Available at: «http://www.europarl.europa.eu/the-president/en/press/press_release_speeches/speeches/sp-2012/sp-2012-january/speeches-2012-january-1».

Schulz, M. (2012c) Speech to European Council, Brussels, 28 October. Available at: «http://www.europarl.europa.eu/the-president/en/press/press_release_speeches/speeches/sp-2012/sp-2012-june/speeches-2012-june-1.html».

Simonian, H. (1985) *The Privileged Partnership: Franco–German Relations in the European Community, 1969–1984* (Oxford: Clarendon Press).

Toshkov, D. and Rasmussen, A. (2012) 'Time to Decide: The Effect of Early Agreements on Legislative Duration in the EU'. *European Integration Online Papers*, Vol. 16, No. 11. Available at: «http://eiop.or.at/eiop/texte/2012-011a.htm».

Van Rompuy, H. *et al.* (2012) 'Towards a Genuine Economic and Monetary Union', 5 December. Available at: «http://www.consilium.europa.eu/uedocs/cms_data/docs/pressdata/en/ec/134069.pdf».

© 2013 The Author(s) JCMS: Journal of Common Market Studies © 2013 John Wiley & Sons Ltd

JCMS 2013 Volume 51 Annual Review pp. 103–123   DOI: 10.1111/jcms.12054

Banking Union as Holy Grail: Rebuilding the Single Market in Financial Services, Stabilizing Europe's Banks and 'Completing' Economic and Monetary Union*

DAVID HOWARTH[1] and LUCIA QUAGLIA[2]
[1] University of Luxembourg. [2] University of York

Introduction

In 2012, the European Commission celebrated the 20th anniversary of the European Union 'single market'. In a climate of trepidation about the future of the European project, the Commission organized a series of events to remind Europeans of the great strides in market integration since the late 1980s. However, the year itself was marked by little progress on internal market legislation. In the context of the ongoing sovereign debt crisis and instability in Europe's banking sector, the one exception to legislative inactivity was in the area of financial services. A series of major pieces of legislation have continued their slow progress through the EU's legislative process. Notably, the capital requirements directive and regulation were the topic of intense debate (European Commission, 2010; see Buckley *et al.*, 2012) and the Member States failed to reach a final agreement on the package details.

The second half of 2012 was dominated by debates surrounding the construction of an EU banking union. In June, the European Council and eurozone summit agreed to deepen economic and monetary union (EMU) creating 'banking union', which was to be based on five components: a single rule book; a single framework for banking supervision; a common deposit guarantee scheme; a single framework for the managed resolution of banks and financial institutions; and a common backstop for temporary financial support. Indeed, the verb officially – and hyperbolically – used was to 'complete' EMU, suggesting that these elements – rarely discussed in European policy-making circles prior to 2012 – were the *sine qua non* of 'full' EMU (European Council, 2012b). The Member States decided to make the creation of the Single Supervisory Mechanism (SSM) the precondition for possible direct recapitalization of banks by the European Stability Mechanism (ESM) – the funding mechanism created to help tackle the sovereign debt crisis.

In September 2012, the Commission adopted a set of legislative proposals as first steps towards banking union: a regulation giving strong powers for the supervision of all banks in the eurozone to the European Central Bank (ECB) (European Commission, 2012a); a regulation with limited specific changes to the regulation setting up the European Banking Authority (EBA) to ensure a balance in its decision-making structures between eurozone and non-eurozone Member States (European Commission, 2012b); and a communication

* Lucia Quaglia wishes to acknowledge financial support from the Leverhulme Trust and the British Academy (SG 120191). This article was written while she was Visiting Fellow at the Hanse-Wissenschaftskolleg.

© 2013 The Author(s) JCMS: Journal of Common Market Studies © 2013 John Wiley & Sons Ltd, 9600 Garsington Road, Oxford OX4 2DQ, UK and 350 Main Street, Malden, MA 02148, USA

on a road map for completing the banking union over the coming years, covering the single rule book, common deposit protection and a single bank resolution mechanism (European Commission, 2012c). The Commission and the French government called for an end-of-year deadline to finalize the first element of banking union (the transfer of supervisory powers to the ECB). However, it became clear in the autumn that implementation would be delayed to the spring of 2014.

The proposals for banking union in several respects amount to a radical initiative to stabilize the EU's national banking systems – exposed directly to the sovereign debt crisis – by breaking the dangerous link between the high and rising sovereign debt in the eurozone-peripheral Member States and domestic banks, which had come to hold an increasing amount of this debt. However, banking union would also bring about a significant transfer of powers from the national to the EU level. While it is unlikely that some elements of the proposals will be adopted in the near future, the December European Council decision to transfer significant supervisory responsibilities to the ECB amounts to a major development in European integration history and, more specifically, in the operation of the single market.

This article is organized as follows. First, we consider the fragmentation of the single market in financial services and the need for banking union to address this fragmentation. We then outline the key elements of banking union as well as the main outstanding issues on which Member States failed to reach an agreement at the December summit. Following that we review the intergovernmental debate on banking union, focusing on the main eurozone Member States and their priorities, and look at the growing reality of a 'two-speed Europe' in addition to the priorities of the eurozone outsiders and notably the United Kingdom. We go on to discuss the stance of the ECB in this policy debate as well as the mostly likely changes that the eurozone's central bank will have to undertake in the near future. Finally, we explore the democratic accountability of the new institutional set-up, mainly focusing on the position of the European Parliament (EP).

I. The Fragmentation of the European Financial Market

The impact of the international financial crisis and then the eurozone sovereign debt crisis on the single market in financial services has been devastating. The fragmentation of the financial services market in turn affects the ability of the ECB to operate effective monetary policy. The ECB thus, not surprisingly, dedicates a sizeable part (almost half) of its 2012 annual report on financial integration in Europe to the benefits of financial integration and the deleterious effects of disintegration on monetary union and the effectiveness of monetary policy. Several measures demonstrate the increasing fragmentation of the EU's financial market (ECB, 2012a): a significant increase in the differentiation of average unsecured inter-bank lending rates across the eurozone Member States; the divergence of eurozone Member State lending rates; a decline in unsecured transactions undertaken with non-domestic counterparties in the eurozone since 2007, both in real terms and relative secured transactions; the increased dispersion in credit default swap premiums across the eurozone Member States for sovereign, bank and telecommunications debt (which multiplied from five to nine times from the end of 2009 to early 2012) (ECB, 2012a, p. 23). Banking markets had also become less integrated since 2008 on a range of measures. The establishment and activity (measured in assets) of foreign

© 2013 The Author(s) JCMS: Journal of Common Market Studies © 2013 John Wiley & Sons Ltd

branches and subsidiaries has dropped marginally since 2008 (ECB, 2012a, p. 27). The cross-border merger and acquisition (M&A) activity of banks – another indicator of market integration – declined sharply from 2008 and remained low in 2012. The share of loans granted to monetary financial institutions (MFIs) by MFIs of other eurozone countries stabilized for two years after a drop from 2008, but then began to decline again in 2011. Although the level of cross-border inter-bank loans in the EU remained relatively high (at around 35 per cent of the total at the end of 2011), this was nonetheless a significant decline from the 45 per cent peak in 2007. The dispersion of bank interest rates applied to new loans to non-financial companies (NFCs) rose considerably from the low of 2007 (ECB, 2012a, p. 29). One glimmer of hope in financial integration concerned cross-border lending (eurozone and EU more generally) to NFCs and households, which was close to peak levels at the end of 2011 – albeit at a tiny percentage of the total (5.1 and 2.8 per cent, respectively) (ECB, 2012a, p. 28) with domestic lending only one percentage point above its lowest level in 2008. On the other hand, two additional sets of figures further indicate the fragmentation in eurozone/EU financial markets. The cross-border bond holdings of eurozone MFIs (as a percentage of the total) declined markedly from the middle of the 2000s with no indication of stabilization prior to 2012 (see Figure 1). In 2005, of the government and corporate bonds held by MFIs, over 40 per cent were cross-border. By 2011 this figure had dropped to 23 per cent. Similarly, the share of cross-border collateral used by eurozone MFIs had dropped from over 50 per cent of the total to approximately 33 per cent (see Figure 2). The eurozone periphery (Italy, Portugal, Spain, Greece and Ireland) was most affected by this retreat to domestic debt, given the

Figure 1: Cross-Border Bond Holdings of European Financial Institutions (Percentage of Total), End-June Figures

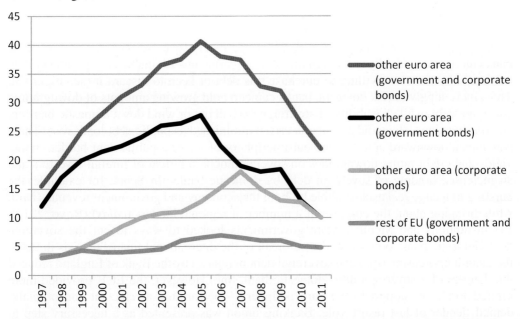

© 2013 The Author(s) JCMS: Journal of Common Market Studies © 2013 John Wiley & Sons Ltd

Figure 2: Share of Domestic and Cross-Border Collateral Used in Eurosystem Operations (Percentages)

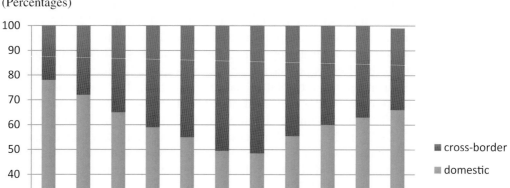

Source: ECB (2012a, p. S10).

declining confidence of non-periphery banks in the value of sovereign and corporate debt issued in the periphery.

A destabilizing sovereign debt–domestic bank loop was created in the euro periphery (BIS, 2011). Higher periphery government spending and rising debt burden increased sovereign risk (Merler and Pisani-Ferry, 2012) and threatened to disrupt the collateral function of sovereign debt, with a resultant damaging effect on bank funding conditions (BIS, 2011). From 2008, the percentage of euro periphery sovereign debt held by domestic banks increased markedly as foreign investors – fearing unsustainable euro periphery debt burdens – became less willing to purchase this debt or keen to discard it (see Figure 3). Thus, increasingly at-risk domestic banks came to hold growing amounts of downgrading sovereign debt, while the ability of sovereigns to bail out or wind down domestic banks in an orderly manner (to avoid a systemic crisis) diminished as public debt loads rose. There was thus a downward spiral in the euro periphery of a rising public debt burden, rising yields and credit rating downgrades on sovereign debt, a retreat of foreign investors and an increased holding of sovereign debt by domestic banks. In Spain, for example, the bursting of a large real estate bubble hit both the economy and government revenues hard, while bringing about the collapse of a number of regional lenders (*cajas*) (Royo, 2013). EU institutions and Member State governments looked to ways to cut the sovereign debt–domestic bank loop. From the outbreak of the international financial crisis in 2008, the quantitative easing (massive sovereign debt purchase) by the Bank of England reduced the dangers of a sovereign debt–domestic bank link. However, the ECB provided more limited forms of support to the euro periphery – performing a reluctant and officially denied 'lender of last resort' role. Banking union was presented as a necessary step to stabilizing euro periphery banking systems and saving EMU.

© 2013 The Author(s) JCMS: Journal of Common Market Studies © 2013 John Wiley & Sons Ltd

Figure 3: Share of Domestic Government Debt in Banks' Total Government Debt Portfolios, Selected Eurozone Member States, June 2010

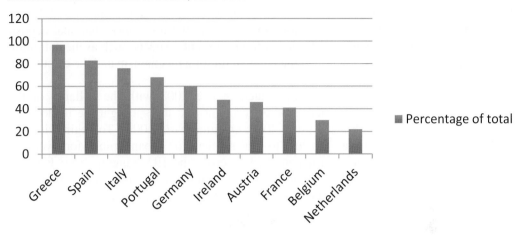

Sources: EBA data.

II. The Main Elements of the Banking Union

'Banking union', as proposed by the European Council in its June conclusions and the Commission in its September legislative proposals and communication, has five main elements: a single EU rule book for financial services (and specifically banks); an SSM for banks; a single framework on bank resolution; a common deposit guarantee scheme; and a common fiscal backstop for struggling banks. A range of scholars and institutions argue that all five of these elements should be adopted to ensure that banking union creates more stability than existing national supervisory systems (Schoenmaker, 2012; Ionnidou, 2012; IMF, 2013). Senior Commission officials have argued that banking union must consist of at least four of the five elements, accepting delays to the construction of a common deposit guarantee scheme given the political difficulties associated with modifying national schemes (Merlin, 2013). A single rule book, which has been advocated by the EU in the aftermath of the global financial crisis, means a set of fully harmonized EU rules applied consistently across the Member States. EU financial legislation is mainly comprised of directives, which need to be adopted by the Member States in order to be implemented. Some of these directives contain several national discretions – that is, they leave open the possibility of national options or 'specificities' in the implementation of EU rules. For example, the Capital Requirements Directive III (CRD III) of 2006 contains more than 100 national discretions (Quaglia, 2010). Partly for this reason, the proposed Capital Requirement IV legislation comprises a directive (European Commission, 2011a); and a regulation, which imposes a maximum harmonization directly applicable in the Member States, thereby leaving little room for manoeuvre in national transposition (European Commission, 2011b; see also Buckley *et al.*, 2012; Howarth and Quaglia, 2013).

The principal logic behind the establishment of deposit guarantee schemes, which reimburse part of the amount of deposits to clients of banks that have failed, is to prevent a 'bank run' – that is, panic withdrawals by customers of their bank deposits because of fear of collapse. There exists long-standing EU legislation on deposit guarantee schemes to decrease the distorting effect to the single market created by different national schemes. The Deposit Guarantee Scheme Directive of 1994 set the minimum level of deposit protection schemes in the EU at €20,000 per depositor (European Commission, 1994). However, as the 1994 directive was based on minimum harmonization, national deposit guarantee schemes continued to differ in several important respects, such as the definition of eligible deposits, the level of cover, the types of funding mechanism and the calculation of bank contributions.

The global financial crisis that accelerated in late 2008 with the collapse of the American investment bank Lehman Brothers brought into the spotlight the inadequacy of the 1994 directive (Ayadi and Lastra, 2010; Quaglia *et al.*, 2009). To begin with, the minimum level (€20,000) was too low to placate fears of a bank run. Moreover, the depositor protection coverage varied markedly across the EU, ranging from €20,000 in most of the new Member States and the United Kingdom to more than €100,000 in Italy and France. Furthermore, unco-ordinated decisions on deposit guarantees taken by some Member States at the height of the crisis in late 2008 (notably in Ireland and Germany) worsened the crisis (Quaglia *et al.*, 2009). It became evident that different national schemes across the EU potentially distorted level playing field competition and created the potential for bank runs because, in the event of financial crises, customers in some Member States were prone to shift deposits to a bank headquartered in those Member States with more generous guarantee schemes.

At the peak of the international financial crisis in late 2008, the Commission proposed legislative changes to the Deposit Guarantee Scheme Directive. These changes – agreed hurriedly in 2009 – represented an emergency measure designed to restore depositors' confidence by raising the minimum level of coverage for deposits from €20,000 to €50,000 and subsequently to €100,000. The need for swift action meant that several controversial issues were not tackled and hence the directive contained a clause providing for a broad review of all aspects of deposit guarantee schemes. By 2010, the deposit guarantee schemes continued to vary markedly across the Member States and only 16 out of 27 applied the coverage level of €100 000, or had legislation in place to do so (European Commission, 2010).

When the sovereign debt crisis broke out in the eurozone in late 2009, the issue of a common deposit guarantee scheme came back onto the agenda. In July 2010, the Commission put forward a legislative proposal to amend the Deposit Guarantee Scheme Directive with a view to promoting the 'harmonization and simplification of protected deposits, a faster pay-out, and an improved financing of schemes' (European Commission, 2010, p. 5). The proposal aimed to establish a network of guarantee schemes as a first step towards a 'pan-European deposit guarantee scheme' to cover all European Union-based banks (European Commission, 2010, p. 5). Such a pan-European scheme however presupposed full harmonization of national schemes and could only enter into force after a minimum fund of 1.5 per cent of eligible bank deposits had been reached in all the Member States.

One of the most contentious provisions in the Commission's proposed 2010 directive was the establishment of a mandatory mutual borrowing facility, whereby if a national deposit guarantee scheme is depleted it can borrow from another national fund. Several Member States tried to remove this provision during negotiations in the Council.[1] The

[1] Interviews with Commission and Permanent Representation officials, Brussels, July 2012.

© 2013 The Author(s) JCMS: Journal of Common Market Studies © 2013 John Wiley & Sons Ltd

mutual borrowing facility could be the first step towards a pan-EU deposit guarantee scheme, which was even more controversial. Indeed, during the preparation of the directive in 2010, the Commission considered the establishment of a single pan-European scheme. However, it soon realized that there were complicated legal issues that needed to be examined (European Commission, 2010) and therefore the idea of a pan-European scheme was shelved for the time being. Ultimately though, the problem was political. The creation of a pan-European deposit guarantee scheme would have implied pooling national sovereignty to an extent not acceptable to the Member States at that time (that is, 2010). The main line of division was between the countries that fear that they would become net contributors to the scheme, such as Germany, and the countries experiencing banking problems (for example, Spain and Ireland) and which were likely to resort to the scheme. Effectively, the German government baulked at the prospect of German taxpayers underwriting depositors in other Member States with unstable banking systems.[2]

The issue of deposit guarantee schemes is interlinked with the discussion on a resolution framework for banks and financial institutions. 'Bank resolution' is the organization of an orderly failure, which involves the continuity of banking service. It is an alternative or complementary mechanism to the deposit guarantee scheme in the event of bank failure. In June 2012, the Commission adopted a legislative proposal for bank recovery and resolution (European Commission, 2012d) with the same scope of application as the CRD III (hence, credit institutions and certain investment firms). The aim of the directive was to create an EU-wide framework on bank resolution.

The proposal distinguished between powers of 'prevention', 'early intervention' and 'resolution'. In the case of prevention, banks would be required to draw up recovery plans and resolution authorities would be required to prepare resolution plans both at group level and for the individual institutions within the group. Authorities could require a bank to change its legal or operational structures to ensure that it could be resolved with the available tools. Financial groups may enter into intra-group support agreements in the form of loans, or the provision of guarantees. The framework envisages early supervisory intervention whereby the authorities could require banks to implement measures set out in the recovery plan and would have the power to appoint a special manager at a bank for a limited period (European Commission, 2012d).

The harmonized resolution tools and powers outlined in the proposed directive were designed to ensure that national authorities in all Member States had a common toolkit and road map to manage the failure of banks. Among the tools considered, there is the bail-in tool, whereby banks would be recapitalized with shareholders wiped out or diluted, and creditors would have their claims reduced or converted to shares. 'Resolution colleges' would be established under the leadership of a clearly identified resolution authority and with the participation of the EBA, which would act as binding mediator if necessary (European Commission, 2012d, p. 15).

The legislation envisaged the creation of resolution funding, which would raise contributions from banks proportionate to their liabilities and risk profiles and would not be used to bail out a bank. There was a link between this piece of legislation and the Deposit Guarantee Scheme Directive, which was to provide funding for the protection of retail depositors. Member States would be allowed to merge these two funds, provided that the

---

[2] *Financial Times*, 13 September 2012.

© 2013 The Author(s) JCMS: Journal of Common Market Studies © 2013 John Wiley & Sons Ltd

scheme remained able to repay depositors in case of failure (European Commission, 2012d). The Commission noted that ideally a single pan-European fund should be established with a pan-European resolution authority to manage its disbursal, but the absence of a single European banking supervisor and insolvency regime would make this unworkable (European Commission, 2012d). As in the case of the Deposit Guarantee Scheme Directive, the obstacles to these far-reaching changes were ultimately political, with the main line of division running between potential net contributors and net beneficiaries. The EU legislative activity on bank recovery and resolution regimes was in line with international regulatory initiatives in this field undertaken by the Financial Stability Board (FSB, 2011) and the Basel Committee on Banking Supervision (BCBS, 2010) which mainly focused on global systemically important cross-border financial institutions.

On the SSM, the Commission proposed that the ECB would be empowered with specific supervisory tasks over eurozone banks in order to help to strengthen confidence in prudential supervision and financial stability. Non-eurozone Member States would be able to participate in the SSM on a voluntary basis (European Commission, 2012a). The main issues and political negotiations concerning the SSM are discussed below.

As for the common fiscal backstop, a link was established between banking union and the ESM in the event that temporary financial support was needed. The ESM is a new EU agency, which was to replace the temporary European financial stability facility (EFSF). It was established in September 2012 and was to have a full lending capacity of €500 billion by 2014. The Member States of the ESM could apply for an ESM bail-out if they were in financial difficulty or their financial sector was a stability threat in need of recapitalization. However, these bail-outs were to be based on strong conditionality and Member States were required to sign the 'Memorandum of Understanding' which would highlight which reforms needed to be undertaken or fiscal consolidation to be implemented in order to restore financial stability. The Commission proposed that the ESM be used to support failing banks directly.

There were several open (and potentially sensitive) issues concerning banking union (see Comporti and Cosimo, 2012; Elliott, 2012; Pisani-Ferry et al., 2012; Veron, 2012). Even on the elements agreed in 2012, and notably the SSM, several issues remained. First, both the Commission's September proposals and the December agreement sidestepped the operational details of the SSM, and notably the relationship between the ECB and national prudential supervision and the responsibilities and powers of the ECB and the EBA and the relationship between these two bodies. Second, many questions remained about the future organization of national supervisory authorities given the potential loss of powers. Furthermore, the relationship among national prudential authorities in the operation of banking union was unclear as was the relationship between these authorities and prudential authorities in EU Member States outside the banking union and those outside the EU.

Perhaps most importantly, the absence of a central EU body responsible for financial crisis management and the lack of a common resolution and deposit insurance scheme cast doubt over the ability of the eurozone to deal effectively with crisis management and resolution. The supervisory power of the ECB still needed to be complemented by a single framework for resolving banks. At the end of 2012, crisis management and resolution remained a national competence. A crisis management body had not yet been proposed at the EU level. Its creation would inevitably be controversial as it would have to be assigned decision-making powers with fiscal implications.

© 2013 The Author(s) JCMS: Journal of Common Market Studies © 2013 John Wiley & Sons Ltd

III. The (Eurozone) Intergovernmental Debate on Banking Union

The debate on banking union was characterized by intense intergovernmental negotiations. As in many episodes of EU institution-building, the main players were France and Germany. However, non-eurozone Member States – first and foremost the United Kingdom – were also active in the debate, which extended to the ECB and the EP. The French, Italian and Spanish governments were the main supporters of banking union and the need to move quickly.[3] The German government was more guarded: it raised several objections in the run-up to the European Council meeting in December and repeatedly pointed out that the need to get the right institutional arrangements in place was more important than to proceed speedily.[4] At the October European Council, German Chancellor Angela Merkel scuppered President François Hollande's ambitious deadline for an agreement on banking union by the end of the year and the meeting of eurozone finance ministers at the start of December failed to overcome major ongoing obstacles.

Effectively, the Franco–German debate on banking union paralleled long-standing debates on eurozone governance and solutions to the sovereign debt crisis. The French sought support mechanisms; the Germans reinforced fiscal policy commitments (sustainable Member State budgets). French efforts stemmed from their limited success in convincing the Germans to agree to other measures to tackle the crisis. The French had pushed for the construction of massive support mechanisms – what David Cameron called the 'Big Bazooka' – able to purchase debt directly from eurozone Member State governments and engage in bank recapitalization.[5] The temporary EFSF and the permanent ESM in operation from late September were endowed with far less firepower than the French would have wanted and more restricted mandates – only the purchase of sovereign debt on secondary markets.[6]

President Hollande insisted that banking union and 'social union' come before the political union (meaning reinforced control over national fiscal and macroeconomic policies) sought by the Germans.[7] Hollande called for further discussions on political union only after the 2014 EP elections. Officially, the French supported banking union because they sought reinforced banking supervision, a eurozone-wide deposit guarantee and a bank resolution fund, which would relieve market worries over unstable banks in the eurozone periphery holding huge quantities of their government's sovereign debt. French interest in banking union also stemmed from a desire to establish a kind of fiscal backstop to the eurozone via a lender-of-last-resort-style support for banks rather than governments per se. Banking union should thus be seen as old wine in a new bottle. The French argued that cutting the sovereign debt–domestic bank loop was crucial in order to rebuild international confidence in the value of sovereign debt of the eurozone periphery. In late November, European Council President Herman Van Rompuy published his paper 'Towards a Genuine Economic and Monetary Union', which largely aligned with French policy preferences (Van Rompuy, 2012). His paper called for the adoption of a legal framework by early 2013 to enable the ESM to begin direct bank recapitalizations by the

[3] *Financial Times*, 5 December 2012.
[4] *Financial Times*, 6 December 2012.
[5] *Financial Times*, 10 October 2011.
[6] For an analysis of France's EU policies and stances in light of Hollande's election, see Lequesne's contribution to this issue.
[7] *Euractiv.com*, 18 October 2012.

© 2013 The Author(s) JCMS: Journal of Common Market Studies © 2013 John Wiley & Sons Ltd

early spring. The French also supported the proposal in the paper to create a eurozone-wide 'shock absorption' fund – effectively an insurance scheme to which all 17 eurozone countries would contribute.

The underlying German and northern European concern remained the fiscal backstop and being forced into a situation of having to contribute more funds to the ESM in order to bail out banks in other countries.[8] Already, by late September, the German, Dutch and Finnish governments made it clear that they opposed any agreement to allow the ESM to recapitalize banks without prior agreement on an adequate regulatory and supervisory framework and reinforced fiscal policy rules (Finnish Ministry of Finance, 2012). These three governments also insisted that the banks in difficulty in those Member States with fragile banking systems – notably Spain and Ireland – remained primarily the responsibility of the governments of those Member States. The ESM was only to be used to help banks facing difficulties in the future, arising under the supervision of the ECB in the new banking union.[9]

The Germans expressed interest in the Van Rompuy paper proposal on a 'shock absorption fund' provided that funds used to help countries absorb shocks in EMU were limited.[10] They insisted that any financing come with thick strings attached (effectively contracts signed) requiring budget discipline and reinforced Commission monitoring, similar to the conditions imposed by the ECB upon countries whose debt it purchases. There was, however, no agreement on the special eurozone fund at the December European Council (2012c).

The German and other northern eurozone Member State governments were also concerned as to the scope of the banking union, in particular whether the ECB should directly supervise all banks in the eurozone or only the main (cross-border) banks. The Germans opposed ECB supervision of the country's public *Landesbanks* and savings banks.[11] These were seen as having a 'public' function in Germany with strong ties to local and regional governments and traditionally reliant on them for financial backing in terms of credit guarantees for the *Landesbanks* (banned since 2007) and long-term covered bond holdings. For these reasons, German policy-makers preferred them to be subject to national supervision.

The Commission and the French government pushed for banking union to cover all eurozone banks. Many argued that the division into larger and smaller banks made little economic sense, given that banking crises often originated with smaller, fast-expanding banks (such as Spanish *cajas*) (Garicano, 2012). The French government expressed concern over unequal treatment of Member States given that its banking system was dominated by five very large institutions which would all end up being directly supervised by the ECB.[12]

Some questioned the ability of the ECB to handle the supervision of all 6,000 eurozone banks – as suggested in the European Commission's September draft of banking union – without a massive transfer of resources.[13] The French and ECB responded that the ECB

[8] *Financial Times*, 12 December 2012.
[9] *Financial Times*, 18 October 2012.
[10] *EUObserver*, 14 December 2012.
[11] *Financial Times*, 5 December 2012.
[12] *Financial Times*, 14 November 2012.
[13] *Financial Times*, 5 December 2012.

© 2013 The Author(s) JCMS: Journal of Common Market Studies © 2013 John Wiley & Sons Ltd

would only have direct responsibility for the supervision of systemically important banks, leaving the rest to national supervisors working according to EU rules. The Germans were also seeking real investigation and auditing powers to be assigned to the ECB – but only over the biggest banks – while the French preferred a 'licensing' system that would enable national supervisors to act on behalf of the ECB.

Despite entrenched Franco–German differences on preconditions for bank recapitalization, in early June, eurozone finance ministers agreed up to €100 billion for the recapitalization of Spanish banks from the eurozone's bail-out funds, without an accompanying austerity programme.[14] The Germans subsequently appeared to backtrack on this commitment in their position on support only to banks with future difficulties under the ECB's watch. The Spanish government feared that the credit line to Spanish banks would count as public debt, thus reinforcing the sovereign debt–bank link and increasing the likelihood of default.[15] However, in early December, the German government announced that it was willing to accept the immediate, and exceptional, recapitalization of four nationalized Spanish banks. The EU leaders agreed on a bail-out plan for Spanish banks using Spain's 'fund for orderly bank restructuring' permitting the transfer of €39.5 billion from the ESM to the fund. This transfer was accompanied by a pledge by Spain to restructure its financial sector. Nonetheless, Wolfgang Schäuble, the German finance minister, insisted that the ESM would not be used for other bank recapitalizations until the banking union was in full operation.[16]

At the June European Council, which took place during a period when Spanish and Italian sovereign bond yields reached dangerously high levels and the situation of many Spanish banks looked particularly fragile, the French secured a commitment on the part of eurozone leaders to reach an agreement on banking union prior to the end of the year. The largest holders of Spanish sovereign debt – Spanish banks – looked fragile. However, in late July, ECB President Mario Draghi announced that the bank was 'ready to do whatever it takes' to save the single currency and would make 'unlimited' purchases of sovereign debt of any eurozone Member State government that agreed to introduce the kinds of austerity reforms introduced in the three bailed-out, so-called 'programme', countries – Greece, Ireland and Portugal.[17] This helped to bring down bond yields. However, it also reduced pressure on eurozone Member State governments to agree far-reaching reforms on banking union.

In the end, the agreement reached at the December European Council foresaw that the ECB would be 'responsible for the overall effective functioning of the SSM' and would have 'direct oversight of the euro area banks' (European Council, 2012a, p. 2). This supervision, however, would be 'differentiated' and the bank would carry it out in 'close cooperation with national supervisory authorities'. Direct ECB supervision was to cover those banks with assets exceeding €30 billion or those whose assets represent at least 20 per cent of their home country's annual GDP.[18] This direct supervision would concern approximately 200 eurozone banks. However, the agreement also permits the ECB to step in, if necessary, and supervise any of the 6,000 banks in the eurozone to bring about the eventual

---

[14] *EUObserver*, 9 June 2012.
[15] *Reuters*, 25 September 2012.
[16] *EUObserver*, 3 December 2012.
[17] *Financial Times*, 26 July 2012. See Hodson's contribution in this issue.
[18] *Financial Times*, 13 December 2012.

© 2013 The Author(s) JCMS: Journal of Common Market Studies © 2013 John Wiley & Sons Ltd

restructuring or closure of banks that found themselves in difficulties. The European Council agreed that the SSM would allow the ESM to recapitalize banks in difficulties directly, subject to 'double majority' voting by both the ECB and the EBA. The SSM was to begin operation on 1 March 2014 or 12 months following the entry into force of the legislation, whichever is later, subject to operational arrangements (European Council, 2012a).

The EU leaders called upon their co-legislators to adopt a directive on a common European resolution fund (to be financed by banks) and the Deposit Guarantee Scheme Directive by June 2013, with implementation 'by the Member States as a matter of priority' (European Council, 2012a, p. 3). The Member State governments failed to agree on how these bank contributions should be calculated (for example, on a proportional basis of bank capital). The December European summit was never likely to agree on a pan-European deposit guarantee scheme which would allow savings to be protected anywhere in the Union or a Union-wide resolution fund to which banks would have to contribute. The German government made clear its opposition to the mutualization of debt, hidden transfer payments and the liability of German taxpayers for foreign bank resolution or for deposit guarantees in other EU Member State banks.[19] The goal of full banking union by 2014 appeared increasingly unrealistic.

IV. Banking Union and Non-Eurozone Member States: The Reinforcement of a 'Two-Speed' EU

The euro-outsiders interested in participating in the SSM were opposed to the European Commission's proposed regulation of September which placed the ECB at the centre of the mechanism. The wording of the draft suggested that non-eurozone Member States would be excluded from decision-making as they lacked a vote on the ECB's governing council. The Commission's draft also appeared explicitly to limit membership by defining 'participating Member State' as a 'Member State whose currency is the euro' (European Commission, 2012a). The euro-outsiders were supported by the EP's economic and monetary affairs committee, which formed its own position on the status of the ten EU Member States not in the eurozone, deciding that 'opt-in' countries should be able to sit on a new ECB supervisory board with equal voting powers but not on the decision-making governing council.[20] The December Council agreement on the SSM satisfied some euro-outsider concerns. The revised regulation changed the definition of 'participating Member State' to 'a Member State whose currency is the euro or a Member State whose currency is not the euro [but] which has established a close co-operation', defined as adopting the necessary legal framework and co-operating with the ECB along the lines codified in the draft regulation. Opening the SSM to non-eurozone Member States made good sense in that more Member States sharing common supervisory frameworks, rules and mechanisms would further strengthen stability.[21] Not including them would potentially create a more difficult situation in case of (financial) problems and the necessity of extra financial assistance. Furthermore, if different rules were to apply in these Member States, the banking union might find itself confronted with regulatory and supervisory arbitrage on its doorstep.

[19] *Financial Times*, 12 December 2012.
[20] *EUObserver*, 29 November 2012.
[21] *EUObserver*, 29 November 2012.

© 2013 The Author(s) JCMS: Journal of Common Market Studies © 2013 John Wiley & Sons Ltd

At the time of writing (April 2013) most non-eurozone Member State governments had yet to take a definitive position on participation in banking union and they are weighing up the pros and cons of membership (Darvas and Wolff, 2013). Among the reasons provided to support membership, participation in the SSM was seen in terms of improving the credibility of national prudential arrangements, overseen by the ECB. The ECB would possess information about the banks' headquarters and subsidiaries, allowing more effective supervision and decision-making. Furthermore, the banking systems of the central and eastern European Member States were dominated by foreign institutions: non-participation in banking union might have a devastating effect on domestic banks as depositors shifted their accounts to banks headquartered in banking union Member States. There were also several reasons not to participate in banking union. Non-eurozone Member States were worried about their second-class status, with limited decision-making power as compared to eurozone members. The ECB might be less prone to focus on the risks building in non-eurozone and smaller Member States. The as yet undetermined implications of full banking union also encouraged some non-eurozone Member States to adopt a cautious position on the SSM.

The majority of non-eurozone Member States either sought to enter banking union or adopted a 'wait and see' policy. This included Denmark, which had a formal opt-out on EMU. By the time of the December European Council, it was clear that the United Kingdom, Sweden and the Czech Republic would opt not to participate in the SSM. The British position is discussed below. The Swedish government's decision not to participate in banking union owed largely to the fact that no major banks in the country were owned by banking groups headquartered in another EU Member State (Darvas and Wolff, 2013). The Swedish government also expressed concern as to the second-class position of non-eurozone Member States in the SSM.[22] Finland and Estonia – with banking systems dominated by Swedish-owned institutions, such as the Hansabank subsidiary of Swedbank – had a strong vested interest in reaching a compromise to ensure Swedish participation. Latvia and Lithuania, also dominated by subsidiaries of Swedish banks, had less interest in joining banking union given Swedish non-membership, although Latvia's intention to enter the eurozone in 2014 pushed its government to support the form of membership on offer.

The main priority of the British government – which had no intention of joining the SSM – was to avoid a potential eurozone bloc within the single financial market. The British, supported by seven other non-eurozone Member State governments, threatened to block banking union if there were insufficient safeguards put in place for the 'euro-outsiders'.[23] Crucially, the British feared the adoption of subsequent financial legislation that would be detrimental to the British financial sector. However, the broader issue of concern was the satisfactory coexistence of a more integrated eurozone core and the non-core Member States. Banking union became a kind of test case for Britain's role in a two-speed Europe.[24] In the EBA – the supervisory body responsible for EU-wide bank stress tests – the British feared a eurozone majority able to impose its rules on non-eurozone members. Hence, as early as the summer of 2012, the British demanded an EBA

---

[22] *Financial Times*, 11 December 2012.
[23] *Financial Times*, 8 November 2012.
[24] *Financial Times*, 13 December 2012.

© 2013 The Author(s) JCMS: Journal of Common Market Studies © 2013 John Wiley & Sons Ltd

voting reform: that any decision by the EBA should be approved by a minimum number of Member States outside the banking union and thus effectively by a 'double majority' of Member States inside and outside the banking union.

Germany, the Netherlands and Austria all broadly accepted British-led requests for so-called 'double majority' voting. However, most eurozone Member States expressed concern that in the event that the number of non-banking union Member States dwindled, the United Kingdom would enjoy effective veto powers.[25] The European Commission opposed EBA reform because it would result in the creation of two forums for decision-making: those inside and outside the eurozone.[26] The outcome was a compromise involving the creation of a double majority system until the number of non-banking union Member States dwindled to less than four. The EP retained amendment and veto powers on the EBA regulation which was to be adopted in 2013.

French policy-makers tended to be the least forthcoming towards British requests. French support for banking union was bolstered by a direct interest to redirect euro trading business and other financial services away from the United Kingdom. In January 2009, then-Finance Minister Christine Lagarde referred to the need for 'euro area clearing'.[27] In February 2009, a 26-page confidential memo by the Bank of France was leaked.[28] The memo advocated the creation of a Paris-based clearing house for credit default swaps (CDS) with the explicit aim of preventing London from dominating the business. Christian Noyer, the governor of the Bank of France, publicly confirmed the long-standing French position in a 2 December 2012 interview with the *Financial Times*: 'Most of the euro business should be done inside the euro area. It's linked to the capacity of the central bank to provide liquidity and ensure oversight of its own currency'. Other eurozone Member States likely agreed on the desirability of redirecting financial transactions from London to the eurozone, but most were less overt in expressing this preference.

The French position also reflected long-standing ECB preference on the location of euro derivatives clearing, stated as early as 2001 (ECB, 2011b). The ECB recommended legislating on this preference for the first time in a July 2011 policy paper (ECB, 2011a), which called for legislation requiring clearing houses to be based in the eurozone if they handled 'sizeable amounts' (that is, more than 5 per cent of the clearer's business) of a euro-denominated financial product. This recommendation came in the context of a long-standing debate over the control and authorization of clearing houses in the European Markets Infrastructure Regulation (EMIR) on which the British government later won an important concession, prohibiting the discrimination against any Member State as a venue for clearing services.

In September 2011, the British government launched its first lawsuit against the ECB through the European Court of Justice on the grounds that the ECB's policy recommendation would restrict the free movement of capital and infringe upon the right of establishment. The rule would disadvantage financial services in the United Kingdom and could force one of the world's largest clearing houses – LCH.Clearnet, which far exceeded the 5 per cent threshold – to move its euro operations to the eurozone.[29] At the

---

[25] *Financial Times*, 8 November 2012.
[26] *Financial Times*, 13 December 2012.
[27] *Financial Times*, 19 February 2009.
[28] *Financial Times*, 19 February 2009.
[29] *Financial Times*, 14 September 2011.

end of 2012, over 40 per cent of euro-denominated transactions took place in London – more than the entire eurozone combined. Further, the British government remained concerned that the ECB would push for new regulation that would contradict British preferences. The ECB responded by a clarification of its clearing house location policy in a November 2011 document (ECB, 2011b), against which, in February 2012, the British government launched a second 'technical' legal challenge.

V. The European Central Bank and Banking Union

Prior to the debate on banking union, some senior ECB officials – for example, Tommaso Padoa-Schioppa – expressed support for the ECB to take over supervisory functions (Howarth and Loedel, 2005). However, this was not official ECB policy. Nonetheless, the ECB endorsed the initial Commission proposal of allocating all supervisory competences to the ECB, regardless of the size of banks. President Mario Draghi made clear that being a decisive supervisor included oversight of all 6,000 banks to ensure a level playing field.[30] Yet in several speeches he also reiterated that day-to-day tasks would remain with national supervisors (see, for example, ECB, 2012c.). He argued that the ECB should be in a position to carry out its new functions 'in a decisive, firm, complete and strong manner without any reputational risks' and 'new tasks should not be mixed with [the central bank's] monetary policy tasks – delivering price stability in the medium term – which for [the central bank] remains the primary task' (ECB, 2012c). The ECB welcomed the 13 December agreement on the SSM.

The impact of banking union upon the size and organization of the ECB remained far from clear. In December, senior ECB figures reported the likely need for approximately 500 new staff members hired from national supervisory bodies, but this was almost certainly an underestimate.[31] President Draghi commissioned a private consultancy firm to prepare a report (published in January 2013) on the necessary steps to prepare the ECB for banking union. The firm recommended that the ECB should more than double its staff, with an expansion of almost 2,000 to be allocated to the operation of the SSM, by 2017 – the date by which the ECB would be supervising up to 200 banks directly.[32] By comparison, there were approximately 1,500 officials working in prudential supervision in Germany (in the Bundesbank and BaFin – the Federal Financial Supervisory Authority).

The consultancy firm also noted the dangers of power struggles with national authorities (some of which are not central banks) over prudential supervision.[33] It proposed that national representatives on supervisory boards should abstain on issues relating directly to their national banks so as to ensure that decisions are objective and pan-European. It was also uncertain where power over supervision would rest in the ECB, although all were agreed that safeguards were needed to ensure a clear separation of the Bank's monetary policy and supervisory policy. However, there were ongoing concerns about the operation of the European Systemic Risk Board (ESRB) – the body established in 2011 to monitor trends in European financial markets – which was chaired by the ECB President and

[30] *Financial Times*, 8 November 2012.
[31] *Financial Times*, 4 February 2013.
[32] *Financial Times*, 4 February 2013.
[33] *Financial Times*, 4 February 2013. See also Howarth (2012).

© 2013 The Author(s) JCMS: Journal of Common Market Studies © 2013 John Wiley & Sons Ltd

supported by the analytical, statistical, administrative and logistical assistance of the ECB. Critics claimed that the close ECB–ESRB ties already gave the central bank a role in macroeconomic supervision that could compromise its monetary policy functions.[34]

The December agreement involved the creation of a planned mediation committee between the banking supervisory board and the ECB governing council. This was a last-minute compromise introduced to satisfy the German government, which was opposed to assigning automatic responsibility to the ECB for mishaps it could not directly supervise.[35] It was agreed that the mediation committee would intervene when the banking supervisory board (which would likely include both eurozone members and non-members) disagreed with the ECB's governing council on the supervision of a specific bank. The consultancy hired by the ECB proposed that the administrative head of the supervisory arm should be a member of the executive board who would also serve as a vice-chair of the supervisory board. This powerful figure would likely come from one of the larger Member States, with Danièle Nouy, a senior official from the Bank of France, a likely candidate.[36]

On the common deposit guarantee scheme, the ECB supported the development of common support tools to manage the failure of financial institutions (ECB, 2012b). It argued that a common deposit guarantee scheme could help to maintain financial stability by discouraging speculation against individual Member States or institutions of the eurozone. The ECB 'fully supports the development of a recovery and resolution framework' (ECB, 2012b, p. 1). In this respect, it called for a rapid establishment of an independent European resolution mechanism (ECB, 2012b, p. 2). ECB President Draghi declared himself to be confident that the resolution mechanism would be in place when the SSM enters into force.[37] However, he claimed that even if this mechanism was not in place, a negative assessment by the SSM of the viability of a bank 'would likely' force national governments to undertake corrective measures.[38] The ECB adopted a positive position on the use of ESM funds to support banks, while its general position had always been that financial assistance should be conditioned by fiscal and macroeconomic reforms (as in the case of Greece, Ireland and Portugal).[39]

The Bundesbank maintained its reputation for rigorous critique on the euro crisis and mooted reforms by issuing an opinion that the December deal on the ECB's role in supervision lacked 'a long-term solid legal basis' and that the mediation committee operating between the bank supervisor and the governing council could be attacked in the courts.[40] Bundesbank President Jens Weidmann also challenged the logic of transforming the ECB into a prudential supervisor and expressed concern that the ECB's new supervisory role would not be sufficiently separate from its monetary policy role (and the goal of price stability) to ensure independence.[41] Many other observers and policymakers, including the EP's economic and monetary affairs committee, expressed similar

[34] *EUObserver*, 1 February 2012.
[35] *Financial Times*, 17 December 2012.
[36] *Financial Times*, 4 February 2012.
[37] *Financial Times*, 14 December 2012.
[38] *Financial Times*, 14 December 2012.
[39] *EurActiv.com*, 4 December; *Der Spiegel*, 6 June 2012.
[40] *Financial Times*, 17 December 2012.
[41] *Financial Times*, 27 September 2012; *WirtschaftsWoche*, 22 December 2012.

concerns.[42] Weidmann, however, argued that at best the ECB should operate as a transitional supervisor, while another entirely independent body was set up. Weidmann was also opposed to the creation of a 'resolution' authority able to use taxpayer money to shut down banks until a fund based on bank contributions was established on the grounds that this would spread risks to taxpayers but without adequate democratic controls.

VI. Banking Union and (the Lack of) Democratic Oversight

Members of the EP from the two main party groups were broadly supportive of banking union and called for adoption of the legal framework by the end of 2012 and for implementation to start in 2013.[43] However, MEPs also expressed the concern that the EP had been sidelined in the design of the banking union proposals and that democracy would suffer as a consequence.[44] The EP only possessed consultative power over the SSM regulation and other potential legislation to reinforce the powers of the ECB – although the EP held equal legislative power with the Council on the directive amending the powers of the EBA in the context of banking union. MEPs thus pushed to maintain an important role in negotiations and for Member States to treat the two pieces of legislation (SSM and EBA powers) equally. MEPs referred to the negotiations in 2011 on the 'Six Pack' reforms to economic governance as a precedent on which the EP enjoyed *de facto* co-decision even though consultation procedures applied to the reforms.[45] MEPs demanded transparency both in the negotiations on banking union and in the future operation of ECB supervisory powers and threatened to block new rules for the EBA if the Council (Member States) refused to negotiate on its SSM demands.[46]

On 29 November, the EP's economic and monetary affairs committee adopted its amendments of the European Commission's September legislative package (EP, 2012) focusing in large part upon improving the democratic accountability of the SSM. The committee demanded a veto over the nominee for chair of the SSM's board (to be located within the ECB), and that MEPs should have greater say over the SSM's budget and full investigative powers over the new board and its operations. At present, the EP has no confirmation power over the appointment of ECB executive board members, which MEPs have compared unfavourably with the power of the United States Congress over the confirmation of nominees to the Federal Reserve Board (Howarth and Loedel, 2005; Jabko, 2003). The new supervisory board would be required to report to the EP and national parliaments. MEPs also forwarded specific positions on a range of matters. MEPs demanded that the SSM regulation include conflict of interest provisions which could prevent members of the SSM's board from also having a mandate as a national regulator and blocking supervisory officials from entering (or returning) to banking jobs (thus avoiding the 'revolving door' phenomenon). MEPs also recommended that the EBA be assigned more powers to carry out stress tests and investigations and that it be relocated to Frankfurt, in order to tighten the authority's links with the ECB and avoid institutional overlap.

---

[42] *Financial Times*, 29–30 November 2012.
[43] *EUObserver*, 29 November 2012.
[44] *EUObserver*, 29 November 2012.
[45] *EUObserver*, 29 November 2012.
[46] *EUObserver*, 1 February 2013.

© 2013 The Author(s) JCMS: Journal of Common Market Studies © 2013 John Wiley & Sons Ltd

Conclusions

Banking union – if adopted in its entirety as proposed by the European Commission – would be the most important step in European integration since the launch of EMU. The adoption of the SSM is, in itself, one of the most significant leaps forward since 1999. Banking union can be seen as a necessary response to the 'asymmetric' design of EMU (a monetary union with a limited form of economic union) and to the fragmentation of the single financial market. It can also be seen as a crisis-driven attempt to address several important issues that were sidestepped or papered over during the negotiations leading to the Maastricht Treaty – principally the allocation of supervisory responsibilities to the ECB and the creation of a fiscal backstop in the eurozone. Other issues (notably the need for a single rule book and the harmonization of deposit guarantee schemes) stemmed from the incomplete nature of the single financial market – despite its heralded re-launch in the early 2000s. The limited integration of financial services markets (and notably banking markets) even after 13 years of EMU is a major weakness in the single market. Finally, other issues, such as the need for a common deposit guarantee and a resolution fund/ authority for the eurozone, were highlighted by the global financial crisis and the sovereign debt crisis. The further disintegration of financial markets since 2007 is the most significant ongoing impact of these crises upon the single market. The banking union proposals are a direct response to this disintegration and thus should be seen as much in terms of reinforcing the single market as stabilizing banks and EMU.

In the summer of 2012, the International Monetary Fund (IMF) came out as a vocal champion of banking union as an essential step to resolve the sovereign debt crisis (Goyal *et al.*, 2013; IMF, 2012, 2013). Like the Bundesbank, the IMF expressed concern over a 'half-finished' project, arguing that the SSM, the single resolution mechanism with common fiscal backstops (mutualization), a single authority with the power to shut down banks and common safety nets were *all* required to ensure a successful banking union. The creation of an SSM prior to the creation of a credible fiscal backstop would leave the former at risk, resulting in 'an architecture that is inferior to the current national one' (Goyal *et al.*, 2013, p. 22).

The sudden push on banking union by the European Commission and certain Member State governments, and notably the French, reflects the limited success of EU-level fiscal policy reinforcement and support mechanism construction in terms of building confidence in the stability of EMU. The half-hearted nature of reform to date owes to fundamental disagreements between France and Germany on how to tackle the crisis. Banking union has thus been embraced by many as an alternative route to stability: a European holy grail. Yet the banking union to be agreed in 2013 was as likely to be an uncomfortable compromise as previous reforms adopted to resolve the sovereign debt crisis. German opposition to the mutualization of financial support for banks would be difficult to overcome. While a major step forward in European economic integration, the reforms adopted would likely fall short of the silver bullet hoped by many to bring the sovereign debt crisis to an end.

References

Ayadi, R. and Lastra, R.M. (2010) 'Proposals for Reforming Deposit Guarantee Schemes in Europe'. *Journal of Banking Regulation*, Vol. 11, pp. 210–22.

© 2013 The Author(s) JCMS: Journal of Common Market Studies © 2013 John Wiley & Sons Ltd

Bank for International Settlements (BIS) (2011) 'The Impact of Sovereign Credit Risk on Bank Funding Conditions'. Committee on the Global Financial System Paper 43 (Basel: BIS).

Basel Committee on Banking Supervision (BCBS) (2010) 'Report and Recommendations of the Cross-Border Bank Resolution Group: Final Paper', March (Basel: BCBS).

Buckley, J., Howarth, D. and Quaglia, L. (2012) 'Internal Market: The Ongoing Struggle to "Protect" Europe from its Money Men'. *JCMS*, Vol. 48, No. 1, pp. 119–41.

Commission of the European Communities (1994) 'Directive on deposit-guarantee schemes'. 94/19/EC, 30 May.

Comporti, C. and Cosimo, R. (2012) 'Sightlines: European Regulatory Developments', 14 September. Available at: «http://www.promontory.com/uploadedFiles/Articles/Insights/Promontory_Sightlines_EU_Roadmap_120914_FINAL.pdf».

Darvas, Z. and Wolff, G. (2013) 'Should Non-Euro Area Countries Join the Single Supervisory Mechanism'. *Bruegel Policy Contribution*, No. 2013/06, March.

Elliott, D.J. (2012) 'Key Issues on European Banking Union Trade-Offs and Some Recommendations'. Global Economy and Development Working Paper 52 (Washington, DC: Brookings Institution).

European Central Bank (ECB) (2011a) 'The Eurosystem's Policy Line with Regard to Consolidation in Central Counterparty Clearing' (Frankfurt: ECB). Available at: «http://www.ecb.int/pub/pdf/other/centralcounterpartyclearingen.pdf».

European Central Bank (ECB) (2011b) 'Standards for the Use of Central Counterparties in Eurosystem Foreign Reserve Management Operations', November (Frankfurt: ECB).

European Central Bank (ECB) (2012a) 'Financial Integration Report', April (Frankfurt: ECB).

European Central Bank (ECB) (2012b) 'Opinion of the European Central Bank of 29 November 2012 on a Proposal for a Directive Establishing a Framework for Recovery and Resolution of Credit Institutions and Investment Firms'. CON/2012/99, 29 November. Available at: «http://www.ecb.europa.eu/ecb/legal/pdf/en_con_2012_99_f_sign.pdf».

European Central Bank (ECB) (2012c) 'Introductory Statement to the Press Conference (with Q&A) Presented by Mario Draghi, President of the ECB and Vítor Constâncio, Vice-President of the ECB at Frankfurt am Main, 6 December. Available at: «http://www.ecb.int/press/pressconf/2012/html/is121206.en.html».

European Commission (2010) 'Proposal for a Directive on deposit guarantee schemes [recast]'. *COM*(2010) 369, *SEC*(2010) 834, *SEC*(2010) 835, 12 July. Available at: «http://ec.europa.eu/internal_market/bank/docs/guarantee/20100712_proposal_en.pdf».

European Commission (2011a) 'Proposal for a Directive on the access to the activity of credit institutions and the prudential supervision of credit institutions and investment firms'. 2011/453/EC, 20 July.

European Commission (2011b) 'Proposal for a Regulation on prudential requirements for credit institutions and investment firms'. 2011/452/EC, 20 July.

European Commission (2012a) 'Proposal for a Council Regulation conferring specific tasks on the European Central Bank concerning policies relating to the prudential supervision of credit institutions'. *COM*(2012) 511 final, 12 September.

European Commission (2012b) 'Proposal for a Regulation establishing a European supervisory authority (European banking authority) [. . .]'. *COM*(2012) 512 final, 12 September.

European Commission (2012c) 'Communication from the Commission to the European Parliament and the Council: A roadmap towards a banking union'. *COM*(2012) 510 final, 12 September.

European Commission (2012d) 'Proposal for a Directive establishing a framework for the recoveryand resolution of credit institutions and investment firms'. *COM*(2012) 280/3, 20 June.

© 2013 The Author(s) JCMS: Journal of Common Market Studies © 2013 John Wiley & Sons Ltd

European Council (2012a) 'Council Agrees Position on Single Supervisory Mechanism'. 17739/
    12, PRESSE 528, 13 December, Brussels. Available at: «http://www.consilium.europa.eu/
    uedocs/cms_data/docs/pressdata/en/ecofin/134265.pdf».
European Council (2012b) 'The European Council Agrees on a Roadmap for the Completion
    of Economic and Monetary Union', 14 December. Available at: «http://www.european
    -council.europa.eu/home-page/highlights/the-european-council-agrees-on-a-roadmap-for-the
    -completion-of-economic-and-monetary-union».
European Council (2012c) 'Conclusions on Completing EMU', 14 December. Available at: «http://
    www.consilium.europa.eu/uedocs/cms_data/docs/pressdata/en/ec/134320.pdf».
European Parliament (EP) (2012) 'Report on the proposal for a Regulation amending Regulation
    (EU) No 1093/2010 establishing a European Supervisory Authority (European Banking
    Authority) [. . .]', 3 December. Available at: «http://www.europarl.europa.eu/sides/getDoc.do?
    pubRef=%2f%2fEP%2f%2fTEXT%2bREPORT%2bA7-2012-0393%2b0%2bDOC%2bXML
    %2bV0%2f%2fEN&language=EN#title1».
Financial Stability Board (FSB) (2011) 'Key Attributes of Effective Resolution Regimes for
    Financial Institutions', November (Basel: FSB).
Finnish Ministry of Finance (2012) 'Joint Statement of the Ministers of Finance of Germany, the
    Netherlands and Finland', Press Release 175/2012, 25 September. Available at: «http://www.
    vm.fi/vm/en/03_press_releases_and_speeches/01_press_releases/20120925JointS/name.jsp».
Garicano, L. (2012) 'Five Lessons from the Spanish Cajas Debacle for a New Euro Wide Super-
    visor'. In Beck, T. (ed.) *Banking Union for Europe: Risks and Challenges* (London: Centre for
    Economic Policy Research).
Goyal, R., Koeva Brooks, P., Pradhan, M., Tressel, T., Dell'Ariccia, G., Leckow, R., Payarbasioglu,
    C. and an IMF Staff Team (2013) 'Banking Union for the Euro Area'. IMF Staff Discussion
    Note SDN/13/01, 13 February (Washington, DC: International Monetary Fund).
Howarth, D. (2012) 'Unity and Disunity among Central Bankers in an Asymmetric Economic and
    Monetary Union'. In Hayward, J. and Wurzel, R. (eds) *European Disunion: The Multidimen-
    sional Power Struggles* (Basingstoke: Palgrave Macmillan).
Howarth, D. and Loedel, P. (2005) *The European Central Bank: The New European Leviathan?*
    (Basingstoke: Palgrave Macmillan).
Howarth, D. and Quaglia, L. (2013) 'Banking on Stability: The Political Economy of New
    Capital Requirements in the European Union'. *Journal of European Integration*, Vol. 35,
    No. 3, pp. 333–46.
International Monetary Fund (IMF) (2012) 'IMF Calls on Eurozone to Take Determined Action
    in Response to Crisis'. *IMF Survey Online, Economic Health Check*, 18 July. Available at:
    «http://www.imf.org/external/pubs/ft/survey/so/2012/int071812a.htm».
International Monetary Fund (IMF) (2013) 'A Banking Union for the Euro Area: Technical
    Background Notes', 13 February (Washington, DC: IMF). Available at: «http://www.imf.org/
    external/pubs/ft/sdn/2013/sdn1301technt.pdf».
Ionnidou, V. (2012) 'A First Step towards a Banking Union'. In Beck, T. (ed.) *Banking
    Union for Europe: Risks and Challenges* (London: Centre for Economic Policy
    Research).
Jabko, N. (2003) 'Democracy in the Age of the Euro'. *Journal of European Public Policy*, Vol. 10,
    No. 5, pp. 710–39.
Merlin, M. (2013) 'The Single Resolution Mechanism: State of Play and Next Steps'. Presentation
    at the high level round table 'Towards Banking Union: Open Issues', College of Europe,
    Bruges, 18 April.
Pisani-Ferry, J. and Wolff, G.B. (2012) 'The Fiscal Implications of a Banking Union'. *Bruegel
    Policy Paper*, 14 September.

© 2013 The Author(s) JCMS: Journal of Common Market Studies © 2013 John Wiley & Sons Ltd

Pisani-Ferry, J., Sapir, A., Véron, N. and Wolff, G.B. (2012) 'What Kind of European Banking Union?' *Bruegel Policy Paper*, 25 June.

Quaglia, L. (2010) *Governing Financial Services in the European Union* (London: Routledge).

Quaglia, L., Eastwood, R. and Holmes, P. (2009) 'The Financial Turmoil and EU Policy Co-operation in 2008'. *JCMS*, Vol. 47, No. S1, pp. 63–87.

Royo, S. (2013) 'A "Ship in Trouble": The Spanish Banking System and the International Financial Crisis'. In Hardie, I. and Howarth, D. (eds) *Market-Based Banking and the International Financial Crisis* (Oxford: Oxford University Press).

Schoenmaker, D. (2012) 'Banking Union: Where We're Going Wrong'. In Beck, T. (ed.) *Banking Union for Europe: Risks and Challenges* (London: Centre for Economic Policy Research).

Van Rompuy, H. (2012) 'Towards a Genuine Economic and Monetary Union', 5 December. Available at: «http://www.consilium.europa.eu/uedocs/cms_Data/docs/pressdata/en/ec/134069.pdf».

Veron, N. (2012) 'Briefing Paper for the European Parliament'. Available at: «http://veron.typepad.com/main/2012/10/briefing-paper-for-the-european-parliament.html».

© 2013 The Author(s) JCMS: Journal of Common Market Studies © 2013 John Wiley & Sons Ltd

JCMS 2013 Volume 51 Annual Review pp. 124–138   DOI: 10.1111/jcms.12041

Justice and Home Affairs

JÖRG MONAR
College of Europe/University of Sussex

Introduction

The year 2012 was an important test of the European Union's capacity to meet its own objectives in the field of justice and home affairs. The 2009–14 'Stockholm Programme' on the EU's 'area of freedom, security and justice' foresaw the completion of the common European asylum system (CEAS) by the end of the year. This objective was missed, but by a narrower margin than the differences between Council and Parliament initially suggested, with political agreement having been reached on two of the still missing four recast legislative acts and only the Directive on asylum procedures and the electronic fingerprint exchange system (Eurodac) regulation still remaining on the negotiation table. The EU's migration policy saw slow progress on the seasonal workers and intra-corporate transferees directives, but the Council redefined priorities for the EU's international action in the field. Judicial co-operation took significant steps forward with the adoption of the recast 'Brussels I Regulation' on jurisdiction, and the recognition and enforcement of judgments in civil and commercial matters and of a new regulation on jurisdiction and mutual recognition in matters of succession as well as – in the criminal justice domain – of a reinforced directive on victims' rights and the right to information in criminal proceedings. In the internal security domain the focus was primarily on the implementation of previously agreed objectives, with implementation again appearing as one of the persisting challenges of EU action in this field.

I. Developments in Individual Policy Areas

Asylum Policy

After an initial fall in the number of asylum applications during the first few months of the year they started to rise again from June 2012 onwards and with 88,970 applications in the third quarter, they exceeded those of the same period last year by 12,000 (Eurostat, 2012). With the strong likelihood of annual applications reaching similar levels to the 300,000 reached in the previous decade, the finalization of the CEAS appeared all the more necessary.

The negotiations between Council and Parliament on the recasting of the 2003 Dublin II Regulation, which established the criteria and mechanisms for determining the Member State responsible for processing an asylum application, progressed slowly, but led eventually to a political agreement endorsed by the Council in December (Council, 2012a): the European Parliament (EP) extracted from the Council a number of concessions in terms of better procedural guarantees for asylum seekers as regards family unity rules, effective

© 2013 The Author(s) JCMS: Journal of Common Market Studies © 2013 John Wiley & Sons Ltd, 9600 Garsington Road, Oxford OX4 2DQ, UK and 350 Main Street, Malden, MA 02148, USA

access to judicial review and protection of particularly vulnerable persons, in particular children, but failed to secure a more restrictive definition of the grounds for detaining asylum seekers. The Council itself had to overcome some internal tensions between particularly geographically exposed Member States – in particular, Cyprus, Greece, Italy and Malta – favouring a revision of the existing criteria for determining responsibility and transfer system, and other Member States having shown a primary interest in border Member States shielding them from some of the pressures on the emerging CEAS by more effective national crisis management capabilities. The extent to which the current system has in fact resulted in a burden-shifting to southern and eastern Member States of first entry was underlined again by Italy reporting that during the previous year 4,665 asylum seekers were transferred back to it under the Dublin system whereas there were only 14 transfers from Italy to other Member States – a ratio of 1:333 (European Network, 2013, p. 21). In the final political compromise the majority of the other Member States secured an almost unchanged continuation of the existing criteria and transfer system, with a new 'mechanism for early warning, preparedness and crisis management' adding even additional pressure on Member States experiencing a surge of applications in that they will in the future be expected to submit first a Commission-monitored 'preventive action plan' and then, in case of deteriorating situation, a Council-monitored 'crisis management action plan'.

This reaffirmation of the primary responsibility of 'frontline' countries for asylum applications could not have passed the Council, however, without a solidarity counterpart. This counterpart was in fact provided – at least to some extent – by the adoption by the Council of 'Conclusions on a common framework for genuine and practical solidarity towards Member States facing particular pressures due to mixed migration flows'. This provides for solidarity measures to be triggered at the 'substantiated request' of Member States facing an emergency situation and consisting primarily of the use of the asylum intervention pool of the European Asylum Support Office (EASO) and 'further solidarity' being offered by other Member States on a bilateral basis (Council, 2012b, pp. 5, 7). While the 'further' solidarity was in that case left rather unspecified, the Council and EP were able to agree in March on a more concrete measure with regard to the resettlement in 2013 of refugees from designated regional protection programme areas outside of the EU and 'priority countries' (such as Congolese refugees in the Great Lakes Region) and of persons being in a particularly vulnerable situation (such as women and children at risk). The legislative decision provides for Member States to receive a lump sum of €4,000 from the European Refugee Fund for each person resettled according to the agreed priorities – and even €6,000 per resettled person if they have not applied to the Fund before (European Parliament/Council, 2012a). Although these sums can only defray a minor part of the costs of a resettlement, the intention is to provide an additional solidarity incentive to Member States to pull their own weight in addressing the plight of refugees in particularly difficult situations outside of the Union.

The importance of further solidarity measures – also in view of the new financial framework 2014–20 – was also highlighted by the increased guarantees, many of which are likely to entail additional costs for at least some Member States, defined for asylum seekers under the political agreement reached on 25 October on the recast 2003 directive laying down minimum standards for the reception of asylum seekers (Council, 2012c). While still leaving a large leeway to Member States in terms of the material reception conditions offered to asylum seekers – new Article 17(5) of the recast directive provides that these shall be determined on the basis of the adequate standards of living foreseen for nationals but still allows for 'less favourable treatment' in some respects – the revised legal instrument brings some distinctive improvements as regards the situation of particularly vulnerable refugees and imposes additional limitations on the detention of asylum seekers, both of which were strongly welcomed by the UNHCR (2012, p. 4). The recast directive provides not only in Article 21 for an extension of the categories of vulnerable persons with special needs to victims of trafficking in human beings, persons with serious illnesses or mental disorders and victims of female genital mutilation, but also introduces in Article 22 a mandatory procedure for the assessment of any special needs after an application for international protection is made as well as a monitoring of the situation of the persons concerned throughout the entire asylum procedure. A greater emphasis is also placed in Article 23 on the protection of the best interests of children. As regards the highly controversial issue of detention, the revised Article 8 stipulates that applicants for international protection should only be detained on the basis of an individual assessment if other less coercive alternative measures cannot be applied effectively. In addition at least one of five listed grounds – which include verification of identity or nationality, implementation of a return procedure and national security or public order requirements – have to apply, and the rights of detained applicants in terms of information, legal assistance and speedy judicial review of their cases have been strengthened. In order to enhance the integration and self-sufficiency of applicants during their asylum procedure the time limit for granting access to the labour market is reduced by Article 15 to nine months instead of the current 12.

The negotiations on the recast Eurodac Regulation remained deadlocked because of the fundamental disagreement between the Council and EP over the question of the access of law enforcement authorities to the electronic fingerprints of asylum seekers in the Eurodac database which Member States kept insisting upon throughout the year. There was some progress on the recasting of the asylum procedures directive – with good chances for a political agreement under the upcoming 2013 Irish Presidency (Council, 2012d) – but there were at the end of the year still disagreements, *inter alia*, over the possible extension of the time limit for asylum procedures beyond six months (the Council was aiming at an additional 12 months), the limitation of the grounds for the application of the so-called 'accelerated' procedures (favoured by the EP, resisted by the Council) and the criteria for determining 'safe third countries'.

Given the EU legislative procedures in the asylum domain failed to meet the 2012 Stockholm Programme deadline for the completion of the CEAS, the common system's most operational element – the EASO – continued to consolidate its young existence and to expand its activities. Based on a 'European asylum curriculum' adopted in January, EASO both provided Member States with learning materials on best practices in asylum procedures and organized a range of training sessions for national officials. It also standardized its procedures and expanded its working groups for 'country of origin information' (COI) which is aimed at strengthening the evidence base for decision-making on asylum cases. The first COI report on a major country of origin (Afghanistan) was published in July, which was complemented in December by a report on insurgent strategies and targeted violence against Afghans (EASO, 2012a). The 'asylum intervention pool' of national experts which can be deployed in the context of 'asylum support teams' (ASTs) to provide emergency support to Member States experiencing particular pressures grew to 345 registered experts from 21 Member States. During the year, 65 ASTs were deployed to Greece to reduce the backlog of asylum cases, improve the registration of asylum claims and provide training (EASO, 2013).

As all aspects of the EASO's work – from operational support over analysis to training – contribute to effective solidarity in EU asylum policy and as it is still in the process of building up its structures, the decision by Council and Commission to cut its projected budget for 2013 from an originally planned €15 million to €11.9 million (later marginally increased to €12.0 million) appeared as another example of the axe of austerity hitting the wrong targets – with the EASO itself making no secret of the consequences (EASO, 2012b). Member States still seem to give preference to solidarity in terms of national pay-outs – as in the case of the European Refugee Fund – over real investments into common solidarity structures.

Migration and Visa Policy

In its annual report on immigration and asylum presented in May, the Commission pointed to a continuing rather modest level of net legal immigration into the EU of 0.17 per cent (0.9 million – 2011 figures), although third-country nationals amounted to 4 per cent of the total EU population (20.2 million). The extent of illegal immigration remained difficult to estimate, but 343,000 refusals of entry and 468,500 apprehensions of persons in an irregular situation within the EU indicated a continuing significant illegal immigration pressure. As before, the Commission made a case for expanding legal immigration channels as a way to address skills shortages and to contribute to economic growth, recognizing, however, that increasing levels of unemployment made Member States focus more on increasing the employability of their own resident population (European Commission, 2012a).

The negotiations on the directives for seasonal workers and intra-corporate transferees – both proposed by the Commission in 2010 – continued their slow progress. With several Member States wanting to retain a maximum of national autonomy in regulating seasonal work by third-country nationals, it took the Council until December to define a comprehensive common position. This position, however, differed on a number of substantial issues (for example, the compensation rights of seasonal workers in the case of EU employers breaching their obligations, the possible access of third-country students to seasonal work, the potential use of national quotas to limit the renewal of seasonal work permits, the maximum period of seasonal work and the right of a seasonal worker to seek new employment in case of a problem with the first employer) from the amendments proposed by the EP. The latter appeared not much more liberal than the Council in terms of access conditions to seasonal employment – no doubt a reflection of constituents' concerns about the protection of employment possibilities of nationals in a period of rising unemployment – but MEPs put a much greater emphasis than the Council on imposing conditions on employers to exclude an adequate treatment of third-country seasonal workers (Council, 2013). As regards the directive on intra-corporate transferees, the EP's position differed from that of the Council in particular on more liberal family reunification conditions, the equivalence of working conditions with those of EU nationals and the possibilities of transferees to move between Member States. However, sufficient common ground seemed to have been reached by the end of the year to make adoption during 2013 likely.

While the adoption of new legislation facilitating legal immigration is clearly one challenge for the EU, the implementation of existing legislation is clearly another. The Commission deplored again the sluggish implementation of the 2009 EU 'blue card' directive facilitating the access of highly skilled third-country nationals to combined work and residence within the EU (European Commission, 2012a). It was symptomatic that Germany (one of the no fewer than 11 Member States against which the Commission had started treaty infringement procedures) passed the necessary implementing legislation only in April and accepted its first blue card applications only from 1 August onwards.[1] The required minimum income threshold of €44,800 in the German case highlighted again the limited reach of this instrument in comparison with, for instance, the American 'green card'.

Migration policy has necessarily an important external dimension, and the European Council had already in 2005 endorsed a corresponding 'global approach to migration'. Responding to the Commission's 2011 evaluation of progress, deficits and new priorities (European Commission, 2011), the Council adopted in May 'Conclusions on the global approach to migration and mobility' (Council, 2012e). In these, the Council defined as the four 'operational priorities': better organized legal migration and the fostering of well-managed mobility; the prevention and combating of illegal migration and the eradication of the trafficking in human beings; maximization of the development impact of migration and mobility; and the promotion of international protection and the enhancement of the external dimension of asylum. The Council used the occasion to emphasize again the importance of 'mobility partnerships' involving closer co-operation on circular migration, visa facilitation and readmission, especially with neighbouring countries, although these are not legally binding and affect only a variable number of Member States. The Conclusions also strongly reiterated the application of EU conditionality by establishing a clear conditional link between the negotiation of visa facilitation and re-admission agreements with countries of origin and/or transit of migration into the EU.

Re-admission agreements and visa facilitation agreements remain the most important external migration policy instruments of the Union. The initialling of the re-admission agreement with Turkey on 21 June was hailed by Commissioner Cecilia Malmström as an 'important development' (European Commission, 2012b). However, the length of the preceding negotiations (the original Council negotiating mandate went back to 2002), their frequent stalling, the persisting doubts in some Member States about full Turkish co-operation on re-admission issues and the continuing dissatisfaction of the Turkish side about the EU's refusal to start visa liberalization talks before the signing of the re-admission agreement had amply shown all the difficulties of arriving at satisfactory arrangements with a major illegal immigration transit country. A 'roadmap toward a visa-free regime', which was submitted to Turkey in December, was met with considerable criticism because of the EU's insistence on the re-admission agreement being signed and fully implemented before concrete steps towards visa liberalization (Council, 2012f). At the end of the year it still seemed uncertain when – and even if – the re-admission agreement would be signed.

[1] *Auswärtiges Amt*, 1 August 2012.

© 2013 The Author(s) JCMS: Journal of Common Market Studies © 2013 John Wiley & Sons Ltd

In the case of the visa facilitation agreement with Cape Verde, which was signed on 29 October, negotiations on the usual parallel re-admission agreement were still continuing. However, the EU had insisted on a clause in the agreement (Article 12(2)), according to which the visa facilitation agreement could only enter into force on the same day as the re-admission agreement (Council, 2012g). The same approach was followed with regard to the visa facilitation agreement signed with Armenia on 17 December (Council, 2012h), emphasizing again the EU's re-admission conditionality with regard to visa facilitation.

Border Policy

The monitoring of the situation at the EU's external borders by Frontex revealed a significant decline in illegal border crossings compared to the year before, which in the third quarter of 2012 even reached 43 per cent, that is, 22,093 instead of 38,500 in the same period the year before. This decrease could partially be ascribed to a 'back to normal' situation after the Arab Spring refugee and migration movements, but partially also, as Frontex pointed out, to a significant strengthening of surveillance and patrolling operations on the Greek–Turkish land border to which the Frontex co-ordinated 'Poseidon Land 2012' operation contributed substantially. However, the detection of illegals staying within the EU remained at a high level (86,562 in the third quarter), as did the refusals of entry (32,278 in the third quarter), so that there was no sign of a general easing of the illegal immigration pressure on the EU's external borders. Other primary security issues at external borders identified and analyzed by Frontex included the smuggling of drugs through the Western Balkans, western Mediterranean and west African routes; the smuggling of tobacco products and petrol over the eastern borders routes; and the smuggling of tobacco, drugs and precious metals over the eastern Mediterranean routes (Frontex, 2013).

While the Frontex risk assessments highlighted the continuing challenges at the external borders, much of the EU's political focus in this field during the year was on internal rather than external borders. This was due to the unresolved issues under which conditions and according to which procedure Schengen Member States should be allowed to reintroduce controls at internal borders in case of risks arising inside the Schengen zone as a result of one or more other Member States failing to ensure adequate external border security. With the original Commission proposal according to which any reintroduction of controls at internal borders would have been dependent on a prior evaluation and authorization by the Commission having met almost unanimous resistance in the Council, the negotiations evolved at the beginning of the year in the direction of a more Member State controlled evaluation mechanism, but risked being deadlocked by the reluctance of the Commission to give ground and by significant opposition in the EP to what many MEPs saw as a subordination of the continuation of border control free travel within the EU to purely national internal security considerations. Several Member States pushed for rapid progress on the issue. On 11 March, French President Nicolas Sarkozy, no doubt partially motivated by the presidential election campaign, threatened to suspend French participation in the Schengen system if there was no decisive progress within the year,[2] and in

[2] *Le Monde*, 11 March 2012.

© 2013 The Author(s) JCMS: Journal of Common Market Studies © 2013 John Wiley & Sons Ltd

April, French Minister of the Interior Claude Guéant and German Minister of the Interior Hans-Peter Friedrich wrote a joint letter to the Danish Presidency in which they declared national control over the reintroduction of the border 'not negotiable' and the final decision over the admissibility of a reintroduction of border controls to be a matter for the Council and not the Commission.[3]

The Danish Presidency, itself in favour of more national autonomy in this field, then worked out a 'Presidency compromise' eventually acceptable to all Member States which consisted of the proposed adoption of two separate legislative texts. The first was a Council Decision (the Commission had proposed an EP/Council regulation) on the establishment of an evaluation and monitoring mechanism to verify the application of the Schengen *acquis* which provided for a much toughened Schengen evaluation mechanism including unannounced inspection visits and an obligation of Member States to adopt action plans on identified deficits and to report on their implementation (Council, 2012i). The second was a regulation establishing common rules on the temporary reintroduction of border controls at internal borders in exceptional circumstances which considerably widened the possibilities of Member States to reintroduce – based on the reports stemming from the toughened Schengen evaluation process and under the control of the Council rather than the Commission – controls at internal borders up to a maximum length of two years (Council, 2012j). Rather daringly, but with the support of most of the Member States and of the Council Legal Service, the Danish Presidency tried to reduce the co-decision powers of the EP by changing the legal base for the evaluation mechanism from Article 77(2)(e) TFEU (measures regarding the absence of controls at internal borders) – requiring co-decision – to Article 70 TFEU (measures on objective and impartial evaluation of the implementation of EU measures within the 'area of freedom, security and justice') – requiring only that the EP is informed about the results of evaluations.

When the Council approved the Schengen package in its session on 7–8 June it tried to soften the pill for the EP by offering a non-mandatory consultation on the evaluation mechanisms decision, but this was not enough to avoid one of the worst breakdowns in co-operation between the Council and the EP in the justice and home affairs domain in recent years. Reactions in the EP ranged from Joseph Daul, President of the EPP Group, qualifying this as 'a breach of the relation of trust with this Parliament' to Guy Verhofstadt, President of the liberal ALDE Group, describing it as a unilateral attempt of the Council to 'renationalize Schengen' (EP, 2012a), and on 14 June the Parliament's Conference of Presidents decided in retaliation to suspend co-operation with the Council not only on the Schengen package, but also on four other justice and home affairs files, the proposed directive on attacks against information systems, the European Investigation Order, the internal security EU budgetary aspects for 2013 and EU passenger name records (EP, 2012b). This unprecedented step was primarily due to all major political groups feeling strongly about the need to protect the EP's democratic prerogatives, but the debates amongst the MEPs also showed a real concern about a progressive dismantling of the Schengen zone of open borders by the reassertion of national control powers and the – in response to populist political dynamics at the domestic level – often exaggerated presentation of migratory movements as a security risk justifying this rolling back of

[3] *EurActiv*, 8 June 2012.

© 2013 The Author(s) JCMS: Journal of Common Market Studies © 2013 John Wiley & Sons Ltd

the Schengen *acquis*. The clash in June blocked any further substantial progress on the Schengen package during the year, although there were signs in December that negotiations between the Council and the EP might resume under the incoming Irish Presidency.

As the European Commission noted in November in its second biannual report on the functioning of the Schengen area, there were again a range of cases in which national police authorities carried out checks in internal border areas where questions arose about the compatibility of those with the absence of border checks according to Schengen rules (European Commission, 2012c). The Dutch Raad van Staate actually requested on 4 June an urgent preliminary ruling by the Court of Justice on the question of whether mobile surveillance checks carried out by the Koninklijke Marechaussée police force close to the Netherlands' internal land borders with Belgium and Germany are compatible with Articles 20 and 21 of the Schengen borders code. In its ruling, the court held that the checks which had been questioned were compatible with Schengen rules as they were of a selective nature with limited intensity and frequency and had not had as their purpose border checks but rather were to establish whether the persons stopped satisfy the requirements for lawful residence applicable in the Member State concerned (European Court of Justice, 2012). This ruling showed again that Member States are already – even without the projected changes to the Schengen system – far from 'defenceless' as regards the 'threat' of illegal immigration across the open internal borders.

The strong reaffirmation of national control possibilities at the Council level and the many instances of checks within border areas clearly indicate that in spite of the significant progress made (primarily via Frontex) in common risk assessments and joint operations at external borders has not been able to stem an increasing degree of distrust within the Schengen system. This distrust, which was fuelled by the Arab Spring migratory pressures and the partial breakdown of effective external border management in Greece during the year before, also contributed much to the continuing postponement during the year – primarily because of the concerns about corruption in the law enforcement services – of the integration of Bulgaria and Romania into the Schengen border system. To some extent this trust problem was addressed by the conclusions regarding guidelines for the strengthening of political governance in the Schengen co-operation, which the Council adopted on 8 March and which placed a strong emphasis on 'necessary political guidance' to be provided at ministerial level in light of political discussions focused on 'serious shortcomings' and the implementation of action plans aimed at tackling those (Council, 2012k). More regular and open discussion of all matters of concern and more sustained collective pressure on Member States failing to live up to their obligations might help to rein in the unravelling of the commitment to the core of the Schengen project, but more solidarity with Member States facing particular difficulties at their external borders is at least equally important and to this issue the Council conclusions made only a passing reference in the preamble.

In a year which overall gave rise to more questions than answers regarding EU border policy a positive note was set by the progress (finally) made with regard to the second-generation Schengen information system (SIS II). In October the Commission reported that 'milestone tests' carried out in May had proved the 'maturity' of the central system and that national compliance tests had – in spite of slight technical difficulties in four Member States – also overall progressed satisfactorily (European Commission, 2012d). By the end of the year it seemed likely that the SIS II, with its enhanced law enforcement information functions, would be able to go live in March or April 2013, which might also make a contribution to restoring confidence in the overall Schengen system.

Judicial Co-operation

In the field of judicial co-operation in civil matters, the adoption by the EP and Council on 12 December of the recast 'Brussels I Regulation' on jurisdiction and the recognition and enforcement of judgments in civil and commercial matters (originally adopted in 2001) marked a significant step forward taken with regard to the acceleration of cross-border litigation as well as the circulation and enforcement of judgments across borders (European Parliament/Council, 2012b). The recast Regulation (EU) 1215/2012, which will become fully applicable in January 2015, ensures that the court to which parties have assigned exclusive jurisdiction in an underlying agreement has priority of jurisdiction over any other court. As a result, any other court seized in a matter relating to the agreement has either to decline jurisdiction or to stay proceedings until the court identified in the agreement declares that it has no jurisdiction (Article 31). This provision reduces the current risk of proceedings being disrupted and/or delayed by contracting parties bringing pre-emptory proceedings in other jurisdictions.

Of at least equal importance is the new provision made by Article 39 of the regulation for a judgment given in a Member State which is enforceable in that Member State being enforceable in the other Member States without any 'declaration of enforceability' being required. This puts an end to the current need in several Member States (such as Germany, France and Spain) for parties seeking enforcement to obtain an '*exequatur*' (enforceability decision) decision by a court in the respective other Member State – a process which can be both costly and lengthy. A contracting party can still apply for a refusal of enforcement in the respective other Member State (Articles 45 and 46), but in that case the burden will be with the objecting party and not the one which has already successfully sought an enforcement decision – which is likely to reduce certain litigation temptations.

Last but not least, the regulation also extends the jurisdiction of Member States' courts to non-EU domiciled parties in cases of consumer contracts (new Article 18(1)), employment contract cases if the employees concerned habitually carry out their work within a Member State (new Article 21(2)) and in cases in which Member States have exclusive jurisdiction such as cases concerning immovable property, tenancies of immovable property, dissolution of companies and the registration or validity of patents, trademarks and designs (new Article 24) – which strengthens the rights and legal certainty of EU consumers and companies.

Progress was also made in a slightly more specific civil justice field with the adoption on 4 July of Regulation (EU) 650/2012 on jurisdiction, applicable law, recognition and enforcement of decisions in matters of succession and on the creation of a European certificate of succession (European Parliament/Council, 2012c). With, according to the Commission, over 450,000 annual cross-border successions of a total estimated value of €120 billion, the facilitation of often legally complex cross-border succession arrangements is of obvious importance not only to the family members concerned but also to cross-border economic ventures. The new regulation, which will become fully applicable in August 2015, does not impose harmonization change on national substantive inheritance laws and national rules regarding inheritance tax liabilities, which are both very

© 2013 The Author(s) JCMS: Journal of Common Market Studies © 2013 John Wiley & Sons Ltd

sensitive fields for the Member States. Instead it establishes clear rules on the determination of jurisdiction and the applicable law and provides for mutual recognition of enforcement decisions in this field. Important principles include the succession to the estate of a deceased person to be dealt with as a whole irrespective of the nature or the location of the assets (Article 1(1)), one single judicial authority being in charge of the succession (Article 4 and 5), and one single law being applicable to the succession (Article 21). The regulation establishes as a fundamental rule that the law applicable to the succession is the law of the Member State of the deceased's habitual residence at the time of death, but under the choice of law clause of Article 22 a person can also choose the law of a state of which she or he is a national.

The regulation also introduces a 'European certificate of succession', which can be issued by a competent court and can be used for stating: the status and/or the rights of each heir or legatee mentioned in the certificate and their respective shares of the estate; the attribution of a specific asset or specific assets forming part of the estate to the heir(s) or legatee(s) mentioned in the certificate; and the powers of the person mentioned in the certificate to execute the will or administer the estate (Article 63). Although the use of the certificate is not mandatory, it should facilitate the settlement of succession issues especially in cases in which property is located in other Member States. While adding a further building-block to the EU's civil justice area, the regulation also added to its differentiation as Denmark, Ireland and United Kingdom decided not to opt in.

Within the EU's criminal justice area the position of victims of crime was strengthened by the adoption on 25 October of Directive 2012/29/EU on minimum standards on the rights, support and protection of victims of crime (European Parliament/Council, 2012d). This directive replaced a former 'third-pillar' framework decision of 2001 as part of the Council's 2011 'Budapest road map' to arrive at a higher level of protection for victims of crime. The new instrument recognizes in its preamble that some victims are particularly at risk of secondary and repeat victimization, of intimidation and of retaliation by the offender during criminal proceedings which can derive from the personal characteristics of the victim or the type, nature or circumstances of the crime. In order to ensure that corresponding specific protection needs can be adequately identified, Article 22 provides for a timely 'individual assessment' which should pay particular attention to victims who have suffered considerable harm due to the severity of the crime, who have suffered a crime committed with a bias or discriminatory motive, and those whose relationship to, and dependence upon, the offender make them particularly vulnerable. In this regard, victims of terrorism, organized crime, human trafficking, gender-based violence, violence in a close relationship, sexual violence, exploitation or hate crime, and victims with disabilities are identified for special consideration. The directive provides for partially extended minimum rights as regards general information and support, the rights of participation in criminal proceedings and the rights to victim protection. The first group includes the right 'to understand and to be understood' (Article 3), to receive information about available support (Article 4), to make complaints (Article 5), to receive information about their case (Article 6), to interpretation and translation (Article 7) and to have free of charge access services to confidential victims support services (Articles 8 and 9). The second includes the right to be heard in criminal proceedings (Article 10), rights in the event of a decision not to prosecute (Article 11), a right to safeguards in the context of restorative justice services (Article 12), to legal aid (Article 13), to the

© 2013 The Author(s) JCMS: Journal of Common Market Studies © 2013 John Wiley & Sons Ltd

reimbursement of expenses (Article 14), to the return of property (Article 15), to compensation by the offender (Article 16) and to measures to facilitate the situation of
victims residing in another Member State. The rights relating to the protection of victims,
finally, obliges Member States to protect victims and their family members from secondary and repeat victimization, from intimidation and from retaliation and to protect the
dignity of victims during questioning and when testifying (Article 18), and provides for
the right of the victim to avoid contact with the offender (Article 19), protective measures
during criminal investigations (Article 20) and the right to privacy (Article 21). An
element of innovation is also the extension of several of these rights, such as that of free
of charge access to support services, also to family members. Although most of these
rights are defined rather vaguely – leaving wide margins of application to Member States
– the extensive list of these rights and their applicability to a wide range of different
categories of victims of crime in this directive can be regarded as the most extensive
'charter of rights' of individuals that has so far emanated from the EU's 'area of freedom,
security and justice'.

On a more modest scale, the EU's promotion of rights also took a step forward with the
adoption on 22 May of the Directive 2012/13/EU on the right to information in criminal
proceedings (European Parliament/Council, 2012e). It provides for suspects or accused
persons to be provided promptly with information concerning at least the right to access
to a lawyer, any entitlement to legal advice free of charge and the conditions for obtaining
it, and the right to be informed about the accusation, the right to interpretation and
translation and the right to remain silent (Article 3). The directive also introduces a 'letter
of rights' to be issued to any person arrested, which, in addition to information on the
aforementioned rights, also should contain minimum information on the rights to: access
to the materials of the case (which is crucial for preparing an effective defence), consular
authorities and one person being informed of the person's arrest; access to urgent medical
assistance; and to know how long the person can be deprived of liberty in the country
concerned before being brought before a judicial authority (Article 4).

On the operational side of criminal justice co-operation, Eurojust reported only a slight
increase in assistance requests from national prosecution authorities from 1,424 to 1,441
in 2011, but a 45 per cent increase in co-ordination meetings held from 141 to 204
(Eurojust, 2012). As these co-ordination meetings enable Eurojust to provide guidance on
and mediate in often complex cross-border prosecution cases, this was a clear indication
that the institution – which celebrated its tenth anniversary during the year – has become
an active and not only a supporting factor in judicial co-operation in criminal matters.

Internal Security Co-operation

The year 2012 was the second year of the implementation of the EU's first three-year
'policy cycle on serious and organized crime' which is aimed at ensuring that co-operation
on cross-border crime phenomena at EU level are based on police intelligence-led priorities
and operational action plans. This first cycle serves as a testing phase for a second 'full'
cycle from 2014 to 2017 which is going to have a much enhanced 'serious organized crime
threat assessment' (SOCTA) to be submitted by Europol as its strategy basis. Yet during the
year the intelligence requirements and the operational priorities were only broadly met as
regards one of the objectives defined for the first cycle in June 2011 – the fight against

© 2013 The Author(s) JCMS: Journal of Common Market Studies © 2013 John Wiley & Sons Ltd

trafficking in human beings – with other important fields, such as action against organized crime in the Western Balkans and drug-trafficking, suffering from a lack of common commitment by Member States. The Commission's evaluation report submitted in January 2013 identified as major problems a significant gap between the decisions taken by the Member States' senior representatives in the Council's standing committee on operational co-operation on internal security (COSI) and their subsequent implementation by national ministries and law enforcement authorities; Member States often appearing as 'passengers' rather than active 'participants' in agreed priority fields and the reluctance to assume (as foreseen by the cycle) responsibility as 'drivers' in certain crime areas in which they have primary expertise; the dissociation of some strategic goals from operational considerations; and the absence of a mechanism to make mid-cycle adjustments to operational action plans (European Commission, 2013). While the progress made in the field of action against trafficking in human beings showed the overall validity of the intelligence-led strategic and operational planning approach, the many identified shortcomings highlighted again the problem of the discrepancy between Member State endorsed European political programming and actual implementation effort at the national level, which obviously is a systemic problem of the Union and not one only affecting internal security co-operation.

Prospects for a more effective role of the Union in the internal security domain were not enhanced by the politics of budgetary austerity which started to impact also on the justice and home affairs field. Although Europol reported in September a further significant increase of 17 per cent of operational support services provided to national authorities in comparison with the previous reporting period (Europol, 2012a) and although Europol had to provide additional resources for the establishment of the new European cybercrime centre (EC3) in January 2013, Europol saw its budget for 2013 cut from €84.15 million in 2012 to €75.18 million although both the Member States and the Commission had agreed in February on a funding need of €90.4 million (Europol, 2012b). The adding, on the one hand, ever more to the tasks of Europol while, on the other hand, cutting its budget can be taken as another indication of the growing gap between EU-level political programming and the willingness to ensure adequate implementation capabilities.

The killings perpetrated by Mohammed Merah in France in March and the terrorist attack on an airport passenger bus at Burgas Airport in July showed again the persistence and diversity of terrorist threats within the EU. In his annual report on the implementation of the EU counter-terrorism strategy, Counter-Terrorism Co-ordinator Gilles de Kerchove highlighted in particular the progress made with a number of measures countering radicalization and recruitment, including that of the newly established radicalization awareness network (RAN) which works on the identification of best practices and includes a technical assistance and support (RAN-TAS) mechanism to provide logistical, technical and administrative support to national authorities. On the protection side, the critical infrastructure warning and information network (CIWIN) became operational, and in October the second European 'cyber incident management exercise' took place in order to test the effectiveness of existing mechanisms and procedures and the information flow between public authorities in Europe in the event of large-scale cyber attacks. However, implementation deficits appeared also in the counter-terrorism field with only 16 Member States having started the automated exchange of electronic DNA profiles and only 14 that of electronic fingerprints, although the deadline for both foreseen in the 2008 'Prüm Decisions' had been 26 August 2011 (Council, 2012l). In his discussion paper on the EU's

© 2013 The Author(s) JCMS: Journal of Common Market Studies © 2013 John Wiley & Sons Ltd

strategy of 23 May, the Counter-Terrorism Co-ordinator also indicated again a number of shortcomings of the information supply of EU agencies by national authorities (Council, 2012m).

Conclusions

This third full year of the implementation of the 2010–14 Stockholm programme saw the EU still struggling to meet some of its strategic objectives – perhaps the most notable example of which was the completion of the CEAS. Tensions between the EP and the Council over new or recast key legislation clearly contributed significantly to the delay in progress in several policy-making fields. While this may be partially ascribed to the EP asserting its role in line with its much strengthened position in this domain after the Lisbon Treaty extension of its co-decision powers,[4] it also highlights the EU's more general, and fundamental, problem of the dissociation between national executive policies and the EP's worthy, although not always consistent, efforts to define and defend common public goods of the EU's citizenry as a whole.

The actual implementation of instruments also remained a serious challenge, which in some cases stretches back to the pre-Stockholm period. Given that the deficits in implementation and capabilities are almost exclusively due to failures at the national level, it seemed ironic that in the debate about the reform of 'Schengen governance' several Member States, including France and Germany, forcefully argued in favour of more national control and autonomy. In justice and home affairs no less than in many other policy domains, the real problem seems not to be a failing Union, but failing Member States.

The year, however, also showed that trouble arising from the national level for the major treaty objective of the 'area of freedom, security and justice' (AFSJ) is not limited to problems associated with implementation. British Prime Minister Cameron's announcement in September that the British government intended to exercise the right conferred exclusively on the United Kingdom by Protocol 36 of the Lisbon Treaty to opt out of EU criminal law and policing measures adopted before that Treaty entered into force (House of Commons, 2013) increased the likelihood of a weakening of the common core of EU action against serious cross-border crime and terrorism – and this, rather ironically, by one of the Member States which over the last decade has contributed most to the introduction and development of EU criminal justice and law enforcement instruments and mechanisms. Domestic politics spillovers of a not always very rational sort should be counted among the main risks for the AFSJ. Although of a very different nature, they are not far behind those of serious cross-border crime in their disruptive effects.

References

Council of the European Union (2012a) 'Proposal for a Regulation of the European Parliament and of the Council establishing the criteria and mechanisms for determining the Member State responsible for examining an application for international protection lodged in one of the Member States [. . .] political agreement'. 16332/12, 21 November.

---

[4] See Dinan's contribution to this issue.

© 2013 The Author(s) JCMS: Journal of Common Market Studies © 2013 John Wiley & Sons Ltd

Council of the European Union (2012b) 'Council Conclusions on a common framework for genuine and practical solidarity towards Member States facing particular pressures due to mixed migration flows'. 7485/12, 9 March.

Council of the European Union (2012c) 'Amended proposal for a Directive of the European Parliament and of the Council laying down standards for the reception of asylum seekers [. . .] political agreement'. 14112/1/12, 27 September.

Council of the European Union (2012d) 'Amended proposal for a Directive of the European Parliament and of the Council on common procedures for granting and withdrawing international protection status (Recast) [. . .] preparation of the seventh informal trilogue'. 17698/12, 17 December.

Council of the European Union (2012e) 'Council Conclusions on the global approach to migration and mobility'. 8361/12, 30 March.

Council of the European Union (2012f) 'Relations with Turkey – Broader dialogue and cooperation framework on justice and home affairs: Roadmap towards a visa-free regime'. 17347/12, 6 December.

Council of the European Union (2012g) 'Agreement between the European Union and the Republic of Cape Verde on facilitating the issue of short-stay visas to citizens of the Republic of Cape Verde and of the European Union'. 14203/12, 3 October.

Council of the European Union (2012h) 'Agreement between the European Union and the Republic of Armenia on the facilitation of the issuance of visas'. 16913/12, 4 December.

Council of the European Union (2012i) 'Amended proposal for a regulation of the European Parliament and of the Council on the establishment of an evaluation and monitoring mechanism to verify the application of the Schengen *acquis*: Revised draft compromise text'. 5754/6/12 REV 6, 4 June.

Council of the European Union (2012j) 'Proposal for a Regulation of the European Parliament and of the Council amending Regulation (EC) No 562/2006 in order to provide for common rules on the temporary reintroduction of border control at internal borders in exceptional circumstances: Revised draft compromise text'. 161/4/12 REV 4.

Council of the European Union (2012k) 'Council Conclusions regarding guidelines for the strengthening of political governance in the Schengen cooperation'. 7417/12, 8 March.

Council of the European Union (2012l) 'Counter-terrorism coordinator: Annual report on the implementation of the EU Counter-Terrorism Strategy'. 16471/12 ADD 1 REV 1, 7 December.

Council of the European Union (2012m) 'EU Counter-terrorism coordinator: EU counter-terrorism strategy discussion paper'. 9990/12, 23 May.

Council of the European Union (2013) 'Proposal for a Directive of the European Parliament and of the Council on the conditions of entry and residence of third-country nationals for the purposes of seasonal employment: Comparative table'. 6312/13, 12 February.

Eurojust (2012) *Annual Report 2011* (The Hague: Eurojust).

European Asylum Support Office (EASO) (2012a) 'EASO country of origin information report on Afghanistan – Insurgent strategies: Intimidation and targeted violence against Afghans', Valetta, December.

European Asylum Support Office (EASO) (2012b) 'EASO work programme 2013'. Valetta, December.

European Asylum Support Office (EASO) (2013) 'EASO newsletter'. Valetta, January/February.

European Commission (2011) 'The global approach to migration and mobility'. *COM*(2011) 743 final, 18 November.

European Commission (2012a) 'Annual report on immigration and asylum'. *COM*(2012) 250, 30 May.

© 2013 The Author(s) JCMS: Journal of Common Market Studies © 2013 John Wiley & Sons Ltd

European Commission (2012b) 'Statement by EU Commissioner Cecilia Malmström on the initialling of the EU–Turkey Readmission Agreement'. MEMO/12/477, 21 June.

European Commission (2012c) 'Second biannual report on the functioning of the Schengen area'. *COM*(2012) 686, 23 November.

European Commission (2012d) 'Progress report from the Commission to the European Parliament and the Council on the development of the second generation Schengen Information System (SIS II)'. *COM*(2012) 587, 19 October.

European Commission (2013) 'Evaluation of the EU policy cycle on serious and organised crime 2011–2013'. *SWD*(2013) 17, 24 January.

European Court of Justice (2012) 'Judgment of the Court in Case-278/12 PPU, *Atiqullah Adil* v *Minister voor Immigratie, Integratie en Asiel*', 19 July. Available at: «http://curia.europa.eu/juris/celex.jsf?celex=62012CJ0278&lang1=en&type=NOT&ancre=».

European Network for Technical Co-operation on the Application of the Dublin II Regulation (European Network) (2013) 'Dublin II Regulation – Lives on hold: European Comparative Report'. Brussels, January.

European Parliament (2012a) 'News release: Schengen: MEPs angry at Council attack on democratic powers', Strasbourg, 12 June.

European Parliament (2012b) 'News release: EP decides to suspend cooperation with Council on five JHA dossiers until Schengen question is resolved', Strasbourg, 14 June.

European Parliament/Council of the European Union (2012a) 'Decision 281/2012/EU [. . .] of 29 March 2012 amending Decision No. 573/2007/EC establishing the European Refugee Fund for the period 2008 to 2013 as part of the general programme "Solidarity and Management of Migration Flows"'. OJ L 92, 30 March.

European Parliament/Council of the European Union (2012b) 'Regulation (EU) 1215/2012 [. . .] of 12 December 2012 on jurisdiction and the recognition and enforcement of judgments in civil and commercial matters (recast)'. OJ L 351, 20 December.

European Parliament/Council of the European Union (2012c) 'Regulation (EU) 650/2012 [. . .] of 4 July 2012 on jurisdiction, applicable law, recognition and enforcement of decisions and acceptance and enforcement of authentic instruments in matters of succession and on the creation of a European Certificate of Succession'. OJ L 201, 27 July.

European Parliament/Council of the European Union (2012d) 'Directive 2012/29/EU [. . .] of 25 October 2012 establishing minimum standards on the rights, support and protection of victims of crime, and replacing Council Framework Decision 2001/220/JHA'. OJ L 315, 14 November.

European Parliament/Council of the European Union (2012e) 'Directive 2012/13/EU [. . .] of 22 May 2012 on the right to information in criminal proceedings'. OJ L 142, 1 June.

Europol (2012a) 'Europol Review 2011'. The Hague, September.

Europol (2012b) 'Europol's Budgetary Requirements in 2013'. File 618015, The Hague, 9 July.

Eurostat (2012) 'Asylum applicants and first instance decisions on asylum applications: Third quarter of 2012'. Data in focus, 14/2012.

Frontex (2013) 'FRAN Quarterly, Issue 3, July–September 2012'. Warsaw, January.

House of Commons, European Union Scrutiny Committee (2013) 'The 2014 Block Optout: Engaging with Parliament, Thirty-seventh Report of Session 2012–13'. HC 798, 22 March.

United Nations High Commission for Refugees (UNHCR) (2012) 'Moving Forward on Asylum in the EU: UNHCR's Recommendations to Ireland for Its EU Presidency' (Brussels: UNHCR).

DOI: 10.1111/jcms.12049

Legal Developments

FABIAN AMTENBRINK
Erasmus University Rotterdam

Introduction

In the view of some, 2012 should first and foremost be remembered as the year in which the European Union (EU) received the Noble Peace Prize. In the opinion of the Nobel Committee: 'The union and its forerunners have for over six decades contributed to the advancement of peace and reconciliation, democracy and human rights in Europe'.[1] It can hardly be denied that the gradual juridification of the idea(l) of the building of Europe through concrete steps, starting with the signing of the Treaty establishing the European Coal and Steel Community (ECSC) in May 1952, has made a – if not *the* most important – contribution in this regard. The geographic advancing of the principles and rules on which European integration was built took place mainly, albeit not exclusively, through the accession of new countries to the European Communities (and later EU). The Union continued on this path also in 2012, as a referendum in Croatia paved the way for its accession to the EU in 2013 and, moreover, candidate status was formally granted to Serbia. The advances also continue on a more substantive level, as Monar's contribution to this issue on developments in the sphere of justice and home affairs highlights.

However, arguably more than anything else, 2012 will be marked as yet another year in which the EU was largely preoccupied with crisis management, as well as the continued reinforcement of economic policy co-ordination in the eurozone and financial market supervision. The Union's and Member States' activities raise profound legal questions *inter alia* concerning the distribution of competences between them and the democratic nature of economic policy in the eurozone. What is more, the continuing debt crisis and – somewhat paradoxically – also the solutions that are sought have triggered, at least in some countries, a much more fundamental debate about the viability of the European project in its present form and the desirability of EU membership. These considerations justify focusing this contribution on legal developments in the area of economic governance in the eurozone and financial market supervision in the EU.

With regard to the former, on 30 January, the Treaty on Stability, Coordination and Governance in the European Union (the 'Fiscal Compact') was signed by all but two Member States, signalling not only the determination of the eurozone members to tighten the reins on economic policy co-ordination, but at the same time the division in the Union that led the United Kingdom and the Czech Republic not to sign. As such, the implications of the Fiscal Compact may reach far beyond its perceived substance.[2] Only a few days

---

[1] Announcement of 12 October 2012. Available at: «http://nobelpeaceprize.org/en_GB/laureates/laureates-2012/announce-2012/».

[2] The Fiscal Compact is not further discussed in this contribution. For further discussion, see Craig (2012) and Hodson's contribution to this issue.

© 2013 The Author(s) JCMS: Journal of Common Market Studies © 2013 John Wiley & Sons Ltd, 9600 Garsington Road, Oxford OX4 2DQ, UK and 350 Main Street, Malden, MA 02148, USA

later, the Treaty establishing the European Stability Mechanism (the 'ESM Treaty') was signed, replacing the European Financial Stabilization Mechanism (EFSM) – the temporary financial rescue mechanism that had been born out of necessity in 2010 to allow for financial assistance for Ireland and Portugal.[3] Similar to the Fiscal Compact, the implications of the ESM Treaty reach beyond its substantive provisions as it raises questions concerning the interpretation of fundamental principles governing European economic and monetary union (EMU) and, moreover, in the view of some, strikes at the heart of national parliamentary budgetary autonomy. In fact, by the end of 2012 several highest national (constitutional) courts in the Member States had reviewed the constitutionality of the ESM Treaty. Moreover, the Court of Justice of the European Union (CJEU) had to evaluate the compatibility of this treaty with Union law on a reference by the Irish Supreme Court, thereby providing important clues for the interpretation of key provisions governing economic governance in the eurozone, such as the prohibition of monetary financing and the no bail-out clause.

The first part of this contribution will therefore discuss the CJEU judgment on the ESM Treaty and the approach to the treaty by some national highest (constitutional) courts with references to decisions by the German Federal Constitutional Court and the Estonian Supreme Court. In the second, shorter part of this contribution, the focus shifts to the major developments that have taken place in 2012 towards the establishment of a banking union.[4] The political agreement on the establishment of a single supervisory mechanism (SSM) with the European Central Bank (ECB) at the helm not only constitutes a major step towards the centralization of banking supervision in the internal financial market; it is also directly linked to the establishment of the ESM, at least in the view of the Union. Both the building of an integrated financial framework as well as an integrated budgetary framework (of which a financial support mechanism may be considered a part) form 'essential building blocks' for 'a stable and prosperous EMU' (Van Rompuy, 2012, p. 3).

I. Judicial Review of New Economic Governance in the Eurozone

The Permanent European Financial Rescue Mechanism in a Nutshell

While the initial financial assistance granted to Greece was made possible by means of bilateral loans by the Member States, shortly thereafter a structured mechanism was set up based on Article 122(2) Treaty on the Functioning of the European Union (TFEU) in the shape of the EFSM.[5] Linked to that was the setting-up of the European Financial Stability Facility (EFSF) in October 2010 through the establishment of a *société anonyme* under Luxembourg law and a framework agreement between the eurozone Member States and the EFSF. The EFSM and EFSF – both of which became operational through the granting of financial assistance under strict conditionality to Ireland and Portugal – were only meant to function as temporary rescue mechanisms. As the crisis lingered on and the need for further rescue measures became very real, in October 2010 the heads of state and government decided to create a permanent crisis mechanism. As the compatibility of such

---

[3] On this mechanism, see Amtenbrink (2012).
[4] See also Howarth and Quaglia's contribution to this issue.
[5] See Council Regulation 407/2010, OJ 2010, L 118/1.

© 2013 The Author(s) JCMS: Journal of Common Market Studies © 2013 John Wiley & Sons Ltd

an instrument with Union law was believed to be uncertain, a clarification of the TFEU in this regard was considered desirable – not least from a political point of view. To this end, a new paragraph 3 was added to Article 136 TFEU by means of the simplified treaty revision procedure provided for in Article 48(6) TFEU.[6] Similar to the regular amendment procedure, this type of treaty revision requires ratification by the signatory Member States in accordance with their constitutional requirements. Signed by the 17 eurozone Member States in February 2012, the ESM Treaty finally entered into force on 8 October 2012. The ESM not only replaced the EFSM, but also the EFSF, although the latter will remain operational until its outstanding loans and bonds have been repaid.

The objective of the ESM Treaty is to provide financial support ('stability support'), under strict conditionality, to eurozone Member States 'which are experiencing, or are threatened by, severe financing problems, if indispensable to safeguard the financial stability of the euro area as a whole and of its Member States' (Article 3, ESM Treaty). The capital stock of the ESM held by the eurozone Member States amounts to €700,000 million, although initially only the 'paid-in shares' of €80,000 million have to be actually forwarded by the Member States (Article 8, ESM Treaty).[7] The remaining €620,000 million (the so-called 'callable shares') only has to be forwarded in case of a unanimous decision by the ESM Board of Governors (Article 9, ESM Treaty). The liability of the ESM Member States is limited, in all circumstances, to their share in the authorized capital stock at its issue price, and Member States are not liable for the obligations of the ESM (Article 8(5), ESM Treaty). Losses that arise from ESM operations are first of all charged against the reserve fund and thereafter against the paid-in capital and, in case this is still not sufficient to cover the losses, against the authorized unpaid capital which is then called in (Article 25, ESM Treaty).

The ESM can grant (precautionary) stability support to Member States subject to economic policy conditionality.[8] For this purpose it is entitled to raise funds by 'issuing financial instruments or by entering into financial or other agreements or arrangements with ESM Members, financial institutions or other third parties' (Articles 3 and 14–18, ESM Treaty). The lending capacity of the ESM is €500,000 million.[9] Spain became the first eurozone Member State to be granted financial assistance by the ESM for the recapitalization of its financial sector based on an agreement under the EFSF of July 2012 for up to €100,000 million.

In principle, financial assistance is granted by a unanimous decision of the ESM Board of Governors, which consists of the finance ministers of the ESM Member States.[10] This body is also in principle responsible for determining the economic policy conditionality attached to any financial assistance, whereby the European Commission can be mandated

---

[6] Council Decision 2011/199, OJ 2011, L 91/1.
[7] The capital subscription of the Member States is based on a contribution key included in Annex 1, ESM Treaty.
[8] This can include precautionary financial assistance in the form of a precautionary conditioned credit line or an enhanced conditions credit line (Article 14), loans (Article 16), loans for the specific purpose of recapitalizing the financial institutions of an ESM Member State (Article 15) or a primary or secondary market support facility (Articles 17 and 18).
[9] Together with the EFSF, which in the transitional period could enter into new operations until mid-2013, the total lending capacity amounts to €700,000 million.
[10] Moreover, according to Article 5(3), ESM Treaty: 'The European Commission is in charge of economic and monetary affairs and the President of the ECB, as well as the President of the Euro Group (if he or she is not the Chairperson or a Governor) may participate in the meetings of the Board of Governors as observers'. Also representatives of non-eurozone Member States and of international organizations can participate on an ad hoc basis without a voting right.

© 2013 The Author(s) JCMS: Journal of Common Market Studies © 2013 John Wiley & Sons Ltd

to negotiate such conditions in liaison with the ECB, which in the end takes the shape of a memorandum of understanding with the ESM Member State in question (Articles 5(6) and 13, ESM Treaty).[11]

The ESM Treaty also foresees an emergency voting procedure that deviates from the unanimity requirement normally applicable for granting financial assistance. Where the European Commission and ECB conclude 'that a failure to urgently adopt a decision to grant or implement financial assistance [. . .] would threaten the economic and financial sustainability of the euro area' the adoption of a decision to grant assistance is taken by a qualified majority of 85 per cent of the votes cast. This special procedure is interesting in a couple of regards. First, the abrogation of the unanimity requirement means that Member States with a larger number of shares in the ESM effectively have greater influence on the decision as Article 4(7) of the ESM Treaty makes clear that the voting rights of each member are equal to the number of shares allocated to it in the authorized capital stock of the ESM. This rule effectively amounts to a weighing of Member States' votes in favour of the larger Member States.[12] In the context of the ratification of the ESM Treaty, the voting procedure applicable in the emergency procedure has led to considerable debates in a number of smaller Member States and, as will be discussed below, in the case of Estonia has also become a central issue in a case before the highest national court. The emergency procedure puts the European Commission and the ECB in a key position to decide on the urgency of the financial situation in an ESM Member State. Considering the factors – namely contagion and instability in the eurozone – that have led to the granting of financial assistance, for example, to Greece, Ireland, Portugal and Cyprus, one may wonder whether there was a threat to the economic and financial sustainability of the eurozone in all past instances of financial assistance. The decision to grant assistance in those cases suggest that the *emergency* procedure may actually become the norm.

Similar to the bilateral loans initially granted to Greece and the establishment of the EFSM and EFSF, the establishment of the permanent rescue mechanism has also become the subject of criticism, for reasons further explored below, in several challenges before national highest (constitutional) courts and – by means of the preliminary ruling procedure – before the CJEU.

Case C-370/12 Pringle[13]

Given the controversies at the European and national levels surrounding the amendment of Article 136 TFEU and the adoption of the ESM outside the Union treaty framework, it is hardly surprising that these measures soon became subject to review by the CJEU. The actual dispute underlying the *Pringle* case was initiated by Thomas Pringle, an independent member of the Irish lower House of Parliament, who originally brought a case before the Irish High Court against the European Council Decision 2011/199 amending Article 136 TFEU and against the ratification by Ireland of the ESM Treaty. When the High Court dismissed the action, Pringle appealed to the Irish Supreme Court, which decided to

[11] According to Article 12(1), 'conditionality may range from a macroeconomic adjustment programme to continuous respect of pre-established eligibility conditions'.
[12] See Annex II, ESM Treaty.
[13] Decision of 27 November 2012 [2012] ECR I-nyp.

© 2013 The Author(s) JCMS: Journal of Common Market Studies © 2013 John Wiley & Sons Ltd

halt proceedings and refer several questions to the CJEU regarding the interpretation and validity of the said decision and the compatibility of the ESM Treaty with primary Union law. The political and legal significance, as well as the urgency, of the case was highlighted by the fact that the European Court was deliberating in plenum and made use of the accelerated procedure provided for in the Statute of the CJEU (Article 23a). Moreover, 12 Member States submitted written observations, including the United Kingdom.

Not all aspects covered by the judgment can be addressed in the limited space available here. Hence, the focus is on the main substantive legal arguments submitted against the validity of the amendment of Article 136 TFEU and the ESM Treaty itself.[14] In fact, the judgment in this regard provides valuable insights into the distribution of competences in EMU and the scope of central provisions of Title VIII TFEU relating to economic and monetary policy governing the eurozone. In interpreting Union law, the CJEU basically had to deal with two issues: the validity of European Council Decision 2011/199 amending Article 136 TFEU; and the compatibility of the ESM Treaty with Union law – namely the central provisions of Title VIII TFEU.

With regard to the amendment of Article 136 TFEU by means of the simplified treaty amendment procedure provided for in Article 48(6) TFEU the main question was whether the new Paragraph 3 allowing for the establishment of a permanent financial rescue mechanism does not in effect encroach upon the exclusive right of the Union in the area of monetary policy and the competences of the Union pertaining to economic policy co-ordination. In fact, Article 48(6) TFEU explicitly excludes its application for the establishment of new competences. It was argued in this context that the stability of the eurozone as pursued by the ESM Treaty really amounts to the preservation of the stability of the single currency, which is an exclusive task of the ECB as monetary policy in the eurozone is an exclusive competence of the Union (Article 3(1) TEU). However, this argument was rejected by the CJEU, which considered that the stability of the eurozone is a different objective than that referred to in Article 127(1) TFEU describing the primary objective of the ECB, even if an economic policy measure such as the granting of financial assistance may 'have indirect effects on the stability of the euro'.[15] The ECJ rejected the idea that the granting of such assistance to a Member State amounts to monetary policy.[16] In fact, in the Court's view the ESM 'falls within the area of economic policy'. However, this is not to say that the Court considered that its establishment curtails any competences of the Union in the area of the co-ordination of the Member States' economic policies. In fact this was denied by the CJEU, which first of all emphasized that given the TFEU's restriction of the empowerment of the EU to economic policy co-ordination, the Treaties 'do not confer any specific power on the Union to establish a stability mechanism'.[17] In this context the Court rightly pointed to Articles 2(3) and 5(1) TFEU, which 'restrict the role of the Union in the area of economic policy to the adoption of coordinating measures'.[18] Yet, in light of these considerations one may wonder what the European Court

---

[14] This is not to say that these issues are not interrelated. For a complete review of the judgment, see, for example, Borger (2013).
[15] Judgment, paragraph 56.
[16] Judgment, paragraph 57.
[17] Judgment, paragraph 64.
[18] Judgment, paragraph 64.

© 2013 The Author(s) JCMS: Journal of Common Market Studies © 2013 John Wiley & Sons Ltd

would have made of the far-reaching legal obligations for the eurozone Member States introduced by means of secondary Union law in the shape of the Six Pack and Two Pack regulations, which can hardly be explained with reference to co-ordination measures (Amtenbrink, 2012). However, this legal regime was clearly not the subject matter of the preliminary ruling procedure.

In the light of the absence of an exclusive or shared competence in the area of economic policy, the CJEU considered that the Member States were indeed 'entitled to conclude an agreement between themselves for the establishment of a stability mechanism of the kind envisaged by Article 1 of Decision 2011/19'.[19] The CJEU in this context did not follow the argument that the new Article 136(3) TFEU increases the competences of the Union in the area of economic policy contrary to Article 48(6) TFEU, and did not perceive this provision as a legal basis (competence). What follows from this is that more than anything arguably Article 136(3) TFEU bears witness to the deep uncertainty among the governments of the Member States at the time of the drafting of the provisions on the ESM about the legal feasibility of a permanent financial rescue mechanism and that has led to the inclusion of a primarily declaratory statement in this provision.

The Court was however quick to emphasize that the Member States under no circumstances may disregard their duties under Union law and thus may not act contrary to the latter. In this context for the first, but certainly not for the last time, in its judgment the Court built a link between the legality of the ESM and the strict conditionality under which financial assistance may be granted to an ESM Member State. In fact, for the Court the reason for this conditionality is precisely 'in order to ensure that that mechanism will operate in a way that will comply with European Union law, including the measures adopted by the Union in the context of the coordination of the Member States' economic policies'.[20] This emphasis on the conditionality attached to financial support, which corresponds with the requirement laid down in Article 136(3) TFEU, runs like a red thread through the judgment and is used by the Court as a major argument in support of the compatibility of the ESM Treaty with Union law. Interestingly in this context, the ESM Treaty is different from, say, the Fiscal Compact[21] as it does not dedicate a provision to the relationship with Union law.[22]

Similar to what was argued for the new Paragraph 3 of Article 136 TFEU, the CJEU also rejected the argument that the ESM Treaty itself amounts to the conduct of monetary policy or an intrusion on the Union's competences pertaining to economic policy co-ordination. The CJEU emphasized once more that the objective of the ESM is not to maintain price stability, but the financial stability of the eurozone as such, whereby any indirect effects of financial assistance on the rate of inflation are not sufficient to establish a price stability objective.[23] Technically speaking, this view may be correct. Nevertheless, from a practical point of view the distinction that the CJEU makes in favour of the ESM Treaty between economic and monetary policy may be somewhat artificial. It is

[19] Judgment, paragraph 64. The CJEU specifically ruled out as legal basis Article 122(2) TFEU, which had been previously used to establish the EFSM, Article 143(2) TFEU, which applies to non-eurozone Member States only, and Article 352 TFEU, which does not create an obligation on the part of the Member States to make use of it.
[20] Judgment, paragraph 69.
[21] See Article 2 of the Fiscal Compact.
[22] See, however, Article 13(3) ESM Treaty on the Memorandum of Understanding underlying any financial assistance, which must be consistent with the measures of economic policy co-ordination under the TFEU.
[23] Judgment, paragraph 97.

© 2013 The Author(s) JCMS: Journal of Common Market Studies © 2013 John Wiley & Sons Ltd

interesting to note that the ECB officials have gone on the record arguing that 'the preservation of financial stability is an integral part of our role as [the] central bank, serving ultimately to fulfill our mandate'.[24] Moreover, the direct link between monetary policy and the stability support by the ESM arguably becomes clear from the fact that the ECB has made interventions in the sovereign bond market as part of its outright monetary transactions programme subject to an application of the Member State in question for financial assistance from the ESM.

Furthermore, the CJEU also considered that the conclusion of an international agreement in the shape of the ESM Treaty does not intrude upon Article 122(2) TFEU or the EFSM regulation based on this provision. Interestingly, in this context the Court emphasized that the Union can continue to exercise its own competences laid down in Article 122(2) TFEU 'in defence of the common interest'.[25] Conversely, the Court stressed that 'nothing in Article 122 TFEU indicates that the Union has exclusive competence to grant financial assistance to a Member State', thereby emphasizing that under the ESM Treaty such assistance is granted by the Member States.[26] This seems to suggest that the Council, on a proposal from the European Commission, could utilize Article 122(2) TFEU in parallel or in addition to the financial assistance granted by the ESM. In the first instance this would amount to a Union measure, whereas in the latter this would be considered a concerted action by the ESM Member States acting outside – albeit not contrary to – the Union framework.

The CJEU also denied the argument brought forward by the claimant in the main proceedings that the conditionality attached to financial assistance granted by the ESM would effectively undermine the Union's competence for the co-ordination of economic policy (Articles 2(3), 119–21 and 126 TFEU). In the view of the Court, the strict conditionality that is attached to financial assistance 'does not constitute an instrument for the coordination of the economic policies of the Member States, but is intended to ensure that the activities of the ESM are compatible with, inter alia, Article 125 TFEU and the coordinating measures adopted by the Union', even if it comes in the shape of a macro-economic adjustment programme.[27] One may observe here that while it is true that the aim of conditionality is not to co-ordinate policies of ESM Member States, it also cannot be denied that on an individual basis conditionality does amount to an instrument to influence the economic policy of a Member State.

Finally, having considered that the provisions of the ESM Treaty do not encroach upon existing competences of the Union, the CJEU turned to what may be considered the core of many legal academic debates since 2010 – namely whether and to what extent the ad hoc and permanent measures that have been taken in response to the eurozone debt crisis are compatible with the central legal provisions of Title VIII TFEU governing economic policy co-ordination in EMU and especially Articles 123 and 125 TFEU.[28]

With regard to Article 123 TFEU, in the view of the CJEU financial assistance which one or more Member States provide to another Member State is simply not covered by this

---

[24] See Asmussen (2012).
[25] Judgment, paragraph 106.
[26] Judgment, paragraphs 119–20.
[27] Judgment, paragraphs 110–14.
[28] With regard to this debate, see Amtenbrink (2011). For a complete review of the judgment, see, for example, Borger (2013).

© 2013 The Author(s) JCMS: Journal of Common Market Studies © 2013 John Wiley & Sons Ltd

provision, which prohibits overdraft facilities and other types of credit facility with the ECB or with national central banks in favor of Union or national government institutions and, moreover, prohibits the purchase by the ECB or national central banks of debt instruments on the primary market.[29] Indeed, as Advocate General Kokott summarized in her view on the case: 'Article 123 TFEU denies to the Member States funding from the central banks'.[30] Moreover, the Court observes that 'there is no basis for the view that the funds provided by the Member States to the ESM might be derived from financial instruments prohibited by Article 123(1) TFEU'.[31]

In the view of the CJEU financial assistance is also not in breach of the much-cited no bail-out clause of Article 125 TFEU.[32] Here the CJEU applied mainly a literal and purposive method of interpretation to conclude that the 'article does not prohibit either the Union or the Member States from granting any form of financial assistance whatever to another Member State'.[33] Indeed, Article 125 TFEU only prohibits the Union or Member States being liable or assuming liability for the *existing* commitments of a Member State.[34]

With reference to its aims and objectives, the CJEU emphasized that Article 125 TFEU intends to subject Member States to market discipline and possible punishment by markets in the case of a loss of credibility. Put differently, this provision is supposed to ensure that Member States remain responsible for their public debt and (re-)finance themselves under market conditions, whereby a loss of market confidence in economic policy may result in a rise of the risk premium which that Member State has to bear. In the view of the Court Article 125 TFEU effectively bars 'the Union and the Member States from granting financial assistance as a result of which the incentive of the recipient Member State to conduct a sound budgetary policy is diminished'.[35] Article 125 TFEU is thus supposed to prevent the emergence of moral hazard in EMU. Yet, while the CJEU emphasized that 'the activation of financial assistance by means of a stability mechanism such as the ESM is not compatible with Article 125 TFEU *unless* it is indispensable for the safeguarding of the financial stability of the euro area as a whole and subject to strict conditions',[36] it fails to explain how in real life strict conditionality can be a sufficient safeguard to rule out moral hazard. In fact, it may be argued that the potential negative (economic) consequences for the eurozone as a whole resulting from the quasi-insolvency of an ESM Member State may make it effectively impossible to ever really enforce conditionality. Given the danger of contagion it is at least questionable, whether and at what point eurozone Member States would be willing to refuse (further) financial assistance in the case of non-compliance of an ESM Member State with conditionality.

With regard to the different types of financial assistance provided for in the ESM Treaty (Articles 14–18), the CJEU rightly pointed out that the granting of credit lines and loans amounts to 'the creation of a new debt, owed to the ESM by that recipient Member State, which remains responsible for its commitments to its creditors in respect of its

---

[29] Judgment, paragraphs 125–6.
[30] View of the AG Kokott delivered on 26 October 2012, paragraph 129.
[31] Judgment, paragraph 127. Arguably this would be the case if such funds would come in the shape of debt instruments.
[32] In favour of such a breach in the case of the bilateral loans to Greece, see, for example, Jeck (2010); Kube and Reimer (2010). Rejecting such a breach is, for example, Herrmann (2010, 2013).
[33] Judgment, paragraph 130.
[34] The Court also points to the less strict wording of Article 125 TFEU compared to Article 123 TFEU.
[35] Judgment, paragraph 136.
[36] Emphasis added. Judgment, paragraph 136. Interestingly, the Court in this context finds support for its view in the ECB opinion on the draft of what became thereafter European Council Decision 2011/199.

© 2013 The Author(s) JCMS: Journal of Common Market Studies © 2013 John Wiley & Sons Ltd

existing debts'.[37] Also the purchasing of bonds of an ESM Member State on the primary and even on the secondary market amounts to a granting of a new loan rather than the assuming of an existing liability of the Member State in question.[38] In the view of the Court, '[d]irect support of the creditors is prohibited, while indirect support, which arises as a result of the support to the debtor Member State, is not prohibited'.[39] Also here the Court emphasized that any financial assistance is granted only exceptionally and subject to strict conditionality.[40]

Overall, in defence of the ESM Treaty and its compatibility with primary Union law the CJEU relied on two main arguments: that financial assistance does not amount to a liability of the ESM Member States for the commitments of one of its members; and that financial support is only granted in exceptional circumstances in which the stability of the eurozone as such is in danger and subject to strict conditionality. With this the CJEU defined clear constitutional markers both for the operation of the existing system as well as the shape of any future system. With regard to the ESM this means that in granting financial assistance sufficient attention must be given not only to the formulation of the conditions under which such support is granted, but arguably also the observation of such conditions by the recipient Member State. Following the reasoning of the Court, non-compliance with such conditions would result in a situation in which financial assistance is no longer compatible with Article 125 TFEU.[41] This puts a lot of pressure on the Union institutions and Member States to ensure that conditionality is indeed enforced. What is more, the Court's emphasis on conditionality arguably has implications for the scope of the current proposals for the establishment of a 'Genuine Economic and Monetary Union' and the plans of the European Commission for the establishment – in the long term – of a so-called 'redemption fund' and the collectivization of government debts in the eurozone.

II. The ESM Treaty before Highest National (Constitutional) Courts

As has been observed above, the CJEU has not been the only court reviewing the ESM Treaty. In fact, the 2012 decisions by the German Federal Constitutional Court (*Bundesverfassungsgericht*)[42] and by the Estonian Supreme Court (*Riigikohus*)[43] highlight that the Irish Supreme Court has only been only one of several national highest courts addressing the validity of the amendment of Article 136 TFEU and of the ESM Treaty with primary Union law. Most importantly, these cases highlight the impact the new system of economic governance can have on the constitutional legal orders of the participating Member States. The central issue in considering the constitutionality of the ESM has been the role of national parliaments and thus the impact of the European system on national parliamentary democracy.[44] Indeed, it was not just in these Member States where the

---

[37] Judgment, paragraph 139.
[38] Judgment, paragraph 141. See also Advocate General Kokott, paragraph 158.
[39] Judgment, paragraph 148.
[40] Judgment, paragraphs 142–3.
[41] For a broader discussion of non-compliance in the EU, see Falkner's contribution to this issue.
[42] Decision of the Federal Constitutional Court of 12 September 2012 – 2 BvR 1390/12, 2 BvR 1421/12, 2 BvR 1438/12, 2 BvR 1439/12, 2 BvR 1440/12, 2 BvE 6/12 –.
[43] Case No. 3-4-1-6-12.
[44] In the case of Germany, the *Bundesverfassungsgericht* already had to address similar issues in the context of a challenge of the constitutionality of the bilateral financial aid to Greece and the German guarantees provided under the EFSM. See BVerfGE 129, 124 (decision of 7 September 2011, Az. 2 BvR 987/10, 2 BvR 1485/10, 2 BvR 1099/10).

criticism could be heard that budgetary rights of national parliaments are effectively hollowed out thanks to parliamentary approval of the general transfer of large amounts of funds to a European body that is thereafter in charge of deciding on the contribution of such funds. In a best-case scenario such a curbing of parliamentary rights could require a constitutional amendment, whereas in a worst-case scenario the establishment of such an effect on the right of parliament could form an insurmountable constitutional barrier. In the case of the German Basic Law of 1949, the principle of democracy, and with it fundamental rights of parliament, are protected by an eternity clause (*Ewigkeitsklausel*) that effectively excludes their amendment.[45]

It is thus hardly surprising that in its 2011 decision on the bilateral loan to Greece the German Federal Constitutional Court emphasized that even in an intergovernmental governance system national parliaments must retain control over fundamental budgetary decisions.[46] The Court confirmed this approach in its decision of September 2012 concerning an application for interim relief against several German federal laws effectively implementing the ESM. With reference to its earlier decision, the Court pointed out that:

> the relevant factor for adherence to the principles of democracy is whether the German Bundestag remains the place in which autonomous decisions on revenue and expenditure are made, including those with regard to international and European liabilities. [. . .] If essential budget questions relating to revenue and expenditure were decided without the mandatory approval of the German Bundestag, or if supranational legal obligations were created without a corresponding decision by free will of the Bundestag, parliament would find itself in the role of mere subsequent enforcement and could no longer exercise its overall budgetary responsibility as part of its right to decide on the budget.[47]

Moreover, the Court made clear that:

> the German Bundestag may not transfer its budgetary responsibility to other entities by means of imprecise budgetary authorisations [and] it may not deliver itself up to any mechanisms with financial effect which [. . .] may result in incalculable burdens with budget significance without prior mandatory consent, whether these are expenses or losses of revenue.[48]

While in its summary review as part of the procedure for interim relief the Court in the end concluded that the ESM Treaty takes account of the provisions in the German constitution that in essence safeguard parliamentary democracy, its more general reflections on the role of a national parliament can be interpreted as a word of caution against any further stripping of the rights of national parliaments for as long as the current constitutional structure of the EU has not been replaced by a more federal structure in which the rights of national parliaments and of the European Parliament are redefined accordingly.

With regard to parliamentary involvement, problems may not only arise in the context of an extensive interpretation of the (financial) commitments of Member States under the ESM Treaty, the professional secrecy rules or the suspension of voting rights of members of the Board of Governors, but also from the decision-making procedures of the Board of

---

[45] See Article 79(3) in conjunction with Articles 20(1) and 20(2) and 38(1), German Basic Law.
[46] BVerfGE 129, 124, paragraph 124.
[47] Extracts from the decision of the Federal Constitutional Court of 12 September 2012 – 2 BvR 1390/12, 2 BvR 1421/12, 2 BvR 1438/12, 2 BvR 1439/12, 2 BvR 1440/12, 2 BvE 6/12 –, paragraph 211.
[48] Decision of the Federal Constitutional Court of 12 September 2012, paragraph 212.

© 2013 The Author(s) JCMS: Journal of Common Market Studies © 2013 John Wiley & Sons Ltd

Governors.[49] Here the application of the 85 per cent majority requirement in case of the application of the above-mentioned emergency procedure effectively threatens to diminish the influence of parliaments of ESM Member States with a relatively small share in the capital of the ESM. While omitted by the *Bundesverfassungsgericht*,[50] the emergency procedure did take centre stage in the constitutional challenge of the ESM Treaty before the Estonian Supreme Court. In fact the provision was considered to interfere with the financial competence of the Estonian parliament, the principle of a democratic state subject to the rule of law and with the state's financial sovereignty.[51] Based only on an analysis of the compatibility of the aims of the ESM Treaty with the Estonian Constitution *en banc*, the Supreme Court came to the conclusion that the interference of Article 4(4) ESM Treaty with the Estonian Constitution:

> is justified by substantial constitutional values. [The] obligation arising from the preamble to and §14 of the Constitution to guarantee the protection of fundamental rights and freedoms [and] that Article 4(4) of the [ESM] Treaty provides for an appropriate, necessary and reasonable measure for the achievement of the objective [i.e.] to guarantee the efficiency of the ESM also in case the states are unable to make a unanimous decision to eliminate a threat to the economic and financial sustainability of the euro area.[52]

III. Towards a Banking Union

As was observed in the 2010 *JCMS Annual Review* (Amtenbrink, 2011), the global economic and financial crisis triggered a major overhaul of the Union's financial market regulatory and supervisory framework. Based on the recommendations of the De Larosière Report, the previous cumbersome Lamfalussy framework was replaced by a new European system of financial supervision, consisting mainly of three new supervisory authorities (ESAs), whereby the aim was the creation of an integrated network of national Union supervisory authorities, rather than a centralized supervisory authority. However, in the course of 2012, both the President of the European Commission as well as the President of the European Council could be seen launching ideas for a further centralization of financial market supervision. European Commission President Barroso (2012) argued in favour of 'the creation of a banking union with a single regulator, common rules and better policy coordination'. This approach was thereafter supported in a June 2012 report entitled 'Towards a Genuine Economic and Monetary Union'[53] produced by the President of the European Council and endorsed by the European Council, the Eurogroup, the European Commission and the ECB. The report called for an 'integrated financial framework to ensure financial stability in particular in the euro area and minimise the cost of bank failures to European citizens' (Van Rompuy, 2012, p. 3).[54]

---

[49] The German Court mainly examined Article 8(5) ESM Treaty on the liability of ESM Member States and Articles 32(5), 34 and 35(2) ESM Treaty on the professional secrecy of the members of the Board of Governors – in both instances applying a restrictive interpretation of these provisions in arguing that the rights of the German parliament are safeguarded.

[50] Germany's share in the ESM capital effectively gives it a right to block any decisions from being taken.

[51] Decision No 3–4–1–6-12, paragraph 153.

[52] Decision No 3–4–1–6-12, paragraphs 169, 209, 179. See also the dissenting opinions of several judges attached to the judgment.

[53] See also Howarth and Quaglia's contribution to this issue.

[54] See also the revised version of this report from 5 December 2012, available at: «http://www.consilium.europa.eu/uedocs/cms_Data/docs/pressdata/en/ec/134069.pdf».

© 2013 The Author(s) JCMS: Journal of Common Market Studies © 2013 John Wiley & Sons Ltd

Based on a September 2012 European Commission proposal for the establishment of a single supervisory mechanism (SSM) for the banking sector,[55] and after the Ecofin Council had agreed on a text in December 2012, in March 2013 a trilogue agreement on the creation of the SSM for the eurozone was reached between the European Parliament, the Council and the European Commission.[56]

At the core of the SSM lies the conferral to the ECB of specific supervisory tasks relating to the prudential supervision of credit institutions established in one of the eurozone Member States. For these Member States the ECB has exclusive competence to carry out supervisory tasks including, *inter alia*, the authorization of and the withdrawal of authorization of credit institutions; to act effectively as competent home state authority in the case of credit institutions that want to establish a branch or provide cross-border services in non-eurozone Member States;[57] to assess applications for the acquisition and disposal of qualified holdings in credit institutions except in the case of banking resolutions; to ensure compliance of credit institutions of prudential requirements (for example, reserve requirements and securitization) and supervisory reviews including stress tests (Article 4(1), SSM Proposal). The ECB is also in charge of applying all relevant Union law, including national legislation transposing EU directives, and in this context has the right to adopt guidelines and recommendations; take decisions subject to, and in compliance with Union law; and adopt regulations necessary to organize and specify the modalities for carrying out its tasks (Article 4(3), SSM Proposal).[58]

National supervisory authorities will continue to fulfil an important role in the SSM, especially with regard to less significant credit institutions established on their territory, but will also act as a sort of executive arm of the ECB in supervisory matters. With the exception of the authorization or withdrawal of authorization and the application for the acquisition and disposal of qualified holdings in credit institutions, the ECB in principle only directly carries out the supervisory tasks for significant credit institutions.[59] Significant credit institutions are those whose total value exceeds €30 billion, or for which the ration of their total assets over the gross domestic product of the Member State of establishment participating in the SSM exceeds 20 per cent of that credit institution, or for which the competent national authority has determined that they are of significant relevance with regard to the domestic economy.[60] Moreover, this also includes credit

---

[55] 'Proposal for a Council Regulation conferring specific tasks on the European Central Bank concerning policies relating to the prudential supervision of credit institutions', *COM* (2012) 511 final, as agreed upon by the Ecofin Council on 14 December (hereafter 'SSM Proposal'); 'Proposal for a Regulation of the European Parliament and of the Council amending Regulation (EU) No 1093/2010 establishing a European Supervisory Authority (European Banking Authority) as regards its interaction with Council Regulation (EU) [. . .] conferring specific tasks on the European Central Bank concerning policies relating to the prudential supervision of credit institutions', *COM* (2012) 512 final, as agreed upon by the Ecofin Council on 14 December.
[56] See statement by Commissioner Michel Barnier following the trilogue agreement on the creation of the single supervisory mechanism for the eurozone, 19 March 2013, MEMO 13/251.
[57] As namely provided by Directive 2006/48 relating to the taking up and pursuit of the business of credit institutions, OJ 2006 L 177/1 (as amended).
[58] See also Article 8. With regard to the role of the ECB in the area of systemic risks, see Article 4a(2)–(2c), SSM Proposal.
[59] Decisions on the authorization of a credit institution are taken based on a draft decision by the competent national supervisory authority, whereby in the case of the non-objection by the ECB within a specified period of time the decision is deemed to be adopted. Withdrawal of authorization can take place on the initiative of the CB or based on a proposal by the competent national authority. See Article 13, SSM Proposal.
[60] According to the proposal, regardless of their size, the ECB in any event always conducts the supervisory tasks for the three most significant credit institutions.

© 2013 The Author(s) JCMS: Journal of Common Market Studies © 2013 John Wiley & Sons Ltd

institutions for which public financial assistance has been requested or received directly from the EFSF or its successor, the ESM.[61] National competent authorities in principle remain in charge of direct supervision of less significant credit institutions (Article 5(6), SSM Proposal), albeit subject to an operational framework to be established by the ECB (Article 5(7), SSM Proposal).[62]

The ECB and the national competent authorities are subject to the duty of co-operation. National authorities are obliged to provide the ECB with the necessary information for the carrying out of its tasks and they are obliged to assist the ECB in fulfilling its tasks. In this context they are subject to the instructions given by the ECB (Article 5(2)–(3), SSM Proposal). The ECB not only has the right to request information from, *inter alia*, credit institutions established in the eurozone and persons belonging to them, but also has a general right of investigation and can carry out 'all necessary on-site inspections at the business premises of the institution under investigation' (Articles 9–11, SSM Proposal).

Non-eurozone Member States can decide to have their competent supervisory authorities enter into close co-operation with the ECB with the aim of having the latter exercise the supervisory tasks foreseen in the SSM (Article 6, SSM Proposal). In such circumstances, the national supervisory authorities of non-eurozone Member States must follow the instructions of the ECB relating to measures to be adopted by the national authority, whereby in the extreme case non-compliance can eventually result in the suspension or even termination of the close co-operation (Articles 5–6, SSM Proposal).

In organizational terms, in placing supervisory tasks with the ECB use is made of the possibility provided for in Article 127(6) TFEU according to which the Council can unanimously decide to 'confer specific tasks upon the European Central Bank concerning policies relating to the prudential supervision of credit institutions and other financial institutions with the exception of insurance undertakings'. Despite the drafters of the provisions on EMU having foreseen the possible transfer of supervisory powers to the ECB, the fact that this is currently actually put into practice is nevertheless remarkable considering the ongoing debate about the pros and cons of vesting micro-prudential supervisory powers in the monetary policy authority.[63]

In several places the SSM Proposal aims at addressing some major objections that have been raised against placing monetary policy and supervisory tasks in a single institution. Thus, the SSM Proposal explicitly states that the ECB independence also extents to its prudential supervisory tasks and thus also includes the members of the Supervisory Board (Article 16, SSM Proposal). A clear distinction between the monetary policy-related tasks and prudential supervision is made (Article 18(2), SSM Proposal), whereby the planning and execution of supervisory-related tasks is assigned to the new body in charge of preparing supervisory decisions, the so-called 'Supervisory Board'. The Board will consist of a chair and vice-chair, four representatives of the ECB not entrusted with any duties directly linked to monetary functions, and one representative

[61] See also Article 5(4), EES Proposal, with regard to credit institutions with banking subsidiaries in more than one SSM Member State.
[62] They are established in consultation with the national authorities and on the basis of a proposal from the Supervisory Board.
[63] For an instructive overview of the arguments for and against, see, for example, ECB (2001).

© 2013 The Author(s) JCMS: Journal of Common Market Studies © 2013 John Wiley & Sons Ltd

of the national supervisory authorities of the eurozone Member States and non-eurozone Member States acting in close co-operation with the ECB (Article 19(1), SSM Proposal). Yet, while the Board is supposed to carry out preparatory works regarding the ECB's supervisory tasks, including the drawing up of draft decisions, it is the Governing Board of the ECB that has to adopt these decisions (Article 19(3), SSM Proposal).

The SSM Proposal even includes two separate provisions on the accountability of the ECB *vis-à-vis* the European Parliament and the parliaments of the Member States participating in the SSM. Apart from reporting requirements, this accountability mainly takes the shape of the possibility of the European Parliament and national parliaments to invite the chair of the ECB Supervisory Board for discussions. There is a notable difference in wording in this context between the European Parliament, where the chair 'may, at the request of the European Parliament, be heard on the execution of its supervisory tasks by the competent committee' and a national parliament, which 'may invite the Chair or a member of the Supervisory Board to participate in an exchange of views in relation to the supervision of credit institutions in that Member State together with a representative of the national competent authority' (Articles 17(5) and 17aa(3), SSM Proposal). In the case of national parliaments it may be argued that an invitation does not as such create a legal obligation on the part of the invited party actually to appear. Moreover, national parliaments apparently are not supposed to question the chair of the Board on broader issues of prudential supervision in the eurozone not directly related to their own country. Yet, it is neither realistic to believe that the ECB would reject an invitation by a national parliament nor that national parliaments will necessarily confine themselves to prudential supervisory issues linked to their own country.

Conclusions

This year's review of legal developments in the EU has exclusively focused on issues linked to European economic and financial market governance. This admittedly one-sided focus is arguably justified mainly by the important implications for the future of the developments in these areas in 2012. With regard to the recent judgment by the CJEU in the *Pringle* case, it can be observed that it has been overlooked by non-legal scholars despite its implications that reach far beyond the ESM Treaty.

Indeed, at a time when the echo of the outrage in some quarters about the Member States' and EU's financial rescue of several eurozone Member States could still be heard, the CJEU has taken a clear position in favour of the compatibility of the ESM with Union law. In the view of the Court, neither the Union's competence to grant financial assistance to a Member State pursuant to Article 122(2) TFEU nor the prohibition of monetary financing (Article 123 TFEU) or the so-called 'no bail-out clause' (Article 125 TFEU) rule out the establishment of a permanent mechanism that in exceptional circumstances grants financial assistance subject to strict conditionality. While the arguments brought forward against a breach of existing provisions of primary Union law are conclusive, the question remains whether the application of conditionality that has been emphasized so strongly by the CJEU can really tame the moral hazard problem arising from the possibility of financial assistance to a Member State in financial distress. Arguably this problem arises regardless of whether legally speaking the Union or Member States take on the commitments of a Member State in financial

© 2013 The Author(s) JCMS: Journal of Common Market Studies © 2013 John Wiley & Sons Ltd

distress or not. Of course, one may argue that the ESM should not be taken for more than a safety net, the utilization of which should remain very rare indeed once the Six Pack and Two Pack regulations, as well as the Fiscal Compact, are fully operational. However, the fact that Member States were not entering new economic governance with a clean sheet (that is, without excessive deficits) means that for the time being financial assistance under the ESM will not remain so exceptional.

To be sure the approval of the ESM Treaty under Union law by the CJEU should not be mistaken as the end of all debates regarding the legality of such measures. As has been highlighted in this contribution, the substance of this mechanism and especially its effects on the position of national parliaments is causing (constitutional) tensions in several Member States. So far the national highest (constitutional) courts seem to have taken a Europe-friendly approach to the interpretation of the ESM Treaty and to the interpretation of their own constitution. However, it is not entirely excluded that in due course, as a result of the way in which the ESM may operate in practice with regard to the enforcement of conditionality, new challenges arise before national courts.

The adoption of the ESM Treaty is part of a broader strategy of the European Commission to work towards the establishment of what may be described as a more sustainable model of economic and monetary integration in the EU. Indeed, considering the direct impact that developments in the financial markets can have on developments in the economic and monetary sphere, the establishment of an SSM can be considered an integral part of an overall strategy to make economic and monetary policy in the eurozone more resilient. Putting the ECB at the helm of prudential supervision in the eurozone can hardly be considered an unexpected step in this context. Yet it remains to be seen how the ECB will deal with this *de facto* double mandate, especially in ensuring that prudential supervision considerations neither in practice nor in the all-important perception of the financial markets take precedence over its monetary policy objective.

References

Amtenbrink, F. (2011) 'Legal Developments'. *JCMS*, Vol. 49, No. S1, pp. 165–86.

Amtenbrink, F. (2012) 'Legal Developments'. *JCMS*, Vol. 50, No. S2, pp. 132–46.

Asmussen, J. (2012) 'Stability Guardians and Crisis Managers: Central Banking in Times of Crisis and Beyond'. Speech delivered at Goethe University, Frankfurt, 11 September. Available at: «http://www.ecb.int/press/key/date/2012/html/sp120911.en.html».

Barroso, J.M. (2012) 'Building Blocks for Deeper Integration'. Available at: «http://ec.europa.eu/commission_2010-2014/president/pdf/integration/index.html».

Borger, V. (2013) 'The ESM and the European Court's Predicament in *Pringle*'. *German Law Journal*, Vol. 14, No. 1, pp. 113–40. Available at: «http://www.germanlawjournal.com/index.php?pageID=11&artID=1498».

Craig, P. (2012) 'The Stability, Coordination and Governance Treaty: Principle, Politics and Pragmatism'. *European Law Review*, Vol. 37, pp. 231–48.

European Central Bank (ECB) (2001) 'The Role of Central Banks in Prudential Supervision' (Frankfurt a.M.: ECB). Available at: «http://www.ecb.int/pub/pdf/other/prudentialsupcbrole_en.pdf».

Herrmann, C. (2010) 'Griechische Tragödie – der währungsverfassungsrechtliche Rahmen für die Rettung, den Austritt oder den Ausschluss von überschuldeten Staaten aus dem Eurogebiet'. *Europäische Zeitschrift für Wirtschaftsrecht*, pp. 413–18.

© 2013 The Author(s) JCMS: Journal of Common Market Studies © 2013 John Wiley & Sons Ltd

Herrmann, C. (2013) 'Legal Aspects of the European Sovereign Debt Crisis'. *Hitotsubashi Journal of Law and Politics*, Vol. 41, pp. 25–40.

Jeck, T. (2010) 'EU-Rettungsschirm bricht EU-recht und deutsches Verfassungsrecht'. Available at: «http://www.cep.eu/fileadmin/user_upload/Kurzanalysen/Euro-Rettungsschirm/CEP-Studie _Euro-Rettungsschirm.pdf».

Kube, H. and Reimer, E. (2010) 'Grenzen des Europäischen Stabilitätsmechanismus'. *Neue Juristische Wochenschrift*, pp. 1911–16.

Van Rompuy, H. (2012) 'Towards a Genuine Economic and Monetary Union'. EUCO 120/12, Brussels, 26 June. Available at: «http://www.consilium.europa.eu/uedocs/cms_data/docs/ pressdata/en/ec/131201.pdf».

JCMS 2013 Volume 51 Annual Review pp. 155–167 DOI: 10.1111/jcms.12055

Stasis in Status: Relations with the Wider Europe

RICHARD G. WHITMAN[1] and ANA E. JUNCOS[2]
[1] Global Europe Centre, University of Kent. [2] University of Bristol

Introduction

The continuation of the eurozone crisis into 2012 ensured that the predominant focus for political energy and effort continued to be focused on the European Union itself rather than on the immediate neighbourhood. Given its current economic and monetary woes, the political impact of the EU is declining in its near abroad. Moreover, the crisis is also having a negative impact on its neighbouring countries, particularly, those of the Western Balkan region. As the European Council on Foreign Relations (ECFR, 2013, p. 76) noted, 'the EU is now exporting the crisis to its already-troubled periphery and this is to some extent undercutting its policy in the region'.

The award of the Nobel Peace Prize in October 2012, in the midst of the worst economic and political crisis since the creation of the EU was, however, also a reminder of what the EU can achieve in its neighbourhood, especially through the enlargement process. Having said that, future enlargement of the EU did not move forward substantively after Croatia signed its accession treaty with the EU in December 2011.

Despite the re-launch of the Union's neighbourhood policies after the Arab Spring, efforts to promote democracy in its neighbourhood have produced meagre results to date (from Morocco to Ukraine; from Syria to Belarus). The overall feeling is one of continuity rather than change in the approach of the EU to the neighbourhood as it continues to deal with problems in a technocratic manner. There is a general lack of EU political imagination – and political will – to make a significant impact in the region through diplomatic and security initiatives. Furthermore, a new initiative – the 'European Endowment for Democracy' – has yet to garner the support of all EU Member States (Kostanyan and Nasieniak, 2012) and in consequence, therefore, lacks the resources to produce any meaningful results.

Our overall assessment of the EU's policies towards the neighbourhood is that the last 12 months has been a period largely of stasis in EU policy. Coming on the back of disappointing policy performance in the preceding two years (Whitman and Juncos, 2011, 2012), the EU's policies for its neighbourhood are in need of substantive reinvigoration. Further, the substantive impact of the European External Action Service (EEAS) on policy formulation and implementation towards the challenges of the EU's neighbouring states remains limited.

I. The Enlargement Process: Progress or Stagnation?

In December 2012, the EU received the Nobel Peace Prize in recognition for over six decades of contribution 'to the advancement of peace and reconciliation, democracy and

© 2013 The Author(s) JCMS: Journal of Common Market Studies © 2013 John Wiley & Sons Ltd, 9600 Garsington Road, Oxford OX4 2DQ, UK and 350 Main Street, Malden, MA 02148, USA

human rights in Europe'.[1] The enlargement policy constitutes the best example of the EU's 'transformative power' (Grabbe, 2006), with the 2004 enlargement to central and eastern Europe being a case in point. Given its past successes and its potential to foster democratic reforms in neighbouring countries, the EU remains officially committed to continue expanding its membership. As recently confirmed by the European Council, 'enlargement remains a key EU policy' (European Council, 2012a).

Notwithstanding the official rhetoric, in 2012 the EU's enlargement policy continued to be beset by popular disillusionment – so-called 'enlargement fatigue' – and the eurozone crisis, as the attention and energies of the Member States were largely focused on how to resolve the problems in the eurozone.[2] The economic crisis is not only reducing the attractiveness of becoming a member of the EU, but also having a negative economic impact on the candidate and potential candidate countries and, in particular, on the Western Balkan countries, which have seen a reduction in the levels of exports to EU countries and foreign direct investment (World Bank, 2012). According to Bechev (2012, p. 1), 'the crisis is relegating the region to the outermost circle in a multi-speed Europe – the periphery of the periphery', it encourages a 'wait-and-see' approach on the part of the EU Member States, undermines the EU's influence and 'encourages competitors' (for example, Russia and China) to develop an increasing role in the region. For this reason, Bechev suggests that the EU should shift its focus 'from a narrative based on security to one based on the economy'. In other words, the Union should focus on economic recovery and it should provide much needed resources to the weak economies of the Western Balkans to prevent potential instability in the region.

Despite this pessimistic state of affairs, there were some encouraging signs in 2012. Croatia is set to become the EU's 28th Member State on 1 July 2013. By December 2012, 21 Member States had ratified Croatia's accession agreement. Other positive steps included Serbia becoming a candidate country in March in recognition of progress made in normalizing relations with Kosovo (see below); accession talks with Montenegro being launched on 29 June;[3] and Kosovo making progress towards the signing of a Stabilization and Association Agreement. Iceland also continued to make headway to EU membership by opening six new more negotiating chapters and provisionally closing one chapter (Competition). Even Albania received a recommendation from the European Commission to be granted conditional candidate status in the Commission's 2012 Enlargement Report (European Commission, 2012a). However, the European Council decided to postpone this decision at its December meeting (European Council, 2012a). In those cases where negotiations remained blocked by the Member States, the European Commission launched a Positive Agenda and a High Level Accession Dialogue with Turkey and Macedonia, respectively, to facilitate the harmonization with the *acquis communautaire* despite the lack of official progress in the negotiations. Similarly, a High Level Dialogue on the Accession Process was launched with Bosnia, where progress had been forestalled by domestic political bickering.

---

[1] See «http://www.nobelprize.org/nobel_prizes/peace/laureates/2012/eu.html».
[2] See Whitman and Juncos (2012) for a discussion of the impact of the eurozone crisis on the neighbourhood.
[3] In line with the new enlargement approach (see Whitman and Juncos, 2012), the first chapters opened during accession negotiations with Montenegro were those dealing with the judiciary, the fight against organized crime and corruption. In December, Montenegro provisionally closed its first chapter (Science and Research).

© 2013 The Author(s) JCMS: Journal of Common Market Studies © 2013 John Wiley & Sons Ltd

As in the previous year, High Representative Catherine Ashton invested a significant amount of diplomatic capital to facilitate a rapprochement between Pristina and Belgrade. These efforts paid off with the so-called 'footnote agreement' regarding Kosovo's participation in regional forums reached in March. The High Representative, supported by the European External Action Service (EEAS), also managed to organize a series of meetings between the two prime ministers, Ivica Dačić of Serbia and Hashim Thaçi of Kosovo, in October–December. However, this progress was marred by the electoral victory of the populist Serbian Progressive Party (SNS) headed by Tomislav Nikolić, who was voted president in May's elections. At least this time the electoral rhetoric was more pro-European than on previous occasions.

As well as progress regarding relations with Serbia, Kosovo advanced on other fronts too. In January, it launched a visa liberalization dialogue with the European Commission and, in June, a road map was adopted with specific steps towards this objective. The European Commission also published a positive feasibility study in June, which might lead to the signing of a Stabilization and Association Agreement. However, there are still considerable obstacles in Kosovo's path towards European integration as five Member States (Spain, Romania, Slovakia, Greece and Cyprus) have yet to recognize this territory. However, pragmatic considerations as well as the effects of the economic crisis are eroding opposition to Kosovo's independence. For instance, Greece and Slovakia have started to accept passports issued by Kosovo's authorities despite not recognizing the state. In addition, the eurozone crisis also seems to have strengthened the pro-independence camp (led by Germany) and weakened the southern Member States opposing Kosovo's independence, which explains some of the progress witnessed throughout 2012 in bringing Kosovo closer to establishing contractual relations with the EU.[4]

Progress was mixed in the case of Bosnia. It started with some signs of optimism with an agreement on the formation of a state-level government after 16 months of deadlock following the October 2010 elections. In February, the parliamentary assembly adopted the state aid law and the census law – two pieces of legislation considered to be critical for the country's integration into the EU. There was even talk of a possible submission of a membership application, 20 years after the beginning of the war. However, by the middle of the year it became clear that this was going to be another period of stagnation as far as progress towards Bosnia's membership of the EU was concerned. Local politics was, once again, to blame for the lack of compliance with EU conditions (see Juncos, 2013). These had been set up in a road map issued by the European Commission in June and included implementation of the Sejdić–Finci decision of the European Court of Human Rights (ECHR), which would end discrimination of those not belonging to any of the three 'constitutive peoples' – Bosniaks, Serbs and Croats. The road map also called on the parties to agree on a co-ordination mechanism to adopt EU-related legislation. These conditions were seen as a necessary step before a membership application could be lodged. However, the Bosnian authorities failed to meet the August deadline to implement the Sejdić–Finci judgment set in the Commission's road map. The issue of the closure of the office of the High Representative was postponed for another year. Some European members of the Peace Implementation Council, such as France, were more vocal about the closure of the office after the establishment of a double-hatted EU Special Representative/

---

[4] *EU Observer*, 17 April 2013.

© 2013 The Author(s) JCMS: Journal of Common Market Studies © 2013 John Wiley & Sons Ltd

Head of EU Delegation in July 2011, but the United States remained opposed to this move – as did other EU Member States such as the United Kingdom.

As far as EU–Turkey relations were concerned, there was some optimism following the election of François Hollande as French president[5] since his predecessor, Nicolas Sarkozy, had been rather hostile to closer EU–Turkish relations and had pressed for a veto on the opening of new negotiating chapters. Hollande's election did not mean a U-turn, although there were some small gestures aimed towards keeping Turkey's EU membership bid alive. First, the European Commission launched a Positive Agenda to facilitate *acquis* harmonization in those areas where negotiations had been blocked. Second, the Council agreed to start negotiations on visa liberalization and on a road map in November. For its part, Turkey initiated a readmission agreement in June. Furthermore, the Cypriot Presidency did not lead to a stalemate in EU–Turkey relations as had been feared by both sides. Yet, the key contentious issues remained: the vetoes were not lifted by France, and Cyprus and Turkey continued to refuse to implement the 2004 Ankara Protocol (extending the customs union between the EU and Turkey to the new EU Member States, including Cyprus). Turkey continued to play a key role as a regional power and is a key actor in the Syrian conflict and in negotiations with Iran. In the case of Syria, Turkey supported the UN–Arab League envoys and was willing to co-ordinate its position with its European partners (for instance, the Turkish Foreign Ministry was in contact with the EEAS on this matter). However, relations with the United States and the North Atlantic Treaty Organization (Nato) continued to be privileged, especially as the Syrian crisis threatened to spill over across Turkey's borders. In December, Nato agreed to deploy Patriot missiles along the Turkish border with Syria.

II. Continued Instability in the EU's Southern Neighbourhood

The year 2012 saw the continuation of the instability on the EU's southern border as the effects of the Arab revolutions could still be felt. Although the EU had revamped its neighbourhood policies as a response to the popular uprisings in the region (see Whitman and Juncos, 2012), this was to some extent another case of 'old wine in new bottles'. The EU continued to prioritize technical co-operation and sought to deal with problems in this part of the world through technocratic means such as new co-operation programmes, launching 'task forces' and resorting to programmatic objectives and benchmarks (ECFR, 2013). By contrast, political issues were hardly ever addressed at the EU level (the western Sahara and EU–Morocco relations is a case in point). These political issues were either completely ignored or dealt with as part of bilateral discussions between individual Member States and neighbouring countries. Hence, despite the strong rhetoric and the promise of 'money, mobility and markets' in the new EU policy towards the neighbourhood (European Union, 2011), progress towards political reform remained slow in countries such as Morocco, Egypt and Tunisia.

The EU's role in Syria is particularly illustrative of the EU's strengths and weaknesses when it comes to promoting democracy in the region and beyond. Throughout 2012, the EU supported a peaceful solution to the conflict, calling for the cessation of governmental repression and the start of a transition process, insisting that President Bashar al-Assad

---

[5] See Lequesne's contribution to this issue.

© 2013 The Author(s) JCMS: Journal of Common Market Studies © 2013 John Wiley & Sons Ltd

leave power. Overall, EU efforts, led by the United Kingdom and France, were however unsuccessful in bringing the conflict to an end. Rather, throughout the year, the conflict continued to escalate, with jihadist fighters reportedly joining the rebels, the number of refugees nearing a million people,[6] growing concerns about the possible use of chemical weapons by the Syrian government, and a risk of spillover of the conflict beyond Syria's borders to other neighbouring countries.

The EU provided humanitarian assistance to Syrian refugees and internally displaced persons, whose number continued to grow at an alarming rate. It also called repeatedly on the Syrian government to allow humanitarian organizations access to provide humanitarian aid where needed. In November, the EU recognized the newly formed Syrian National Coalition as the 'legitimate representatives of the aspirations of the Syrian people'. At the international level, the EU worked alongside other international partners, and in particular the United States, to achieve its objectives through the creation of the 'Friends of Syria' group in February and supporting the UN–Arab League peace envoys (Kofi Annan and, from August 2012, Lakhdar Brahimi). However, these efforts were thwarted by Russia and China, which also goes to show the lack of real 'partnerships' between the EU and these countries despite the official rhetoric (Portela, 2012). These two countries vetoed subsequent United Nations Security Council (UNSC) Resolutions on Syria in February and July. Russia, in particular, opposed any UN or western interference in the conflict which could damage one of its main allies in the Middle East region (and also one of the main destinations of Russian weapons). Arguably, western efforts to oust President Bashar al-Assad were also unsuccessful because of the half-hearted support given to the Syrian opposition. It was only at the end of 2012 that France, Spain and the United Kingdom recognized the new Syrian National Coalition opposition body as the sole legitimate representative of the Syrian people, with other Member States following suit in December. More significantly, western governments were reluctant to support any initiative that might require military involvement, with it being only a year after the Nato-led Libyan intervention.

Throughout the Syrian crisis, common foreign and security policy (CFSP) activities and the role of the High Representative Catherine Ashton were relegated to the margins as bilateral dealings between the Member States and the main actors in the conflict took place. The case of Syria provides another example of Franco–British leadership of European foreign policy. As had been the case in Libya, these two countries were at the forefront of the international effort to deal with the crisis, but they did not always act within an EU framework. France and the United Kingdom actively co-operated with the United States on issues such as the provision of non-lethal arms to the rebels, the creation of the Friends of Syria group, and the establishment of the more centralized and inclusive Syrian National Coalition in November, with other Member States joining these efforts afterwards. France and the United Kingdom (particularly the former) also threatened the Syrian government with more robust action, including the establishment of a no-fly zone and arming the Syrian rebels.[7] The latter option was strongly resisted by other Member States such as Germany, which meant that the EU arms embargo was renewed in

---

[6] Data from Syria Regional Refugee Response. Available at: «http://data.unhcr.org/syrianrefugees/regional.php».
[7] In May, President François Hollande said that military action was possible, but under the auspices of a UNSC Resolution (*EU Observer*, 30 May 2012).

© 2013 The Author(s) JCMS: Journal of Common Market Studies © 2013 John Wiley & Sons Ltd

December for another three months. However, as the conflict deepened in Syria, the option of arming the resistance became more of a reality, with the possibility that an EU agreement to except the Syrian National Coalition from the arms embargo could be achieved in 2013.[8] According to statements by French and British governments in 2012, arming the rebels was the only way to bring President Assad to the negotiating table and to achieve a political solution.

An exception to the bilateralism witnessed in the case of Syria is the role that the EU as a whole played in the imposition of sanctions. Because of the Russian and Chinese veto, and unlike in the case of Libya, these sanctions were adopted without the approval of a UNSC Resolution. The EU deployed the whole range of sanctions to end the conflict in Syria[9] and it did so at an incredible speed. The latter is particularly remarkable since the EU has often been criticized for its slow response to conflicts (Portela, 2012). As has become the practice, the EU applied targeted sanctions to individuals and companies directly involved in the repression with a travel ban and a freezing of financial assets. Other sanctions included an arms embargo, a selective trade ban and an oil embargo. The arms embargo, which has been in place since May 2011, was being monitored by EU national authorities that must search Syrian-bound vessels suspected of carrying weapons as agreed in July 2012. At the time of writing (May 2013), the effectiveness of the arms embargo was still questionable as most of the weapons used by the regime were provided by Russia, which was not willing to enforce the EU's sanctions.[10] The trade embargo has been more effective, but according to Clara Portela (2012), it constitutes a departure from the EU's practice of targeted (or smart) sanctions since it can affect people that are not directly involved in the perpetration of atrocities. The most interesting type of sanction is the oil/energy embargo that the EU had previously used only in very few occasions (for example, against Serbia during the Kosovo crisis). The oil embargo can, and has had, a significant impact on the regime, depriving the government of one of its key sources of income. It has also had an impact on EU Member States, and particularly those more dependent on Syria's oil such as Italy.

These kinds of sanctions provide evidence that the EU is willing to sacrifice economic interests in order to achieve security interests (to end the conflict). This was rarely done in the past and constitutes an important precedent (Portela, 2012). Overall, despite the swiftness and range of sanctions imposed on Damascus and the fact that they had an impact on the economic situation of the regime (in particular, the trade and oil embargoes), EU sanctions did not make the position of Assad's government untenable and did not force it to come to the negotiating table. Hence, one can conclude that, by the end of 2012, these sanctions had not been successful in achieving the EU's objectives, among other reasons, because of the continued support of Russia and Iran.

The EU's role in the Middle East peace process represented another missed opportunity for European diplomacy, despite Catherine Ashton and the EEAS' activism.[11] The EU failed to achieve a return to peace talks and to stop Israel's settlement expansion in the Occupied Territories. With Barack Obama preoccupied with presidential re-election, international efforts to reinvigorate the peace negotiations were virtually absent in 2012.

---

[8] *European Voice*, 21 March 2013.
[9] For a full list, see Blockmans (2012, p. 2).
[10] *EU Observer*, 20 July 2012. On Russia–EU relations, see Lavrov's contribution to this issue.
[11] For more discussion on the EEAS, see Hadfield and Fiott's contribution to this issue.

© 2013 The Author(s) JCMS: Journal of Common Market Studies © 2013 John Wiley & Sons Ltd

Despite these disappointing facts, EU diplomacy was more successful in achieving a more co-ordinated response to events in the region. First, EU Member States seemed more united during the UN General Assembly vote on Palestinian observer status, with 14 Member States voting in favour and 12 abstaining from the vote. Just one Member State (the Czech Republic) voted against Palestine's observer status. Although the lack of unity was still evident, it represented an improvement compared to the Unesco vote in December 2011. In total nine Member States changed their votes to 'yes' or abstained since the Unesco vote. Some Member States, like Germany, abstained to show their dismay at continued Israeli settlement expansion and the launch of Operation Pillar of Defence (see below).

Related to this, EU diplomacy was also active in seeking a more unified response to settlement expansion. Catherine Ashton made clear to the Israeli government on several occasions that settlement expansion was illegal under international law and also threatened the peace process. Similarly, the EEAS, through the political reports of the EU delegations in Jerusalem, Ramallah and Tel Aviv, repeatedly criticized Israeli activities in the Occupied Territories. In 2012, progress was achieved in the drafting of a voluntary code of conduct for labels of products originating from settlement territories that could provide a better guide for EU consumers to boycott these products. Furthermore, a proposal was discussed by the ambassadors to the political and security committee (PSC) to explore the possibility of denying access of 'violent settlers' to EU territory.[12] EU Member States sitting in the UNSC also criticized Israeli plans for new settlements in a Declaration in December 2012. These political gestures, however, seemed to have little impact on Israeli activities, especially since EU Member States continued to be reluctant to agree on sanctions against Israel or a compulsory ban of imports from settlement territories.

During Operation Pillar of Defence, launched by Israel in November 2012, the EU was again unable to play any meaningful role as a mediator in the conflict and had to witness an increasing role of Egypt's new Islamist President Mohammed Morsi in negotiating a ceasefire. The EU's policy on Hamas (listed as a terrorist organization in 2003) made any role of the EU as a mediator between the parties difficult, if not impossible – as had already been the case during Operation Cast Lead in 2009. On the positive side, an agreement was achieved to reactivate the EU's border assistance mission (EUBAM) at Rafah at the end of the year.

III. Eastern Neighbourhood

In contrast to the instability in the EU's southern neighbourhood, the east persisted in its ongoing processes of political atrophy with the continuation of political trends of all countries to the EU's east. Armenia, Georgia and Moldova were the only countries in which there was positive political change, with Ukraine further backtracking from political reform and continuing to present considerable challenges for the EU. Belarus also continued to remain impervious to EU attempts to encourage reform. Relations with countries in the south Caucasus remained hostage to political instability and the unresolved frozen conflicts of South Ossetia and Nagorno-Karabakh. Developments

---

[12] *EU Observer*, 26 November 2012.

© 2013 The Author(s) JCMS: Journal of Common Market Studies © 2013 John Wiley & Sons Ltd

in Azerbaijan were particularly worrying regarding continuing violations of freedom of expression and assembly, with non-governmental organizations reporting increasing levels of harassment of political opponents, activists and journalists in the country. Despite some statements by High Representative Catherine Ashton, the position of the EU remains a difficult case given Member States' economic interests in the country's energy resources.[13]

The most dramatic political development in the eastern neighbourhood was the defeat in parliamentary elections in October 2012 of President Mikheil Saakashvili's ruling United National Movement by the billionaire businessman Bidzina Ivanishvili's Georgian Dream Movement. This was Georgia's first peaceful transfer of power through elections since gaining independence in 1991. The EU judged the elections to be generally free and fair, and they led to an improvement in the assessment of its political rights rating by Freedom House (2013). The EU's negotiations with Georgia for an Association Agreement proceeded and negotiations were on track to meet the EU–Georgia road map objective that negotiations on a Deep and Comprehensive Free Trade Agreement (DCFTA) would be well advanced if not finalized by the autumn of 2013. In November 2012, Georgia was invited to enter into negotiations on a framework participation agreement to govern its participation in common security and defence policy (CSDP) missions and operations.

The new Armenian electoral code adopted in 2011 provided a basic democratic framework for the May 2012 parliamentary elections. The EU positively evaluated (with minor qualifications) the elections, which saw the ruling Republican Party retaining power and the opposition Armenian National Congress gaining seats for the first time (European Union, 2012a). However, relations with neighbouring Azerbaijan deteriorated with border clashes and the controversial extradition from Hungary of Ramil Safarov convicted of the murder of an Armenian army officer while attending a Nato-sponsored course in Budapest in 2004. The hero's welcome received by Safarov on his return home threatened to halt peace talks between the two neighbours over Nagorno-Karabakh. The EU remained a bystander to the diplomatic process. By the end of 2012, three rounds of negotiations with Armenia on a DCFTA had been held and good progress was made. This progress means the EU is on track to meet the road map objective of DCFTA negotiations with Armenia, alongside Georgia and Moldova, with possible finalization by the autumn of 2013. The EU and Armenia also signed a visa facilitation agreement at the co-operation council meeting on 17 December. In October, the Armenian government signed a decree abolishing visa requirements for EU citizens by January 2013.

The EU's relationship with Belarus remained difficult in the absence of substantive political change in the country. Belarus remains outside the bilateral track of the EU's Eastern Partnership (EaP). The parliamentary elections in Belarus of September 2012, which resulted in no opposition members entering parliament, drew EU condemnation. Catherine Ashton and Štefan Füle's joint statement stated that the election was 'another missed opportunity' (European Union, 2012b). EP President Martin Schulz described the vote as 'a mockery of a democratic ballot' and urged the EU to 'finally devise an effective strategy [of] how to deal with Belarus' that would support civil society while sanctioning

---

[13] 'Europe's Caviar Diplomacy with Azerbaijan Must End'. *EU Observer*, 26 November 2012. Available at: «http://euobserver.com/opinion/118320».

© 2013 The Author(s) JCMS: Journal of Common Market Studies © 2013 John Wiley & Sons Ltd

the country's leaders (Schultz, 2012). Sanctions against members of the Lukashenka regime were renewed by EU foreign ministers in October banning Belarusian officials from the EU and their assets frozen. In addition, 29 companies belonging to three businessmen linked to the regime were subject to sanctions. At the time of writing (May 2013), diplomats in Brussels said that there is no doubt that the sanctions will be renewed before they expire on 31 October.

The elections followed the 'teddy bear affair' expulsion of Swedish diplomats, including the ambassador, in early August and the subsequent expulsion of Belarusian counterparts from Stockholm. The dispute came after a Swedish advertising agency, Studio Total, airdropped teddy bears in Belarus in July with parachutes and placards calling for free speech. The ambassador's expulsion was a rerun of events in February 2012 when the EU and the Polish ambassadors to Minsk were expelled because the EU imposed sanctions on an oligarch friend of Lukashenka. The EU Member States temporarily pulled out all of its ambassadors from Belarus in solidarity with Poland. These ambassadors, however, trickled back a few weeks later to resume work. EU Member States did not respond in the same manner in August and kept their ambassadors in Minsk as they were keen to retain diplomatic representation on the ground to monitor the September parliamentary elections.

Moldova remained the EU's best performing partner in 2012. The indirect election of Nicolae Timofti as president in March 2012 ended a political crisis which had persisted since April 2009. The August 2012 visit by German Chancellor Angela Merkel and the first visit by José Manuel Barroso to Chisinau in November 2012 highlighted the EU's desire to mark Moldova's progress. This was on the back of a speech by Commissioner Füle in October 2012 seeing EU accession as a proposition for Moldova (Füle, 2012). The country rated top of the indices of the Eastern Partnership Index for the most EU integrated states of the EaP produced by the International Renaissance Foundation (2012). Moldova continued to make progress in the negotiation of an Association Agreement in 2012. Negotiations on all 24 chapters covering economic and sectoral co-operation and five chapters on the people-to-people contacts were closed. Negotiations on other chapters were either provisionally closed or are very well advanced. Negotiations on a DCFTA were anticipated to start in early 2013. Moldova made substantial progress on the implementation of the Visa Liberalization Action Plan (VLAP) and the first phase benchmarks were met, in line with the road map. This required Moldova to adopt several important legislative acts reforming the judiciary and fighting discrimination. In December, Moldova also signed a framework participation agreement enabling its participation in CSDP missions and operations.

Negotiations on the EU–Ukraine Association Agreement were finalized and it was initialled in March 2012. However the agreement was stymied by the requirement of Ukraine to comply with the conditions set out in the Foreign Affairs Council Conclusions of 10 December 2012 (European Council, 2012b) and raised in the 2012 ENP progress report (European Commission, 2013). The EU was seeking changes in three areas: the compliance of the 2012 parliamentary elections with international standards and follow-up actions; Ukraine's progress in addressing the issue of selective justice and preventing its recurrence; and implementation of the reforms defined in the jointly agreed association agenda.

The EU's position on the 28 October parliamentary elections in the Ukraine was that they were flawed and that standards had deteriorated from those of previous elections.

It was subsequently made clear that shortcomings identified in the final report by the OSCE-ODIHR needed to be fully addressed by implementing its recommendations and dealing with the observed shortcomings (ODIHR, 2012). The EU's concern with selective justice and politically motivated convictions of members of the former government concerned most especially the treatment of Yulia Tymoshenko after trials which the EU viewed as not respecting international standards regarding fair, transparent and independent legal process and preventing opposition leaders from standing in the parliamentary elections. Concerns about Tymoshenko resulted in the EP sending medical experts to assess her health and treatment in May 2012.

EU–Ukraine relations continued to be complicated by the EU's relationship with Russia, especially following President Putin's return to the Russian presidency in March 2012 on the back of flawed elections to the Duma in December 2011. Russia's diplomatic pressure upon the Ukraine to join a customs union with Russia, Belarus and Kazakhstan can be viewed as an attempt to frustrate the EU's efforts to deepen its relationship with Ukraine (Dragneva and Wolczuk, 2012).

On implementing reforms defined in the jointly agreed association agenda, the EU has set a further set of conditions for the Ukraine on electoral, judicial and constitutional reforms in line with international standards. Further, the country needs to prepare for establishing a DCFTA by making sustained efforts in the fight against corruption and public finance management reform, improving the deteriorating business and investment climate, and stressing the importance of inclusive reforms through constructive engagement between government, parliamentary opposition and civil society. The Council made the signing of the already initialled Association Agreement dependent on the determined action and tangible progress in the three areas mentioned above by the time of the Eastern Partnership summit in Vilnius in November 2013.

The EU's policy vehicle for its relationship with its neighbours – the EaP – continued to develop in 2012. The multilateral agenda for it was largely devoted to preparations for the biennial partnership summit due in the autumn of 2013. The joint communication from the European Commission and High Representative for Foreign and Security Policy/ European Commission Vice-President (European Commission and HR/VP, 2012a) and the two accompanying joint staff working documents (European Commission and HR/VP, 2012b, c) were the substantive documents prepared by the EU as the basis for preparations for the summit. These were considered by the EaP foreign ministers meeting in July 2012 to monitor the implementation of the objectives set out in the previous Prague and Warsaw EaP summit declarations and with the road map intended to be implemented in advance of the next summit in Vilnius in autumn 2013.

In June 2012, the new EaP Integration and Co-operation (EaPIC) programme was launched to make additional resources available to countries that make progress in building deep and sustainable democracy and in implementing related reform objectives under the 'more for more' principle (European Commission, 2012b). The EaPIC programme provides additional funding of €130 million for the period 2012–13 on top of the €1.9 billion already committed. A first round of country allocations was announced to benefit Moldova (€28 million), Georgia (€22 million) and Armenia (€15 million). EaPIC contributes to new or existing projects targeting democratic transformation and institution-building, sustainable and inclusive growth, and economic development. Although the bilateral track of the EaP is the locus for most of the activity, the parallel

© 2013 The Author(s) JCMS: Journal of Common Market Studies © 2013 John Wiley & Sons Ltd

multilateral track also saw progress in 2012. The multilateral track is intended to provide a forum for the exchange of best practice between the six partner countries (and understood as approximation to EU standards). The four thematic multilateral platforms provide the main arrangement for the multilateral strand and work continued in the four areas of democracy, good governance and stability; economic integration and convergence with EU sector policies; energy security; and contacts between people. In addition, in all six EaP countries Civil Society Forum (CSF) national platforms have been set up, providing civil society organizations with a chance to engage in the implementation of the EaP at country level. Moreover, the CSF is now a regular and active participant in most EaP meetings.

The proposal for a European Endowment for Democracy (EED) was taken further forward in 2012 (European Council, 2011). The plan is for the EED to be come fully operational in 2013 on the basis of €15 million of funding (of which €6 million is contributed by the European Commission and the remaining from the Member States) and to function as an independent European non-profit foundation, with the participation of representatives of Member States, the EP, the European Commission, the High Representative and civil society organizations (see Kostanyan and Nasieniak, 2012).

Conclusions

The EU's neighbourhood is currently a region in which the EU's political and economic influence has plateaued. The continuing economic difficulties of the majority of Member States' economies and the eurozone crisis have limited the EU's capacities for substantive political initiatives within the region. The events in the aftermath of the Arab Spring in the southern neighbourhood are unfolding with the EU apparently unable, and unwilling, to envision political and economic innovation in its response to events. The EU's policy towards its eastern neighbours is largely dictated by the lack of political reform within the partner countries. The EaP is making modest gains in advancing relationships with the bulk of the EU's eastern neighbours, but relationships remain vulnerable to the vicissitudes of political events on the ground as demonstrated in relations with Ukraine.

The accession process has moved at a glacial pace within the last 12 months and predicting a date for the next enlargement beyond Croatia is impossible under current circumstances. Rather, real questions arise as to whether the EU's capacity for soft power influence through enlargement has been expended in its ability to effect reform in the applicant states. The promise of the EEAS to deliver greater connectivity between the different strands of the EU's external action is still largely under-demonstrated in the policy towards the EU's neighbouring states. This is anticipated to remain unchanged until the EU's internal difficulties are resolved and allow for greater political energy and financial resources to be released to greater ambitions for the neighbourhood.

References

Bechev, D. (2012) 'The Periphery of the Periphery: The Western Balkans and the Euro Crisis'. Policy Brief (London: European Council on Foreign Relations).

Blockmans, S. (2012) 'Preparing for a Post-Assad Syria: What Role for the European Union?' *CEPS Commentary*, 2 August.

© 2013 The Author(s) JCMS: Journal of Common Market Studies © 2013 John Wiley & Sons Ltd

Dragneva, R. and Wolczuk, K. (2012) 'Russia, the Eurasian Customs Union and the EU: Cooperation, Stagnation or Rivalry?' REP BP 2012/01 (London: Chatham House).

European Commission (2012a) 'Communication from the Commission on enlargement strategy and main challenges, 2012–13'. *COM*(2012)600 final, 10 October.

European Commission (2012b) 'Commission implementing Decision of 26 June 2012 on the Eastern Partnership integration and co-operation programme 2012–13 in favour of the eastern neighbourhood to be financed under Article 19 08 01 03 of the general budget of the European Union. Available at: «http://ec.europa.eu/europeaid/documents/aap/2012/aap-spe_2012_enpi -e_en.pdf».

European Commission (2013) 'ENP country progress report 2012: Ukraine', 20 March. Available at: «http://europa.eu/rapid/press-release_MEMO-13-257_en.htm».

European Commission and HR/VP (2012a) 'Joint Communication on the Eastern Partnership: A roadmap to the autumn 2013 summit'. SWD(2012) 108 final, SWD(2012) 109 final, JOIN(2012) 13 final, 15 May. Available at: «http://ec.europa.eu/world/enp/docs/2012_enp_pack/e_pship _roadmap_en.pdf».

European Commission and HR/VP (2012b) 'Joint staff working document: Eastern Partnership roadmap 2012–13 – the bilateral dimension'. SWD(2012) 109 final, 15 May. Available at: «http://ec.europa.eu/world/enp/docs/2012_enp_pack/e_pship_bilateral_en.pdf».

European Commission and HR/VP (2012c) 'Joint staff working document: Eastern Partnership roadmap 2012–13 – the multilateral dimension'. SWD(2012) 108 final, 15 May. Available at: «http://ec.europa.eu/world/enp/docs/2012_enp_pack/e_pship_multilateral_en.pdf».

European Council (2011) 'Council Conclusions on the European Endowment for Democracy', 3130th Foreign Affairs Council Meeting, Brussels, 1 December. Available at: «http://www .consilium.europa.eu/uedocs/cms_data/docs/pressdata/EN/foraff/126505.pdf».

European Council (2012a) '3210th General Affairs Council Meeting Minutes', 11 December.

European Council (2012b) 'Council Conclusions on Ukraine', 3209th Foreign Affairs Council Meeting, Brussels, 10 December. Available at: «http://www.consilium.europa.eu/uedocs/cms _data/docs/pressdata/EN/foraff/134136.pdf».

European Council on Foreign Relations (2013) *European Foreign Policy Scorecard, 2013* (Berlin: ECFR). Available at: «http://www.ecfr.eu/scorecard/2013».

European Union (2011) 'The EU's Response to the "Arab Spring"'. Europa Press Releases RAPID, MEMO/11/918, 16 December. Available at: «http://europa.eu/rapid/press-release _MEMO-11-918_en.htm».

European Union (2012a) 'Statement by High Representative Catherine Ashton and Commissioner Štefan Füle on the Parliamentary Elections in Armenia', 8 May. Available at: «http:// www.europarl.europa.eu/meetdocs/2009_2014/documents/depa/dv/nest_20120523_14_/nest _20120523_14_en.pdf».

European Union (2012b) 'Statement by the High Representative Catherine Ashton and Commissioner Štefan Füle on the Parliamentary Elections in Belarus', 24 September. Available at: «http://europa.eu/rapid/press-release_MEMO-12-706_en.htm».

Freedom House (2013) *Freedom in the World 2013*. Available at: «http://www.freedomhouse.org/ report/freedom-world/freedom-world-2013».

Füle, S. (2012) 'Speech Delivered at EU–Moldova Forum Organised by Deutsche Gesellschaft für Auswärtige Politik', Berlin, Germany, 22 October. Available at: «http://europa.eu/rapid/press -release_SPEECH-12-753_en.htm».

Grabbe, H. (2006) *The EU's Transformative Power: Europeanization through Conditionality in Central and Eastern Europe* (Houndmills: Palgrave Macmillan).

International Rennaisance Foundation (2012) *European Integration Index*. Available at: «http:// www.eap-index.eu/sites/default/files/EaP%20Index%202012_0.pdf».

© 2013 The Author(s) JCMS: Journal of Common Market Studies © 2013 John Wiley & Sons Ltd

Juncos, A.E. (2013) *EU Foreign and Security Policy in Bosnia: The Politics of Coherence and Effectiveness* (Manchester: Manchester University Press).

Kostanyan, H. and Nasieniak, M. (2012) 'Moving the EU from a Laggard to a Leader in Democracy Assistance: The Potential Role of the European Endowment for Democracy'. *CEPS Policy Brief* (Brussels: Centre for European Policy Studies).

Office for Democratic Institutions and Human Rights (ODIHR) (2012) *Ukraine Parliamentary Elections, 28 October 2012: OSCE/ODIHR Election Observation Mission Final Report* (Warsaw: ODIHR). Available at: «http://www.osce.org/odihr/98578».

Portela, C. (2012) 'The EU's Sanctions against Syria: Conflict Management by Other Means'. Security Policy Brief 38 (Brussels: Egmont Royal Institute for International Relations).

Schultz, M. (2012) 'Schulz on Belarus Elections: Mockery of Democratic Ballot'. Press Release, 24 September. Available at: «http://www.europarl.europa.eu/the-president/en/press/press_release_speeches/press_release/2012/2012-september/press_release-2012-september-13.html».

Whitman, R.G. and Juncos, A.E. (2011) 'Relations with the Wider Europe'. *JCMS*, Vol. 49, No. S1, pp. 187–208.

Whitman, R.G. and Juncos, A.E. (2012) 'The Arab Spring, the Eurozone Crisis and the Neighbourhood: A Region in Flux'. *JCMS*, Vol. 50, No. S1, pp. 147–61.

World Bank (2012) 'From Recession to Reform: The Western Balkans and the Impacts of a Double Dip Recession' (Washington, DC: World Bank). Available at: «http://www.worldbank.org/en/news/feature/2012/12/18/from-recession-to-reform-western-balkans-and-impacts-of-double-dip-recession».

JCMS 2013 Volume 51 Annual Review pp. 168–182   DOI: 10.1111/jcms.12052

Europe and the Rest of the World

DR AMELIA HADFIELD[1] and DANIEL FIOTT[2]
[1] Canterbury Christ Church University. [2] Vrije Universiteit Brussels

Introduction

There were a number of *leitmotifs* by which to identify the European Union's activities in 2012. The first of these was the eurozone crisis.[1] A second theme was the change (or not) of key personnel: the election of François Hollande in France,[2] the re-election of American President Barack Obama in October, the generational change of leadership in China and the return of Vladimir Putin as Russian president. Third was the United States' 'pivot' away from two wars in Iraq and Afghanistan towards the Pacific region. The fourth *leitmotif* related to the deepened crises in the Sahel, North Africa and the Middle East. Finally, there were the activities of the European External Action Service (EEAS) and the development of the High Representative/Vice-President (HR/VP) position held by Baroness Catherine Ashton. Against this background, the EU in 2012 displayed an observable if uneven consolidation of its international identity, while the EEAS itself produced a range of muted but generally organized responses, the sum total of which suggested at least an emerging strategic vision for the EU.

The development of the EEAS constituted the major narrative of EU foreign affairs in 2012, and hence forms much of the connecting thread for this contribution, reviewing key developments throughout the year. Accordingly, we first assess the degree to which the institutional composition of the EEAS, and the strategic vision inherent in the HR/VP post constituted a progressive or regressive influence on its overall ability to construct and implement key EU foreign policies, and the consequential emergence of a medium-term strategic plan for EU diplomacy. The following sections then consider the Union's response to various international crises and the implementation of the 'comprehensive approach' within the CSDP (the closer integration of the EU's civilian and military capabilities and institutions), before concluding with an overview of the EU's progress in regional diplomacy, and in consolidating its writing produced on the strategic partnerships with the United States and Brazil, Russia, India, China and South Africa[3] (the 'BRICS').

I. The High Representative and the EEAS

The year 2012 was key from the standpoint of analytical writing produced on the EEAS. A variety of reports and academic articles emerged (for example, Hemra *et al.*, 2011; O'Sullivan, 2012a; Petrov *et al.*, 2012; EP, 2013a; Helwig *et al.*, 2013), all assessing

---

[1] See the contributions of Hodson, and Howarth and Quaglia to this issue.
[2] See Lequesne's contribution to this issue.
[3] South Africa was not initially considered part of the original grouping of the BRIC countries, although following the third BRIC summit – organized by the BRIC members in Sanya, China, in April 2011 – South Africa was formally invited to join the annual summits and the acronym thus changed to 'BRICS'.

© 2013 The Author(s) JCMS: Journal of Common Market Studies © 2013 John Wiley & Sons Ltd, 9600 Garsington Road, Oxford OX4 2DQ, UK and 350 Main Street, Malden, MA 02148, USA

challenges facing the EEAS, including institutional design, budgetary matters and regional strategy-making. For policy-makers and academics alike, the emergence of such evaluations is a particularly important means of distilling expectations regarding the EEAS' overall strategic ability, and examining its substantive goal of crafting foreign policy. Statements by senior EEAS staff and independent commentators throughout 2012 assessing the Service's procedural developments are equally helpful in this respect. Both outputs provide a baseline of various criteria by which to judge the progress of the EEAS and the HR/VP. By providing an *institutional* focus, the reports generally weigh the procedural requirements versus the substantive dynamics at work in the Service, while the *strategic* focus found in public statements explains the ability of the EEAS and the HR/VP to variously capitalize on external policy-making opportunities and contend with the countervailing challenges imposed by the eurozone crisis.

From a reactive, lacklustre stance in 2011 to the dramatic events of the Arab Spring, the EEAS entered 2012 in a constrained mode as a result of the financial crisis. This imposed severe material spending limits on European governments and undermined political solidarity on a number of fronts, including the consolidation and expansion of the EU's international identity. To regain ground lost to these initial challenges, the EEAS had to undertake both procedural and substantive overhauls to keep its house in order. However, the reports and articles that assessed these changes were critical of the performance of the EEAS in these respects (for example, Petrov *et al.*, 2012; EP, 2013a). They were however more enthusiastic about various external opportunities seized by the EEAS, as well as with the new-found methods of moving beyond the constraints of the EU's financial crisis, including cost-saving measures at the EU Delegation level such as the joint action between the EEAS and the Member States to lower translation, hotel and accommodation costs (House of Lords, 2013a, p. 24). Overall changes undertaken by the EEAS and the HR/VP in 2012 can thus be identified in two main areas: internal institutional cohesion and inter-institutional relations.

In terms of internal institutional cohesion, the EEAS continued to make poor use of its 'coherence mandate' as established by Article 18(4) Treaty on European Union (TEU) (EP, 2013a, p. 84). As such, for the HR/VP and the EEAS there was a mixed record in 2012 in terms of streamlining the procedural substructures of the EEAS and enhancing the tools by which to construct and enact substantive policy. Much of the problem stems from its initial institutional set-up, in which the *sui generis* existence of the EEAS, separate from the Council and Commission, is viewed as 'an indeterminate entity' with a split personality disorder, at once a Commission Directorate-General (DG) and a Council General Secretariat. Consequently, there is at present 'no shared understanding among stakeholders outside or within the EEAS on the role, mandate and position of the Service within the EU external action architecture' (EP, 2013a, p. 83). Overhauling the top-heavy internal structure of the EEAS is key to tackling its indeterminate identity; a better division of labour must be implemented by eradicating duplication, unclear vertical chains of command and opaque inter-departmental relations. Added to this is the problem that the HR/VP post remains an impossibly unwieldy mixture of tasks for one person to manage adequately.

In the absence of procedural clarity and the substance that could have been afforded by a simple, 'clear vision and an agreed framework strategy on the EU's road map', 2012 saw some frenzied but unfocused activity and much representation, but with little in-depth preparation (Blockmans, 2012, p. 7). Again, a lack of foundational principles was to

© 2013 The Author(s) JCMS: Journal of Common Market Studies © 2013 John Wiley & Sons Ltd

blame. The late 2011 report by the HR/VP identified only the need to 'consolidate the capacity to deliver policy substance', but failed to provide a decent guiding rationale for the conduct of foreign policy in 2012 (EEAS, 2011, p. 12).[4] As such, there was little clear understanding as to *which* common foreign and security policy (CFSP) themes should emerge as priorities; the method of their enactment; the modes connecting CFSP and non-CFSP external relations; methods of diminishing inter-institutional factionalism; and principally the guiding role of the HR/VP.

Unsurprisingly, senior EEAS staff painted a more positive picture. Chief Operating Officer David O'Sullivan, for instance, argued that the HR/VP and EEAS registered many successes in 2012, including the facilitated dialogue between Belgrade and Pristina, the Swiss-mediated efforts aimed at Russia's World Trade Organization (WTO) accession, spearheading the E3+3 negotiations with Iran, participating in both the stalled Middle East peace process negotiations and the Cairo group, and providing a renewed focus on the Neighbourhood after the 2012 review (O'Sullivan, 2012b, p. 6). From this perspective, Baroness Ashton certainly shuttled admirably between sundry areas of external affairs. However, there is little sense that such frenetic activity generated more light than heat, and instead rather confirmed the observation that the EEAS is operating widely, but ineffectively, due chiefly to its 'contradictory mandates': busy demonstrating policy entrepreneurship, but without overtly challenging national foreign policy (Balfour and Raik, 2013, p. 13).

In terms of leadership, a variety of positives can certainly be noted. The Danish and Cypriot EU Presidencies passed with little fanfare,[5] cementing the EEAS' position as the overall co-ordinator of the EU's external relations agenda. More substantively, HR/VP leadership was demonstrated (but not without considerable pressure from the EP) by the drafting of a strategic framework on human rights and democracy, leading to the appointment of an EU Special Representative for Human Rights on 25 July. The question, of course, is whether these successes typified a new adaptive mode of delivering a European message, or are examples of reactive shuttle diplomacy that merely cover as much ground as possible, rather than providing strategic and substantive policy solutions in each of these areas.

EEAS staffing also remained an issue in 2012. As interviews with EEAS staff revealed, tensions remain between staff transferred from the Council, European Commission and national foreign ministries. In addition, staffing cost pressures have led to the hiring of more contractual agents, undermining the construction of an EEAS institutional memory and muddying prospects for a clear Service career path.[6] EEAS officials also intimated the need for a viable, harmonized reporting database, whereby Service staff could access policy-relevant documents from the national foreign ministries.[7] Staff training was also raised as an area for further action by the EEAS hierarchy, despite the 'closer training ties' developed with DG DEVCO.[8] Overall, the Service in 2012 suffered rather than benefited from the

---

[4] Instead, the 2011 EEAS report comprises a loose overview of key policy hotspots (North Africa, Horn of Africa, Western Balkans), and a general update on past and future organizational development.
[5] For accounts of the Danish and Cypriot Presidencies, see Manners and Christou in this issue.
[6] Interview with two senior EEAS staff members, Brussels, 14 and 20 February 2013.
[7] Interview with a senior EEAS staff member, Brussels, 20 February 2013.
[8] Email interview with Professor Simon Duke, EIPA, 7 April 2013. DG DEVCO is the European Commission's Directorate-General responsible for Development and Co-operation.

© 2013 The Author(s) JCMS: Journal of Common Market Studies © 2013 John Wiley & Sons Ltd

'diverse professional backgrounds of its members, the absence of standard operating procedures, and the lack of an *esprit de corps*' (Vanhoonacker and Pomorska, 2013, p. 13).

The EEAS did better at channelling the Member States' foreign policies than in the previous year, with half of the EU's diplomatic information flows now originating 'in Brussels rather than in EU Member States' capitals' since the establishment of the EEAS (Bicchi, 2012, p. 93). This suggests an increased concentration of diplomatic communication emanating, and indeed co-ordinated from EU rather than national levels, indicating that the EEAS contributes positively to the expansion of information-sharing. Nevertheless, challenges remain regarding the joined-up nature of the Member States' foreign policies, both in Brussels and abroad, which in turn relates to the EU Delegations. As observed by the European Parliament, the majority of EU Delegation officials – 'with the exception of Delegations in multilateral forums and Delegations in capitals of significant partners – come from the Commission, this creates an apparent shortage of staff [from the EEAS] working on political issues' (EP, 2013a, p. 65), enhancing the sense of an EU–national foreign policy disconnect.

Following the foreign policy axiom that absence speaks as loudly as presence, it should be noted that the majority of strategic speeches delivered by the EU in the capitals of major partners such as the United States and China in 2012 came from either or both of 'the Presidents' or other European Commissioners, and not from the HR/VP. Herman Van Rompuy and Jose Manuel Barroso thus actively represented the EU at most of the high-level meetings during the year rather than Baroness Ashton.

Some have interpreted this as a sensible division of labour between the European Council, the HR/VP and European Commission. For others, it suggested a power vacuum to be filled. Accordingly, some EU Member States began to initiate strategic projects. In one instance, it was left to German Foreign Minister Guido Westerwelle and ten of his EU counterparts to launch a process about the 'Future of Europe' in March 2012. In another strategic initiative, the European global strategy was launched in July 2012 by the foreign ministries of Sweden, Spain, Poland and Italy with the aim of shifting the terms of the strategic debate in the EU away from security threats to how the EU can capitalize on global opportunities. While such initiatives point to the fact that the appetite for a renewed European security strategy – even a 'grand strategy' – remains strong (Biscop, 2012), it does suggest the HR/VP is largely absent from the process of forging both a clear strategic vision for the EEAS, and a sharp understanding of its role as a catalyst of this overall process.

Turning to inter-institutional cohesion, the EEAS is designed to be 'a facilitating vehicle for the EU institutions and Member States by weaving together our knowledge of foreign policy with the different instruments' (O'Sullivan, 2012b, pp. 2–3). From a procedural perspective, inter-institutional coherence stems from the chairmanship of the Foreign Affairs Council (FAC), and an explicit use of the 'VP' side of the HR/VP job description. In 2012, the former ambition gained some traction, but the latter remained badly mired in institutional jostling between the Council, Commission, the Member States and the EEAS, creating something akin to a latter-day Berlin Wall between DG Trade and DG DEVCO, on the one hand, and the EEAS, on the other. This remains a significant problem for 2013, because the ability of the EEAS to demonstrate any genuine policy entrepreneurship 'depends crucially on the integration of "community" policies in the policy mix' (Balfour and Raik, 2013, p. 14).

© 2013 The Author(s) JCMS: Journal of Common Market Studies © 2013 John Wiley & Sons Ltd

Substantively, the point of the HR/VP post is the establishment of a necessarily demanding and unique method of supporting both the Council and Commission in order to ensure coherence and consistency across the varied areas of EU external action. A post that conducts, contributes and ensures compliance on foreign security and defence policies looks good on paper; however, the European Council remains the 'primary authority' for the initial policy choices that set out the working blueprint in all these areas, while 'the Commission remains responsible for policy initiation, implementation and external representation in other domains of EU external action' (Blockmans, 2012, p. 7). From this perspective, the HR/VP position was, from its inception, rather perversely condemned to a Janus-faced existence, compelled to act in a second-hand, convoluted capacity on behalf of the European Council to carry out CFSP/CSDP policy concessions grudgingly given over by the Member States, and persistent turf wars with the European Commission in attempting to gain ground, or even opportunities to co-operate, on all other areas of EU external action.

The relationship with the Member States plays a critical role in shaping the results that the EEAS can deliver. Foreign ministers have contributed to strengthening diplomatic channels with the EEAS, but also symbolize active opposition 'by producing public "alternative" proposals or letters on how foreign policy can be improved'; initiatives such as the 17 September 2012 Final Report of the Future of Europe Group of the Foreign Ministers of Austria, Belgium, Denmark, France, Italy, Germany, Luxembourg, the Netherlands, Poland, Portugal and Spain, which was 'perceived to mine the ground on which the HR/VP and the EEAS are standing' (Balfour and Raik, 2013, p. 21).

The year 2012 also saw continued tension between the EEAS and the Commission. As stated by the EEAS' Executive Secretary General, Pierre Vimont to the United Kingdom's House of Lords: '[W]e have a problem [. . .] [t]he EEAS is not a fully-fledged institution; we are an administration. For the Commission, as such we do not have the legal status to deal with the different operational and financial resources that it manages' (House of Lords, 2013b, p. 12). While Ashton's relative absence from Commission College meetings has not helped inculcate a co-operative spirit between the two bodies, there is still significant debate in the Commission itself as to whether policy areas such as 'development', 'peace-building' and 'humanitarian aid' should be considered as 'foreign policy' (Spence, 2012, pp. 122, 132). As one member of the Service confirmed, the EEAS is now more of a political institution in its working assumptions and objectives than DG RELEX ever was.[9]

This certainly speaks to the need for a more judicious exploitation of the HR/VP's various roles; the HR, VP and FAC Chair roles should visibly feed into the EEAS and its respective Commission and Council dimensions, both within the EEAS itself, and horizontally to boost inter-institutional co-operation. While the replacement of the rotating six-month Presidencies by the HR/VP as FAC Chair has allowed individual Member State priorities to be 'replaced by long-term actions translating overall European objectives', little genuine forward movement took place in converting Presidency objectives into decent EU outputs (O'Sullivan, 2012b, p. 4), and the problem of ensuring a continued 'buy-in' on the part of the Member States remained largely unresolved. Furthermore, while the EU Delegations performed decently in 2012, the EEAS as a whole was unable

---

[9] Interview with two senior EEAS staff members, Brussels, 14 and 20 February 2013.

© 2013 The Author(s) JCMS: Journal of Common Market Studies © 2013 John Wiley & Sons Ltd

to fully emerge as the primary 'diplomatic entrepreneur in EU external action'. Only by striking a 'new deal' with the Commission, garnering serious Member State support and eschewing budget neutrality would it realistically stand a chance of decent improvement in 2013 (EP, 2013a, p. 84).

II. The EEAS and International Crises

The success or failure of the HR/VP and the EEAS in 2012 can be benchmarked in terms of a number of pressing international crises. The ongoing dynamic political transition in Libya, for example, made the EU's engagement with the country difficult. The year saw continued clashes between former rebel forces and the National Transitional Council (NTC), local militias in remote parts of the country were involved in killings; then followed the election of the General National Congress in July, and government by October, and the death of Ambassador Christopher Stevens and three other American citizens. Under such circumstances, it was difficult for the 'new ENP' (European neighbourhood policy) to have an impact. While the immediate concern for the EU was stability in the country, it was quick to engage with the key issue of immigration. In this regard, the EU deployed a capability assessment team to Libya in March, with a view to eventually deploying a border management and capacity-building mission under the CSDP.

The HR/VP's reaction times to dynamic crisis situations were also highlighted. In Egypt, for example, the HR/VP saw the election of the Muslim Brotherhood's Mohamed Morsi as largely compatible with a democratic transition in the country. But the EU soon found itself in a difficult position when Morsi announced sweeping constitutional powers on 22 November that saw the removal of the prosecutor general, and the weakening of the Constitutional Court; MEPs subsequently criticized Ashton for her tardiness in condemning Morsi's actions (EP, 2013b). The EEAS' subsequent response has been mainly of a diplomatic nature, aimed at assisting with dialogue in Egypt. It is, however, a manifestly cautious approach – or, as the HR/VP has stated, one of 'strategic patience' – with high-level individuals such as the EU Special Representatives for Egypt and Human Rights and the EEAS' Political Director meeting regularly with relevant parties in the country.

Prioritizing EU action in crisis situations highlighted the challenges inherent in garnering international support. As demonstrated in Syria, where there is substantial international indecision about a course of action, there is even less room for the EU to act. After frictions caused by the intervention in Libya of the North Atlantic Treaty Organization (Nato), EU Member States quickly removed the military option regarding Syria, especially given the EU's inability to convince Russia and China of the need for a United Nations Security Council Resolution on the situation. Consequently, the EU response took the form of sanctions on the Bashar al-Assad regime, and humanitarian assistance to Syria via Lebanon and Jordan.

The successful November 2012 vote by the UN General Assembly to recognize Palestine as a state further tested EU unity. While the HR/VP stated that the 'EU has repeatedly expressed its support and wish for Palestine to become a full member of the [UN] as part of a solution to the conflict', the schism between EU Member States on the Israel–Palestine conflict was all too clear (European Union, 2012). The Czech Republic joined the United States, Canada and six other states to reject the motion, with Bulgaria,

Estonia, Germany, Hungary, Latvia, Lithuania, the Netherlands, Poland, Romania, Slovakia, Slovenia and the United Kingdom among of the 41 abstaining states. Only 14 EU Member States voted in favour of Palestine.

A more positive 2012 outcome for the EU was the resumption of nuclear talks with Iran. Ashton, as the lead negotiator for the E3+3 countries (the United Kingdom, the United States, China, France, Germany and Russia) was regarded as a pivotal go-between in diffusing difficult relations, particularly after International Atomic Energy Agency (IAEA) inspectors who had detailed the development of Iranian weapons-grade material were denied access to the Parchin nuclear site. While some 'in the Delegations and outside of the EEAS are of the opinion that the Iranians are in reality looking to the USA, with the EU merely playing the role of a middleman', it cannot be denied that Iran's chief nuclear negotiator, Saeed Jalili, has reasonable respect and trust for the HR/VP as a result of work undertaken in 2012 (EP, 2013a, p. 26).

III. The Comprehensive Approach and the CSDP

The 'comprehensive approach' continued to play a key role in defining EU external affairs. Defined by Smith (2012, pp. 265–6) as 'a stress on preventive action using a full range of EU policy tools directed towards a single target/problem' with a spectrum of tools including 'military, policing, law, human rights, and economic development resources', the comprehensive approach is now an emerging 'trademark' for the EU in its foreign, security and defence policies. More than improved functionality, the comprehensive approach is now fundamental to the 'EU's conception of itself as a responsible global actor' (Smith, 2012). Given that Ashton will not take up a second term as HR/VP, the comprehensive approach will also form part of her legacy. With the potential to create a substantive symbiosis in the EU's military and civilian tools, 2012 witnessed much energy by the HR/VP in cultivating the comprehensive approach as a permanent centrepiece of EU foreign policy.

Part of this process included the ongoing review of the EU's crisis management procedures, and the elaboration of a process labelled the 'Kermabon proposals'. Broadly, the proposals build on the identified need to further integrate CSDP and EEAS tools, to speed up crisis management planning (CMP) processes and to standardize operational planning procedures. Equally however, the 'CMP review is ultimately about the political direction of the CSDP', and its ability to intelligently underwrite the EU's growing arsenal of foreign policy tools (Mattelaer, 2012, p. 3). The development of the comprehensive approach should also halt suggestions that the CSDP will transform the EU into a wholesale military actor like Nato. Buttressed by the expectation from the European Council that the EEAS and the European Commission will publish a joint communication on the comprehensive approach for the middle of 2013, what remains unclear is whether this plan will improve the EU's overall effectiveness in crisis situations such as that witnessed in Libya (Simón, 2012). In the meantime, however, there has been no shortage of international crises by which to test EU responsiveness and the viability of its newly discovered foreign policy 'trademark'.

Indeed, there were a number of cases where this policy symbiosis showed promise. In the Horn of Africa, the EU's first naval CSDP mission – Operation Atalanta – continued to combat piracy and secure vital humanitarian aid deliveries into Somalia. The second mandate given to the EU in 2012 to train Somali troops in Uganda (EUTM Somalia) assisted the African Union's operation to regain control of Somalia, operating alongside the ongoing regional maritime capacity-building mission (EUCAP Nestor) to Somalia, Djibouti, Kenya, the Seychelles and Tanzania. The EU's first Operations Centre was activated to help co-ordinate these missions, and the HR/VP appointed an overall Special Representative to the region in January 2012, further buttressed by approximately €198 million in humanitarian aid. While the country is still extremely fragile, the fact that Somalia has moved from an impending food crisis and a failed government to tackling justice reform is credibly due in part to the EU's sufficiently comprehensive and necessarily sustained engagement in the region.

In response to the deepening crisis in the Sahel, which resulted in violence in northern Mali and approximately 450,000 displaced persons, the EU allocated €172 million in humanitarian aid to the country, and drafted a Sahel strategy for security and development. The EU also set in motion the deployment of a Training Mission to Mali (EUTM Mali) to help train the country's army, but deployment did not occur due to the intense violence that ultimately toppled the government in Bamako by rebel groups in May 2012. In this case, the EEAS' comprehensive approach was ultimately ineffective in tackling a situation that eventually required French military intervention in February 2013. Indeed, no comprehensive action on a par with French intervention through the CSDP was forthcoming in 2012; and 2012 plans for EU development assistance remained stymied by the rebels' control of northern Mali. As such, the Sahel region and Mali remains an open-ended test case for the comprehensive approach.

While 2012 signalled the end of a nearly decade-long EU police mission (EUPM) presence in Bosnia and Herzegovina,[10] it was a busy year for the deployment of three new CSDP missions in Africa: EUCAP Sahel Niger, designed to improve Niger's security forces' capacity to tackle terrorism and crime, an EU aviation security mission (EUAVSEC) to south Sudan to provide security support at Juba International Airport, and EUCAP Nestor building maritime capacity in the Horn of Africa. Such activities did not, however, prevent an 'ongoing debate about the rationale' of the CSDP in 2012 (Fiott, 2013, p. 49), especially after the failure to reach a coherent EU military response to the Libya crisis in 2011. The same questions have already been asked of the EU regarding Mali in 2013. The EU's CSDP 2012 action in Mali thus remains a complicated blend of evolving security and development policies that highlight the need for a 'comprehensive approach', but are largely disappointing in terms of implementing the approach, as well as the ongoing internal divisions between EU Member States on the overall issue of the use of force.

IV. The Strategic Partnerships

The EU's relations with established partners such as the United States were marked by the re-election of President Barack Obama in October, the troop drawdown in Iraq and Afghanistan and a refocusing by the United States towards the Pacific region in what is widely termed the 'Pacific pivot'. The pivot itself has prompted questions regarding the potential for an increased EU political and security role in the Asia Pacific region.

[10] See Whitman and Juncos' contribution to this issue.

© 2013 The Author(s) JCMS: Journal of Common Market Studies © 2013 John Wiley & Sons Ltd

Substance to such queries was added in July 2012, when the HR/VP participated in an Association of Southeast Asian Nations (ASEAN) regional forum for the first time. This was followed by an EU–US joint statement on the Asia Pacific region which clearly indicated 'the interest, and the readiness, of the EU to be more involved in the region' (Casarini, 2012). Even though the EU is a non-security actor in Asia, interest remains as to the shape and extent of European engagement in the region, with potential for EU diplomatic capabilities drawn upon to diffuse issues such as the 2012 Sino–Japanese dispute over the ownership of the Senkaku/Diaoyu islands.

The 'Pacific pivot' also raised questions about the EU's defence policies, with some responses generated in 2012. Following the initial 2011 warning by former Secretary of Defence Robert Gates (echoed in observations by his successor, Leon Panetta, in early 2013) of European defence cutbacks and American disinclination to involve themselves in the EU's (wider) neighbourhood, the European Defence Agency (EDA) stepped up its 'pooling and sharing' efforts by initiating air-to-air refuelling and airworthiness projects; supporting projects tackling chronic European capability shortfalls, including helicopters; and proposing a code of conduct on pooling and sharing. Crucially, the 'Pacific pivot' prompted Herman Van Rompuy to announce in December 2012 that the EU would hold a dedicated Council meeting at the level of heads of state and government on the 'state of European defence' in December 2013. Tellingly, Van Rompuy delivered the EU's keynote speech at the May 2012 Nato summit in Chicago, rather than Ashton. Consequently, what remains unclear is the nature of the HR/VP's involvement in catalyzing and leading on European defence projects.

In terms of building bridges with strategic partners, the HR/VP did develop a solid and cordial working relationship with the former American Secretary of State Hillary Clinton on issues regarding the Western Balkans.[11] Indeed, as political and economic infighting in the region continued, the two undertook a joint visit to the region. EU–US efforts in the Balkans came to symbolize a solution achieved during Hillary Clinton's tenure for the perennial American problem of 'whom to phone in Europe', highlighting in the process the importance of personality in constructing a viable transatlantic relationship. Whether the lines will remain open under new Secretary of State John Kerry remains to be seen.

Negotiations to conclude a transatlantic trade and investment partnership (TTIP) constituted another crucial development in EU–US relations. The proposed free trade pact aims to abolish tariffs and non-tariff barriers and to enhance the compatibility of trade regulations and standards in goods, services and investments, estimated to boost American gross domestic product (GDP) by 1 per cent and that of the EU by 0.4 per cent (European Commission, 2013). The prospective TTIP thus has the potential to boost significantly American and EU economies, and to secure the transatlantic relationship against the ongoing vagaries of the global economy. As reported by the EU–US high level working group on jobs and growth on 19 June 2012, the body tasked with exploring the feasibility of the trade deal, 'such an initiative [the TTIP] could promote a forward-looking agenda for multilateral trade liberalization' and further transatlantic co-operation (European Commission, 2012). To some extent, the TTIP aims to consolidate both the EU and the United States in relation to other trade blocs and actors, including the BRICS. As European Trade Commissioner Karel De Gucht stated recently, one of the reasons why the

---

[11] See Whitman and Juncos' contribution to this issue.

© 2013 The Author(s) JCMS: Journal of Common Market Studies © 2013 John Wiley & Sons Ltd

EU and America need a TTIP now 'is because the world has changed. China, India and Brazil play a much different role in the global economy today than they did fifteen, ten or even five years ago. The global centre of economic gravity is shifting' (De Gucht, 2013, p. 3). Taken together, a strategy tackling the economic challenges faced by both the EU and the United States, alongside the 'Pacific pivot' provide a rationale by which to effectively shore up western powers against costly internecine squabbles, allowing them to focus on the opportunities and challenges to be met in new regions. However, such a perspective needs to be tempered with a sober analysis of the EU's relations with key strategic players in Asia.

Apart from evaluating the implications of the generational leadership change in China, the major strategic issue of 2012 constituted Chinese restrictions on exports of rare earth elements to the EU.[12] The EU Commissioners for Trade and Industry crafted the EU's response, which involved reporting China to the WTO along with the United States and Japan, while exploring methods of recycling the EU's rare earth stocks and pushing forward research into rare earth substitutes. Falling almost entirely within the policy area of trade, neither the HR/VP nor the EEAS played a role in this area.

The rest of the 2012 trade picture showed mixed results. Despite trade differences, the EU–China strategic partnership benefited from an ambitious 14th summit in February 2012, making strong commitments to foster closer people-to-people dialogue while remaining stymied by the failure to negotiate a settlement to China's full market economy status (MES) for the purposes of the WTO. While China will automatically attain MES by 2016, it is not currently treated as a market economy, resulting in a variety of trade restrictions with other WTO members that adversely impact the prices of Chinese exports.

The major point of EU–China discussion remained the eurozone crisis. German Chancellor Angela Merkel visited China in February 2012, ahead of the EU–China summit, principally to shore up Chinese financial support for the eurozone bail-out mechanism – the European Stability Mechanism – in the face of continuing Chinese governmental misgivings over the public perception inherent in underwriting years of European economic decadence. Despite a warning from China that the EU 'does its homework' on the eurozone crisis, it continued to make modest investments in the eurozone throughout 2012, highlighting the increasingly interdependent nature of EU–China relations. Crisis, however, appears to have spawned opportunity. Despite the crippling problems of the eurozone crisis, the EU remains China's largest export market and a major source of business for Chinese industrial and consumer goods exports, including luxury products hotly desired by the growing Chinese middle class. Satisfying increasing domestic economic demand, and thereby the continued domestic legitimacy of the Chinese Communist Party, the EU, in both economic and political terms, has emerged from the tremors of 2012 to impress upon Chinese leadership the vital need for its own continued economic growth. While issues such as trade and human rights remain a source of EU–China tension, these issues played a minimal role in Beijing's increasing recognition that the structural well-being of the global economy – and the EU as a major source of this well-being – trumped all other such considerations.

EU–China security and defence issues also saw progress in 2012. The HR/VP met Chinese Defence Minister Liang Guanglie in July to discuss co-operation on

---

[12] A number of sectors of the European economy are nearly 100 per cent dependent on rare earth materials.

© 2013 The Author(s) JCMS: Journal of Common Market Studies © 2013 John Wiley & Sons Ltd

counter-terrorism and piracy, concluding an agreement to hold regular high-level security and defence dialogues. In the same month, the EU naval force (EUNAVFOR) Atalanta commander met his Chinese counterpart on the EUNAVFOR flagship.

Interdependence-driven EU–China diplomacy set the stage for EU trade relations throughout Asia. Building on its free trade agreement (FTA) with South Korea in 2011, the EU commenced its seventh round of FTA negotiations with Malaysia in April 2012, set up a framework for FTA negotiations with Japan in May 2012, launched FTA negotiations with Vietnam in June 2012 and finalized trade negotiations with Singapore for a bilateral trade deal on 16 December 2012. While these trade deals form part of a response to the resurgent Asian economy, they also constitute agreements with countries with whom the EU has few human rights concerns. The trend therefore appears clear: FTA agreements depend on the extent to which human rights impact, positively or negatively, on trade relations between the EU and other Asian states. Given the potential range of trade agreements the EU could undertake with Asia and other regions, the 'west against the rest' narrative inherent in the proposed EU–US TTIP remains uneasily imprecise.

Enhanced relations between the EU and China were not necessarily reflected in relations with India, with whom the EU became strategic partners in 2004. EU–India engagement in 2012 focused on EU support for health and education, including funding fellowships for Indian students and professors to Europe. The 12th EU–India summit took place on 10 February in New Delhi. It was an ambitious meeting in terms of conclusions reached on a wide range of policies including security, energy and trade, but major issues remained, including the opening of negotiations for an EU–India bilateral trade deal. This announcement was overshadowed by the lack of consensus on Iran's nuclear programme. Given its high energy dependency upon Iran, India unsurprisingly refused to follow the EU and the United States in implementing sanctions. A maritime incident involving two Italian marines who shot dead two Indian fishermen, thinking them to be pirates, led to strained relations between the Italian and Indian governments following the arrest of the Italian marines and the subsequent Indian claim that they should be tried criminally.

Such divisions seem to underline Allen's (2013) observation that a coherent EU–India strategic partnership remains elusive. Frictions mark all the EU's strategic partnerships, but it is noteworthy that the two largest democracies in the world have not as yet struck an easy partnership on any significant areas. Indeed, the EU's relationship with China – a single-party state – appears to function at a deeper level. One explanation for this apparent mismatch is the significant differences in trade between China and India in their relations with the EU. As one Indian MP has stated, while the EU is India's second largest trading partner and accounts for 20 per cent of India's global trade, 'Europe's contribution to India's overall global trade has been shrinking even while the Indian economy grows' (Tharoor, 2012). The challenge for the EU is thus to exert leverage in its strategic relations while economic and trade relations remain in an unhelpful state of flux.

One region where the EU successfully built up economic ties in 2012 was Latin America. On 26 June the EU signed a trade agreement with Colombia and Peru, with plans to extend the trade deal to Ecuador and Bolivia. The deal removes European tariff barriers in areas such as sugar, flowers, coffee, bananas and beef, with reciprocal tariff lowering by Columbia in its automotive, chemicals, pharmaceuticals, telecoms, textiles,

© 2013 The Author(s) JCMS: Journal of Common Market Studies © 2013 John Wiley & Sons Ltd

alcoholic beverages and services sectors. On 29 June, the EU signed an association agreement with Costa Rica, El Salvador, Guatemala, Honduras, Nicaragua and Panama, which will, once ratified, open up European agricultural markets and Central American automotive, pharmaceutical, chemical and textile sectors. Such trade deals, and the norms and standards they initiate and inculcate, have traditionally been seen as a way to extend the EU's transformational power. While 2012 was something of a watershed year in this respect, more time is needed to see if the EU genuinely exhibits any transformative power in this region and with what effect (García, 2012).

Another key trade initiative in Latin America was the October summit between EU and Mercosur ministers to discuss a comprehensive FTA, which could bilaterally liberalize key industrial, agricultural and service sectors. In order to increase political co-operation between the actors, the proposed EU–Mercosur FTA will also include regular, formalized, political dialogue. The potential EU-Mercosur deal takes place at a time when EU–Brazil strategic relations themselves are developing. The importance of Brazil as a strategic partner for the EU was underlined in February 2012 when the HR/VP met the Brazilian foreign minister to discuss various global issues, including the Rio+20 meeting and regional co-operation with and throughout Mercosur.

Given its increasingly hegemonic role in Latin America, the EU is caught between garnering a closer bilateral relationship with Brazil, while simultaneously cultivating regionalism through Mercosur. A recurrent theme in EU–Brazil strategic relations is the balance the two players maintain between bilateralism and regionalism, and indeed whether such 'isms' can remain compatible. While 'Brazil has ceased to be a "natural partner" for the EU' in the eyes of some, the Union will need Brazil in order to boost its own influence and legitimacy with countries in the region who are not considered to be truly emerging economies (Gratius, 2012, p. 12). However, Mercosur–EU relations do not themselves constitute a simple region-to-region strategy. The proposed EU–Mercosur FTA has already encountered friction as a result of Argentina's insistence that future negotiations take into consideration the economic asymmetry between the EU and Latin America.

Turning to the east, the EU's relationship with Russia in 2012 was marked by the return of Vladimir Putin as president and the subsequent Union-wide condemnation of Putin's crackdown on civil society organizations. While the EU had little impact on the human rights situation in Russia during 2012, the EU did find renewed resolve in trade matters by opening an antitrust case against Russian energy giant Gazprom in September. Rather surprisingly, this did not provoke a major gas supply cut-off. However, the proposed American ballistic-missile defence shield continued to cause friction between the EU and Russia, and with negotiations for a review of the strategic partnership now stalled, the EU concluded 2012 with the bleak prospect of having to find new ways to tackle the most impasse-ridden of its strategic relationships.

Finally, 18 September 2012 saw the organization of the fifth EU–South Africa summit in Brussels, with a full menu of issues to be tackled by the strategic partnerships. Overshadowed to some extent by the tragedy of the Marikana miners' strike, in which 34 people lost their lives at the hands of South Africa's police service, the summit concluded a new formal dialogue on human rights, with strong commitments by both sides to completing the arms trade treaty. However, differences between the EU and South Africa remain, including the latter's reticence over the former's involvement in a number of

© 2013 The Author(s) JCMS: Journal of Common Market Studies © 2013 John Wiley & Sons Ltd

international crises, such as Libya in 2011 and Syria in 2012, raising South African fears that economic sanctions would eventually turn into military action.

Conclusions

The EU's role as a global actor was put to the test in many ways throughout 2012. This annual review has revealed a mixed picture as to the EU's overall responsiveness, and concludes with a few observations. First, the EU cannot implement a 'one size fits all' response to international crises in places such as North Africa, the Middle East and beyond. Crises in the Horn of Africa and the Sahel, which have elicited better strategic thinking on the part of the EU, still threaten to challenge the EU's crisis management capacities. Second, regarding its strategic partnerships, the Union's diplomatic activities were caught between continued adjustment to a changing world marked by the rise of the BRICS and the American 'Pacific pivot'. Whether the EU attempts to increase its diplomatic presence in Asia, regionally and bilaterally, remains to be seen; but it is clear that the majority of its existing strategic partnerships require more focused and concerted attention. The BRICS in particular 'have not cohered into a group where there is a common agenda with which the EU can engage', and as such, the EU is unable to promote a generic diplomatic response that could apply effectively to the substantial economic and political differences between each individual state within the group.[13]

Finally, 2012 saw a measure of strategic and institutional consolidation on the part of the HR/VP and the EEAS. Institutional problems persist in the EEAS, but the HR/VP oversaw a number of important appointments and strategic decisions. If in 2013 the EEAS can transform itself into a 'professional and efficient diplomatic service at European level' it has the opportunity to generate genuine confidence in its offices with both Member States and EU institutions, which in turn 'can be the catalyst for a "Europeanization" of foreign and security policy' (O'Sullivan, 2012b, p. 7). If not, the danger is that Member States will swiftly begin to use all available opportunities 'to assert national priorities within the Service', resulting in the attenuation of precisely the integrative foreign policy-making mechanics that the EEAS is designed to foster.[14]

References

Allen, D. (2013) 'The EU and India: Strategic Partners but Not a Strategic Partnership'. In Christiansen, T., Kirchner, E. and Murray, P. (eds) *The Palgrave Handbook of EU–Asia Relations* (Basingstoke: Palgrave Macmillan).

Balfour, R. and Raik, K. (2013) 'Equipping the European Union for the 21st century'. FIIA Report 36, FIIA Occasional Report 1 (Helsinki: Finnish Institute of International Affairs).

Bicchi, F. (2012) 'The European External Action Service: A Pivotal Actor in EU Foreign Policy Communications?'. *Hague Journal of Diplomacy*, Vol. 7, No. 1, pp. 81–94.

Biscop, S. (2012) 'EU Grand Strategy: Optimism is Mandatory'. Egmont Security Policy Brief 36 (Brussels: Royal Institute for International Relations).

Blockmans, S. (2012) 'The European External Action Service One Year On: First Signs of Strengths and Weaknesses'. CLEER Working Paper 2012/2 (The Hague: Centre for the Law of EU External Relations).

---

[13] Email interview with Professor Richard Whitman, University of Kent, 21 March 2013.
[14] Email interview with Professor Simon Duke, EIPA, 7 April 2013.

© 2013 The Author(s) JCMS: Journal of Common Market Studies © 2013 John Wiley & Sons Ltd

Casarini, N. (2012) 'EU Foreign Policy in the Asia Pacific: Striking the Right Balance between the US, China and ASEAN'. *EUISS Analysis*, September. Available at: «http://www.iss.europa.eu/uploads/media/US-China-and-ASEAN_01.pdf».

De Gucht, K. (2013) 'A European Perspective on Transatlantic Free Trade'. Speech delivered at a Harvard Kennedy School European Conference, Cambridge, MA. Available at: «http://trade.ec.europa.eu/doclib/docs/2013/march/tradoc_150707.pdf».

European Commission (2012) 'Interim Report to Leaders from the Co-chairs EU–US High Level Working Group on Jobs and Growth'. Available at: «http://trade.ec.europa.eu/doclib/docs/2012/june/tradoc_149557.pdf».

European Commission (2013) 'Recommendation for a Council decision authorising the opening of negotiations on a comprehensive trade and investment agreement, called the Transatlantic Trade and Investment Partnership, between the European Union and the united States of America'. *COM*(2013) 136 final, 12 March.

European External Action Service (EEAS) (2011) 'Report by the High Representative to the European Parliament, the Council and the Commission'. Brussels, 22 December. Available at: «http://www.eeas.europa.eu/images/top_stories/2011_eeas_report_cor.pdf».

European Parliament (EP) Directorate-General for External Policies, Directorate B Policy Department (2013a) *The Organisation and Functioning of the European External Action Service: Achievements, Challenges and Opportunities*. EXPO/B/AFET/2012/07, PE 457.111, Brussels.

European Parliament (EP) (2013b) 'Motion for a Resolution on the Situation in Egypt'. Available at: «http://www.europarl.europa.eu/sides/getDoc.do?type=MOTION&reference=B7-2013-0099&language=EN».

European Union (2012) 'Declaration by the High Representative on behalf of the European Union on the Middle East Peace Process'. 16079/2/12. Available at: «http://www.consilium.europa.eu/uedocs/cms_Data/docs/pressdata/en/cfsp/133902.pdf».

Fiott, D. (2013) 'Improving CSDP Planning and Capability Development: Could There be a "Frontex Formula?"'. *European Foreign Affairs Review*, Vol. 18, No. 1, pp. 47–62.

García, M. (2012) 'The European Union and Latin America: "Transformative power Europe" versus the Realities of Economic Interests'. *Cambridge Review of International Affairs*. Available at: «http://www.tandfonline.com/doi/abs/10.1080/09557571.2011.647762?journalCode=ccam20#.UZ4aVrVJOAg».

Gratius, S. (2012) 'Brazil and the European Union: Between Balancing and Bandwagoning'. European Strategic Partnerships Observatory Working Paper 2. Available at: «http://www.egmontinstitute.be/papers/12/sec-gov/ESPO_WP2_Brazil_and_the_EU.pdf».

Helwig, N., Ivan, P. and Kostanyan, H. (2013) *The New EU Foreign Policy Architecture: Reviewing the First Two Years of the EEAS* (Brussels: Centre for European Policy Studies).

Hemra, S., Raines, T. and Whitman, R. (2011) 'A Diplomatic Entrepreneur: Making the Most of the European External Action Service'. Report (London: Chatham House).

House of Lords (2013a) 'The EU's External Action Service: Report'. Report by the European Union Committee, 11th Report of Session 2012–13. Available at: «http://www.publications.parliament.uk/pa/ld201213/ldselect/ldeucom/147/147.pdf».

House of Lords (2013b) 'Unrevised Transcript of Evidence Taken before the Select Committee on the European Union Inquiry on the European External Action Service, Evidence Session 9 (22 January)'. Available at: «http://www.parliament.uk/documents/lords-committees/eu-sub-com-c/EEAS/ucEUC220113ev9.pdf».

Mattelaer, A. (2012) 'Reviewing the EU's Crisis Management Procedures'. IES Policy Brief 4 (Brussels: Institute for European Studies).

O'Sullivan, D. (2012a) 'The EEAS, National Foreign Services and the Future of European Diplomacy'. EPC Policy Dialogue, 6 September (Brussels: European Policy Centre).

O'Sullivan, D. (2012b) 'EPC Breakfast: The European External Action Service One Year On'. Brussels, 25 January. Available at: «http://www.eeas.europa.eu/images/top_stories/2012_dos _speech.pdf».

Petrov, P., Pomorska, K. and Vanhoonacker, S. (eds) (2012) 'Special Edition: The Emerging EU Diplomatic System'. *Hague Journal of Diplomacy*, Vol. 7, No. 1.

Simón, L. (2012) 'CSDP, Strategy and Crisis Management: Out of Area or Out of Business?' *International Spectator*, Vol. 47, No. 3, pp. 100–15.

Smith, M.E. (2012) 'Developing a "Comprehensive Approach" to International Security: Institutional Learning and the CSDP'. In Richardson, J. (ed.) *Constructing a Policy-Making State? Policy Dynamics in the EU* (Oxford: Oxford University Press).

Spence, D. (2012) 'The Early Days of the European External action Service: A Practitioner's View'. *Hague Journal of Diplomacy*, Vol. 7, No. 1, pp. 115–34.

Tharoor, S. (2012) 'Reconsider Relations with the European Union'. *India Today*. Available at: «http://indiatoday.intoday.in/story/european-union-india-ties-india-eu-joint-action-plan/1/ 189252.html».

Vanhoonacker, S. and Pomorska, K. (2013) 'The European External Action Service and Agenda-Setting in European Foreign Policy'. *Journal of European Public Policy*. DOI:10.1080/ 13501763.2012.758446.

JCMS 2013 Volume 51 Annual Review pp. 183–200   DOI: 10.1111/jcms.12044

The Eurozone in 2012: 'Whatever It Takes to Preserve the Euro'?

DERMOT HODSON
Birkbeck College

Introduction

The year 2012 was a proverbial game of two halves for the eurozone. The first half saw eurozone authorities trailing behind financial markets as confidence in Greece's economy waned in spite of an agreement in May on a second €130 billion package of loans. This was followed in June by an agreement between eurozone finance ministers to offer Spain up to €100 billion to help cover the cost of recapitalizing the country's banks. The second half of the year saw the eurozone fight back against financial markets. In July, European Central Bank (ECB) President Mario Draghi (2012a) hit the back of the net by promising to do 'whatever it takes to preserve the euro', paving the way for a programme of unlimited government bond purchases. The ECB's outright monetary transactions (OMT), as this programme was called, brought the game into extra time but sudden death for the single currency remains a possibility at the time of writing in April 2013 as Member States struggle to solve the underlying causes of the euro crisis. Whether plans for banking union and an embryonic fiscal federation, which were unveiled by European Council President Herman Van Rompuy in December, provide the required remedy in this regard is a moot point. Progress towards these projects had, in any case, already encountered serious problems by the year's end.

This article takes stock of these and other key developments in its review of the eurozone for 2012. Section I discusses the eurozone's poor economic performance and Member States' attempt to promote recovery through a new growth compact. Section II focuses on the ECB's change of heart over bond purchases and notes a controversy with the European Parliament (EP) over a lack of gender balance in appointments to the Bank's executive board. Section III evaluates the European Systemic Risk Board's (ESRB) emerging approach to financial supervision. Section IV looks at economic policy co-ordination in the eurozone and asks what difference the Six Pack made to macroeconomic surveillance in 2012. Section V explores the eurozone's interaction with selected international financial institutions in 2012. Section VI discusses running repairs to European monetary union's institutional architecture including the entry into force of the Fiscal Compact and the European Stability Mechanism Treaty and emerging plans for European banking union.

© 2013 The Author(s) JCMS: Journal of Common Market Studies © 2013 John Wiley & Sons Ltd, 9600 Garsington Road, Oxford OX4 2DQ, UK and 350 Main Street, Malden, MA 02148, USA

I. The Economic Situation in 2012

Having slowed in 2011, real gross domestic product (GDP) in the eurozone contracted by 0.6 per cent in 2012 (see Table 1).[1] Quarterly GDP growth stagnated between January and March and turned negative thereafter. The drivers of this double-dip recession – for this was the second time that the eurozone had experienced at least two successive quarters of negative GDP growth since 2008 – were both domestic and foreign in origin. As regards domestic factors, tight credit conditions in the eurozone continued to weigh on private consumption and corporate investment, as did the effects of continued fiscal consolidation on demand. In terms of foreign factors, eurozone exporters were hard hit by the continuing challenges facing their three most important trading partners in 2012: the United Kingdom, which recorded zero growth; China, which saw growth continue to moderate; and the United States, which experienced a stop-start recovery.

The economic outlook in individual eurozone members was little better. Having experienced modest rates of GDP growth in 2010 and 2011, France experienced no growth at all in 2012. French firms' preference for running down inventories rather than ordering new stock was a key factor behind this stagnation. Economic conditions were also disappointing in Germany, which saw its impressive recovery from the recession of 2009 peter out due to weak consumer demand and a sharp fall in private sector investment. Among the Member States at the epicentre of the eurozone crisis, Ireland fared the least worst. Although Irish GDP slowed from 1.4 per cent in 2011 to 0.7 per cent in 2012 this slowdown was not as bad as feared due to a stronger than expected export performance and, encouragingly, increased capital investment among Irish firms. Greece, too, put in an impressive export performance but its domestic demand remained in a state of free fall as the government continued to push through swingeing expenditure cuts and emergency tax increases in an effort to get government borrowing under control. In 2012, Greek GDP fell by 6.4 per cent – the fifth successive year in which the economy contracted.[2]

Against this backdrop, it is not surprising that the eurozone labour market struggled in 2012 (see Table 2). In the eurozone as a whole, the number of people unemployed as a percentage of the civilian labour force reached 11.4 per cent. The worst performers here were Spain and Greece, with the rate of joblessness standing at a staggering 25 per cent in both countries. Young people bore the brunt of this tragedy, with the rate of unemployment among 16–24-year-olds exceeding 50 per cent in Spain and Portugal in 2012.[3] Germany continues to buck European trends. The rate of youth unemployment in the eurozone's largest economy was just 8.1 per cent in 2012. The overall rate of unemployment in Germany, meanwhile stood at 5.4 per cent in 2012, the lowest rate achieved since unification in 1991.

Faced with negative growth rates and rising unemployment, it is not surprising that the harmonized rate of consumer price inflation in the eurozone fell from 2.7 per cent in 2011 to 2.5 per cent in 2012 (see Table 3). Here, eurozone inflation also benefited from a benign international environment thanks, in part, to falling prices for oil, minerals and

---

[1] Unless otherwise stated, the macroeconomic data cited in this article are taken from the Commission's Winter Economic Forecast 2013 (European Commission, 2013).
[2] See De Grauwe and Ji's contribution to this issue.
[3] Source: European Union Labour Force Survey (Eurostat). Available at: «http://epp.eurostat.ec.europa.eu/portal/page/portal/labour_market».

© 2013 The Author(s) JCMS: Journal of Common Market Studies © 2013 John Wiley & Sons Ltd

Table 1: Real GDP Growth (% Annual Change) – Eurozone, 2008–13

	2009	*2010*	*2011*	*2012*	*2013[f]*
Belgium	−2.8	2.4	1.8	−0.2	0.2
Germany	−5.1	4.2	3.0	0.7	0.5
Estonia	−14.1	3.3	8.3	3.2	3.0
Ireland	−5.5	−0.8	1.4	0.7	1.1
Greece	−3.1	−4.9	−7.1	−6.4	−4.4
Spain	−3.7	−0.3	0.4	−1.4	−1.4
France	−3.1	1.7	1.7	0.0	0.1
Italy	−5.5	1.8	0.4	−2.2	−1.0
Cyprus	−1.9	1.3	0.5	−2.3	−3.5
Luxembourg	−4.1	2.9	1.7	0.2	0.5
Malta	−2.4	2.7	1.6	1.0	1.5
Netherlands	−3.7	1.6	1.0	−0.9	−0.6
Austria	−3.8	2.1	2.7	0.7	0.7
Portugal	−2.9	1.9	−1.6	−3.2	−1.9
Slovenia	−7.8	1.2	0.6	−2.0	−2.0
Slovakia	−4.9	4.4	3.2	2.0	1.1
Finland	−8.5	3.3	2.8	−0.1	0.3
Eurozone	−4.4	2.0	1.4	−0.6	−0.3

Source: European Commission (2013, p. 112, table 1).
Note: Forecasts are denoted by *f*.

Table 2: Unemployment (% of the Civilian Labour Force) – Eurozone, 2008–13

	2009	*2010*	*2011*	*2012*	*2013[f]*
Belgium	7.9	8.3	7.2	7.3	7.7
Germany	7.8	7.1	5.9	5.5	5.7
Estonia	13.8	16.9	12.5	10.0	9.8
Ireland	12.0	13.9	14.7	14.8	14.6
Greece	9.5	12.6	17.7	24.7	27.9
Spain	18.0	20.1	21.7	25.0	26.9
France	9.5	9.7	9.6	10.3	10.7
Italy	7.8	8.4	8.4	10.6	11.6
Cyprus	5.5	6.5	7.9	12.1	13.7
Luxembourg	5.1	4.6	4.8	5.0	5.4
Malta	6.9	6.9	6.5	6.5	6.4
Netherlands	3.7	4.5	4.4	5.3	6.3
Austria	4.8	4.4	4.2	4.4	4.5
Portugal	10.6	12.0	12.9	15.7	17.3
Slovenia	5.9	7.3	8.2	9.0	9.8
Slovakia	12.1	14.5	13.6	14.0	14.0
Finland	8.2	8.4	7.8	7.7	8.0
Eurozone	9.6	10.1	10.2	11.4	12.2

Source: European Commission (2013, p. 123, table 24).
Note: Forecasts are denoted by *f*.

© 2013 The Author(s) JCMS: Journal of Common Market Studies © 2013 John Wiley & Sons Ltd

Table 3: Inflation Rates (% Change on Preceding Year) – Eurozone, 2008–13

	2009	2010	2011	2012	2013[f]
Belgium	0.0	2.3	3.5	2.6	1.6
Germany	0.2	1.2	2.5	2.1	1.8
Estonia	0.2	2.7	5.1	4.2	3.6
Ireland	−1.7	−1.6	1.2	1.9	1.3
Greece	1.3	4.7	3.1	1.0	−0.8
Spain	−0.2	2.0	3.1	2.4	1.7
France	0.1	1.7	2.3	2.2	1.6
Italy	0.8	1.6	2.9	3.3	2.0
Cyprus	0.2	2.6	3.5	3.1	1.5
Luxembourg	0.0	2.8	3.7	2.9	1.7
Malta	1.8	2.0	2.5	3.2	2.2
Netherlands	1.0	0.9	2.5	2.8	2.6
Austria	0.4	1.7	3.6	2.6	2.2
Portugal	−0.9	1.4	3.6	2.8	0.6
Slovenia	0.9	2.1	2.1	2.8	2.2
Slovakia	0.9	0.7	4.1	3.7	1.9
Finland	1.6	1.7	3.3	3.2	2.5
Eurozone	0.3	1.6	2.7	2.5	1.8

Source: European Commission (2013, p. 120, table 17).
Note: Forecasts are denoted by *f*.

metals and the failure of a foreseen hike in world food prices to materialize. Among eurozone members, Greece recorded the lowest rate of inflation (1.0 per cent) and Estonia recorded the highest (4.2 per cent). In the case of the latter, a rapid increase in wages since 2009 (particularly in the construction sector) was among the key drivers of inflation in 2012. That Estonia finds itself in this position just one year after joining the eurozone brings home the challenges of running an economic policy without an autonomous monetary policy. It could equally be seen as a form of Maastricht fatigue, whereby national economic authorities are prone to economic indiscipline once the convergence criteria for entering the eurozone have been met (see Wyplosz, 2003).

The eurozone budget deficit fell from 4.2 per cent of GDP in 2011 to 3.5 per cent in 2012 (see Table 4). The pace of fiscal consolidation was greatest in Ireland, which cut its deficit from 13.4 per cent to 7.3 per cent, although this figure masked an increase in general government debt as a percentage of GDP from 106.4 per cent to 117.2 per cent. Belgium, Greece, Italy and Portugal also recorded triple-digit debt levels in 2012. Of these Member States, only Belgium avoided the wrath of financial markets in 2012 thanks, in part, to the fact that its budget deficit, at 3.0 per cent, was among the smallest in the eurozone. Germany, meanwhile, posted a budget surplus of 0.1 per cent, making it the most prudent country in the eurozone in 2012 once again. France, in contrast, posted a budget deficit of 4.6 per cent in 2012.

Diverging fiscal performances go some way towards explaining Franco–German differences over how to handle the eurozone crisis in 2012. Whereas German Chancellor Angela Merkel remained steadfast in her commitment to fiscal austerity, the newly elected French President, François Hollande came to office in May arguing that more needed to

© 2013 The Author(s) JCMS: Journal of Common Market Studies © 2013 John Wiley & Sons Ltd

Table 4: Net Lending (+) or Net Borrowing (−) General Government Balance (% of GDP) – Eurozone, 2008–13

	2009	2010	2013	2012^f	2013
Belgium	−5.5	−3.8	−3.7	−3.0	−3.0
Germany	−3.1	−4.1	−0.8	0.1	−0.2
Estonia	−2.0	0.2	1.1	−0.5	−0.4
Ireland	−13.9	−30.9	−13.4	−7.7	−7.3
Greece	−15.6	−10.7	−9.4	−6.6	−4.6
Spain	−11.2	−9.7	−9.4	−10.2	−6.7
France	−7.5	−7.1	−5.2	−4.6	−3.7
Italy	−5.4	−4.5	−3.9	−2.9	−2.1
Cyprus	−6.1	−5.3	−6.3	−5.5	−4.5
Luxembourg	−0.8	−0.8	−0.3	−1.5	−0.9
Malta	−3.8	−3.6	−2.7	−2.6	−2.9
Netherlands	−5.6	−5.1	−4.5	−4.1	−3.6
Austria	−4.1	−4.5	−2.5	−3.0	−2.5
Portugal	−10.2	−9.8	−4.4	−5.0	−4.9
Slovenia	−6.0	−5.7	−6.4	−4.5	−5.1
Slovakia	−8.0	−7.7	−4.9	−4.8	−3.3
Finland	−2.5	−2.5	−0.8	−1.7	−1.5
Eurozone	−6.3	−6.2	−4.2	−3.5	−2.8

Source: European Commission (2013, p. 129, table 36).
Note: Forecasts are denoted by f.

be done at the EU level to promote growth (Hollande, 2012, p. 12).[4] In so doing, he struck a chord with a number of other EU leaders who agreed in June 2012 on a new 'compact for growth and jobs'. The term 'compact' here was misleading since a growth-friendly rewrite of the EU's Fiscal Compact was off-limits for Merkel and others. What was agreed instead was a set of new(ish) policy commitments, including an increase in the European Investment Bank's (EIB) lending capacity by €60 billion, an agreement to divert unused EU structural funds to projects targeted at businesses and unemployed people, and a new project bond initiative, which will see the EIB offer (partial) guarantees for large-scale infrastructure projects.[5] Together these commitments amounted to €120 billion for enhancing growth, too small a sum to make much difference to the eurozone's growth prospects, but sufficient to show that EU leaders are capable of imagining a 'Plan B' if the outlook for the European economy remains moribund.[6]

II. Monetary Policy in 2012

Eurozone monetary policy has been cautious in the extreme since the global financial crisis struck. The ECB, it is true, was ahead of the curve in providing emergency liquidity

[4] Hollande's manifesto was a model of ambiguity. Strictly speaking, he promised a pact for 'responsibility, governance and growth' and to renegotiate the Fiscal Compact while leaving open the question of how these objectives related. Following his election, Hollande focused on the first of these goals and quietly dropped his commitment to the second, allowing France to ratify the Fiscal Compact in October 2012. For an account of France's EU policy under Hollande, see Lequesne in this issue.
[5] See EurActiv (2012) for a sceptical view about the compact for growth and jobs.
[6] By way of comparison, the American Recovery and Reinvestment Act (2009) increased borrowing by the American government to the tune of US$831 billion over the period 2009–19.

© 2013 The Author(s) JCMS: Journal of Common Market Studies © 2013 John Wiley & Sons Ltd

support in August 2007 (see Trichet, 2010) but the eurozone monetary authority has been much more hesitant than other central banks about cutting interest rates and, when interest rates could not fall much further, embracing so-called 'unconventional monetary policies'. Whereas the United States Federal Reserve started cutting interest rates in September 2007 and then launched a full-scale programme of government bond buying in March 2009, the ECB waited until October 2008 to cut interest rates and until May 2010 to begin buying government bonds. Even then the ECB's securities markets programme (SMP) was seen as having limited effectiveness because of its emphasis on buying bonds on secondary markets rather than directly from governments (Buiter and Rahbari, 2012, p. 29).

The year 2012 produced a more decisive response from the ECB, in part because of the resignation of two key critics of bond purchases – Bundesbank President Axel Weber and ECB Executive Board Member Jürgen Stark – but primarily because of the leadership shown by ECB President Mario Draghi. Following the end of Jean-Claude Trichet's eight-year term of office in November 2011, Draghi – a surprise choice to lead the ECB after Axel Weber ruled himself out (Hodson, 2012) – quickly won the confidence of markets by launching a new long-term refinancing operation (LTRO), which provided more than €1 trillion in cheap three-year loans to European banks. In retrospect, the LTRO served only as a sticking plaster for European banks, which remain in a fragile state, as evidenced by the slow speed at which they have sought to repay these loans. The LTRO served as a powerful tonic for the ECB, however, by allowing the bank to counter protracted criticism over its perceived failure to go far enough in response to the crisis. Decisive too was the ECB governing council's unanimous decision in July 2012 to cut interest rates on its deposit facility to 0.00, its main financing rate to 0.75 and its marginal lending facility to 1.50, their lowest ever levels.

In the end, the LTRO and interest rate cuts served as mere sideshows to the ECB's main event in 2012: the launch at long last of an unlimited programme of bond purchases. As discussed in last year's review of the eurozone, Draghi refused to commit to such a programme after assuming the ECB Presidency in November 2011 but he left himself some wiggle room (Hodson, 2012). The room for manoeuvre was duly exploited in July 2012, when Draghi (2012a) told a conference of international investors in London that the ECB would do 'whatever it takes to preserve the euro'. The soothing effect of these seven words on financial markets was almost instantaneous. In Spain, for instance, the interest rate on ten-year government bonds fell from 7.62 to 6.75 per cent within a week of Draghi's speech and to 5.27 per cent by the end of the year. A similar effect could be observed in other eurozone members, with the comparable interest rate in Italy falling from 6.06 to 4.50 between late July and the end of December.

Precisely what the ECB President had in mind by 'whatever it takes' became clearer if not entirely clear-cut in August 2012 with the launch of a successor to the SMP, known as 'outright monetary transactions' (OMT). Simply put, the OMT confirms the ECB's *de facto* role as lender of last resort subject to three caveats. First, the ECB's purchase of government bonds will be limited to secondary markets, although unlike the SMP the OMT allows, in principle, for the unlimited purchase of government bonds. Second, the OMT is subject to strict conditionality. Member States that benefit from ECB bond purchases must first seek financial support from the EU and are expected to seek assistance from the International Monetary Fund (IMF), which means that these countries will have committed themselves to a prior programme of fiscal consolidation and economic reform. For champions of the OMT, the ECB's commitment to unlimited bond purchases stopped the eurozone sovereign debt crisis from getting worse even if it did not tackle the root causes of eurozone fiscal imbalances (De Grauwe, 2012). For critics of the OMT, the conditionality attached to ECB bond purchases lacks credibility in as much as Member States that are most likely to benefit from this instrument will find it hardest to meet the requirements for fiscal consolidation or other hard-to-implement economic reforms (Lombardi, 2012).

The OMT has yet to be used at the time of writing in April 2013 – indeed, it became clear in the turmoil over the financial rescue of Cyprus in March 2013 that the legal documentation associated with this programme was not yet complete (Draghi, 2013) – but it remains a source of controversy within the ECB's governing structures. The Bundesbank has emerged once again as critic-in-chief of bond purchases, with Axel Weber's successor, Jens Weidmann, voting against the OMT in August 2012 and questioning its potential effectiveness thereafter (see, for example, Weidmann, 2012). That the ECB has shown itself capable of acting without the support of the Bundesbank could be interpreted as a sign of growing institutional maturity; prior to the launch of the euro, some commentators foresaw the possibility of German hegemony in EMU (see Feldstein, 1997). That said, the diverging preferences of the ECB and the Bundesbank raise questions over how long the single currency will retain legitimacy in Germany. Angela Merkel, for one, has played her cards carefully here, defending Bundesbank President Jens Weidmann's right to criticize the OMT, but without endorsing the substance of his criticisms (Bryant, 2012).

Turning from questions of policy to institutional matters, 2012 was marked by yet more controversy over appointments to the ECB executive board. Although the Treaty imposes no nationality requirement on the occupants of this six-seat body, which runs the ECB on a day-to-day basis, a convention emerged in the early years of EMU whereby the four largest eurozone members – France, Germany, Italy and Spain – reserved seats for their nominees while leaving the other two to be rotated between smaller eurozone members. The appointment to the ECB executive board in January 2012 of one German, Jörg Asmussen, to replace another, Jürgen Stark, was in keeping with this tradition. The choice in November 2012 of Yves Mersch, a Luxembourger, to replace José Manuel González-Páramo, a Spaniard, was not. Welcome though Mersch's appointment was from the point of view of the ECB's independence from large Member States, it was opposed by the EP. The EU legislature was rightly critical in this regard of the absence of women on the board following the retirement of Gertrude Tumpel-Gugerell in May 2011. Why not one suitable woman could be found to replace González-Páramo is unclear – former Spanish Finance Minister Elena Salgado was among the names mentioned, but she failed to win support from Madrid – especially when it is noted that the seven-person board of governors of the Federal Reserve has three female members.[7] In any event, the EP failed to overturn Mersch's nomination since the European Council is required to consult rather than co-decide with the EP on appointments to the ECB executive board (Article 283,

---

[7] That there are no female national central bank governors in the eurozone at present is a poor excuse here since the ECB executive board would only gain from economists with experience from beyond the world of central banking. Of the three female members of the Fed's governing board, only one (Janet L. Yellen) has prior experience as head of one of the Federal Reserve Banks.

© 2013 The Author(s) JCMS: Journal of Common Market Studies © 2013 John Wiley & Sons Ltd

TFEU). EU leaders' lack of regard for the outcome of this consultation speaks to long-standing concerns about the eurozone monetary authority's lack of accountability compared to other central banks (Verdun, 1998).

III. Financial Supervision in 2012

Last year's review of the eurozone provided details on the make-up of the ESRB – a new EU financial supervisor launched in the light of the global financial crisis (Hodson, 2012). The initial meetings of this body were low-key affairs, it was noted, but the ESRB became more vocal about systemic threats to financial stability as the year progressed. Mario Draghi took over where Jean-Claude Trichet left off as ESRB chair by using his regular appearances before the EP as a bully pulpit from which to preach about the financial risks facing the EU as a whole. In his first visit of the year to the EP as ESRB Chair, Draghi (2012b) described a 'grave state of affairs' in which a worsening economic outlook and continued concerns over fiscal sustainability were impairing the normal functioning of financial markets. By the end of the year, Draghi (2012c) offered an upbeat but not exactly optimistic assessment thanks to the OMT.

In October 2011, the ESRB made its first recommendation to national supervisors with the test case involving lending in foreign currency. Such recommendations rely on peer pressure insofar as Member State authorities are required to 'act or explain' – that is, comply or give public reasons for non-compliance with the guidance of the ESRB. Peer pressure can be problematic as an instrument of policy co-ordination, especially when naming and shaming imposes costs on the sanctioning institution as well as the sanctioned party (see Hodson, 2011a, ch. 5). Quite why it was so reluctant to have a public debate over compliance with its first recommendation is unclear, but by late 2012 the ESRB was prepared only to say that it was 'processing the replies received from the addressees of its recommendations'.[8]

Inauspicious though this start was, it did not stop the ESRB from issuing three recommendations in 2012 concerning money market funds, the US-dollar-denominated funding of credit institutions and the funding of credit institutions more generally. Another important milestone was the publication in September 2012 of the first ESRB 'Risk Dashboard', a quarterly database of quantitative indicators of systemic risk covering, *inter alia*, money, equity, bond and foreign exchange markets.[9] Welcome though the launch of the Risk Dashboard was, it too betrayed a reluctance to sound the alarm against individual Member States. The notes accompanying updates to the Risk Dashboard were bland affairs that included only general references to developments in Member States. Little forewarning was given here, for example, of the systemic problems that came to light in Cyprus in early 2013. For its part, the ESRB has been at pains to stress that the Risk Dashboard should not be treated as an early warning system – a disclaimer that invites the question of when or whether such a system will be developed.

Institutionally, the ESRB found itself in the odd position in 2012 of establishing itself as an EU financial supervisor while Member States took forward plans for a radical overhaul of EU financial supervision. Such moves were welcomed rather than resisted by

[8] On the broader issues of compliance in the EU, see Falkner's contribution to this issue.
[9] Issues of the ESRB Risk Dashboard are available at: «http://www.esrb.europa.eu/pub/html/index.en.html».

© 2013 The Author(s) JCMS: Journal of Common Market Studies © 2013 John Wiley & Sons Ltd

the ESRB general board, which called in December 2012 for 'a consistent implementation of the agreements on the banking union, including the speedy adoption of the Council regulations concerning the establishment of a single supervisory mechanism' (ESRB, 2012). Key to this support was the Commission's proposal in September 2012 that national central banks and/or national financial supervisors should have a seat on a new ECB supervisory board. This decision, which is reminiscent of the Maastricht Treaty's empowerment of national central banks through their membership of the ECB governing council, ensures for better or worse that the multitude of national supervisors present on the ESRB general board will retain their seat at the table. This holds true for eurozone and non-eurozone members alike, with representatives of the latter given the possibility of participating in the ECB's new supervisory board.

IV. Economic Policy Co-ordination in 2012

The Stability and Growth Pact

The Six Pack, which consists of half a dozen legislative reforms to EU economic policy co-ordination enacted in response to the sovereign debt crisis, took effect in December 2011 (see Hodson, 2012; Amtenbrink, 2012; Dinan, 2012). The centrepiece of these reforms was an overhaul of the Stability and Growth Pact, a combination of political agreement and secondary legislation for, *inter alia*, speeding up and clarifying the Treaty's excessive deficit procedure (Article 126, TFEU). The Stability and Growth Pact mark III – the original agreement having been signed in 1997 and revised in 2005 – shifts the emphasis from peer pressure to pecuniary sanctions inasmuch as eurozone members face the possibility of financial penalties at an earlier stage of the excessive deficit procedure. The new pact also makes it harder for finance ministers to avoid such penalties, as occurred in November 2003 when a set of Commission recommendations concerning France and Germany failed to gain a qualified majority of support in the Economic and Financial Affairs Council (Ecofin). The Six Pack introduces a new principle of reversed qualified majority voting whereby a Commission recommendation to impose sanctions will be carried unless it is vetoed by a qualified majority of Member States.

Significant though the Six Pack has the potential to be, it made surprisingly little difference to eurozone fiscal surveillance in 2012. For the 14 eurozone members that began the year in a state of excessive deficit – that is, all countries except Estonia, Finland and Luxembourg – one of two fates was in store. The first group, which comprised Germany and Malta, escaped from purgatory after the Commission recommended and the Council agreed under Article 126(12) to close the excessive deficit procedure on the grounds that budget deficits had been sustainably reduced below the 3 per cent of GDP threshold. The second group, which included Austria, Belgium, Cyprus, France, Greece, Ireland, Italy, the Netherlands, Portugal, Slovakia, Slovenia and Spain avoided fire and damnation after the Commission recommended and the Council agreed under Article 126(7) that Member States had taken effective action in response to earlier recommendations. In some cases this agreement was tacit; Ireland, for example, remains bound by an Article 126(7) recommendation that remains unchanged since December 2010. In other cases agreement was more explicit. Portugal, for instance, was subject to a second Article 126(7) recommendation in September 2012 – the first one having been issued in December 2009.

© 2013 The Author(s) JCMS: Journal of Common Market Studies © 2013 John Wiley & Sons Ltd

For all the talk of pecuniary sanctions under the new Stability and Growth Pact, no eurozone member with budget deficits in excess of 3 per cent of GDP faced financial penalties in 2012. The working assumption, it would seem, remains that Member States in a state of excessive deficit will not face financial penalties under Article 126(11) providing they comply with (repeated) Article 126(7) recommendations. The principle of reverse qualified majority voting makes little direct difference here since conventional qualified majority voting applies for this stage of the excessive deficit procedure under the Six Pack.

When it comes to assessing compliance with and/or revising Article 126(7) recommendations, the Commission and Ecofin continue to exercise considerable discretion under the Six Pack. A case in point concerns the treatment of Spain – a Member State that had been given until 2012 to get government borrowing below 3 per cent of GDP under an Article 126(7) recommendation endorsed by Ecofin in April 2009. This deadline was extended to 2013 in December 2011 because of 'unexpected adverse economic events' before the Article 126(7) recommendation was revised yet again in July 2012 to allow for a new deadline of 2014 for correcting the excessive deficit.[10] Where the Six Pack did make a difference here was in the timetable for following up on this recommendation, with Spain being given three months rather than the usual six to take effective action given the gravity of the situation.

Excessive Imbalance Procedure

Another key element of the Six Pack was the launch of a new macroeconomic imbalance procedure. This close cousin of the Stability and Growth Pact is designed to prevent and correct for the kinds of cross-country growth and inflation differences, credit booms, housing bubbles and other forms of imbalance that accumulated during the first decade of the single currency and which amplified the effects of the global financial crisis when it struck. The Commission hit the ground running in 2012 by launching a new scoreboard for measuring macroeconomic imbalances and a set of indicative thresholds for judging such imbalances to be excessive. The metrics employed here include current account balances, unit labour costs and the evolution of house prices. The thresholds include, for instance, current account deficits in excess of 4 per cent of GDP, current account surpluses in excess of 6 per cent of GDP, percentage change in unit labour costs in excess of 9 per cent and real house price increases in excess of 6 per cent.

As with debates about the Maastricht Treaty's convergence criteria two decades ago (Buiter *et al.*, 1993) questions can be asked about whether the precise numbers used in these indicators have a meaningful economic rationale. Particularly problematic in this regard is the excessive imbalance procedure's greater tolerance for current account surpluses compared to current account deficits – a politically convenient asymmetry given the reluctance of German authorities to countenance measures that could hinder the country's external competitiveness.[11] That said, evidence that composite measures of macroeconomic imbalances could have provided an effective early warning for the eurozone in

[10] For details on the various steps taken in relation to Spain under the excessive deficit procedure, see: «http://ec.europa.eu/economy_finance/economic_governance/sgp/deficit/countries/spain_en.htm».
[11] A case in point is Wolfgang Schäuble's speech at Chatham House in October 2011 in which the German finance minister castigated some eurozone members for running persistent current account deficits while rejecting the idea that those Member States running persistent current account surpluses should be punished for their competitiveness (Schäuble and Niblet, 2011).

© 2013 The Author(s) JCMS: Journal of Common Market Studies © 2013 John Wiley & Sons Ltd

advance of the global financial crisis (Knedlik and Von Schweinitz, 2012) suggests that the excessive imbalance procedure is an economically worthwhile exercise.

Compared to the EFSB's financial stability dashboard, the Commission's macroeconomic imbalance scorecard is, furthermore, a model of clarity. Following the publication of the Commission's first Alert Mechanism Report in February 2012, seven eurozone members (Belgium, Spain, France, Italy, Cyprus, Slovenia and Finland) were selected for an in-depth review because of concerns over the risks posed by macroeconomic imbalances. These reviews fed, in turn, into a set of country-specific recommendations on macroeconomic imbalances endorsed by Ecofin in July 2012. As with the EFSB's Dashboard, however, the Commission's scoreboard suggested a reluctance to be too critical of errant Member States. Of the seven countries subject to in-depth review in 2012, the EU executive cited none for having excessive imbalances. This includes Cyprus which was adjudged to be facing imbalances that were 'very serious' but 'not excessive' in May 2012 even though the country exceeded a number of the indicative thresholds associated with the macroeconomic imbalance procedure scorecard (European Commission, 2012a). The Commission's reluctance to exert more pressure was an opportunity missed given the systemic banking crisis that erupted in Cyprus in March 2013, although it should be noted that the Commission went further than Ecofin in expressing concerns over this Member State in 2012. Whereas the Commission published a detailed report on macroeconomic imbalances in Cyprus in July 2012 that raised specific concerns over the country's precarious financial model, the Council of Ministers adopted a set of country-specific recommendations on Cyprus that conveyed insufficient urgency over this problem and offered limited ideas about how to remedy it (Council of the European Union, 2012).

V. The Eurozone as a Global Actor in 2012

The global financial crisis allowed the EU to show an unprecedented degree of leadership in international financial institutions and forums but, as noted in last year's review, this momentum has been difficult to sustain as the eurozone has become part of the problem for the world economy rather than part of the solution (Hodson, 2012). In 2012, the EU and its Member States continued to speak with one voice on major international economic issues but in so doing their tone became decidedly defensive. At the G20 summit in Los Cabos in June 2012, for instance, the eurozone came under increasing pressure to put its house in order, as evidenced by Canadian Prime Minister Stephen Harper's sharp criticisms of Europe's 'half-done' monetary union[12] and Australian Prime Minister Julia Gillard's unsolicited sermon about what Europe could learn from the Australian economic model (Cullen, 2012). José Manuel Barroso responded to such criticisms with uncharacteristic terseness. The EU had not come to Los Cabos, the Commission President told the G20 press pack, 'to receive lessons in terms of democracy and in terms of how to run an economy' (Wintour et al., 2012). The summit conclusions themselves ventured no such lessons – a testament, for better or worse, to Europe's collective influence behind the scenes.

Perhaps the most significant outcome of the Los Cabos summit was the G20's decision to support a US$450 billion increase in the resources available to the IMF (Group of Twenty, 2012). The fund does not earmark money for particular regions, but it is plain

[12] See *Canadian Press*, 8 June 2012.

© 2013 The Author(s) JCMS: Journal of Common Market Studies © 2013 John Wiley & Sons Ltd

that these additional resources were put in place to deal with the eurozone's worsening sovereign debt crisis. That Brazil, Russia, India, China and South Africa committed an estimated US$75 billion to this sum was symptomatic of the growing importance of emerging powers within the IMF. It also drew attention to the under-representation of these countries in the Fund as reflected in the G20's calls at Los Cabos for movement on the quota and voice reforms agreed in 2010. No such movement was forthcoming at the annual meeting of the IMF in Tokyo in October 2012. This outcome was frustrating for emerging powers but beneficial in the short term for EU Member States insofar as the former stood to gain greater influence within the IMF at the expense of the latter under the 2010 reforms (see Hodson, 2011b).

Last year's review noted the ease with which eurozone members ensured that their preferred candidate, Christine Lagarde, secured the post of managing director of the IMF. This year saw an altogether less sure-footed approach by the eurozone when it came to choosing a new president of the EBRD. The EU is a shareholder of this lesser-known but important international financial institution, which played a key role in supporting investment projects in central and eastern Europe in the 1990s and 2000s and which has seen its role reinvigorated by the global financial crisis and the Arab Spring. Since the EBRD's establishment in 1991 the presidency has been occupied by a candidate from either France or Germany but this convention was broken in May 2012 after the United Kingdom's nominee, Suma Chakrabarti, won the backing of a majority of EBRD governors to secure the top job. Chakrabarti was without doubt a worthy candidate – he served as permanent secretary in the United Kingdom's Department for International Development – but his appointment owed a debt to the EU's failure to agree on a suitable Franco–German candidate. Thomas Mirrow, the German incumbent, had a strong claim to reappointment here – not least because of his efforts to stabilize banks in central and eastern Europe after the global financial crisis intensified in late 2008. Germany did not push for Mirrow's reappointment, however, reportedly because of a deal to back French nominee, Philippe de Fontaine Vive Curtaz. The Frenchman failed to win the backing of all EU Member States, however, leaving Chakrabarti to emerge as a compromise candidate backed by the United Kingdom, the United States, Australia and Canada. Quite why de Fontaine Vive Curtaz, a well-respected vice-president of the European Investment Bank, failed to win the EU's backing is uncertain, but there may have been a concern about giving France undue influence over the EBRD's new programme of investment in North Africa following the Arab Spring (Buckley, 2012). If true, this raises the question of why France and Germany did not throw their weight behind Mirrow or look to a nominee from another eurozone member. To lose one suitable candidate under such circumstances was unfortunate. To lose two looked like carelessness.

VI. The Reform of Eurozone Governance

'We are like sailors who on the open sea must reconstruct their ship but are never able to start afresh from the bottom', wrote the philosopher W.V.O. Quine (1960). These words come to mind when recalling the frenetic efforts to reform eurozone governance since the global financial crisis struck. Last year's review of the eurozone noted the conclusion of negotiations over the Six Pack, which as discussed above saw its first full year in operation in 2012, along with ongoing negotiations over the Fiscal Compact – an intergovernmental

© 2013 The Author(s) JCMS: Journal of Common Market Studies © 2013 John Wiley & Sons Ltd

agreement to intensify economic policy co-ordination among a subset of EU Member States in the light of the financial crisis – and the European Stability Mechanism (ESM) Treaty – an intergovernmental agreement on a new permanent crisis resolution mechanism for the eurozone.

The Fiscal Compact was signed in March and by the end of the year had been ratified by all eurozone members except Belgium, Malta, Luxembourg and the Netherlands. This was sufficient for it to enter into force in January 2013 as the Treaty required only 12 eurozone members to deposit their instruments of ratification for it to become law. For all the fuss over the Fiscal Compact, it remains to be seen whether it will make any meaningful difference to eurozone governance. Among the Treaty's most significant provisions is the agreement that Member States will adopt a set of fiscal rules designed to codify in national law the Stability and Growth Pact's limits on government deficits and debt. Whether numerical fiscal rules help or hinder the pursuit of fiscal discipline is a matter of debate within the political economy literature with a key question being how such rules will interact with national budget processes (see Hallerberg *et al.*, 2009; Hodson, 2011a, ch. 4).

Also significant are the Fiscal Compact's provisions on the establishment of a euro summit, which will bring together the heads of state or government of eurozone members with the presidents of the ECB and Commission invited to take part too. Such summits have been a familiar if ad hoc feature of the eurozone's response to the global financial crisis, which has emphasized an intensive, informal and deliberative approach to economic decision-making among heads of state or government in a domain where finance ministers in general and the Eurogroup in particular previously reigned supreme (Puetter, 2012). Further evidence of this presidentialization of eurozone governance[13] is the Fiscal Compact's stipulation that the euro summit should appoint a chair for a two-and-a-half-year term of office (Hodson and Puetter, 2013). This chair will usually be appointed at the same time as the President of the European Council and Herman Van Rompuy was duly elected as the first President of the euro summit in March 2012. The decision to appoint Van Rompuy was an obvious one given the Belgian's preoccupation with the euro crisis during his first term as President of the European Council.

Whether the posts of Presidency of the European Council and euro summit will continue to be merged in the future is an interesting question. To the extent that they are, it will ensure that eurozone members have a lock on the Presidency of the European Council since it would be highly problematic to put a politician from a non-eurozone country in charge of eurozone affairs. To the extent that they are not, it will ensure that eurozone members form a powerful caucus within the European Council just as eurozone finance ministers do within the Economic and Financial Affairs Council (see Pisani-Ferry, 2006).

The ESM Treaty, meanwhile, was signed for the second time in February 2012 after eurozone members agreed to widen the remit of this crisis resolution mechanism. Under the original agreement, which was initialled in July 2011, the ESM was authorized to lend to eurozone members facing severe financial difficulties. A key change under the amended version of the Treaty is that the ESM will be allowed to provide precautionary financial assistance to Member States, to purchase bonds on secondary markets or directly from national governments and to support Member States' efforts to recapitalize financial

---

[13] See Desmond Dinan's contribution to this issue.

© 2013 The Author(s) JCMS: Journal of Common Market Studies © 2013 John Wiley & Sons Ltd

institutions. The precise modalities of how the ESM would support such recapitalization is not spelled out in the Treaty, with a key question here being whether loans would be provided directly to financial institutions or channelled via national governments. The answer to this question is of the utmost importance since it will determine the extent to which financial institutions are backed by individual governments or collective guarantees by eurozone members.

In June 2012, eurozone members took a major step forward towards the second of these scenarios by agreeing that 'the ESM could [. . .] have the possibility to recapitalize banks directly' but there were two key catches (Euro Area Summit, 2012). The first catch was that the agreement did not conclusively state whether the ESM could be used to recapitalize banks retroactively – an approach that would drastically reduce government borrowing in both Ireland and Spain, two Member States that entered the global financial crisis with comparatively low levels of debt only to find themselves on the brink of sovereign default after bailing out commercial banks.[14] The second catch is that eurozone members agreed that the ESM should be allowed to recapitalize banks only after a so-called 'single supervisory mechanism' had been established, thus committing the EU to a radical rewrite of financial supervision provisions a little over 18 months after the ESRB opened its doors.

The Commission wasted little time in coming forward with plans for a single supervisory mechanism. In September 2012, the EU executive put forward a proposal that called for the ECB to be given overall responsibility for supervising credit institutions in the eurozone. This proposal went well beyond the soft co-ordination role entrusted to the ESRB by arguing that the ECB should assume responsibility under the single supervisory mechanism for, *inter alia*, granting licences to enforce capital requirements among certain categories of eurozone financial institutions. In so doing, the Commission jettisoned one of the key guiding principles underpinning EMU: that the ECB should be allowed to focus more or less exclusively on monetary policy to the benign (or, as it turned out, malevolent) neglect of financial markets (Eichengreen, 2012). This raises the question of how the eurozone monetary authority will reconcile its mandate under the treaties to pursue price stability above all other goals with the more nebulous task of maintaining financial stability. The Commission's September 2012 proposal assumes that the ECB's monetary and supervisory functions will be kept separate although the feasibility of such an arrangement is unclear (European Commission, 2012b).

Building on this issue linkage between the ESM and the single supervisory mechanism, Herman Van Rompuy (2012) argued in a report prepared at the request of EU leaders and published in December 2012 that such reforms to EU financial supervision should be embedded within a three-stage plan for a so-called 'genuine EMU'. The first stage of the Van Rompuy plan envisages, *inter alia*, a deal on the creation of a single supervisory mechanism and the modalities of bank recapitalization via the ESM by the end of 2013. The second stage calls for the creation of an independent authority to oversee the resolution of failed banks by the end of 2014 as well as raising the possibility of 'temporary, targeted and flexible financial support' to encourage Member States to undertake structural reforms. The final stage would involve the launch post-2014 of 'a

[14] In Ireland, government transfers to Anglo Irish Bank, and the Nationwide Building Society and EBS Building Society saw the country's budget deficit for 2010 increase by an astonishing 20.2 percentage points (Eurostat, 2012).

© 2013 The Author(s) JCMS: Journal of Common Market Studies © 2013 John Wiley & Sons Ltd

well-defined and limited fiscal capacity to improve the absorption of country-specific economic shocks, through an insurance system set up at the central level'.

The Van Rompuy plan, which would set EMU on a course to fiscal federalism via a fully fledged banking union,[15] will have come as music to the ears of those supranationalists who champion more Europe as the solution to the euro's current woes. Mattli and Stone-Sweet (2012, p. 14) express this position succinctly when they describe the global financial crisis as 'revealing the striking absence of what Europe needs most: strong political leadership capable of forging a more federal EU'. The problem with such supranationalist logic is that it downplays the economic and political downsides to imposing one-size-fits-all policy solutions on diverse Member States while overplaying the extent to which supranational institutions can, or perhaps even want to, influence negotiations in such a high-stakes game.

That a European banking union would make future financial crises less likely, much less help to end the current crisis, cannot be taken for granted. For Masciandaro *et al.* (2011, p. 19), delegating responsibility for macro financial supervision to central banks is the surest response to the supervisory failures that preceded the global financial crisis but 'it is misleading', they suggest, 'to believe that supervisory governance arrangements can be defined and implemented in such a way that each and every possibility of political, industry and self-capture can be eliminated'. The jury is long since out, meanwhile, on whether fiscal federations help or hinder adjustment to regional imbalances. The Mezzogiorno's arrested economic development in spite of a steady stream of fiscal transfers from the north of Italy – not to mention structural funds from the EU – illustrates the difficulties in this regard of designing a well-functioning fiscal federation. Such functional arguments should also be weighed against normative concerns, which would take on an added significance as EMU moves beyond the (potentially) pareto efficient world of stabilization and efficiency into the realm of cross-border burden-sharing and redistribution. Van Rompuy's plan is not ignorant of this fact, but its calls for greater involvement in eurozone governance from the EP and national parliament show limited appreciation for the scale of the legitimation challenge entailed by such reforms.

For liberal intergovernmentalists the point here is not so much whether the reforms envisaged by the Van Rompuy plan are necessary, but whether they are compatible with the preferences of national governments, which in turn reflect the interest of key socio-economic groups (see Moravcsik, 2012). Viewed in these terms, the European Councils in June, October and December 2012 entailed an asymmetric bargain in which Germany held and played the most important cards. At the first of these summits, Angela Merkel made it clear that as majority shareholder in the ESM this fund would be used to recapitalize banks only if the ECB's authority over financial supervision was significantly beefed up. At the second summit, the German chancellor secured a concrete timetable for launching the single supervisory mechanism – EU finance ministers and the EP signed off on the Commission's proposal in March 2013 – while delaying discussions of the ESM's role until after Germany's general election. At the final summit, the chancellor protected Germany's smaller savings and regional banks from ECB oversight by striking a deal that

---

[15] For a discussion of banking union, see Howarth and Quaglia's contribution to this issue.

© 2013 The Author(s) JCMS: Journal of Common Market Studies © 2013 John Wiley & Sons Ltd

the single supervisory mechanism would apply to banks with assets in excess of €30 billion. Not content with this concession, Merkel also moved to minimize the exposure of European (or more specifically, German) taxpayers to any EU bank resolution mechanism and to kick talk of a fiscal federation into touch. On the first of these points, the European Council's conclusions in December invited the Commission to come forward with proposals on a single resolution mechanism 'based on contributions by the financial sector' (European Council, 2012). On the issue of fiscal federalism, the conclusions said nothing at all, in spite of the best efforts of France and the Commission.

Conclusions

Trying to determine what is going on in the eurozone through a review of the year gone by is, to paraphrase the screenwriter Ben Hecht, like trying to tell the time by watching the second hand of a clock. Without the benefit of historical perspective it is impossible to know precisely where the eurozone economy was headed in the last 12 months and which policy initiatives during this period were most significant for the functioning and evolution of eurozone governance. With this caveat in mind, this contribution has offered some tentative thoughts about what students of EMU can learn from the tumultuous events of 2012. This was, above all, the year in which the ECB bought time by agreeing to do whatever it takes to preserve the eurozone while eurozone members looked to the future with yet another round of reform proposals for strengthening EMU's institutional architecture.

In the monetary sphere, the most significant development was the OMT, which saw the ECB commit to a programme of unlimited government bond purchases – albeit with significant strings attached. This move produced a sigh of relief from financial markets and provided breathing space for Spain, Italy and other eurozone members, although doubts remain as to whether the strict conditionality imposed on Member States seeking access to the OMT will be workable in practice. In the sphere of financial supervision, the ESRB continued to define its operational framework, but it did little to warn about the financial imbalances that would emerge in Cyprus in March 2013. In the sphere of economic policy co-ordination, the new excessive imbalance procedure was more audible in this regard, although EU policy-makers were reluctant to apply peer pressure on authorities in Cyprus and elsewhere. The entry into force of the Six Pack, meanwhile, made limited difference to fiscal surveillance in 2012 insofar as EU policy-makers continued to rely on peer pressure rather than pecuniary sanctions for Member States posting excessive budget deficits. In the external relations sphere, the eurozone encountered criticisms within the G20 for its failure to stem the sovereign debt crisis, pressure within the IMF over its perceived over-representation and a political misstep over the appointment of a new EBRD president.

Negotiations over a new-look EMU also caught the eye in 2012. The entry into force of the ESM Treaty and Fiscal Compact over the course of the year did little to discourage talk of further institutional reform, as evidenced by Herman Van Rompuy's three-stage plan for a fully fledged banking union and an embryonic fiscal federation. Negotiations over the details of this plan were ongoing at the year's end. Whereas political agreement on the creation of a single supervisory mechanism was in sight, discussions over other aspects of banking union and a centralized budgetary instrument for the eurozone proved altogether more contentious.

© 2013 The Author(s) JCMS: Journal of Common Market Studies © 2013 John Wiley & Sons Ltd

References

Amtenbrink, F. (2012) 'Legal Developments'. *JCMS*, Vol. 50, No. S2, pp. 132–46.

Bryant, C. (2012) 'Merkel Supports Bundesbank Chief'. *Financial Times*, 26 August.

Buckley, N. (2012) 'EBRD Presidency: A Sporting Guide'. Available at: «http://blogs.ft.com/beyond-brics/2012/04/05/ebrd-presidency-a-sporting-guide/#axzz2PK6UTgQf».

Buiter, W.H. and Rahbari, E. (2012) 'The ECB as Lender of Last Resort for Sovereigns in the Eurozone'. *JCMS*, Vol. 50, No. S2, pp. 6–35.

Buiter, W., Corsetti, G. and Roubini, N. (1993) 'Excessive Deficits: Sense and Nonsense in the Treaty of Maastricht'. *Economic Policy*, Vol. 8, No. 16, pp. 57–100.

Council of the European Union (2012) 'Council Recommendation on the National Reform Programme 2012 of Cyprus and delivering a Council opinion on the stability programme of Cyprus'. Brussels, 6 July.

Cullen, S. (2012) 'Europe Fires Back over G20 Criticism'. Available at: «http://www.abc.net.au/news/2012-06-19/europe-fires-back-at-g20/4079008».

De Grauwe, P. (2012) 'The ECB was Right to Intervene as Lender of Last Resort, but Structural Reforms are Still Needed to Save the Eurozone'. Available at: «http://blogs.lse.ac.uk/europpblog/2012/09/12/ecb-eurozone».

Dinan, D. (2012) 'Governance and Institutions: Impact of the Escalating Crisis'. *JCMS*, Vol. 50, No. S2, pp. 85–98.

Draghi, M. (2012a) Speech by Mario Draghi, President of the European Central Bank, given at the Global Investment Conference, London, 26 July.

Draghi, M. (2012b) 'Introductory Statement by Mario Draghi, Chair of the European Systemic Risk Board (ESRB), Brussels, 16 January' (Frankfurt am Main: ESRB).

Draghi, M. (2012c) 'Introductory Statement by Mario Draghi, Chair of the European Systemic Risk Board (ESRB), Brussels, 9 October' (Frankfurt am Main: ESRB).

Draghi, M. (2013) 'Introductory Statement to the Press Conference (with Q&A)' (Frankfurt am Main: European Central Bank).

Eichengreen, B. (2012) 'European Monetary Integration with Benefit of Hindsight'. *JCMS*, Vol. 50, No. S1, pp. 123–36.

EurActiv (2012) 'Questions Marks over €12 Billion EU "Growth Pact"'. Available at: «http://www.euractiv.com/euro-finance/question-marks-120-eu-growth-pac-news-513652».

Euro Area Summit (2012) 'Euro Area Summit Statement', Brussels, 29 June.

European Commission (2012a) 'Macroeconomic Imbalances: Cyprus'. European Economy Occasional Paper 101, Brussels, July.

European Commission (2012b) 'Proposal for a Council regulation conferring specific tasks on the European Central Bank concerning policies relating to the prudential supervision of credit institutions'. *COM*(2012) 511 final.

European Commission (2013) 'European Economic Forecast, Winter 2013'. European Economy 1 (Brussels: DG ECFIN).

European Council (2012) 'European Council Conclusions'. EUCO 205/12.

European Systemic Risk Board (ESRB) (2012) 'ESRB General Board Meeting in Frankfurt', Press Release, 20 September (Frankfurt am Main: ESRB).

Eurostat (2012) 'Supplementary Table for the Financial Crisis', Background Note, April (Luxembourg: European Commission).

Feldstein, M. (1997) 'EMU and International Conflict'. *Foreign Affairs*, Vol. 76, No. 6, pp. 60–73.

Group of Twenty (2012) 'G20 Leaders Declaration', Los Cabos, Mexico, 19 June.

Hallerberg, M., Strauch, R. and Von Hagen, J. (2009) *Fiscal Governance in Europe* (Cambridge: Cambridge University Press).

© 2013 The Author(s) JCMS: Journal of Common Market Studies © 2013 John Wiley & Sons Ltd

Hodson, D. (2011a) *Governing the Euro Area in Good Times and Bad* (Oxford: Oxford University Press).

Hodson, D. (2011b) 'The Eurozone in 2010'. *JCMS*, Vol. 49, No. S1, pp. 231–49.

Hodson, D. (2012) 'The Eurozone in 2011'. *JCMS*, Vol. 50, No. S2, pp. 178–94.

Hodson, D. and Puetter, U. (2013) 'The European Union and the Economic Crisis'. In Cini, M. and Pérez-Solórzano Borragán, N. (eds) *European Union Politics* (4th edition) (Oxford: Oxford University Press).

Hollande, F. (2012) 'Le changement c'est maintenant'. Socialist Party Manifesto (Paris: Socialist Party).

Knedlik, T. and Von Schweinitz, G. (2012) 'Macroeconomic Imbalances as Indicators for Debt Crises in Europe'. *JCMS*, Vol. 50, No. 5, pp. 726–45.

Lombardi, D. (2012) 'IMF + ECB = OMT'. Available at: «http://www.brookings.edu/research/articles/2012/11/imf-ecb-lombardi».

Masciandaro, D., Pansini, R. and Quintyn, M. (2011) 'The Economic Crisis: Did Financial Supervision Matter?' IMF Working Paper WP/11/261 (Washington: International Monetary Fund).

Mattli, W. and Stone Sweet, A. (2012) 'Regional Integration and the Evolution of the European Polity: On the Fiftieth Anniversary of the Journal of Common Market Studies'. *JCMS*, Vol. 50, No. S1, pp. 1–17.

Moravcsik, A. (2012) 'Europe after the Crisis: How to Sustain a Common Currency'. *Foreign Affairs*, Vol. 91, No. 3, pp. 54–68.

Pisani-Ferry, J. (2006) 'Only One Bed for Two Dreams: A Critical Retrospective on the Debate over the Economic Governance of the Euro Area'. *JCMS*, Vol. 44, No. 4, pp. 823–44.

Puetter, U. (2012) 'Europe's Deliberative Intergovernmentalism: The Role of the Council and European Council in EU Economic Governance'. *Journal of European Public Policy*, Vol. 19, No. 2, pp. 161–78.

Quine, W.V.O. (1960) *Word and Object* (Cambridge, MA: MIT Press).

Schäuble, W. and Niblet, R. (2011) *Achieving Sustainable Growth: Fiscal Consolidation and Financial Market Regulation* (London: Chatham House).

Trichet, J.C. (2010) 'State of the Union: The Financial Crisis and the ECB's Response between 2007 and 2009'. *JCMS*, Vol. 48, No. S1, pp. 7–19.

Van Rompuy, H. (2012) *Towards a Genuine Economic and Monetary Union* (Brussels: European Council).

Verdun, A. (1998) 'The Institutional Design of EMU: A Democratic Deficit?' *Journal of Public Policy*, Vol. 18, No. 2, pp. 107–32.

Weidmann, J. (2012) Interview with *Neue Zürcher Zeitung*. Available at: «http://www.bundesbank.de/Redaktion/DE/Interviews/2012_09_26_weidmann_nzz.html».

Wintour, P., Traynor, I. and Smith, H. (2012) 'G20 Summit: Barroso Blames Eurozone Crisis'. *The Guardian*, 19 June.

Wyplosz, C. (2003) 'Policy Challenges under EMU'. In Baimbridge M. and Whyman P. (eds) *Economic and Monetary Union in Europe: Theory, Evidence and Practice* (Cheltenham: Edward Elgar).

JCMS 2013 Volume 51 Annual Review pp. 201–218   DOI: 10.1111/jcms.12050

Developments in the Economies of Member States Outside the Eurozone

RICHARD CONNOLLY
University of Birmingham

Introduction

The ongoing post-financial crisis correction continued to weigh heavily on economic activity and employment in the European Union (EU), with 2012 proving to be a particularly turbulent year. In the first half of the year, domestic demand across the European economy continued to contract. This occurred amid a wider slowdown in the global economy, with growth slowing in east Asia, Russia and Latin America. Although growth in Japan was much stronger than in 2011, this was largely due to the recovery from the economic damage inflicted by the Fukushima earthquake. Of the major economies, only the United States performed significantly better than the previous year – growing at over 2 per cent annually compared to around 1.8 per cent in 2011 – although the pace of the recovery from the recession of 2009 remained well below previous recoveries in the post-war period. Nevertheless, the fact that the American recovery was driven by investment rather than consumption augured well for the necessary rebalancing of the world's largest economy. By the summer of 2012, fears over sovereign debt across the eurozone, as well as concerns about the wider debt burdens – both public and private – across the continent, weighed heavily on consumer and investor sentiment. Although concerted action by the European Central Bank (ECB) in the summer quelled fears of an imminent default in Greece, Spain and Italy, the future fragmentation of the eurozone remained a distinct possibility.[1] Overall, the EU was forecast to experience a small annual contraction in GDP growth, although this average concealed considerable variation in performance within the group.

Against this unsettled backdrop, the economies of the Member States outside the eurozone reacted in different ways as uncertainty spread across the continent. The slowdown in the eurozone contributed to a contraction in economic activity in the Czech Republic, Hungary and the United Kingdom, while the economies of Latvia and Lithuania grew at a reasonably fast rate. For the other countries, the picture was one of modest growth. In all cases, economic growth rates remain well below pre-crisis rates. Although this is to be expected – and even encouraged – as some countries repair damaged balance sheets, the fact that growth remained so anaemic in nearly all cases was a serious concern.

This year's *Annual Review* article looks at the non-eurozone economies from two perspectives. The next section gives an overview of key economic performance indicators, while the following section summarizes key developments in each of the ten European economies outside the eurozone, focusing on whether domestic demand and/or external

---

[1] On developments in the eurozone, see Hodson in this issue.

© 2013 The Author(s) JCMS: Journal of Common Market Studies © 2013 John Wiley & Sons Ltd, 9600 Garsington Road, Oxford OX4 2DQ, UK and 350 Main Street, Malden, MA 02148, USA

demand have driven output growth in these economies. The third section explores the long-term growth prospects in the both the non-eurozone economies and in the economies of the wider EU by assessing the current state of their national innovation capacities (NICs), which are of crucial importance to long-run growth performance because they act as useful predictors of a country's potential for innovation and productivity growth (for example, Freeman, 1982; Nelson, 1998; Radosevic, 2004).

I. Economic Performance Outside the Eurozone: Main Economic Indicators

Economic Growth

Because of the instability in the eurozone described above, GDP growth rates in the non-eurozone were considerably slower than rates recorded in 2011, albeit with significant variation observed within the group. The data presented in Table 1 reveal the heterogeneity of the recovery across the countries outside the eurozone. Sweden and Poland again were among the fastest growing of the larger economies from within the group, with both economies growing significantly faster than the EU and eurozone average, although growth was much slower than the previous year. Latvia and Lithuania continued to enjoy robust gross domestic product (GDP) growth, although again it was slower than in 2011. Bulgaria, Denmark and Romania managed to register modest GDP growth rates of under 1 per cent, which was still a better performance than the eurozone and EU averages. Elsewhere, and in line with performance in the eurozone, Czech Republic, Hungary and the United Kingdom all experienced a contraction in annual GDP, although this was less severe in the United Kingdom. Overall, the fact that many of the countries with the lowest levels of per capita income in the EU (that is, the countries of central and eastern Europe) were recovering at such sluggish rates continued to be a source of concern. These countries experienced some of the deepest recessions in the world during the 2008–09 crisis and were therefore expected to make much sharper recoveries (Connolly, 2012). In most cases, however, output remained well below the heights reached in 2008.

Table 1: Real GDP Growth (% Annual Change) – Non-eurozone (2007–12)

	2007	2008	2009	2010	2011	2012
Bulgaria	6.2	6.0	−5.5	0.2	1.7	0.8
Czech Republic	6.1	2.5	−4.7	2.7	1.9	−1.3
Denmark	1.6	−1.2	−5.2	1.7	0.8	0.6
Latvia	10.0	−4.6	−17.7	−0.3	5.5	4.3
Lithuania	9.8	2.8	−14.8	1.4	5.9	2.9
Hungary	1.0	0.6	−6.8	1.3	1.6	−1.2
Poland	6.8	5.0	1.6	3.9	4.3	2.4
Romania	6.3	6.2	−6.6	−1.9	2.5	0.8
Sweden	2.6	−0.2	−5.2	5.6	3.9	1.1
United Kingdom	2.6	−1.1	−4.4	1.8	0.9	−0.3
Eurozone	2.8	0.6	−4.2	1.9	1.4	−0.4
EU average	3.0	0.5	−4.2	2.0	1.5	−0.3

Source: European Commission (2012, p. 148, table 1).
Note: The figures for 2012 are estimates.

© 2013 The Author(s) JCMS: Journal of Common Market Studies © 2013 John Wiley & Sons Ltd

Employment

Compared to pre-crisis levels, unemployment remained high in all non-eurozone econo-mies (Table 2). Moreover, unemployment levels continued to grow in most countries, with significant declines in unemployment levels observed in only Latvia, Lithuania and Hungary. Within the non-eurozone economies there are two distinct groups. The first group, comprising Bulgaria, Hungary, Latvia and Lithuania, all exhibited unemployment rates significantly higher than the EU average. Indeed, in the two Baltic economies of Latvia and Lithuania, unemployment remained at levels not seen since the 'transition depression' of the 1990s – more than twice as high as that observed during the pre-crisis boom. The second group of countries, including all the other countries of the non-eurozone, registered unemployment rates lower than both the eurozone average and the overall EU average. In the one country that defies this simple categorization – Poland – unemployment rose for the fourth year running despite the country experiencing better GDP growth rates than nearly all of its neighbours.

Inflation

Between 2009 and 2011, inflation rose across the economies of the non-eurozone (Table 3). This was supported by a rise in global commodity prices throughout 2010 and 2011, fuelled by political instability in major energy producing regions as well as by loose monetary policy in the world's major economies (including by the ECB). While com-modity prices remained high in 2012, the rate of growth was more moderate than in previous years. Coupled with much weaker output growth, the uniform increase in inflation was halted in 2012 as some countries began to experience slower price rises.

Prices rose faster than the previous year in only two of the ten non-eurozone economies: the Czech Republic and Hungary – despite the fact that both countries registered negative GDP growth in 2012. In the Czech Republic, this rise in inflation was caused largely by one-off value-added tax adjustments and was expected to moderate in 2013 (IMF, 2012). In Hungary, however, rising inflation was caused by sharp increases in the price of food,

Table 2: Unemployment (% of the Civilian Labour Force) – Non-eurozone (2007–12)

	2007	2008	2009	2010	2011	2012
Bulgaria	6.9	5.6	6.8	10.8	11.3	12.7
Czech Republic	5.3	4.4	6.7	7.3	6.7	7.0
Denmark	3.8	3.3	6.0	7.4	7.6	7.7
Latvia	6.0	7.5	17.1	18.7	16.2	15.2
Lithuania	4.3	5.8	13.7	17.8	15.4	13.5
Hungary	7.4	7.8	10.0	11.2	10.9	10.8
Poland	9.6	7.1	8.2	9.6	9.7	10.1
Romania	6.4	5.8	6.9	7.3	7.4	7.4
Sweden	6.1	6.2	8.3	8.4	7.5	7.5
United Kingdom	5.3	5.6	7.6	7.8	8.0	7.9
Eurozone	7.5	7.5	9.5	10.1	10.1	11.3
EU average	7.2	7.0	8.9	9.7	9.7	10.5

Source: European Commission (2012, p. 159, table 23).
Note: The figures for 2012 are estimates.

© 2013 The Author(s) JCMS: Journal of Common Market Studies © 2013 John Wiley & Sons Ltd

Table 3: Inflation Rate[a] (% Change on Preceding Year) – Non-eurozone (2007–12)

	2007	2008	2009	2010	2011	2012
Bulgaria	7.6	12.0	2.5	3.0	3.4	2.5
Czech Republic	3.0	6.3	0.6	1.2	2.1	3.6
Denmark	1.7	3.6	1.1	2.2	2.7	2.4
Latvia	10.1	15.3	3.3	−1.2	4.2	2.4
Lithuania	5.8	11.1	4.2	1.2	4.1	3.4
Hungary	7.9	6.0	4.0	4.7	3.9	5.6
Poland	2.6	4.2	4.0	2.7	3.9	3.8
Romania	4.9	7.9	5.6	6.1	5.8	3.5
Sweden	1.7	3.3	1.9	1.9	1.4	1.0
United Kingdom	2.3	3.6	2.2	3.3	4.5	2.7
Eurozone	2.1	3.3	0.3	1.6	2.7	2.5
EU average	2.4	3.7	1.0	2.1	3.1	2.7

Source: European Commission (2012, p. 156, table 17).
Notes: The figures for 2012 are estimates. [a]Harmonized index of consumer prices.

tobacco and fuel. Given the weakness of domestic demand in Hungary, the rapid growth in inflation was a source of considerable concern to the National Bank of Hungary.

In the other eight economies of the non-eurozone, inflation subsided as regional and global concerns dampened output growth. In countries such as the Bulgaria, Latvia, Lithuania, Romania and the United Kingdom, this moderation in price rises was welcome as concerns had been expressed that inflation was approaching excessive levels in 2011. As such, the rates of inflation observed in these countries during 2012 represented a return to more normal and desirable levels. However, in Sweden inflation growth continued to slow, reaching just 1 per cent in 2012.This was primarily due to the strength of the Swedish krona, which continued to appreciate throughout 2012.

Public Finances

The state of public finances, and the issue of sovereign debt, continued to be a particularly important issue across the world in 2012 – not least in Europe where concerns over the solvency of Greece, Italy, Portugal and Spain were responsible for the decline in economic sentiment across the region. Although the focus was on the eurozone periphery countries, it was clear that a failure to demonstrate sufficient standards of sovereign fiscal rectitude might invite financial turbulence elsewhere. As Table 4 illustrates, government balances across the non-eurozone varied quite dramatically in 2012. The only country where the budget was balanced was Sweden, where a relatively strong economic performance in recent years has helped support government revenues. All other countries from within the non-eurozone registered budget deficits, although these ranged from the very small, as in Bulgaria and Latvia, to substantially larger than the EU and eurozone average, as in the United Kingdom. Indeed, despite an improvement in the level of net borrowing since 2008, the United Kingdom's level of net borrowing remained among the highest in the world, and certainly within the group of rich OECD countries (OECD, 2012).

Of perhaps more importance than the levels of government borrowing was the change in trajectory for some countries from within the non-eurozone. While budget deficits

© 2013 The Author(s) JCMS: Journal of Common Market Studies © 2013 John Wiley & Sons Ltd

Table 4: Net Lending (+) or Net Borrowing (–), General Government Balance (% of GDP) – Non-eurozone (2007–12)

	2007	2008	2009	2010	2011	2012
Bulgaria	0.1	1.8	–4.7	–3.1	–2.0	–1.5
Czech Republic	–0.7	–2.1	–5.8	–4.8	–3.3	–3.5
Denmark	4.5	3.4	–2.7	–2.6	–1.8	–3.9
Latvia	–0.3	–4.1	–10.2	–8.3	–3.4	–1.7
Lithuania	–1.0	–3.2	–9.2	–7.0	–5.5	–3.2
Hungary	–5.0	–3.8	–4.4	–4.2	4.3	–2.5
Poland	–1.9	–3.6	–7.2	–7.8	–5.0	–3.4
Romania	–2.5	–5.5	–8.6	–6.9	–5.5	–2.8
Sweden	3.8	2.5	–0.9	0.2	0.4	0.0
United Kingdom	–2.7	–5.0	–11.4	–10.3	–7.8	–6.2
Eurozone	–0.6	–2.0	–6.3	–6.2	–4.1	–3.3
EU average	–0.9	–2.3	–6.8	–6.6	–4.4	–3.6

Source: European Commission (2012, p. 165, table 36).
Note: The figures for 2012 are estimates.

Table 5: Gross General Government Debt (% of GDP) – Non-eurozone (2007–12)

	2007	2008	2009	2010	2011	2012
Bulgaria	18.2	14.1	14.7	16.3	16.3	19.5
Czech Republic	29.0	30.0	35.3	37.6	40.8	45.1
Denmark	26.8	33.5	41.5	43.7	46.6	45.4
Latvia	9.0	19.5	36.7	44.7	42.2	41.9
Lithuania	16.9	15.6	29.5	38.0	38.5	41.6
Hungary	65.9	72.9	78.4	81.3	81.4	78.4
Poland	45.0	47.2	50.9	54.9	56.4	55.5
Romania	12.6	13.6	23.9	31.0	33.4	34.6
Sweden	40.5	38.0	41.9	39.7	38.4	37.4
United Kingdom	44.2	52.0	68.2	79.9	85.0	88.7
Eurozone	66.0	61.5	79.1	85.6	88.1	92.9
EU average	58.8	61.8	74.0	80.3	83.0	86.8

Source: European Commission (2012, p. 168, table 42).
Note: The figures for 2012 are estimates.

continue to narrow in Bulgaria, Latvia, Lithuania, Poland, Romania and the United Kingdom, the reverse was observed in Czech Republic, Denmark, Hungary and Sweden. This was of particular concern in Hungary where the stock of government debt was already high. Notwithstanding this reversal of fortunes in several countries, the level of government borrowing tended, with the exception of the United Kingdom, to remain at around or below the levels observed in the eurozone (Table 5).

Continued flows of government borrowing resulted in an increase in the stock of government debt in half of the ten countries of the non-eurozone in 2012. Stocks of gross government debt declined in Denmark, Latvia, Hungary, Poland and Sweden. Government debt rose in Bulgaria, the Czech Republic, Lithuania, Romania and the United Kingdom, although the total levels of government debt were lower than eurozone average in all cases, and with the exception of the United Kingdom, lower than the EU average. Unfortunately, the fact that private debt levels tended to be much higher in the non-eurozone meant that sovereign default risk was not necessarily any less likely. This was because public balance sheets were exposed to the contingent liabilities of the private sector, leading to a worsening of the overall consolidated balance sheets of these economies (Roubini and Setser, 2004). Moreover, because per capita income was lower in central and eastern Europe – and with almost universally negative demographic prospects (that is, populations were forecast to become smaller and older; see Magnus, 2009) – the sustainable level of government debt was likely to be considerably lower than in richer EU neighbours.

Competitiveness

Competitiveness – that is, the potential to increase exports due to lower comparative production costs – remained an important consideration for policy-makers in 2012. With substantial private and public sector debt burdens dampening domestic demand, the potential for achieving faster economic growth (sufficient to reduce overall debt-to-GDP ratios) was most likely to come from rapid net export growth. Increasing competitiveness through a reduction in production costs was of particular importance in those countries that experienced large increases in the real effective exchange rate (REER) in the pre-crisis boom, especially Bulgaria, Latvia and Romania (Table 6). In all three cases, the REER in 2012 depreciated, going some way to regaining cost competitiveness. Similar tendencies were observed across the non-eurozone, with unit labour costs adjusted for nominal exchange rate movements declining in every country except Sweden and the United Kingdom. 2012 saw the United Kingdom's competitiveness significantly eroded as a REER appreciation of 6.7 per cent contrasted with a eurozone average REER depreciation of –4.8 per cent. Indeed, the REER depreciation observed in the eurozone outpaced the gains to competitiveness observed in every one of the non-eurozone economies, suggesting that the competitive position of non-eurozone economies had deteriorated relative to their largest trading partners despite significant cost reductions.

Table 6: Real Effective Exchange Rate (% Change on Preceding Year) – Non-eurozone (2007–12)

	2007	2008	2009	2010	2011	2012
Bulgaria	11.0	12.5	10.6	3.0	1.8	−0.2
Czech Republic	3.4	13.5	−5.6	3.1	3.0	−1.6
Denmark	3.8	5.2	3.9	−4.4	−1.3	−3.7
Latvia	23.0	19.1	−9.3	−11.6	2.5	−1.6
Lithuania	3.0	5.1	−2.1	−8.1	−1.0	−1.3
Hungary	9.0	1.2	−9.6	−1.0	−0.4	−0.2
Poland	3.8	12.8	−19.3	8.1	−3.2	−3.5
Romania	19.4	8.0	−13.0	6.6	1.3	−4.4
Sweden	3.2	−3.3	−8.0	5.1	3.4	1.2
United Kingdom	2.8	−14.0	−9.4	2.2	−0.6	6.7
Eurozone	1.6	3.4	3.9	−7.6	0.0	−4.8
EU average	6.0	1.6	−3.4	−7.8	0.3	−5.0

Source: European Commission (2012, p. 164, table 34).
Note: The figures for 2012 are estimates.

© 2013 The Author(s) JCMS: Journal of Common Market Studies © 2013 John Wiley & Sons Ltd

Overall, the economic performance of the Member States from outside the eurozone worsened over the course of 2012. The fear that some members of the eurozone might default on large amounts of sovereign debt was the most obvious source of instability during the year. This was compounded by slower growth in China, where efforts to shift towards a less investment-based economic growth model looked likely to reduce GDP growth for years to come. A slowing regional and global economy restricted the opportunities for the countries of the non-eurozone to adopt net export-led growth models. Exogenous factors, however, were not the only cause of slower growth. First, many countries continued to exhibit large stocks of debt – in the non-eurozone economies this tended to be located in the private sector, especially the household and financial sectors – which looked likely to restrain domestic private demand growth for years to come. Second, the absence of expansionary fiscal policies across the region, even where public sector debt levels were relatively modest, acted as another drag on growth prospects. Finally, government policies also shaped growth prospects across the region, with some policy choices – such as the populist actions of the Hungarian government – generating political instability and a concomitant decline in investor and consumer sentiment.

II. Economic Developments in Non-Eurozone Countries[2]

Bulgaria

GDP growth moderated compared with the previous year, and was estimated to have grown by less than 1 per cent. This meant that Bulgaria continued to recover from the long and deep recession that started in 2008 (which continued into 2010), although given the depth of the recession the rebound from recession was still relatively slow. Whereas in 2011, the modest recovery was driven by external demand (net exports make the largest contribution to GDP growth in 2011), in 2012 domestic demand took over as the main driver of growth. Net exports turned negative as the external environment worsened. A recovery in private consumption (up 3 per cent) was the main factor behind the leading role of domestic demand, along with growth in inventories (contributing 0.7 per cent to GDP growth). Perhaps most promising was a modest increase in investment activity (up 0.2 per cent) – the first such increase in over three years. This increase in investment was supported mainly by public projects and some recovery in foreign direct investment (FDI), especially in the energy sector. However, unemployment continued to rise, despite the fact that the labour force shrank due to negative demographic trends that were forecast to continue for years to come.

Czech Republic

The previous year the Czech economy grew almost entirely because of growth in external demand, with net exports driving GDP growth of 1.8 per cent in 2011. However, as the regional macroeconomic environment deteriorated in early 2012, this external demand slackened, causing the Czech economy to enter another recession. As an open economy (trade openness of 142 per cent of GDP in 2007) that was tightly integrated into international production networks (IPNs) focused on machinery exports, the Czech economy was

---

[2] All data presented in this section are taken from European Commission (2012).

© 2013 The Author(s) JCMS: Journal of Common Market Studies © 2013 John Wiley & Sons Ltd

especially susceptible to developments elsewhere in Europe, especially in Germany. Household consumption declined at a rate of –2.8 per cent – the sharpest since 1996, while real disposable incomes also contracted due to sluggish growth in wages and elevated inflation, generated by a one-off increase in the lower rate of VAT from 10 to 14 per cent. Investment contracted by 1.7 per cent, and with capacity utilization running well below its long-run average, did not look likely to recover soon. Exports grew at an annual rate of 3.9 per cent, exceeding imports, which grew at 1.1 per cent, to ensure that the recession in the Czech Republic was not even more severe.

Denmark

After a year of modest export-driven growth in 2011, during which domestic demand contributed negatively to economic activity, the Danish economy experienced another year of slow growth at a rate of 0.6 per cent compared with 0.8 per cent in 2011. Because of the slow and protracted recovery in Europe and elsewhere, demand for Danish exports was subdued, growing at just 2.5 per cent in 2012. Furthermore, the regional uncertainty surrounding European sovereign debt resulted in tighter credit conditions in Denmark, thereby adversely affecting the propensity of businesses and households to invest and consume. Private consumption grew by just 0.9 per cent, while gross fixed capital investment grew by 1.6 per cent. Although these growth rates were an improvement on the previous year, they remained well below pre-crisis levels. Public consumption also grew, albeit by only 0.2 per cent, reversing the trend of previous years. Unemployment remained stable, with the moderate growth in output generated by an increase in labour productivity towards the pre-crisis level. Looking to the future, wage growth was lower than in Denmark's trading partners as productivity growth continued to approach pre-crisis levels. This depreciation of the real effective exchange rate contributed to an improvement in Denmark's competitive position.

Hungary

After GDP growth of 1.6 per cent in 2011, the Hungarian economy entered into recession in the first half of 2012. This renewed recession was caused by a sharp drop in domestic demand (making a negative contribution of 2 per cent to GDP), while investment declined for the fourth consecutive year (contracting by 5.4 per cent). As fiscal policy was tightened, public consumption fell by 2.8 per cent. Against this backdrop, moderate growth in exports (2 per cent) cushioned the wider economy from the drop in domestic demand. The banking sector continued to face higher funding costs and tighter liquidity, limiting access to finance for the wider economy. In addition, instalment payments on foreign-currency-denominated loans surged as the forint depreciated, depressing consumption: around 65 per cent of household loans from banks were denominated in foreign currencies – predominantly Swiss francs. Against a backdrop of weak domestic demand and faltering external demand as the eurozone sovereign debt crisis deepened, Hungarian unemployment remained stable at 10.8 per cent.

Latvia

Latvia experienced one of the most severe recessions in the world during the course of 2008–10, although its economy began to grow over 2010 and 2011. This recovery

© 2013 The Author(s) JCMS: Journal of Common Market Studies © 2013 John Wiley & Sons Ltd

continued into 2012, with growth of 4.3 per cent making Latvia the fastest growing economy in Europe. This recovery continued to be driven by domestic demand, with gross fixed capital formation growing by 9.2 per cent. Private consumption rose by 4.7 per cent, while public consumption also rose, albeit at a slower rate of 1.1 per cent, despite continued government efforts to reduce the budget deficit. Altogether, domestic demand as a whole made a positive contribution of 5.7 per cent, with net exports exerting a gentle drag on GDP growth, as imports grew faster (5.3 per cent) than exports (5.1 per cent). After several years of deflation, prices rose by 2.4 per cent in 2012. This boosted domestic demand, but in the long run threatened to reduce Latvian competitiveness in export markets, despite the fact that real unit costs continued to fall (−1.8 per cent). However, the fact that unemployment fell from a peak of 19.8 per cent in 2010 to 15.2 per cent in 2012 augured well for a continued recovery.

Lithuania

As in Latvia, a recovery in domestic demand acted as the engine of growth in a country that had also experienced a deep and protracted recession in 2008–09, with the Lithuanian economy growing at a relatively fast rate of 2.9 per cent in 2012. Private consumption grew by 4.2 per cent, supported by a recovering labour market and reduced debt-servicing costs. Growth was also helped by a rise in investment, although at 3.1 per cent this was much slower than the 18.9 per cent observed in 2011, suggesting that Lithuanian corporate sector sentiment was adversely affected by external events. Public consumption made a negative contribution to GDP growth, contracting by 1.5 per cent. Exports grew (5.0 per cent) at a faster rate than imports (4.1 per cent), causing net exports to make a modest contribution to GDP growth. The continued fall in unemployment from a peak of 17.8 to 13.5 per cent in 2012 meant that the prospects for continued growth in domestic demand look positive despite persistent uncertainty in the wider European economy.

Poland

The Polish economy, which was the only EU economy to avoid recession in 2008–09, continued to grow, although the pace slowed somewhat to 2.4 per cent, down from 4.3 per cent in 2011. Public consumption, which had driven growth in 2010 and 2011, peaked in the first quarter of 2012 when major transport infrastructure projects and projects linked to the 2012 European football championships were completed, resulting in a slowdown in public investment thereafter. Indeed, investment more widely grew by just 1.7 per cent – significantly slower than the 9 per cent growth observed in 2011. As the labour market weakened and consumer sentiment worsened, private consumption growth was sluggish, growing at just 1.6 per cent. Against this weakening of private sector demand, the contraction in public spending caused by fiscal consolidation meant that net exports emerged as the primary driver of growth in Poland. Exports grew at a rate of 3 per cent, while imports contracted by 0.2 per cent, both supported by the lagged effect of the depreciation of the złoty in 2011. Despite the still healthy pace of GDP growth, unemployment continued to grow, rising from 9.7 per cent in 2011 to 10.1 per cent in 2012. Output growth and fiscal consolidation helped the government reduce the fiscal deficit from −5.0 per cent of GDP in 2011 to −3.4 per cent in 2012, helping reduce pressure on the public finances.

© 2013 The Author(s) JCMS: Journal of Common Market Studies © 2013 John Wiley & Sons Ltd

Romania

Romania continued to be highly exposed to negative developments in the eurozone. Growth in 2012 was subdued at 0.8 per cent, with public consumption continuing to shrink (–2.3 per cent), but aided by an increase in private consumption (0.8 per cent) and rapid investment growth (6.7 per cent). However, exports barely grew at all (0.2 per cent), causing net exports to make a modest negative contribution to GDP. A severe drought in the summer, waning consumer confidence and renewed difficulties in absorbing EU funds all contributed to this weak performance, although this did at least curb import demand, keeping the current account deficit broadly stable. The most significant risks continued to remain in the fiscal sector. The budget deficit target was revised from 1.9 to 2.2 per cent of GDP in 2012. The IMF approved an increase in the deficit target to account for an increase in public wages (8 per cent in June; to bring up to a total of 15 per cent increase by the end of the year) and the repayment to pensioners of illegally collected tax revenues. The fact that the IMF programme (a 24-month precautionary standby arrangement of €3.4 billion signed in March 2011) remained on track provided some comfort.

Sweden

The final quarter of 2011 saw the Swedish economy contract by 1.1 per cent in the wake of the eurozone sovereign debt crisis and global slowdown. However, in the first half of 2012 vigorous growth returned, supported by resilient household consumption, robust investment and a positive contribution from net exports. In the second half of 2012, however, increased uncertainty regarding sovereign risk in the eurozone and its implications for economic growth sapped business and consumer confidence, which fell sharply to levels usually observed in connection with very slow or even negative output growth. As a result, the Swedish economy stagnated in the second half of the year. Industrial confidence dropped from April onwards, reflecting a low level of new domestic orders and the expected effect of the strong krona on Swedish exports. Financing conditions remained favourable, supported by low domestic policy rates and wide access to foreign funding for Swedish banks. Thus, in a year of two halves, overall public consumption grew by 1.5 per cent, compensating for slow growth in private consumption, which expanded by just 0.8 per cent. Despite the fall in the second half of the year, investment still grew at 4 per cent, making it the primary driver of growth in Sweden. Overall, this was the worst year for the Swedish economy since 2009.

United Kingdom

After registering only modest GDP growth in 2011 of 0.9 per cent, the British recovery continued to lose momentum in 2012, contracting on an annual basis by 0.3 per cent. Despite the continuation of exceptionally loose monetary policy, economic activity was slow and volatile. Much of the United Kingdom's weakness was related to weak private consumption, which, weighed down by a large debt burden, grew by just 0.5 per cent in 2012. Investment, which had contracted in 2011, grew by 1.9 per cent and was forecast to continue growing for the next few years. With the private sector remaining weak, the government continued to implement a severe fiscal austerity package, unprecedented in depth and scope. Nevertheless, because only a small proportion of government spending

© 2013 The Author(s) JCMS: Journal of Common Market Studies © 2013 John Wiley & Sons Ltd

cuts was implemented by the end of 2012, public consumption made a positive contribution to GDP growth, growing by 0.5 per cent. Despite this fiscal retrenchment, it appeared that the government would miss its target of having national debt fall as a share of GDP by 2015–16. The other hope for the United Kingdom's economic recovery – a growth in net exports – showed few signs of materializing throughout the year. Exports grew by just 0.2 per cent, while imports expanded by over 2 per cent. As a result, net exports made a negative contribution to growth. The weak and volatile nature of economic activity in the United Kingdom remained stable, dropping slightly from 8.0 to 7.9 per cent.

III. Prospects for Long-Term Growth: National Innovation Systems in the EU

This section considers the current level of national innovation capacities across the EU, with a focus on assessing the distance between non-eurozone economies and those from the eurozone. The longer lasting effects of the 2008–09 crisis include, in many cases: large stocks of private sector debt which may take years to decline to sustainable levels; functionally impaired financial systems caused by both excessive pre-crisis domestic credit booms and by foreign banks' exposure to wider sovereign debt risks across Europe; and a slowdown in the rate of domestic consumption growth. In addition, many countries of the region, especially in central and eastern Europe, also face a projected shift in demographic profiles in which dependency ratios are expected to rise dramatically and population sizes are expected to decline (Magnus, 2009).

If the countries of the region are to overcome the challenges associated with both the immediate effects of the ongoing global economic slowdown and the longer-term challenge of demographic change, productivity levels will need to rise rapidly. Such a rapid increase in productivity is unlikely to occur without the accumulation of higher levels of technology and the development of more knowledge-intensive industries. This is because there is considerable evidence that overall economic development (that is, per capita income) is, in the long run, associated with patterns of structural transformation. Countries which expand the range and sophistication of activities in which they are active tend to experience faster productivity growth, and as a result, faster growth in per capita incomes (for example, Hausmann et al., 2008; McMillan and Rodrik, 2011).[3] With this aim in mind, it is essential that countries develop national systems of innovation (NSI) that will enable them to upgrade their productive capabilities.

National Systems of Innovation

The concept of 'national systems of innovation', as first described by Christopher Freeman (1982), is based on the assumption that national innovation processes should be treated in a systemic manner, with the flows of technology and information between people, enterprises and institutions viewed as key to the innovative process. The NSI concept is closely related to (neo-)Schumpeterian growth theory (Aghion and Howitt, 1998), which suggests that policies and institutions exert a powerful effect on economic growth, and that different types of policies and institutions are appropriate under certain

---

[3] McMillan and Rodrik (2011) argue that structural transformation is a key determinant of productivity growth and explains two-thirds of the difference between superior east Asian growth and more muted Latin American growth in the past two decades.

© 2013 The Author(s) JCMS: Journal of Common Market Studies © 2013 John Wiley & Sons Ltd

types of conditions, especially a country's position relative to the technology frontier. Of perhaps even greater importance, however, is the fact that (neo-)Schumpeterian growth theory does not reduce productivity growth in countries simply to rates of observable technological change. Instead, the NSI approach argues that what is important in shaping the prospects for long-run productivity growth is the interaction of a wider set of variables beyond simple measures of research and development (R&D) supply and the absorption of R&D results (see, for example, Nelson, 1998). Other such sets of variables include, for example, measures of technology diffusion and local demand for new technologies. More broadly, these variables interact in a complex and country-specific manner, with innovation institutions (such as universities, enterprises and other research institutes) 'embedded in a much wider socio-economic system in which cultural influences as well as economic policies help to determine the scale, direction and relative success of all innovative activities' (Freeman, 2002, p. 194). An important consequence of this approach to innovation is that a single ideal NSI that fits different countries' specific socio-economic, political and cultural backgrounds does not exist (Varblane *et al.*, 2007).

Measuring National Systems of Innovation

The complex and institutionally framed nature of NSI demands measurement through a composite indicator that measures the different sets of components of countries' innovation capacities. Accordingly, this section of the article employs the approach utilized by Radosevic (2004), who organizes national systems of innovation (or what he labels 'national innovative capacities') into four subgroups (R&D supply, absorptive capacity, diffusion and demand) and one aggregate measure of national innovation capacity. In line with existing research on NSI, this approach is based on the assumption that 'the innovative capacity of an economy depends not only on the supply of R&D, but also on the capability to absorb and diffuse technology and on the demand for its generation and utilization' (Radosevic, 2004, p. 646).

According to Radosevic, each subgroup measures an essential component of a national innovation system. First, *absorptive capacity* measures the ability of an economy to absorb new knowledge and adapt imported technologies, crucial capabilities in catch-up economies (Cohen and Levinthal, 1989). Second, the *supply of R&D* is equally important not only to generate new knowledge, but also as an additional mechanism to absorb it (Cohen and Levinthal, 1990). Third, *diffusion* is a key mechanism for ensuring that increased R&D supply and more effective absorption capacities result in tangible economic gains for domestic enterprises (Davies, 1979). Finally, *demand* for R&D and innovation is included because of its importance in initiating wealth-generation processes in R&D, absorption and diffusion activities (Easterly, 2002).

Each of the four sub-components comprises six indicators, leading to a total of 24 indicators. Data are presented for all EU countries. All data are taken from the 2012 World Bank Knowledge Assessment Methodology (KAM). The KAM consists of 148 structural and qualitative variables for 146 countries to measure their performance on a range of knowledge economy measures. The data are taken from the most recent year for which they are available. Data for 27 countries and 24 variables should result in 648 observations. However, 41 observations (6.3 per cent of the data set) are missing. Missing observations are replaced by regression estimates. Because the KAM indicators contain a mixture of subjective (for example, rankings and scores based on expert perceptions) and objective data, the indicators used are not perfect.

Each sub-component comprises the following indicators.

Absorptive capacity: Indicators of absorptive capacity are human capital measures capturing levels of education, lifelong learning and firm-level technology absorption capabilities. They include:

1. Science and engineering enrolment ratio, 2009
2. Firm-level technology absorption, 2010
3. Public spending on education (% of GDP), 2009
4. Tertiary school completion (% of population aged 15+), 2010
5. Local availability of specialized research and training services, 2010
6. Manufactured trade (% of GDP), 2009

R&D supply: Indicators of R&D supply measure the extent to which a country is engaged in the generation and protection of R&D. They include:

1. Researchers in R&D (per million people), 2009
2. Total R&D expenditure (% of GDP), 2008
3. Science and engineering journal articles (per million people), 2007
4. Patents granted by the United States Patents and Trademarks Office (USPTO) (per million people), average 2005–09
5. Private sector spending on R&D, 2010
6. Intellectual property protection, 2010

Diffusion: Indicators of technology and innovation diffusion capture the extent to which an economy is capable of ensuring that the gains from R&D supply and absorptive capacities result are appropriated by domestic enterprises. They include:

1. University–company research collaboration, 2010
2. Professional and technical workers (% of the labour force), 2008
3. Extent of staff training, 2010
4. Computers (per 1,000 people), 2008
5. Internet users (per 1,000 people), 2009
6. Information and communication technology (ICT) expenditures (% of GDP), 2008

Demand: Indicators of demand include proxies for financial depth, trade and investment, competition and macroeconomic stability. They include:

1. Gross capital formation (% of GDP), average of 2005–09
2. Trade openness (% of GDP), 2009
3. Intensity of local competition, 2010
4. Domestic credit to private sector (% of GDP), 2009
5. FDI inflows (% of GDP), average of 2004–08
6. Unemployment rate (% of labour force), average 2005–09

Summary measure of national innovation capacities: Aggregation raises the problem of establishing how one should weight each of the sub-components to reach a single summary measure. Essentially, there are two choices. First, one can assign weights that correspond with a sound theoretical framework. Alternatively, one can use data reduction methods, such as principal components analysis (PCA) or factor analysis. Here, the weights are chosen according to the first method, assigning weights grounded in a conceptual framework that emphasizes the equal importance of the four sub-components described above. Aggregate values for each sub-component are calculated using equal weights for each indicator. In turn, each of the four sub-components is assigned equal weights in calculating the aggregate NSI indicator. The results using this method are not substantially different from the results using data reduction methods.[4] Indicators are normalized on a scale of 0 to 10 relative to all other countries in the comparison group. The standardized values calculated in the KAM sample of 146 countries are used in this article.

The summary indicator summarizing national innovation capacities (NIC) for each country is defined as follows:

$$\phi_c^{NIC} = \alpha_1\phi_c^{ABS} + \alpha_2\phi_c^{R\&D} + \alpha_3\phi_c^{DFS} + \alpha_4\phi_c^{DMD} \tag{1}$$

where ϕ_c^{ABS} is a country's coefficient for absorptive capacity, $\phi_c^{R\&D}$ is a country's coefficient for R&D supply, ϕ_c^{DFS} is a country's coefficient for diffusion and ϕ_c^{DMD} is a country's coefficient for demand. The alphas are the weights described above, and these weights sum to one.

Observations on the Prospects for Innovative Growth

The national innovative capacities for 58 countries from across the world are plotted against per capita income levels in Figure 1. This shows that there is a very close association between national innovation capacities and income levels (Pearson's r correlation coefficient of 0.77). Rich countries, such as the United States, Japan, Norway, Singapore and Switzerland are located in the top right quadrant. Poorer countries, such as Albania, Bolivia, Indonesia and the Philippines are located in the bottom right quadrant. What are perhaps most interesting are those countries that deviate significantly from the regression line. In those instances where a country possesses better national innovation capacities than its income level would suggest, we might expect to see better growth prospects in the future. Globally, countries like Brazil, China, India, Malaysia and South Korea are included in this group. Conversely, where countries are located behind the regression line (that is, their income levels are higher than their national innovation capacities would suggest) they might be expected to experience slower growth in the future. Such countries include Argentina, Mexico, Russia and Turkey.

The national innovative capacities for only the countries of the EU are plotted against per capita income levels in Figure 2. Here, the association between national innovation capacities and income is weaker (Pearson's r correlation coefficient of 0.62), primarily because there are two clusters of outliers either side of the regression line. The richest countries of the EU are, as expected, located in the top right quadrant. From the non-eurozone we can see the United Kingdom and Sweden – both countries with sophisticated national innovation capacities. In the bottom left quadrant, two countries from the new

---

[4] For example, the correlation coefficient between the aggregate indicator using the weights described above and those derived from PCA is 0.92.

© 2013 The Author(s) JCMS: Journal of Common Market Studies © 2013 John Wiley & Sons Ltd

Figure 1: Index of National Innovation Capacities and Per Capita Income ($US) in 58 Countries across the World, 2008–10

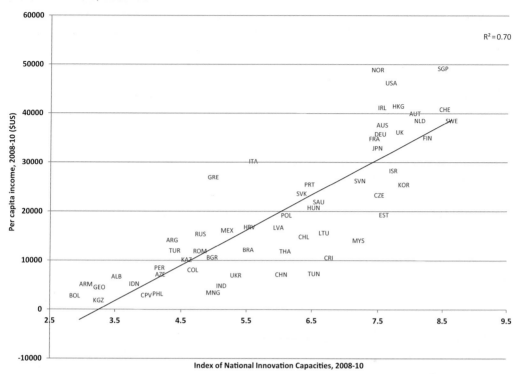

Source: Author's own calculations.

Member States display the lowest income levels and among the weakest national innovation capacities. These countries will need to upgrade their innovation systems if they are to enjoy convergence with EU average income levels in the future. Several other countries located close to the middle of the regression line – Hungary, Latvia and Poland – are from the non-eurozone. In all cases, income levels are where their national innovation capacities would predict them to be. They will need to improve their innovation systems, but the distance to travel is not as far as Bulgaria and Romania.

The most interesting cases are located significantly to the left and right of the regression line. The first group, located to the left, includes the four countries where sovereign debt concerns in the EU are perhaps highest: Greece, Italy, Portugal and Spain. The poor state of their national innovation capacities would suggest that the four countries should have lower levels of income than those observed in 2008–10. The fact that income levels are higher than their innovation systems would predict may be due to the fact that government borrowing in recent years has inflated incomes beyond levels consistent with their productivity levels. To the right of the regression line, on the other hand, the Czech Republic, Estonia and Lithuania all exhibit much higher scores for their national innovation capacities than their income levels would suggest. This could well prove to be good news in the future as it suggests that the conditions to support rapid productivity and income growth are present.

© 2013 The Author(s) JCMS: Journal of Common Market Studies © 2013 John Wiley & Sons Ltd

Figure 2: Index of National Innovation Capacities and Per Capita Income ($US) in 27 EU Countries, 2008–10

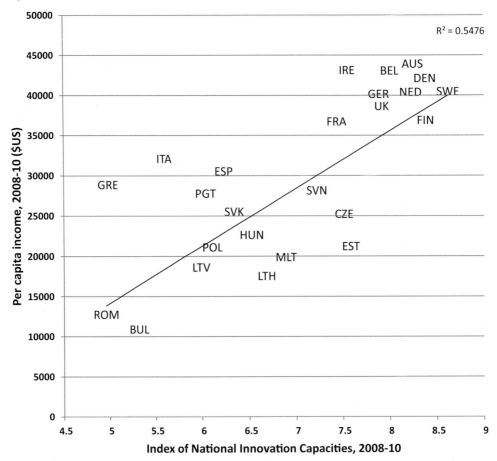

Source: Author's own calculations.

Policy-makers in Europe, and indeed elsewhere, have expressed a desire to upgrade the innovation capacities of their respective countries. In Europe, the goal of fostering growth in innovative industries has been an ambition of a number of EU policies, such as the Lisbon strategy, the Europe 2020 strategy and other programmes aimed at education and regional development. In addition, national policies from each of the Member States have supplemented EU policies. Such policies are usually considered necessary both so that European countries can stay in touch with global leaders in innovation, such as the United States and Japan, and also to prevent lower income countries, such as China and Russia, who have invested large sums on innovation from catching up and ultimately overtaking European countries. As a result, the heterogeneity of NICs within Europe, and the rapid progress made by large low- and middle-income countries, may prove to be a growing source of concern to policy-makers in the future.

However, despite significant investment – both in terms of financial and political capital – the slow pace of positive change in many European countries suggests that upgrading

© 2013 The Author(s) JCMS: Journal of Common Market Studies © 2013 John Wiley & Sons Ltd

NICs is difficult to achieve. Why should that be the case? The reason is likely to be that because national innovation systems are complex and institutionally framed, significant change will only occur alongside wider political, social and cultural change. Within Europe it is perhaps no surprise that the countries which have made the most rapid progress were those that abandoned state planning of economic activity two decades ago. Those that made the most progress in wider institutional development also tended to be the same countries that experienced faster growth in innovation capabilities.[5] By contrast, NIC development has been much slower in countries where domestic institutional change has been much slower. Countries like Greece, Portugal, Spain and Italy have made enormous progress in recent decades which should not be ignored. However, 'easy' credit-fuelled economic growth since 2000 masked the necessity for deeper structural reforms aimed at, for example, increasing economic competition and reforming inefficient public sectors. If the link between wider institutional development and more narrowly conceived technological change is as strong as suggested here, the implication is that laggard countries should think more broadly (that is, than mere technocratic solutions to, say, R&D funding or higher education policy) when considering how to foster economic innovation.

Conclusions

Because of the instability in the eurozone and beyond, the year 2012 saw the economies of the non-eurozone continue to make an uncertain and unsteady recovery from the severe recession of 2008–09. After all the countries under review here registered positive GDP growth in 2011, several slipped back into recession or if not experienced slower growth in 2012. As a result, the pace of recovery continued to be much slower than is usual after a recession. As growth faltered, unemployment was still either high or rising (in some cases both). Against this backdrop, a number of countries saw government debt rise, with little progress made in reducing private sector debt. Gains in cost competiveness achieved between 2009 and 2011 began to be reversed in 2012. The prospect of further strains in the eurozone sovereign debt markets did not disappear, despite the actions of the ECB, as shown in early 2013 by events in Cyprus. However, while the short-term economic prospects for the countries of the non-eurozone continued to appear uncertain, the longer-term prospects appear brighter, for some countries at least, due to progress made in recent years in upgrading national innovation capacities. This provided some of the economies of the non-eurozone with an excellent opportunity to enjoy rapid productivity gains in the future if and when the wider macroeconomic environment improves.

References

Aghion, P. and Howitt, P. (1998) *Endogenous Growth Theory* (Cambridge, MA: MIT Press).
Cohen, W.M. and Levinthal, D. (1989) 'Innovation and Learning: The Two Faces of R&D'. *Economic Journal*, Vol. 99, No. 397, pp. 569–96.
Cohen, W.M. and Levinthal, D. (1990) 'Absorptive Capacity: A New Perspective on Learning and Innovation'. *Administration Science Quarterly*, Vol. 35, No. 1, pp. 128–52.
Connolly, R. (2012) 'The Determinants of the Economic Crisis in Post-Socialist Europe'. *Europe-Asia Studies*, Vol. 64, No. 1, pp. 35–67.

---

[5] Outside Europe, this would also be true for countries like Brazil, China and India.

© 2013 The Author(s) JCMS: Journal of Common Market Studies © 2013 John Wiley & Sons Ltd

Davies, S.W. (1979) *The Diffusion of Process Innovations* (Cambridge: Cambridge University Press).

Easterly, W. (2002) *The Elusive Quest for Growth: Economists' Adventures and Misadventures in the Tropics* (Cambridge, MA: MIT Press).

European Commission (2012) *European Economic Forecast: Autumn 2012* (Brussels: Ecofin).

Freeman, C. (1982) *The Economics of Industrial Innovation* (2nd edition) (London: Pinter).

Freeman, C. (2002) 'Continental, National and Sub-national Innovation Systems: Complementarity and Economic Growth'. *Research Policy*, Vol. 31, No. 2, pp. 191–211.

Hausmann, R., Hwang, J. and. Rodrik, D. (2008) 'What You Export Matters', Harvard University. Available at: «http://ksghome.harvard.edu/~drodrik/hhr.pdf».

International Monetary Fund (IMF) (2012) 'Czech Republic – 2012 Article IV Consultation Concluding Statement'. Available at: «http://www.imf.org/external/np/ms/2012/022712.htm».

Magnus, G. (2009) *The Age of Ageing* (Singapore: Wiley & Sons).

McMillan, M. and Rodrik, D. (2011) 'Globalization, Structural Change, and Productivity Growth'. Kennedy School of Government, Harvard University, February. Available at: «http://www.hks.harvard.edu/fs/drodrik/research.html».

Nelson, R. (1998) 'The Agenda for Growth Theory: A Different Point of View'. *Cambridge Journal of Economics*, Vol. 22, No. 4, pp. 497–520.

Organization for Economic Co-operation and Development (OECD) (2012) *World Economic Outlook* (Paris: OECD).

Radosevic, S. (2004) 'A Two-Tier or Multi-tier Europe? Assessing the Innovation Capacities of Central and East European Countries in the Enlarged EU'. *JCMS*, Vol. 42, No. 3, pp. 641–66.

Roubini, N. and Setser, B. (2004) *Bail-Outs or Bail-Ins? Responding to Financial Crises in Emerging Economies* (Washington, DC: Institute for International Economics).

Varblane, U., Dyker, D., Tamm, D. and von Tunzelmann, N. (2007) 'Can the National Innovation Systems of the New EU Member States be Improved?' *Post-Communist Economies*, Vol. 19, No. 4, pp. 399–416.

JCMS 2013 Volume 51 Annual Review pp. 219–224　　　　　　　　　　　　DOI: 10.1111/jcms.12045

Chronology: The European Union in 2012

FABIAN GUY NEUNER
University of Michigan

At a Glance

Presidencies of the EU Council: Denmark (1 January–30 June) and Cyprus (1 July–31 December).

January

1	Denmark takes over the EU Council Presidency.
1	New Hungarian constitution enters into force.
13	Rating agency Standard & Poor's (S&P) downgrades the credit rating of nine EU Member States, including France and Italy.
16	S&P downgrades the credit rating of the European Financial Stability Facility (EFSF) to AA+.
17	German Socialist MEP Martin Schulz is elected President of the European Parliament.
17	The European Commission launches infringement proceedings against Hungary over legislation that came into force under the new constitution.
22	Croatians vote in favour of joining the EU in an accession referendum.
23	EU foreign ministers adopt new sanctions against Iran, in the form of an oil embargo, over the country's nuclear programme.
23	Intergovernmental ministerial meeting reaches agreement on the new European Stability Mechanism (ESM) Treaty and on the draft Fiscal Compact Treaty.
30	The Erasmus programme celebrates its 25th anniversary.
30	At a summit in Brussels all EU Member States except the United Kingdom and the Czech Republic endorse the final version of the Treaty on Stability, Coordination and Governance in the Economic and Monetary Union (Fiscal Compact) and the ratification process begins.

February

2	The new version of the ESM Treaty is signed.
5	Saul Niinistö is elected president of Finland.
6	Romanian Prime Minister Emil Boc resigns following protests over austerity measures.
8	Commission publishes proposals for a 'European Statute for Foundations'.
10	Slovenian parliament confirms Janez Janša's government.
10	12th EU–India summit in New Delhi.
12	In a move to secure a second EU/IMF (International Monetary Fund) bail-out and avert bankruptcy, the Greek parliament passes austerity measures amid popular protests.

© 2013 The Author(s) JCMS: Journal of Common Market Studies © 2013 John Wiley & Sons Ltd, 9600 Garsington Road, Oxford OX4 2DQ, UK and 350 Main Street, Malden, MA 02148, USA

13	Rating agency Moody's downgrades six eurozone members' credit ratings.
14	14th EU–China summit in Beijing.
14	Commission publishes first alert mechanism report on macroeconomic imbalances in the Member States.
17	German President Christian Wulff resigns over corruption claims.
18	Latvians vote against making Russian a second national language in a referendum.
22	Commission proposes suspending €495 million worth of cohesion funds for Hungary over the country's failure to curb its excessive deficit.
22	Commission requests that the European Court of Justice (ECJ) assesses whether the Anti-Counterfeiting Trade Agreement (ACTA) violates fundamental human rights.
27	S&P downgrades Greece's credit rating to 'selective default'.
28	EU withdraws all Member State ambassadors from Belarus after the country had told the ambassadors of the EU and Poland to leave the country following renewed EU sanctions.
29	The European Central Bank (ECB) agrees to provide €530 billion in low-interest loans to banks across the Member States.
29	Commission proposes central securities depositories regulation.

March

1–2	European Council. Discussion centred on the implementation of EU economic strategy and the completion of the single market. The Treaty on Stability, Coordination and Governance in the Economic and Monetary Union (Fiscal Compact) was signed. Further, Serbia was granted candidate status and Herman Van Rompuy was re-elected as the Council's President.
4	Vladimir Putin is elected president of Russia.
10	Robert Fico's Smer Social Democracy Party wins an absolute majority of seats in the parliamentary election in Slovakia.
13	Council adopts a decision to suspend €495.2 million in cohesion funds for Hungary due to the country taking insufficient steps to correct its budget deficit.
13	Eurozone finance ministers approve second Greek bail-out deal worth €130 billion.
16	Nicolae Timofti, an independent, is elected president of Moldova by a parliamentary vote.
18	Joachim Gauck is elected president of Germany in an indirect election.

April

1	First day for the submission of proposals through the European citizens' initiative (ECI).
2	President of Hungary Pál Schmitt resigns over a plagiarism scandal.
16	EU 'Sustainable Energy for All' summit in Brussels.
18	Commission adopts a communication on growth and jobs for Greece.

© 2013 The Author(s) JCMS: Journal of Common Market Studies © 2013 John Wiley & Sons Ltd

| 23 | Dutch Prime Minister Mark Rutte announces the resignation of his coalition government after no agreement was reached on austerity measures. |
| 25 | Commission presents its proposal for the EU budget for 2013. |

May

2	Fidesz Party candidate János Áder is elected president of Hungary in an indirect election.
2	S&P upgrades Greece's credit rating to CCC.
6	François Hollande is elected president of France in the second round, beating incumbent Nicolas Sarkozy.
6	Parliamentary elections in Serbia. Socialist Party leader Ivica Dačić becomes prime minister heading a coalition with United Serbia and the Party of United Pensioners of Serbia.
6	Antonis Samaras' New Democracy Party wins a plurality in the Greek legislative elections.
9	Spain partially nationalizes Bankia group.
9	Commission officially launches the first ECI to coincide with Europe day.
18–19	38th G8 summit in Camp David.
20	Tomislav Nikolić is elected president of Serbia in a second round run-off election.
31	The Irish vote in favour of an amendment to the country's constitution to enable ratification of the European Fiscal Compact in a referendum.
31	Brussels Economic Forum.

June

4	Commission starts talks on visa liberalization with Georgia.
9	Spanish government announces request for financial assistance for up to €100 billion.
11	Bujar Nishani is elected president of Albania in the fourth round of an indirect election
11	Inaugural EU–Iraq framework agreement signed.
17	The Socialist Party wins an absolute majority in the French legislative elections.
17	After attempts to form a government following the May elections failed, a new legislative election took place in Greece returning New Democracy as the largest party.
18–19	7th G20 summit held in Mexico.
22	The leaders of Germany, France, Italy and Spain agree to a blueprint for a European growth pact worth €130 billion.
25	Cyprus becomes the fifth eurozone country to request a bail-out.
28–29	The European Council approved a 'compact for growth and jobs', and held discussions on the multi-annual financial framework. Moreover, it was decided to open EU accession negotiations with Montenegro.
30	Ólafur Ragnar Grímmson is elected president of Iceland.

| 30 | The EU completes its police mission in Bosnia and Herzegovina, thereby marking the end of the first mission launched under the European security and defence policy (ESDP) banner. |

July

1	Cyprus takes over the EU Council Presidency.
4	The European Parliament rejects the Anti-Counterfeiting Trade Agreement (ACTA).
4	French President François Hollande announces plans for tax increases, including a 75 per cent top rate of income tax.
5	The ECB cuts interest rates to 0.75 per cent.
11	Spanish Prime Minister Mariano Rajoy announces €65 billion in spending cuts.
18	Commission decides on draft negotiation directives to start dialogue on possible EU–Japan Free Trade Agreement.
26	Ireland returns to financial bond markets for the first time since September 2010.
29	After having been suspended from office earlier in the month, Romanian President Traian Băsecu survives a popular referendum on his impeachment.

August

1	France unilaterally introduces a financial transactions tax (FTT).
5	Commission, ECB and IMF monitoring visit to Greece to discuss the country's economic recovery.
28	Commission announces that Europe and Australia will be linking their emissions trading systems.

September

6	ECB President Mario Monti announces unlimited bond buying in the secondary market as a means of regaining control over the spreads between government bond interest rates in the eurozone.
10	The International Civilian Office (ICO), monitoring the implementation of the Ahtisaari plan in Kosovo, ceases to exist after it determined that Kosovo had fulfilled the obligations laid out in the plan.
11	The Commission and the Organisation for Economic Co-operation and Development (OECD) publish the 2012 'Education at a Glance' report.
12	Commission President José Manuel Barroso gives his State of the Union address.
12	Commission proposes new single supervisory mechanism (SSM), which would enhance supervisory role of the ECB.
12	German Constitutional Court rules that the ESM does not contravene the country's constitution.

© 2013 The Author(s) JCMS: Journal of Common Market Studies © 2013 John Wiley & Sons Ltd

12	Mark Rutte's People's Party for Freedom and Democracy wins a plurality in the Dutch general election. In November, Rutte becomes prime minister after entering into coalition with the Labour Party.
18	EU–South Africa summit.
20	15th EU–China summit.
27	Germany ratifies the ESM Treaty, thereby ensuring that the ratification threshold is surpassed and the treaty can enter into force.

October

1	Bidzina Ivanishvili's Georgian Dream coalition wins a majority of seats in the Georgian parliamentary election.
2	The Liikanen Report of the European Commission's High-level Expert Group on Bank Structural Reform is published. It recommends strengthening governance and control of banks and separation of activities.
8	ESM commences operations with its inaugural meeting.
9	Koen Lenaerts is elected Vice-President of the ECJ.
10	Commission enlargement progress reports are published. It is recommended that Albania be granted candidate status.
14	Milo Đukanović's Coalition for a European Montenegro wins the plurality of votes in the Montenegrin parliamentary election.
14/28	Lithuanian parliamentary election sees the Social Democratic Party win a plurality of seats.
16	European Commissioner for Health and Consumer Policy John Dalli resigns following an anti-fraud investigation.
18–19	European Council discussions centre on economic recovery, the situation in Greece and EMU governance. Further, the Council discusses relations with strategic partners.
20	Voters in Iceland approve six proposals in a non-binding constitutional referendum.
28	Prime Minister Mykola Azarov's Pro-Presidential Party of the Regions wins a plurality of the vote in the Ukrainian parliamentary elections.

November

5–6	9th Asia–Europe meeting.
7	EU–EIB (European Investment Bank) project bond initiative launched.
13	Greek parliament approves another austerity package worth €13.5 billion.
16	Croatian Generals Mladen Markač and Ante Gotovina are acquitted by the International Criminal Tribunal for the Former Yugoslavia (ICTY).
22	Special European Council in order to reach agreement on the terms of the multi-annual financial framework.
27	Eurozone finance ministers and the IMF reach a deal on Greek bail-out.
28	Commission publishes 'Blueprint for a deep and genuine economic and monetary union'.
29–30	2nd European Gender summit.

© 2013 The Author(s) JCMS: Journal of Common Market Studies © 2013 John Wiley & Sons Ltd

December

2	Borut Pahor is elected president of Slovenia in the second round of a run-off (direct) election.
5	Commission antitrust regulators fine several electronic companies €1.47 billion over two decade-long cartels.
5	Fourth EU–US Energy Council in Brussels.
9	The Social Liberal Union Party of Prime Minister Victor Ponta wins an absolute majority of seats in both chambers in the Romanian legislative elections.
10	The EU receives the 2012 Nobel Peace Prize.
12	The EP adopts a uniform patent system.
12	The EP awards the 2012 Sakharov Prize to two Iranian activists.
13–14	The European Council agrees a road map for the completion of EMU through deeper integration, and launches the 2013 European Semester.
18	S&P upgrades Greece's credit rating and sets its outlook to stable.
20	Commission withdraws ACTA referral to ECJ.
20–21	30th EU–Russia summit in Brussels.
21	Italian Prime Minister Mario Monti announces his resignation after the country's parliament passed the budget for the following year.

© 2013 The Author(s) JCMS: Journal of Common Market Studies © 2013 John Wiley & Sons Ltd

Index

Note: Italicized page references indicate information contained in tables.

© 2013 The Author(s) JCMS: Journal of Common Market Studies © 2013 John Wiley & Sons Ltd, 9600 Garsington Road, Oxford OX4 2DQ, UK and 350 Main Street,
Malden, MA 02148, USA

© 2013 The Author(s) JCMS: Journal of Common Market Studies © 2013 John Wiley & Sons Ltd

ENABLE
DISCOVERY

WILEY ONLINE LIBRARY
Access this journal and thousands
of other essential resources.

Featuring a clean and easy-to-use interface, this online service delivers intuitive navigation, enhanced discoverability, expanded functionalities, and a range of personalization and alerting options.

Sign up for content alerts and RSS feeds, access full-text, learn more about the journal, find related content, export citations, and click through to references.

WILEY
ONLINE LIBRARY
wileyonlinelibrary.com

Author Services

Committed to providing the best possible service to journal authors

Visit the Author Services website at http://authorservices.wiley.com for:

● Online article tracking through production with optional e-alerts at key stages

● Information on how to **nominate up to 10 colleagues** to receive FREE online access to your article

● Author **guidelines** by journal

● **Resources**, FAQs and tips on article preparation, submission, artwork, copyright, offprints etc.

● **Free online access** to your article when it is published online

● **25% discount** on Wiley books

WILEY-BLACKWELL

http://authorservices.wiley.com